Iran is a land of contradictions. It is an Islamic republic, but only 1.4 percent of the population attend Friday prayers. Iran's religious culture includes some of the most censorious and dogmatic Shi'a Muslim clerics in the world, and yet Iran's great heritage of poetry insistently dwells on the joys of life—wine, beauty, love, and desire. Iranian women are subject to one of the most restrictive dress codes in the Islamic world, but make up over 60 percent of students entering university.

In clear and engaging prose, Michael Axworthy explains the effect that Iran's complex history of empire, foreign invasion, and religious revolution has had on the Iranian national identity. He illuminates the role that cultural, literary, religious, and intellectual movements—and the personalities and ideas that shaped them—have played in one of the oldest continuing civilizations in the world.

Concluding with an assessment of the great changes the nation has undergone since the revolution in 1979, *A History of Iran* is essential for anyone seeking to understand the past, present, and future of this troubled and enigmatic nation.

A History of Iran

A History of
IRAN
Empire of the Mind

Michael Axworthy

A Member of the Perseus Books Group
New York

Published by Basic Books,
A Member of the Perseus Books Group

Books published by Basic Books are available at special discounts for bulk purchases in the United States by corporations, institutions, and other organizations. For more information, please contact the Special Markets Department at the Perseus Books Group, 2300 Chestnut Street, Suite 200, Philadelphia, PA 19103, or call (800) 810-4145, ex. 5000, or email special.markets@perseusbooks.com.

Designed by Timm Bryson
Set in 12 point Adobe Jenson by the Perseus Books Group

Library of Congress Cataloging-in-Publication Data
Axworthy, Michael.
A history of Iran : empire of the mind / Michael Axworthy.
p. cm.
Includes bibliographical references and index.
ISBN 978-0-465-00888-9 (alk. paper)
1. Iran—History. I. Title.

DS272.A94 2008
955—dc22

2007049157

10 9 8 7 6 5 4 3 2 1

To my wife Sally

Das Ewig-Weibliche zieht uns hinan

Contents

. . . However, when I began to consider the reasons for these opinions, all these reasons given for the magnificence of human nature failed to convince me: that man is the intermediary between creatures, close to the gods, master of all the lower creatures, with the sharpness of his senses, the acuity of his reason, and the brilliance of his intelligence, the interpreter of nature, the nodal point between eternity and time, and, as the Persians say, the intimate bond or marriage song of the world, just a little lower than angels, as David tells us. I concede these are magnificent reasons, but they do not seem to go to the heart of the matter. . . .

. . . Euanthes the Persian . . . writes that man has no inborn, proper form, but that many things that humans resemble are outside and foreign to them: "Man is multitudinous, varied, and ever changing." Why do I emphasize this? Considering that we are born with this condition, that is, that we can become whatever we choose to become, we need to understand that we must take earnest care about this, so that it will never be said to our disadvantage that we were born to a privileged position but failed to realize it and became animals and senseless beasts. . . . Above all, we should not make that freedom of choice God gave us into something harmful, for it was intended to be to our advantage. Let a holy ambition enter into our souls; let us not be content with mediocrity, but rather strive after the highest and expend all our strength in achieving it.

—Pico della Mirandola, *Oration on the Dignity of Man*
(translated by Richard Hooker)

Preface

The Remarkable Resilience of the Idea of Iran

Har kas ke bedanad va bedanad ke bedanad
Asb-e kherad az gombad-e gardun bejahanad
Har kas ke nadanad va bedanad ke nadanad
Langan kharak-e khish be manzel beresanad
Har kas ke nadanad va nadanad ke nadanad
Dar jahl-e morakkab 'abad od-dahr bemanad

Anyone who knows, and knows that he knows,
Makes the steed of intelligence leap over the vault of heaven.
Anyone who does not know, but knows that he does not know,
Can bring his lame little donkey to the destination nonetheless.
Anyone who does not know, and does not know that he does not know
Is stuck for ever in double ignorance

(Anonymous, attributed to Naser od-Din Tusi (1201–1274); anticipating Donald Rumsfeld by perhaps seven centuries)

Iranian history is full of violence and drama—invasions, conquerors, battles, and revolutions. Because Iran has a longer history than most countries, and is bigger than many, there is more of this drama. But there is more to Iranian history than that. There are religions, influences, intellectual movements, and ideas that have changed things within Iran, but also outside Iran and around the world. Today Iran demands attention again, and the new situation poses questions: Is Iran an aggressive power, or a victim? Is

Iran traditionally expansionist, or traditionally passive and defensive? Is the Shi'ism of Iran quietist, or violent and revolutionary? Only history can suggest answers to those questions. Iran is one of the world's oldest civilizations, and has been among the world's most thoughtful and complex civilizations from the very beginning. There are aspects of Iranian civilization that, in one way or another, have touched almost every human being on the planet. But the story of how that happened, and the full significance of those influences, is often unknown and forgotten.

Iran is replete with paradoxes, contradictions, and exceptions. Most non-Iranians think of it as a country of hot deserts, but it is ringed with high, cold mountains. It has rich agricultural provinces, and others full of lush subtropical forests. Reflecting its wide climatic variations, Iran has a diverse and colorful range of flora and fauna. Between Iraq and Afghanistan, Russia and the Persian Gulf, Iranians speak an Indo-European language in the midst of the Arabic-speaking Middle East. Iran is commonly thought of as a homogeneous nation, with a strong national culture, but minorities like the Azeris, Kurds, Gilakis, Baluchis, and Turkmen make up nearly half the population. Since the 1979 revolution, Iranian women have been subject to one of the most restrictive dress codes in the Islamic world, yet partly in consequence, Iranian families have released their daughters to study and work in unprecedented numbers. More than sixty percent of students entering university now are female, and many women—even married women—have professional jobs.

Iran has preserved some of the most stunning Islamic architecture in the world, as well as traditions of artisan metalworking, rug making, and bazaar trading: a complex and sophisticated urban culture. And yet its capital, Tehran, has slowly smothered itself in concrete, traffic congestion, and pollution. Iranians glory in their literary heritage and above all in their poetry, to a degree one finds in few other countries, with the possible exception of Russia. Many Iranians can recite lengthy passages from their favorite poems, and phrases from the country's great poets are common in everyday speech. It is poetry that insistently dwells on the joys of life—themes of wine, beauty, flowers, and sexual love. And yet Iran also has an intense popular tradition of Shi'ism, which in the mourning month of Moharram (when Shi' Muslims mourn the death of the Emam Hosein) emerges in religious processions dominated by a mood of gloom, and a powerful sense of betrayal and injustice. Iran's religious culture also encompasses the world's most forbidding, censorious, and dogmatic Shi'a Muslim clerics. It is an Islamic republic, but one in which only 1.4 percent of the population attends Friday prayers.

One thing is best explained at the start—another apparent paradox. Iran and Persia are the same country. The image conjured up by the name *Persia* is one of romance—roses and nightingales in elegant gardens, fast horses, flirtatious women, sharp sabers, jewel-colored carpets, melodious music. But in the cliché of Western media presentation, the name *Iran* conjures a rather different image—frowning mullahs, black oil, women's blanched faces peering from under dark chadors, grim crowds burning flags, chanting "death to. . . ."

In the south of Iran there is a province called Fars. Its capital is Shiraz and the province contains Iran's most ancient and impressive archaeological sites, Persepolis and Pasargadae (along with Susa, in neighboring Khuzestan). In ancient times the province was called Pars, after the people who had settled there—the Persians. When those people created an empire that dominated the whole region, the Greeks called it the Persian Empire. Later, the term Persia was applied by the Greeks, Romans, and other Europeans to all the dynastic states that followed in that region—the territory that is Iran today: Sassanid Persia in the centuries before the Islamic conquest, Safavid Persia in the sixteenth and seventeenth centuries, Qajar Persia in the nineteenth century. But all through that time the people of those empires called themselves *Iranians*, and their land *Iran*. The word derives from the very earliest times, apparently meaning "noble." It is cognate both with a similar word in Sanskrit, and with the term "Aryan"—the word used and abused in the racial ideologies of the late nineteenth and early twentieth centuries.[1]

In 1935 Reza Shah, wanting to distance his state from the decadent, ineffectual Qajar government he had displaced, instructed his embassies overseas to require foreign governments henceforth to call the country Iran in official communications. But many people, including some Iranians outside

Iran, still prefer the term Persia because it retains the ancient, often happier, connotations. My practice is to use both terms, but with a preference for Iran when dealing with the period after 1935, and for Persia for the preceding centuries, when it was the word used for the country by English-speakers. Iranians themselves call their language *Farsi* because it originated in the Iranian dialect spoken in Fars province. The language is now spoken not just in Iran but also extensively in Tajikistan; in Afghanistan (as the Dari dialect); and it has had a strong influence on the Urdu language spoken in Pakistan and northern India. In the earlier chapters of this book, the term *Iranian* is used also to cover the non-Persian peoples and languages of the wider region, like the Parthians, Sogdians, and Medes.

There are many books available on contemporary Iran, and on earlier periods of Iranian history. Several cover the whole history of Iran from the earliest times—notably the monumental seven-volume *Cambridge History of Iran*, and the huge project of the *Encyclopedia Iranica* (the latter is as yet incomplete but nonetheless incomparable for the range and depth of knowledge of Iranian history it pulls together—and much more than history). This book does not attempt to compete with those, but tries rather to present an introduction to the history of Iran for a general readership, assuming little or no prior knowledge. In addition it aims to explain some of the paradoxes and contradictions through the history—probably the only way that they can be properly understood. And beyond that—especially in Chapter 3, which explores some of the treasury of classical Persian poetry—it attempts to give the beginnings of an insight into the way the intellectual and literary culture of Iran developed, and has had a wider influence, not just in the Middle East, Central Asia, and India, but throughout the world.

Acknowledgments

The title of this book, if not the idea of it altogether, is unusual in that it originated at a public event—a panel discussion in front of an invited audience, arranged to inaugurate the *Forgotten Empire* exhibition at the British Museum in the autumn of 2005. The panel was chaired by the journalist Jon Snow and included the Iranian ambassador, Seyyed Mohammad Hossein Adeli (recalled to Tehran shortly afterward), Haleh Afshar of York University, Ali Ansari from the University of St. Andrews, and Christopher de Bellaigue, author of *In the Rose Garden of the Martyrs*. Neil MacGregor, the director of the British Museum, made an introductory presentation.

The discussion ranged widely but centered on the question of continuity in Iranian history, and on the enduring power of the idea of Iran, the influence of its literary and court culture on the other powers and linguistic cultures of the region, and its resilience over millennia despite war, invasion, religious change, and revolution. Then Jon Snow asked the audience to put questions to the panel. I asked a question toward the end—to the effect that if, as members of the panel had suggested, the center of Iranian culture had moved at different times from Fars in southern Iran to Mesopotamia, to Khorasan in the northeast and Central Asia, and to what is now called Azerbaijan in the northwest; and given its strong influence far beyond the land of Iran itself, into Abbasid Baghdad and Ottoman Turkey, for example, on the one side and into Central Asia and Moghul India on the other; then perhaps we should set aside our usual categories of nationhood and imperial culture and think instead of Iran as an Empire of the Mind? The panel seemed to like this suggestion, and someone in the audience called out that it would make a good book. So, here it is.

I have benefited greatly from the generous help and advice of a number of people, especially Baqer Moin, Ali Ansari, Willem Floor, Sajjad Rizvi, Lenny Lewisohn, Hashem Ahmadzadeh, Chris Rundle, Touraj Daryaee, Michael Grenfell, Peter Melville, Duncan Head, Haideh Sahim, and Mahdi Dasht-Bozorgi, and one anonymous reviewer, who read all or part of it in advance of publication; but also my father Ifor Axworthy and my sister Janet Axworthy, Peter Avery, Frances Cloud, Gordon Nechvatal, Shaghayegh Azimi, Paul Luft, and Paul Auchterlonie, as well as the other staff at the University Library in Exeter, and at the London Library. I should also thank my other friends and colleagues in the Institute of Arab and Islamic Studies in Exeter for their help and support, especially Tim Niblock, Rasheed El-Enany, Gareth Stansfield, James Onley, and Rob Gleave, as well as Michael Dwyer (simply the best editor it has been my good fortune to encounter), Maria Petalidou, and their colleagues at Hurst; Lara Heimert at Basic Books; Jim Morgan; my agent Georgina Capel; and (not just last but not least this time) my wife Sally for her unfailing cheerfulness and encouragement.

The author and publisher wish to thank the following for kindly agreeing to reproduce copyrighted material included in this book. Penguin Books Ltd., for permission to reproduce the quotations from Arthur Koestler's *Darkness at Noon*, © Penguin Books, 1969, and from *The Conference of the Birds*, by Farid al-Din Attar, translated by A. Darbandi and D. Davis, © Penguin Classics, 1984; Ibex Publishers, for permission to reproduce the poem on p. 116 from *A Thousand Years of Persian Rubaiyat*, translated by Reza Saberi, © Ibex Publishers, 2000; The University of Washington Press for permission to reproduce the excerpt from *The Tragedy of Sohrab and Rostam*, translated by J. W. Clinton, © The University of Washington Press, 1996.

Transliteration

The transliteration of names and other terms from Persian into English is an awkward problem, and it is not possible to be fully consistent without producing text that will sometimes look odd. As with my previous book, on Nader Shah, I have used a transliteration scheme that leans toward modern Iranian pronunciation, because I did not want to write a book on Iranian history in which the names and places would read oddly to Iranians. But there are inconsistencies, notably over the transliteration of names that have had a life of their own in Western writing—Isfahan, Fatima, Sultan, mullah, for example. Other, less justifiable inconsistencies, of which there will doubtless be some, are in all cases my fault rather than that of those who tried to advise me on the manuscript in its different stages of completion.

I

Origins

Zoroaster, the Achaemenids, and the Greeks

> *O Cyrus . . . Your subjects, the Persians,*
> *are a poor people with a proud spirit*
>
> —King Croesus of Lydia,
> according to Herodotus

The history of Iran starts with a question: Who are the Iranians? The question concerns not just the origins of Iran, but echoes, in one form or another, in the history of the country and its people down to the present day.

The Iranians were one branch of the Indo-European family of peoples who moved out of what are today the Russian steppes to settle in Europe, Iran, Central Asia, and northern India, in a series of migrations and invasions in the latter part of the second millennium BC. This explains the close relationship between the Persian language and other Indo-European languages—particularly Sanskrit and Latin, but also modern languages like Hindi, German, and English. Any speaker of a European language who is learning Persian soon encounters a series of familiar words: *pedar* (father, Latin *pater*); *dokhtar* (daughter, girl, German *tochter*); *mordan* (to die, Latin *mortuus*, French *mourir, le mort*); *nam* (name); *dar* (door); and perhaps the most familiar of all, the first-person present and singular of the verb *to be,* the suffix—*am* (I am—as in the sentence "I am an Iranian"—*Irani-am*). An English-speaker who has attempted to learn German will find Persian grammar both familiar and blessedly simple by comparison. There are no genders or grammatical cases for nouns. Persian, like English, has evolved since ancient times into a simplified form, dropping the heavily inflected grammar of old Persian. It has no structural relationship with Arabic or the other Semitic languages of the ancient Middle East (though it took in many Arab words after the Arab conquest).

Long before the migrants who spoke Iranian languages arrived from the north, there were other people living in what later became the land of Iran. People lived on the Iranian plateau as early as 100,000 BC, in what is known as the Old Stone Age, and by 5000 BC agricultural settlements were flourishing in and around the Zagros mountains—the area to the east of the great Sumerian civilization of Mesopotamia. Excavation of one of these settlements, at Hajji Firoz Tepe, has produced the remains of the world's oldest-known wine jar, complete with grape residue and traces of resin that were used as a flavoring and a preservative, indicating that the wine would have tasted something like Greek retsina.[1] Before and during the period of the Iranian migrations, an empire—the empire of Elam—flourished in the area that later became the provinces of Khuzestan and Fars, based in the cities of Susa and Anshan. The Elamites spoke a language that was neither Mesopotamian nor Iranian, but they were influenced by the Sumerians, Assyrians, and Babylonians, and transmitted elements of their culture on to the later Iranian dynasties. Elamite influence spread beyond the area usually associated with its empire. An example of this is in Tepe Sialk, just south of modern Kashan, where a ziggurat—an ancient Mesopotamian temple—shows all the forms of an Elamite settlement. This ziggurat at Tepe Sialk has been dated to around 2900 BC.

Recent DNA-based research in other countries has tended to emphasize the relative stability of the genetic pool over time, despite conquests, migrations, and what look from historical accounts to be mass settlements or even genocides. It is likely that the Iranian settlers or conquerors were relatively few in number, compared to the pre-existing peoples who later adopted their language and intermarried with them. And probably ever since that time, down to the present day, the rulers of Iran have ruled over at least some non-Iranian peoples. From the very beginning then, the Idea of Iran was as much about culture and language—in all their complex patterns—as about race or territory.

From the beginning there was always a division (albeit a fuzzy one) between Iran's nomadic or semi-nomadic peoples and its settled, crop-growing agriculturists. Iran is a land of great contrasts in climate and geography, and in addition to areas of productive agricultural land (expanded by ingenious use of irrigation from groundwater), there are more extensive areas of rugged mountain and semi-desert, worthless for crops but suitable for grazing, even if only for a limited period each year. Over these lands the nomads moved their herds. The early Iranians seem to have herded cattle in particular.

In the pre-modern world, pastoralist nomads had many advantages over settled peasant farmers. Their wealth was their livestock, which meant their wealth was movable and they could escape from threats of violence with little loss. Other nomads might attack them, of course, but peasant farmers were always much more vulnerable. If threatened with violence at harvest time, the farmers stood to lose the accumulated value of a full year's work and be left destitute. In peaceful times nomads were happy to trade meat and wool with the peasants in exchange for grains and other crops, but the nomads always had the option of adding direct coercion to purely economic bargaining. Nomads have had the upper hand from the time the Indo-European pastoralist Iranians first entered the Iranian plateau, right up to the twentieth century.

From such circumstances a system of tribute—what the twentieth-century Mafia would call protection—developed. The peasants paid a portion of their harvest in order to be left alone. From another perspective, augmented with a bit of presentational subtlety and tradition, this system could be called government taxation. Most of the historical rulers of Iran originated from the nomadic tribes (including from non-Iranian nomads who arrived in later waves of migration), and animosity between the nomads and the settled population has persisted into modern times. The settled population (particularly later, when towns and cities developed) regarded themselves as more civilized, less violent, and less crude. But the nomads saw the settled population as soft and devious, while considering themselves, by contrast, as hardy, tough, and self-reliant, exemplifying a kind of rugged honesty. There would have been elements of truth in both caricatures, but the attitudes of the early Iranian elites partook especially of the latter.

Medes and Persians

The Iranian-speakers who migrated into the land of Iran and the surrounding area in the years before 1000 BC were not one single tribe or group. In time some of their descendants became known as Medes and Persians, but there were Parthians, Sogdians, and others, too, who only acquired the names known to us later in their history. And even the titles Mede and Persian were themselves simplifications, lumping together shifting alliances and confederacies of disparate tribes.

From the beginning, the Medes and Persians are mentioned together in historical sources, suggesting a close relationship from the very earliest times. The first such mention is in an Assyrian record of 836 BC—an account of an extended military campaign by the Assyrian king Shalmaneser III and several of his successors that was waged in the Zagros mountains and as far east as Mount Demavand, the high, extinct volcano in the Alborz range. The accounts they left behind listed the Medes and Persians as tributaries—those paying tribute to the stronger Assyrians. The heartlands of the Medes were in the northwest, in the modern provinces of Azerbaijan, Kurdistan, Hamadan, and Tehran. In the region of the Zagros south of the territories occupied by the Medes, the Assyrians encountered the Persians in the region they called Parsuash, which has been known ever since as Pars or Fars.[2]

Within a century or so, however, the Medes and Persians were fighting back, attacking Assyrian territories. Later traditions recorded by Herodotus in the fifth century BC mention early kings of the Medes, called Deioces and Cyaxares, who appeared in the Assyrian accounts as Daiaukku and Uaksatar; and a king of the Persians called Achaemenes, who the Assyrians called Hakhamanish. By 700 BC the Medes—with the help of Scythian tribes—had established an independent state, which later grew to become the first Iranian Empire. In 612 BC the Medes destroyed the Assyrian capital, Nineveh (adjacent to modern Mosul, on the Tigris). At its height the Median Empire stretched from Asia Minor to the Hindu Kush, and south to the Persian Gulf, ruling the Persians as vassals as well as many other subject peoples.

The Prophet Who Laughed

But before the first mentions of the Iranians and their kings appear in the records, another important historical figure lived—Zoroaster or Zarathustra (modern Persian *Zardosht*). It is generally accepted that Zoroaster lived and was not just a man of myth or legend. His dates are unknown and experts have disagreed radically about when he lived. Compared with Jesus, Mohammad, or even Moses, Zoroaster is a much more indistinct figure. Little is known for sure about his life—the best evidence suggests he lived in the northeast, in what later became Bactria and later still, in Afghanistan. But another tradition has suggested he came from what is now Azerbaijan, around the river Araxes. As a religious thinker and a key figure in the history of world religions, Zoroaster certainly ranks in importance with the other prophets. But for the same reason that the details of his life are obscure, it is also difficult to establish the precise import of his teaching. The Zoroastrian religious texts that are the main source for both (notably the *Avesta*) were written down in the form they are known to us only much later, in the Sassanid period.[3] The stories about Zoroaster they contain are little more than fables. Some of the stories correspond with information from classical Greek and Latin commentators and show their genuine antiquity. For example, there is the story that at birth the infant Zoroaster did not cry, but laughed. And the theology combines what are undoubtedly ancient elements with innovations that were incorporated and developed much later.

So although Zoroastrian tradition places Zoroaster's birth at around 600 BC, most scholars now believe he lived earlier. It is still unclear just when, but it is reasonable to think it was around 1200 or 1000 BC, at the time of, or shortly after, the migrations of Iranian cattle herders to the Iranian plateau. This view is based on the fact that the earliest texts (the *Gathas*, traditionally considered to be hymns first sung by Zoroaster himself) show significant differences with the later liturgical language associated with the period around 600 BC. Other clues come from the characteristics of the pastoral way of life reflected in the texts, and the absence in them of references to the Medes or Persians or the names of kings or other people known from that later time.

It seems plausible that Zoroaster's religious revelation arose in the context of the changes, new demands, and new influences associated with the migration, including the self-questioning of a culture faced with new neighbors and unfamiliar pressures. The religion, then, was the result of an encounter with a new complexity. While it was to some extent a compromise with that new complexity, it was also an attempt to govern it according to new principles.

Other evidence supports the view that Zoroaster did not invent a religion from nothing. Instead, he reformed and simplified pre-existing religious practices (against some resistance from traditional priests), infusing them with a much more sophisticated philosophical theology and a greater emphasis on morality and justice. This view is supported by the existence of an early tradition that held writing to be alien and demonic—suggesting that the Iranians associated it with the Semitic and other peoples among whom they found themselves in the centuries after the migration.[4] More evidence that Zoroaster reformed pre-existing religions is that the Persian word *div*—cognate with both Latin and Sanskrit words for the gods—in the Zoroastrian context was used for a class of demons opposed to Zoroaster and his followers, suggesting that the reforming prophet reclassified at least some previous deities as evil spirits.[5] The demons were associated with chaos and disorder—the antithesis of the principles of goodness and justice represented by the new religion. At the more mundane level the demons also lay behind diseases of people and animals, bad weather, and other natural disasters.

At the center of Zoroaster's theology was the opposition between Ahura Mazda, the creator-god of truth and light, and Ahriman, the embodiment of lies, darkness, and evil.[6] This dualism became a persistent theme in Iranian thought for centuries. Modern Zoroastrianism is much more strongly monotheistic, and to make this distinction more explicit many scholars refer to the religion in this early stage as Mazdaism. Other pre-existing deities were incorporated into the Mazdaean religious structure as angels or archangels—notably Mithra, a sun god, and Anahita, a goddess of streams and rivers. Six Immortal archangels (the *Amesha Spenta*) embodied animal life, plant life, metals and minerals, earth, fire, and water. The names of several of these archangels—for example Bahman, Ordibehesht, Khordad—survive as months in the modern Iranian calendar, even under the Islamic republic. Ahura Mazda himself personified air, and in origin paralleled the Greek Zeus, as a sky-god.

The modern Persian month Bahman is named after the Mazdaean archangel Vohu Manu—the second in rank after Ahura Mazda, characterized as Good Purpose and identified with the cattle who were the second class of beings to be created by Ahura Mazda, after man himself. Part of the creation myth in Zoroastrianism holds that after all was created good by Ahura Mazda, the evil spirit Ahriman (accompanied by six evil spirits matching the six Immortals) assaulted creation, murdering the first man, killing the sacred bull Vohu Manu, and polluting the pure elements of water and fire. The importance of cattle to the nomadic early Iranians is shown by the frequent appearance of bulls and cattle in sculpture and iconography from the Achaemenid period—but many of these images may have a more specific religious significance, referring to Vohu Manu.

The name Ahura Mazda means Lord of Wisdom, or Wise Lord. The dualism went a long way toward resolving the problem of evil that presents such difficulties for the monotheistic religions (the origin of evil in the world was Ahriman, against whom Ahura Mazda struggled for supremacy) and at least initially permitted a strong attachment to the ideas of free will (arising out of the necessity of human beings choosing between good and evil), goodness emerging in good actions, judgment after death, and heaven and hell. Some scholars have suggested that within a few centuries (but before 600 BC) Mazdaism developed a theory of a Messiah—the Saoshyant, who would be born miraculously at the end of time from a virgin mother and the seed of Zoroaster himself.[7] But the dualism implied other difficulties, which emerged later. One was how Ahura Mazda and Ahriman themselves came into existence. To explain this, some later followers of the Iranian religion believed in a creator-god, Zurvan (identified with Time or Fate), who prayed for a son and was rewarded with twins. The twins became Ahura Mazda and Ahriman. This branch of Mazdaism has been called Zurvanism.

It was a characteristic of the new religion that philosophical concepts or categories became personified as heavenly beings or entities—indeed these seem to have proliferated, a little like characters in John Bunyan's *Pilgrim's Progress*. One example is the idea of the *daena*. According to one later text, a beautiful maiden appeared to the soul of a just man after his death. She was the personification of all the good works he had done in life, and she said to him,

> For when, in the world, you saw someone sacrificing to the demon, you instead started adoring God; and when you saw someone carrying out violence and robbery and afflicting and despising good men and gathering in their substance with evil actions, you instead avoided treating creatures with violence and robbery; you took care of the just and welcomed them and gave them lodgings and gifts. Whether your wealth came from near or from afar, it was honorably acquired. And when you saw people give false judgments and allowed themselves to be corrupted with money and commit perjury, you instead undertook to tell the truth and speak righteously. I am your righteous thoughts, your righteous words, your righteous actions, thought, spoken, done by you.[8]

Elsewhere the word daena was used to signify religion itself. Another example of personification in Mazdaism is the identification of five separate entities belonging to each human being—not just body, soul, and spirit, but also *adhvenak* and *fravashi*. Adhvenak, the heavenly prototype for each human being, was associated with semen and regeneration. The fravashi were more active, associated with the strength of heroes, the protection of the living in life (like guardian angels), and the collection of souls after death (rather like the Valkyries in Germanic mythology). These and other personifications prefigure the role of angels in Judaism, Christianity, and Islam, but also have obvious connections to the idea of forms in Platonism. Many scholars believe Plato was strongly influenced by Mazdaism.

Paralleling Ahura Mazda and Ahriman were two principles, sometimes translated as good and evil but more precisely as Truth and the Lie—*asha* and *druj*. These terms recur insistently in the Avestan texts, along with the concept of justice. They also show up in surviving inscriptions (in old Persian, the words became *arta* and *drauga*) and in Western classical texts describing Iran or events in Iran. In the centuries after Zoroaster, there were different currents and separate sects within the Mazdaean tradition, representing both innovations and survivals from the pre-Zoroastrian religions, as well as various compromises between them. The priestly class, the Magi (listed by Herodotus as a distinct tribe within the Medes) survived from before the time of Zoroaster. As all priests do, they interpreted and adapted doctrine and ritual to suit their own purposes, while remaining remarkably faithful to the central oral tradition.

The history of the relationship between Iranians and Jews is almost as old as the history of Iran itself. After the conquest of the northern Kingdom of Israel by the Assyrians around 720 BC, large numbers of Jews were removed to Media, among other places, setting up long-lived Jewish communities, notably in Ecbatana/Hamadan. A second wave of deportations, this time to Babylonian territory, took place in the 590s and 580s BC under Nebuchadnezzar, who destroyed the temple of Solomon in 586. Babylon came under Persian control in the 530s, and thereafter many of the Jews eventually returned home. Some scholars believe that Judaism changed significantly under Mazdaean influence in the period of the Babylonian exile (the logical corollary, the possibility of Judaic influence on Mazdaism, seems to have received less attention). The trauma of the Babylonian exile was never forgotten, and it marked a watershed in Jewish history in several ways. One of the leaders of the return from Babylon, the scribe Ezra, is believed to have been the first to write down the books of the Torah (the first five books of the Bible, the books of Moses). He did so in a new script different from the one used by the Jews before the exile. This is the Hebrew script used ever since. Post-exile Judaism laid greater emphasis on adherence to the Torah, and on monotheism.

For hundreds of years thereafter, first under the Persian Empire and later under Hellenistic rulers, diaspora Jewish and Mazdaean religious communities lived adjacent to one another in cities all over the Middle East.[9] It seems plain that many religious ideas became common currency, and the Qumran scrolls (the Dead Sea scrolls) indicate some crossover of religious concepts from Mazdaism.[10] It is a controversial subject, and the relative obscurity of Mazdaism and Zoroastrianism in Western scholarship until recent times has helped to conceal the influence of Mazdaism on Judaism; but as further work is done, the more significant it is likely to be found. Perhaps the strongest indicator is the positive attitude of the Jewish texts toward the Persians.

There are a number of contradictions between the later practice of Zoroastrianism, as it has come down to us in the written scriptures, and the apparent norms of the Mazdaean religion at this earliest stage. Many of the problems are difficult to resolve. It is a complex picture. But the concepts of heaven and hell, of free human choice between good and evil, of divine judgment, of angels, of a single creator-god—all appear to have been genuine early features of the religion, and all were hugely influential for religions that originated later. Mazdaism was the first religion—in this part of the world, at least—to move beyond cult and totemism to address moral and philosophical problems with its theology, emphasizing personal choice and responsibility. In that limited sense, Nietzsche was right—Zoroaster was the first creator of the moral world we live in. *Also sprach Zarathustra.*

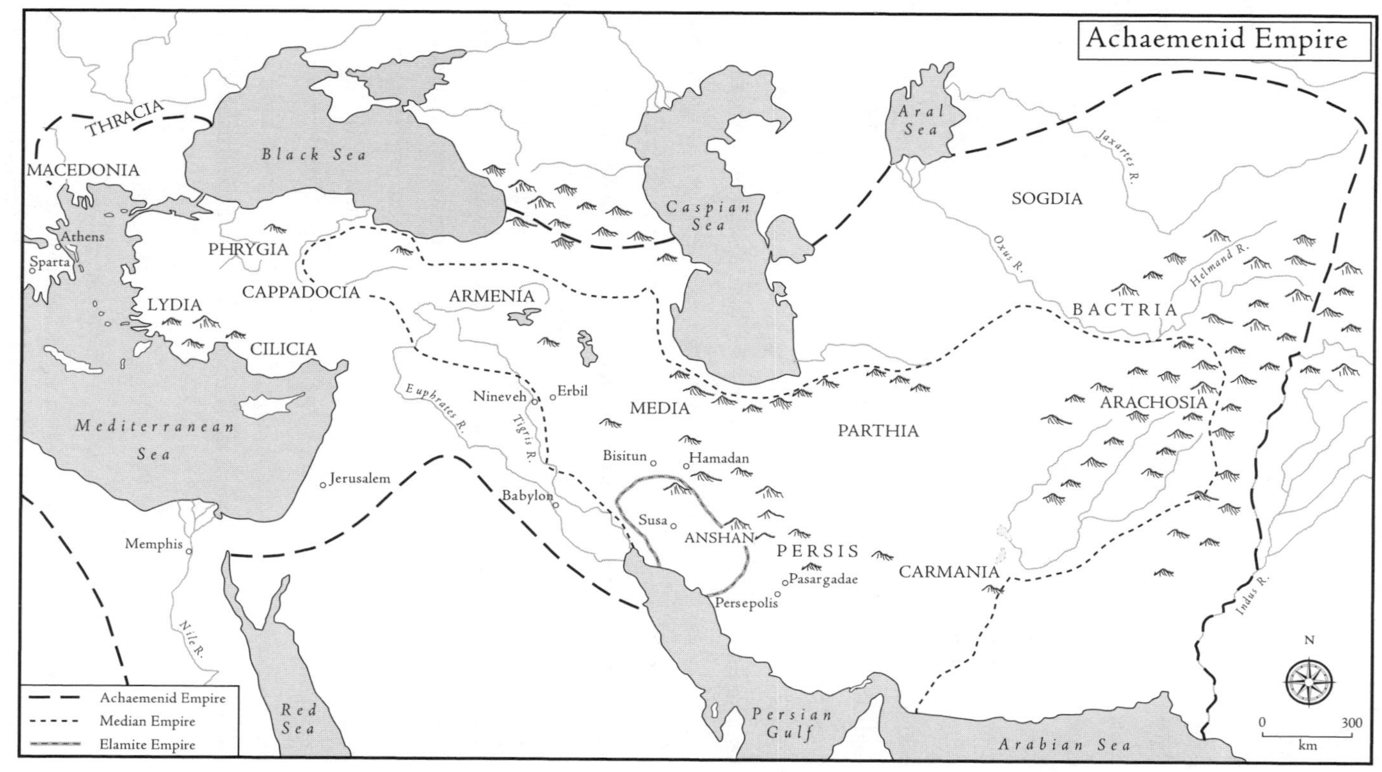

Achaemenid Empire
THRACIA
MACEDONIA
Black Sea
Athens
Sparta
PHRYGIA
CAPPADOCIA
LYDIA
CILICIA
Mediterranean Sea
Jerusalem
Memphis
Nile R.
Red Sea
ARMENIA
Euphrates R.
Tigris R.
Nineveh
Erbil
Babylon
Caspian Sea
MEDIA
Bisitun
Hamadan
Susa
ANSHAN
PERSIS
Pasargadae
Persepolis
Persian Gulf
PARTHIA
CARMANIA
Aral Sea
SOGDIA
Jaxartes R.
Oxus R.
BACTRIA
Helmand R.
ARACHOSIA
Indus R.
Arabian Sea
N
0 300
km
Achaemenid Empire
Median Empire
Elamite Empire

Cyrus and the Achaemenids

Around 559 BC a Persian prince named Cyrus (modern Persian *Kurosh*), claiming descent from the royal house of Persia and from its progenitor Achaemenes, became king of Anshan upon the death of his father. Persia and Anshan, at that time, were still subject to the Median Empire, but Cyrus led a revolt against the Median king Astyages, and in 549 BC captured the Median capital, Ecbatana (modern Hamadan). Cyrus reversed the relationship between Media and Persia—he crowned himself king of Persia, making Persia the center of the empire and Media the junior partner. But he did not stop there. He went on to conquer Lydia, in Asia Minor, taking possession of the treasury of King Croesus, legendary for his wealth. He also conquered the remaining territories of Asia Minor, as well as Phoenicia, Judaea, and Babylonia. This created an enormous empire that stretched from the Greek cities on the eastern coast of the Aegean Sea to the banks of the river Indus—in extent perhaps the greatest empire the world had seen up to that time.

Cyrus's empire took on much of the culture of previous Elamite, Assyrian, and Babylonian empires, notably in its written script and monumental iconography. But without romanticizing Cyrus unduly, it seems that he aspired to rule an empire different from others that had preceded it in the region. Portentous inscriptions recording the military glory of kings and the supposed favor of their terrible war-gods were commonplace in the Middle East in the centuries preceding Cyrus's accession. In the nineteenth century an eight-sided clay object (known since as the Taylor Prism, after the man who found it), measuring about 15 inches long by 5.5 inches in diameter, covered in cuneiform script, was discovered near Mosul. When the characters were eventually deciphered, it was found to record eight campaigns of the Assyrian king Sennacherib (705 BC–681 BC). An excerpt reads:

> Sennacherib, the great king . . . king of the world, king of Assyria, king of the four quarters . . . guardian of right, lover of justice, who lends support, who comes to the aid of the needy, who performs pious acts, perfect hero, mighty man, first among all princes, the flame who consumes those who do not submit, who strikes the wicked with the thunderbolt; the god Assur, the great

> mountain, has entrusted an unrivaled kinship to me . . . has made powerful my weapons . . . he has brought the black-headed people in submission at my feet; and mighty kings feared my warfare. . . .
>
> In the course of my campaign, Beth-Dagon, Joppa, Banaibarka, Asuru, cities of Sidka, who had not speedily bowed in submission at my feet, I besieged, I conquered, I carried off their spoils. . . . I approached Ekron and slew the governors and nobles who had rebelled, and hung their bodies on stakes around the city. . . .
>
> As for Hezekiah the Jew, who did not submit to my yoke: 46 of his strong, walled cities . . . by means of ramps and by bringing up siege-engines . . . I besieged and took them. 200,150 people, great and small, male and female, horses, mules, asses, camels, cattle and sheep without number, I brought away from them and counted as spoil. . . .[11]

The way the pharaohs of Egypt celebrated their rule and their victories was very similar to this, and although Hezekiah, the king of Jerusalem, appears on the Taylor Prism as a victim, some parts of the Bible describing the Israelites and their God smiting their enemies do not read very differently, either.

By contrast, another clay object, about 9 inches by 4 inches, also discovered in the nineteenth century and covered in cuneiform script, tells a rather different story. The Cyrus cylinder, now in the British Museum, was found where it had been deliberately placed—under the foundations of the city wall of Babylon. It has been described as a charter of human rights for the ancient world, which is an exaggeration and a misrepresentation. But the message of the cylinder, particularly when combined with what is known of Cyrus's religious policy from the books of Ezra and Isaiah, is nonetheless remarkable. The kingly preamble from the cylinder is fairly conventional:

> I am Cyrus, king of the world, great king, rightful king, king of Babylon, king of Sumer and Akkad, king of the four quarters (of the earth), son of Cambyses, great king, king of Anshan, grandson of Cyrus, great king, king of Anshan, descendant of Teispes, great king, king of Anshan, of a family that always exercised kingship. . . .

But it continues, describing the favor shown to Cyrus by the Babylonian god Marduk:

> When I entered Babylon as a friend and when I established the seat of the government in the palace of the ruler under jubilation and rejoicing, Marduk, the great lord, induced the magnanimous inhabitants of Babylon to love me, and I was daily endeavouring to worship him. My numerous troops walked around in Babylon in peace, I did not allow anybody to terrorize any place of the country of Sumer and Akkad. I strove for peace in Babylon and in all his other sacred cities . . .

and concludes:

> As to the region . . . as far as Assur and Susa, Agade, Eshnunna, the towns of Zamban, Me-Turnu, Der as well as the region of the Gutians, I returned to these sanctuaries on the other side of the Tigris, the sanctuaries of which had been ruins for a long time, the images which used to live therein and established for them permanent sanctuaries. I also gathered all their former inhabitants and returned to them their habitations. Furthermore, I resettled upon the command of Marduk, the great lord, all the gods of Sumer and Akkad whom Nabonidus had brought into Babylon to the anger of the lord of the gods, unharmed, in their former chapels, the places that make them happy.[12]

Like the proud declarations of Sennacherib, this is propaganda—but it is propaganda of a different kind. It shows Cyrus in a different light, and according to a different scale of values. Cyrus chose to present himself showing respect to the Babylonian deity, Marduk. Perhaps it would have been different if Cyrus had conquered Babylon by force, rather than marching into it unopposed (in 539 BC) after its inhabitants revolted against the last Babylonian king, Nabonidus. Cyrus was a ruthless, ambitious man; no one ever conquered an empire without those characteristics in full measure. But we know that he permitted freedom of worship to the Jews, too. Cyrus and his successors permitted them to return home from exile and to rebuild the temple in Jerusalem. For those acts they were accorded in the Jewish scriptures a unique status among gentile monarchs.

The logic of statecraft alone might have suggested that it would be more sustainable in the long run to let subjects conduct their own affairs and worship as they pleased. But that policy had to be acceptable to the Iranian elite, including the priests—the Magi. Leaving aside the question of Cyrus's personal beliefs, which remain unclear, it is reasonable to see in the policy some of the spirit of moral earnestness and justice that pervaded the religion of Zoroaster. The presence of those values in the background helps to explain why the Cyrus cylinder is couched in such different terms from the militaristic thunder and arrogance of Sennacherib. The old answer was terror and a big stick, but the Persian Empire would be run in a more devolved, permissive spirit. Once again, an encounter with complexity, acceptance of that complexity, and a response. This was something new.

Unfortunately, according to Herodotus, Cyrus did not end his life as gloriously as he had lived it. Having conquered in the west, he turned to campaign east of the Caspian. According to one account he was defeated and killed in battle by Queen Tomyris of the Massagetae, another Iranian tribe who fought mainly on horseback, like the Scythians.

The Massagetae are interesting because they appear to have maintained some ancient Iranian customs that may shed light on the status of women in Persian society under the Achaemenids. There are signs in Herodotus (Book 1:216) that the Massagetae showed some features of a matrilineal, polyandrous society, in which women might have a number of spouses or sexual partners, but men only one. Patricia Crone has suggested that this feature may resurface in men's apparent holding of women in common as practiced later by the Mazdakites in the fifth century AD, and by the Khorramites after the Islamic conquest.[13] Mazdaism certainly permitted a practice whereby an impotent man could give his wife temporarily to another in order to obtain a child; it also sanctioned the marriage of close relatives. But in general, Persian society seems to have leaned toward limiting the status of women, following practices elsewhere in the Middle East. Royal and noble women may have been able to own property in their own right—and even, on occasion, to exert some political influence. But this seems to have been an exception associated with high status rather than indicative of practices prevalent in society more widely.[14]

Cyrus's body was brought back to Persia, to Pasargadae, his capital, to rest in a tomb there. That tomb, which can still be seen (though its contents have long since disappeared), is massively simple rather than grandiose—a sepulchre the size of a small house on a raised, stepped plinth. This tomb burial has raised some questions about the religion of Cyrus and the other Achaemenid kings. Many of his successors were placed in tombs of a different type—rock tombs halfway up a cliff face. Tomb burial was anathema to later Zoroastrians, who held it to be sacrilege to pollute the earth with dead bodies. Instead they exposed the dead on so-called Towers of Silence, to be consumed by birds and animals. Could the Achaemenid kings really have been Zoroastrians if they permitted tomb burial?

Some have explained the inconsistency by suggesting that different classes of Iranian society followed different beliefs—different religions, effectively. As we have seen, there probably was some considerable plurality of belief within the broad flow of Mazdaism at this time. But it seems more likely that the plurality was socially vertical rather than horizontal—a question of geography and tribe rather than of social class. Perhaps an earlier, pre-Zoroastrian tradition of burial still lingered and the elevated position of all the royal tombs was a kind of compromise. Halfway between heaven and earth—itself a strong metaphor. Around the tomb of Cyrus lay a paradise, a garden watered by irrigation channels (our word *paradise* comes, via Greek, from the Old Persian *paradaida*, meaning a walled garden). Magian priests watched over the tomb and sacrificed a horse to Cyrus's memory each month.[15]

Cyrus had been a conqueror, but a conqueror with imagination and vision. He was at least as remarkable a man as that other conqueror, Alexander, whose career marks the end of the Achaemenid period just as that of Cyrus marks the beginning. Maybe as a youth Cyrus had a Mazdaean tutor as remarkable as Aristotle, who taught Alexander.

Religious Revolt

Cyrus was succeeded by his son Cambyses (Kambojiya), who extended the empire by conquering Egypt, but in a short time gained a reputation for harshness. He died unexpectedly in 522 BC—by suicide, according to one source—after he had been given news of a revolt in the empire's Persian heartlands.

An account of what happened next appears on an extraordinary rock relief carving at Bisitun, in western Iran, about twenty miles from Kermanshah, above the main road to Hamadan. According to the text of the carving (executed in Old Persian, Elamite, and Babylonian), the revolt was led by a Magi, Gaumata, who claimed falsely to be Cambyses's younger brother, Bardiya. Herodotus gives a similar version, saying that Cambyses had murdered the true Bardiya years earlier. The revolt led by Gaumata seems to have drawn force from social and fiscal grievances, because one of his measures to gain popularity was to order a three-year remission of taxes. Another was to end military conscription.[16] Pressure had built up over decades of costly foreign wars under Cyrus and Cambyses. But Gaumata also showed strong religious intolerance, destroying the temples of sects he did not approve of.

An Iranian revolution, led by a charismatic cleric, seizing power from an oppressive monarch, asserting religious orthodoxy, attacking false believers, and drawing support from economic grievances—how modern that sounds. But within a few months, Gaumata was dead, killed by Darius (Daryavaush) and a small group of Persian confederates—a killing that sounds more like an assassination than anything else.

The carving at Bisitun was made at Darius's orders and it presents his version of events, as put together after he had made himself king and the revolt had finally been crushed. The carving itself says that copies of the same text were made and distributed throughout the empire. And what a revolt it had been—Babylon revolted twice, and Darius declared that he fought nineteen battles in a single year. It was really a series of revolts, affecting all but a few of the eastern provinces of the empire. The Bisitun carving illustrates this by showing a row of defeated captives, each representing a different people or territory. Whatever the true nature of the rebellion and its origins, it was no simple palace coup, affecting only a few members of the elite. It was just the first of several religious revolutions, or attempted revolutions, in Iran's history. And it was no pushover.

Bisitun was chosen for Darius's grand rock-carving because it was a high place, perhaps already associated with the sacred, close by where he and his companions had killed Gaumata/Bardiya. The site at Bisitun is a museum of Iranian history in itself. Aside from the Darius rock relief, there are caves that had been used by Neanderthals forty thousand years earlier, and by many generations after them. Among other relics and monuments, there is a rock-carving of a reclining Hercules from the Seleucid period, a Parthian carving depicting fire worship, a Sassanian bridge, some remains of a building from the Mongol period, a seventeenth-century *caravanserai*, and, not far away, some fortifications apparently dating from the time of Nader Shah in the eighteenth century.

Many historians have been suspicious about the story of the false Bardiya. The Bisitun carving is a contemporary source, but it is plainly a self-serving account to justify Darius's accession. It is confirmed by Herodotus and other Greek writers, but they all wrote later and would naturally have accepted the official version of events if other dissenting accounts had been stamped out. Darius was not a natural successor to the throne. He was descended from a junior branch of the Achaemenid royal family, and even in that line he was not preeminent—his father was still living. Could a Magian priest have successfully impersonated a royal prince some three or four years after the real man's death? Is it not rather suspect that Darius also discredited other opponents by alleging that they were imposters?

If the story was a fabrication, Darius was certainly brazen in the presentation of his case. In the Bisitun inscriptions, the rebel leaders are called liar kings, and Darius, appealing to religious feeling and Mazdaean beliefs about *arta* and *druj*, declares,

> [. . .] you, whosoever shall be king hereafter, be on your guard very much against Falsehood. The man who shall be a follower of Falsehood—punish him severely . . .

and,

> [. . .] Ahura Mazda brought me aid and the other gods who are, because I was not disloyal, I was no follower of Falsehood, I was no evil-doer, neither I nor my family, I acted according to righteousness, neither to the powerless nor to the powerful, did I do wrong . . .

and again,

> This is what I have done, by the grace of Ahura Mazda have I always acted. Whosoever shall read this inscription hereafter, let that which I have done be believed. You must not hold it to be lies.

Perhaps Darius protested a little too much. Another inscription in Darius's words, from another site, reads,

> By the favor of Ahura Mazda I am of such a sort that I am a friend to right, I am not a friend to wrong. It is not my desire that the weak man should have wrong done to him by the mighty; nor is it my desire that the mighty man should have wrong done to him by the weak. What is right, that is my desire. I am not a friend to the man who is a lie-follower [. . .] As a horseman I am a good horseman. As a bowman I am a good bowman both afoot and on horseback . . .[17]

The latter part of this text, though telescoped here from the original, echoes the famous formula from Herodotus and other Greek writers, that Persian youths were brought up to ride a horse, shoot a bow, and tell the truth. Darius was pressing every button to stimulate the approval of his subjects. Even if one doubts the story of Darius's accession, the evidence from Bisitun and his other inscriptions of his self-justification, and the use of religion by both sides in the intensive fighting that followed the death of Cambyses, nonetheless stands. It is a powerful testimony to the force of the Mazdaean religion at this time. Even the suppressors of the religious revolution had to justify their actions in religious terms. Although Darius by the end reigned supreme, the inscriptions give a strong sense that he himself was nonetheless subject to a powerful structure of ideas about justice, truth and lies, and right and wrong. that was distinctively Iranian—and Mazdaean.

The Empire Refounded

Darius's efforts to justify and dignify his rule did not end there. He built an enormous palace in his Persian homeland, at what the Greeks later called Persepolis (City of the Persians)—thus starting afresh, away from the previous capital of Cyrus at Pasargadae. Persepolis is so big that a modern visitor, wandering bemused between the sections of fallen columns and the massive double-headed column capitals that crashed to the ground when the palace burned, finds it difficult to become oriented, much less make sense of it. The magnificence of the palace served as a further prop to the majesty of Darius and the legitimacy of his rule. But it helped in turn to create a lasting tradition, a mystique of magnificent kingship that might not have come about but for the initial doubts over his accession. A dedicatory inscription at Persepolis played again on the old theme:

> May Ahura Mazda protect this land from hostile armies, from famine, and from the Lie.

The motif of tribute and submission is also repeated from Bisitun. Row upon row of figures representing subjects from all over the empire are shown queuing up to present themselves, frozen forever in stone relief. The purpose of the huge palace complex at Persepolis is not entirely clear. It may be that it was intended as a place for celebrations and ceremonies at the time of the spring equinox, the Persian New Year (*Noruz*—celebrated on and after March 21 each year, today as then). The rows of tribute-bearers depicted in the sculpture suggest that it may have been the place for annual demonstrations of homage and loyalty from the provinces. Whatever the reason for the grandeur of Persepolis, it was never the main, permanent capital of the empire. That was at Susa, the old capital of Elam.

This, again, shows the syncretism of the Persian regime. Cyrus had been closely connected with the royal family of the Medes, and the Medes had a privileged position with the Persians as partners at the head of the empire. But Elam, too, was important and central, and not least for its language, as used in administration and monumental inscriptions. This was an empire that always preferred to flow around and *absorb* powerful rivals, rather than to confront, batter into defeat, and force submission. The guiding principles of Cyrus persisted under Darius and at least some later Achaemenid rulers.

Darius's reign saw the Achaemenid Empire in effect re-founded. It could have gone under altogether in the rebellions that followed the death of Cambyses. But Darius maintained Cyrus's tradition of tolerance, permitting a plurality of gods to be worshipped as before. He also maintained the related principle of devolved government. The provinces were ruled by satraps, governors who returned a tribute to the center but ruled as viceroys (two other officials looked after military matters and fiscal administration in each province, to avoid too much power being concentrated in any one pair of hands). The satraps, who often inherited their offices from predecessors within the same family, ruled their provinces according to pre-existing laws, customs, and traditions. They were, in effect, provincial kings, while Darius was king of kings (*Shahanshah* in modern Persian). The empire did not attempt, as a matter of policy, to Persianize as the Roman Empire, for example, later sought to Romanize.

The certainties of religion, the principle of sublime justice that they underpinned, and the magnificent prestige of kingship—these were the bonds that held together this otherwise diffuse constellation of peoples, languages, and cultures. A complex empire was accepted as such, and was subjected to a controlling principle. The system established by Darius worked, proved resilient, and endured.

Tablets discovered in excavations at Persepolis show the complexity and administrative sophistication of the system Darius established. Although Darius established a standard gold coinage, and some payments were made in silver, much of the system operated by payments in kind. These were assessed, allocated, and receipted from the center. State officials and servants were paid in fixed quantities of wine, grain, or animals; but even members of the royal family received payments in the same way. Officials in Persepolis gave orders for the levying of taxes in kind in other locations, and then gave orders for payments in kind to be made from the proceeds in the same locations. Couriers were given tablets to produce at post stations along the royal highways, so they could get food and lodging for themselves and their animals. These tablets recording payments in kind cover only a relatively limited period, from 509 to 494 BC. There are several thousand of them, and it has been estimated that they cover supplies to more than fifteen thousand different people in more than one hundred different places.[18]

It is significant that the tablets were written mainly in Elamite, not in Persian. We know from other sources that the main language of administration in the empire was neither Persian nor Elamite, but Aramaic, the Semitic *lingua franca* of Mesopotamia, Syria, and Palestine. The Bisitun inscription states directly that the form of written Persian used there was new, developed at Darius's own orders for that specific purpose. It is possible that he and the other Achaemenid kings discouraged any record of events other than their own monumental inscriptions, but these are all strong echoes of the Iranian distaste for writing that we encountered earlier in Mazdaism, and it may go some way to explain an apparent anomaly—the lack of Persian historical writing for the Achaemenid period. It is possible that histories were recorded, that poems were written down, and that all sorts of other literature once existed and have since been simply lost. But later Persian literary culture was strongly associated with a class of scribes, and the fact that the scribes in the Achaemenid system wrote their accounts and official records in other languages suggests that the literature was not there, either. There was no Persian history of the Achaemenid Empire because the Persian ruling classes either (the Magi) regarded writing as wicked or (the kings and nobles) associated writing with inferior peoples—or both. To ride, to shoot the bow, to tell the truth—but not to write it.

That said, no histories as such have survived from the Egyptian, Hittite, or Assyrian empires, either. It is more correct, in the context of the fifth century BC, to call the innovation of history writing by the Greeks an anomaly.

To ourselves, at our great remove of time, awash with written materials and dominated by the getting and spending of money, a human system that was largely nonliterate and operating for the most part on the basis of payments in kind, not cash, seems primitive. But the history of human development is not linear. We should not regard the oral tradition of sophisticated cultures like that of Mazdaism as unreliable, flawed, or backward, something we have gone beyond. The Persians were not stupidly trying, with the wrong tools, to do something we can now, with the right tools, do incomparably better. They were doing something different, and they had evolved complex and subtle ways of doing it very well indeed, which our culture has forgotten. To try to grasp the reality of that, we have to step aside a little from our usual categories of thought—despite the apparent familiarity of concepts like angels, a Day of Judgment, heaven and hell, and moral choice. The Achaemenid Empire was an empire of the mind, but a different kind of mind.

The Empire and the Greeks

In general, Darius's reign was one of restoration and consolidation. It was not a reign of conquest like those that had been pursued by Cyrus and Cambyses. But Darius did campaign into Europe in 512 BC, conquering Thrace and Macedonia, and toward the end of his life, after a revolt by the Ionian Greeks of the Aegean coast of Asia Minor, his subordinates fought a war with the Athenian Greeks that ended with a Persian defeat at the Battle of Marathon in 490 BC. This ushered in what the Greeks called the Persian wars, the shadow of which has affected our view of the Achaemenid Empire, and perhaps our views of Persia, Iran, and the Orient in general. From a Persian perspective, the more serious event was a revolt in Egypt in 486 BC. Before he could deal with this, Darius died.

The standard Greek view of the Persians and their empire was complex, and not a little contradictory. The Greeks regarded the Persians, as they regarded most non-Greeks, as barbarians (the term *barbarian* is thought to come from a disparaging imitation of Persian speech—"ba-ba"), and therefore ignorant and backward. The Greeks were aware that the Persians had a great, powerful, wealthy empire—but one, to their minds, run on tyrannical principles and redolent of vulgar ostentation and decadence. The Persians were therefore both backward and decadent. Here, we may be irresistibly reminded of the contemporary French view of the United States. Perhaps the view of the Greeks also was better explained in terms of a simple resentment or jealousy that the Persians, rather than the Greeks, were running such a large part of the known world.

This is a caricature of the Greek opinion of the Persians, and cannot have been, for example, Plato's attitude or the attitude (openly, at any rate) of the many Greeks who worked for or were allies of the Persians at various times.[19] The Greeks were also an imperialistic or at least a colonizing culture of pioneering Indo-European origin. Perhaps the hostility between the Persians and the Greeks had as much to do with similarity as with difference. But in contrast to the Persians, the Greeks were not a single, unified power. They were composed of a multiplicity of rival city-states, and their influence was maritime rather than land-based. Greeks had established colonies along almost all parts of the Mediterranean coast not previously colonized by the Phoenicians, including places that later became Tarragona in Spain, Marseilles in France, Cyrenaica in Libya, and large parts of Sicily and southern Italy. They had done the same on the coast of the Black Sea. Unlike the Persians, their spread was based on physical settlement, rather than on the control of indigenous peoples from afar.

Just as Persians appear in Greek plays and on Greek vases, there are also examples showing the presence of the Greeks in the minds of the Persians. As well as vases that show a Greek spearing a falling or recumbent Persian, there are engraved cylinder seals showing a Persian stabbing a Greek or filling him with arrows.[20] But it is fair to say the Persians were more present to the Greeks—at least initially—than the Greeks to the Persians. Persian power controlled important Greek cities like Miletus and Phocaea in Asia Minor—only a few hours' rowing away from Athens and Corinth—as well as Chalcidice and Macedonia on the European side of the Bosphorus. In Persepolis, Susa, and Hamadan, by contrast, Greece would have seemed half a world away, and events in other parts of the empire—Egypt, Babylonia, and Bactria—were equally or rather more pressing.

Darius was succeeded by his son, Xerxes (Khashayarsha). The set-piece of Xerxes's reign in the historical record was the great expedition to punish Athens and its allies for their support of the Ionian revolt. But at least as important for Xerxes himself would have been his successful reassertion of authority in Egypt and Babylon, where he crushed a rebellion and destroyed the temple of Marduk that Cyrus had restored. Xerxes is believed (on the authority of Herodotus) to have taken as many as two million men with him to attack Athens in 480 BC. His troops wiped out the rearguard of Spartans and others at Thermopylae, killing the Spartan king Leonidas in a protracted struggle that left many of the Persian troops dead. Xerxes's men then took Athens, his hardy soldiers scaling the Acropolis and burning it. But his fleet was defeated at Salamis, leaving his armies overextended and vulnerable. Xerxes then withdrew to Sardis, his base in Asia Minor, and his forces suffered further defeats the following year at Plataea and Mycale (479 BC). Among other effects of the Persian defeat was the loss of influence on Macedon and Thrace on the European side of the Bosphorus, permitting the subsequent rise of Macedon.

Xerxes's son Artaxerxes (Artakhshathra) succeeded him in 465 BC and reigned for some forty years. The building work at Persepolis continued through the reigns of both, and it was under these two kings that many of the Jews of Babylonia returned to Jerusalem, under the leadership of Ezra and Nehemiah. Nehemiah was Artaxerxes's court cupbearer in Susa, and both Ezra and Nehemiah eventually returned to the Persian court after their efforts to rebuild Jerusalem. The books of Ezra and Nehemiah give a different picture of the Persian monarchy to contrast with the less flattering image in the Greek accounts.

The wars that continued between the Persians and the Greeks ended at least for a time with the peace of Callias in 449 BC, but thereafter the Persians supported Sparta against Athens in the terribly destructive Peloponnesian wars. These conflicts exhausted the older Greek city-states and prepared the way for the hegemony of Macedon. At the death of Artaxerxes, palace intrigues resulted in the murders of several kings or pretenders in succession. In the reign of Artaxerxes II (404–359 BC) there were further wars with the Greeks, and a sustained Egyptian revolt that kept that satrapy independent until Persian rule was restored under Artaxerxes III in 343 BC. But then a particularly lethal round of political intrigue orchestrated by the vizier or chief minister Bagoas caused the deaths of both Artaxerxes III and his son Arses, bringing Darius III to the throne in 336 BC.

The Iranians must have changed their way of life considerably over the two centuries between the reigns of Cyrus and Darius III. One indicator of social change was the constitution of their armies. Prior to and during Xerxes's invasion of Greece, large numbers of Medes and Persians fought on foot, but by the time of Darius III the armies were dominated by large numbers of horsemen. The impression is that the wealth of the empire had enabled the Iranian military classes to distribute themselves across the empire and supply themselves with horses, changing the nature of Persian warfare. There seems also to have been a deliberate policy of military garrisoning and military colonies, notably in Asia Minor. According to Herodotus, Cyrus had warned that if the Persians descended to live in the rich lands of the plain (he probably had Babylonia particularly in mind), they would become soft and incapable of defending their empire. It is too neat to suggest that this is precisely what happened. It may be somewhat the contrary—that by the time of Darius III, taxes had risen too high and the Iranians, having had their expectations raised, had become impoverished and demoralized. But whatever their exact nature, fundamental changes had taken place, and Iran had already moved closer to the social and military patterns of the later Parthian and Sassanid empires.

Macedonia—Strange Fruit

Who were the Macedonians? Some have speculated that they were not really Greeks, but more closely related to the Thracians. Or perhaps they descended from some other Balkan people influenced by the arrival of Indo-European Greeks. They had come under heavy Greek influence by the time of Philip and Alexander—but even at that late stage the Macedonians made a strong distinction between themselves and the Greek hangers-on who accompanied Alexander's eastern adventure. In the fifth century BC, Macedonians were normally, like other non-Greeks, excluded from the Olympic games. But the Persians seem to have referred to them as "Greeks with hats" (they were known for their wide-brimmed hats), and Herodotus too seems to have accepted them as of Greek origin. Like the Medes and Persians in the time of Cyrus, as well as many other militant peoples from mountainous or marginal areas, the Macedonians had a strong sense of their collective superiority—but they also sustained many private feuds among themselves. They were notoriously difficult to manage.

Few stories from the classical world are better known than that of Philip of Macedon and his son Alexander. Often the importance of the father to the success of the son is neglected in favor of the latter's more dramatic victories. Philip was born around 380 BC, became king of Macedon in 359 BC, and immediately set about the expansion of his kingdom. One essential contribution to the success of Macedon was his creation of a new, tightly drilled infantry corps, equipped with a longer spear or pike than was normal in Greece at the time. In favorable conditions this army usually swept aside or rolled over conventionally armed infantry. Having established himself as the prime power in northern Greece and Thrace, Philip defeated the alliance of Athens and Thebes at the Battle of Chaeronea in 338 BC, and then set up the League of Corinth, which established Macedonian hegemony and effectively ended the independence of the Greek city-states, with the exception of Sparta. When Philip demanded submission of the Spartans, saying that he would come to Sparta and wreck their farms, kill the people, and destroy their city, the Spartans replied: "If." Philip and his son left the Spartans alone—perhaps not least for the sake of the legend of Thermopylae.

Philip had other plans in any case—plans to invade the Persian Empire. His preparations were quite open, and were justified in pan-Hellenic terms by reference to the Persian desecration of Athenian temples in the invasion of 480 BC. But in 336 BC, before Philip could put his invasion plans into effect, he was murdered. The circumstances of the murder are murky and were disputed at the time—some have suggested that Alexander and his mother Olympias were involved, but it is possible that the Persians instigated the killing.

Alexander continued where his father had left off. He consolidated his authority in Greece, quickly crushing a rebellion in Thebes, and then, in 334 BC, crossed into Asia Minor. He defeated a Persian army at the Granicus River (near the Dardanelles), conquered the towns of the Ionian coast—including the Persian regional base at Sardis—and then marched east. The following year he defeated Darius at the Battle of Issus (on the Mediterranean coast near the modern border between Syria and Turkey), leading the decisive attack personally at the head of his companion cavalry (*hetairoi*). Alexander then marched south, taking the coastal cities, conquering Egypt and founding Alexandria. Moving east again, in 331 BC Alexander defeated Darius in a third battle, at Gaugamela, near Mosul and Irbil in what is now Iraqi Kurdistan. Darius left the battlefield and was killed some time after by Bessus, the satrap of Bactria.

This is not the place to consider Alexander's conduct of war in any detail, but his military brilliance illustrates something that may appear at first counter-intuitive—the feminine nature of military genius at the highest level. Successful high command has little or nothing to do with masculine attributes like brute force, bravado, machismo, arrogance, or even courage, except insofar as it may be necessary to advertise these from time to time to inspire the troops. Rather, it has to do with what one might regard as more feminine characteristics—sensitivity, subtlety, intuition, timing, an indirect approach, an ability quietly to assess strength and weakness (based perhaps on an intuitive grasp for the opponent's likely behavior as much as factual information) to avoid and baffle strength, to flow around it, to absorb its force and strike unexpectedly at the weak spot at precisely the right moment. Military history shows again and again that predictable male behavior, manifest in frontal attacks and reliance on strength alone, is at best a liability and at worst catastrophically wasteful at the command level. The maximum effectiveness of military force is achieved only by the more subtle methods associated with what one might call a feminine approach. Without making any crass connection to Alexander's bisexuality, his conduct of warfare exemplifies this well.

Alexander continued on to Babylon, Susa, and finally Persepolis, which he burned to destruction in 330 BC after some weeks and months of celebrations. One story says that a courtesan accompanying the army, Thaïs, persuaded Alexander to destroy the palaces while he was drunk, in revenge for the burning of the Athenian Acropolis by Xerxes, and threw in the first torch herself. But it is likely that the destruction was a deliberate political act, to show that the Achaemenid dynasty was over for good. Notwithstanding the destruction of Persepolis, Alexander had been presenting himself, at least since Gaugamela, not so much as the revenger of Greece but as the successor to the Achaemenians.[21] From now on he appears to have followed a deliberate Persianizing policy, encouraging his troops to marry local women and settling them in colonies. He himself married several Persian princesses, including Statira, the daughter of Darius III, and later Roxana (whose name is cognate with the modern Persian word *roshan*, meaning "light"), daughter of Oxyartes of Bactria. Alexander continued with his campaigns, into the farthest reaches of the former empire, wiping out all resistance, and then beyond, into India and what is now the Punjab. But his troops grew increasingly weary of the never-ending wars, and disaffected with his perceived pro-Persian policy.

Alexander died in Babylon in 323 BC, probably of natural causes, after a session of heavy drinking. The succession to his empire was left unclear, and the result was a lengthy series of wars between his generals to divide up his conquests. In these, the murderous unruliness of the Macedonians emerged with full force. Alexander's secretary Eumenes of Cardia had some temporary success in reunifying the centrifugal elements in support of Alexander's young son, born to Roxana after his death. But the other generals and soldiers disliked Eumenes because he was a Greek and a scholar, and in 316 BC he was betrayed and killed. Within a few years Roxana and Alexander's son were also murdered.

Despite his early death, Alexander's aim—to bring Greek influence into Persia, Persian influence into Greece, and to create a blend of Eastern and

Western civilizations—was realized to a startling extent. But ultimately it failed. For more than a century after Alexander's death, Persia was ruled by the descendants of Seleucus, one of Alexander's generals, and Greek influence persisted after that. But the kings of the Seleucid period ruled more in a grand Persian rather than a Greek style. This was arguably also the case for the Ptolemies who ruled in Egypt. When Rome rose to dominate the entire Mediterranean basin, the Roman Empire was divided between the Greek east and the Latin west—but still the style of the Greek east showed the influence of the vanished Achaemenid Empire, and in turn influenced Romans with imperial ambitions from Pompey to Elagabalus.

Although the Iranians submitted to foreign rule—not for the last time in their history—Greek influence was ultimately passing and superficial despite the presence of colonies of Greek ex-soldiers. The Mazdaean religion persisted and consolidated, serving as a focus for hostility to the Greeks, and to the memory of Alexander.

It is generally recognized that the historical accounts we have of Alexander and his life are partial, written mainly by authors writing at second hand and in awe of their subject. They are all Western accounts, and although there is an Eastern tradition of Alexander (*Iskander*) as a warrior-hero, the Zoroastrian tradition about him is very negative, suggesting a different side to the story. There is little in the Western sources about measures Alexander took to establish or consolidate his rule, but the Zoroastrian record says he killed many Magi and teachers, and that the sacred flames in many fire temples were extinguished. This may simply reflect the incidental killing and destruction of the plundering Macedonian armies. But it is likely that the Magian priests, proprietors as they were of the religion that underpinned the Achaemenian state and therefore the most likely center for any continued resistance or revolt, would have been a target for repression in any case.

Whatever exactly happened, it is unlikely that the Iranians cooperated as submissively in Alexander's pacification policies as the Western historians later suggested. In later Zoroastrian writings Alexander is the only human to share with Ahriman the title *guzastag*—meaning "accursed."[22]

2

The Iranian Revival

Parthians and Sassanids

We have made enquiries about the rules of the inhabitants of the Roman empire and the Indian states. . . . We have never rejected anybody because of their different religion or origin. We have not jealously kept away from them what we affirm. And at the same time we have not disdained to learn what they stand for. For it is a fact that to have knowledge of the truth and of sciences and to study them is the highest thing with which a king can adorn himself. And the most disgraceful thing for kings is to disdain learning and be ashamed of exploring the sciences. He who does not learn is not wise.

—Khosraw I Anushirvan
(according to the Byzantine historian Agathias)

The empire established by Seleucus Nicator in 312 BC looked to be the most powerful of the successor states that emerged out of the collection of territories conquered by Alexander. It controlled Syria, Mesopotamia, and the lands of the Iranian plateau—as well as (at least in theory) other territories further east. Initially the capital was established at Babylon, and later at a new site at Seleuceia on the Tigris River. Finally it moved to Antioch on the Mediterranean Sea.

The Seleucid kings pursued the easternizing policy of Alexander. They established Greek military and trading colonies in the east and used Iranian manpower in their armies, but their political attention was on the west—particularly on their rivalry with the other major eastern Macedonian/Greek dynasty, that of the Ptolemies in Egypt. In the east, outlying satrapies like Sogdiana and Bactria gradually became independent princedoms, the latter creating an enduring culture in what is now northern Afghanistan, fusing eastern and Greek cultures under Greek successor dynasties.

Warrior Horsemen

The horse-based cultures of the northeast had given Alexander problems, and the Achaemenids before him. Tribes like the Dahae and the Sakae, who spoke languages in the Iranian family group, would always be very difficult for any empire to dominate. With their military strength entirely on horseback, they were highly mobile and able, when threatened, to disappear into the great expanses of desert and semi-desert south of the Aral Sea. Within two generations of Seleucus Nicator's death in 281 BC, one tribe or group of tribes among the Dahae—the Parni—established their supremacy in Parthia and other lands east of the Caspian. They supplanted the local Seleucid satrap, Andragoras—who around 250 BC had rebelled and tried to make himself an independent ruler in Parthia—and began to threaten the remaining territories of the Seleucids in the east. The Parni ruling family named themselves Arsacids after Arshak (Arsaces), the man who had led them to take control of Parthia. But as the Arsacids expanded their dominion, they were careful to preserve the wealth and culture of the Greek colonies in the towns. Parthian kings later used the title *philhellenos* (friend of the Greeks) on their coinage.

Several Seleucid kings carried out expeditions to the east to restore their authority in Parthia and Bactria, and the Parthian Arsacids occasionally chose to ally with them or even to submit, rather than to confront them. But the Seleucids were always drawn back to the west, and in the reign of the Arsacid Mithradates I (171–138 BC) the Parthians renewed their expansion, taking Sistan, Elam, and Media. Then they captured Babylon in 142 BC and, one year later, Seleuceia itself.

In the decades that followed, the Parthians were attacked by the Sakae in the east and by the Seleucids in the west. Fortunes swung either way. At one point in 128 BC the Parthians defeated a Seleucid army, captured it, and attempted to use the prisoners against the Sakae—only to find that the Seleucid troops had made common cause with the Sakae. Together, they defeated and killed the Parthian king, Phraates. But Mithradates II (Mithradates the Great) was able to consolidate and stabilize Parthian rule in a long reign from about 123 to 87 BC, subduing enemies in both east and west. He also took the title King of Kings, a deliberate reference back to the Achaemenid monarchy. This, along with other indicators, suggests a new Iranian self-confidence.

Concealed behind the long struggle between the Seleucids and the Parthians lie the origins of the silk trade, which was to be of central importance for many Iranian towns and cities for more than a millennium. The initial involvement of Greeks and Greek cities in the silk business may go some way toward explaining both the survival of Greek culture in the Parthian period, and the Parthian kings' respect for it. They were friends to the Greeks not out of aesthetic sensibility or deference to a superior culture, but because they wanted to protect the goose that laid the golden egg.[1]

Mithradates had diplomatic contacts with both the Chinese Han emperor Wu Ti and with the Roman republic under the dictator Sulla. In order to establish a lasting presence in Mesopotamia, either he or his successor Gotarzes founded a new city at Ctesiphon, near Seleuceia. Ctesiphon was to continue as the capital for more than seven hundred years, though Seleuceia, on the other side of the Tigris, was often used as the center of administration, and Ecbatana/Hamadan as the summer capital.

The Parthians established a powerful empire and ruled successfully for several centuries, but they did so with a relatively light touch, assimilating the practices of previous rulers and being content to tolerate the variety of religious, linguistic, and cultural patterns of their subject provinces. A system of devolved power (*parakandeh shahi,* also called *muluk al-tawa'if* in later Arab sources) through satraps continued, often keeping in power families that had ruled under the Seleucids.[2] Parthian scribes continued to use Aramaic, as in the time of the Achaemenids, and there appears to have been a continued diversity of religion. Names like Mithradates and Phraates (the latter a name thought to be related to the fravashi of the *Avesta*) show the Mazdaean allegiances of the Arsacids themselves, but Babylonians, Greeks, Jews, and others were allowed to follow their own religious traditions. As before, Mazdaism itself seems to have encompassed a variety of practices and beliefs. In Jewish tradition, the Parthians are recorded and remembered (with the important exception of the reign of one later king) as tolerant and friendly toward the Jews.[3] This may reflect the fact that the rise of the Parthians in the east was helped by the prolonged struggle between the Maccabean Jews and the Seleucids in Palestine.

The Parthians were not just crude nomads assuming the culture of their subjects for lack of any of their own—or, at least, they did not remain so. Parthian sculpture, with its own particular style that included a strong emphasis on frontality, was different in kind from any predecessor. Parthian architecture—as excavated at Nisa, for example (in what is now Turkmenistan)—shows for the first time the emergence of the audience hall or *ivan,* a feature to be of great importance later, in Sassanid and Islamic architecture. The Parthians exemplified the best of Iranian genius—the recognition, acceptance, and tolerance of the complexity of the cultures and influences over which they ruled, while retaining a strong central principle of identity and integrity.

Rome's Great Rival in the East

The Parthians were also masters of the art of war, as they would show in the next period of conflict, with Rome. Driven on to ever-wider conquests by the ambitions of mighty patricians like Pompeii, Lucullus, and Crassus,

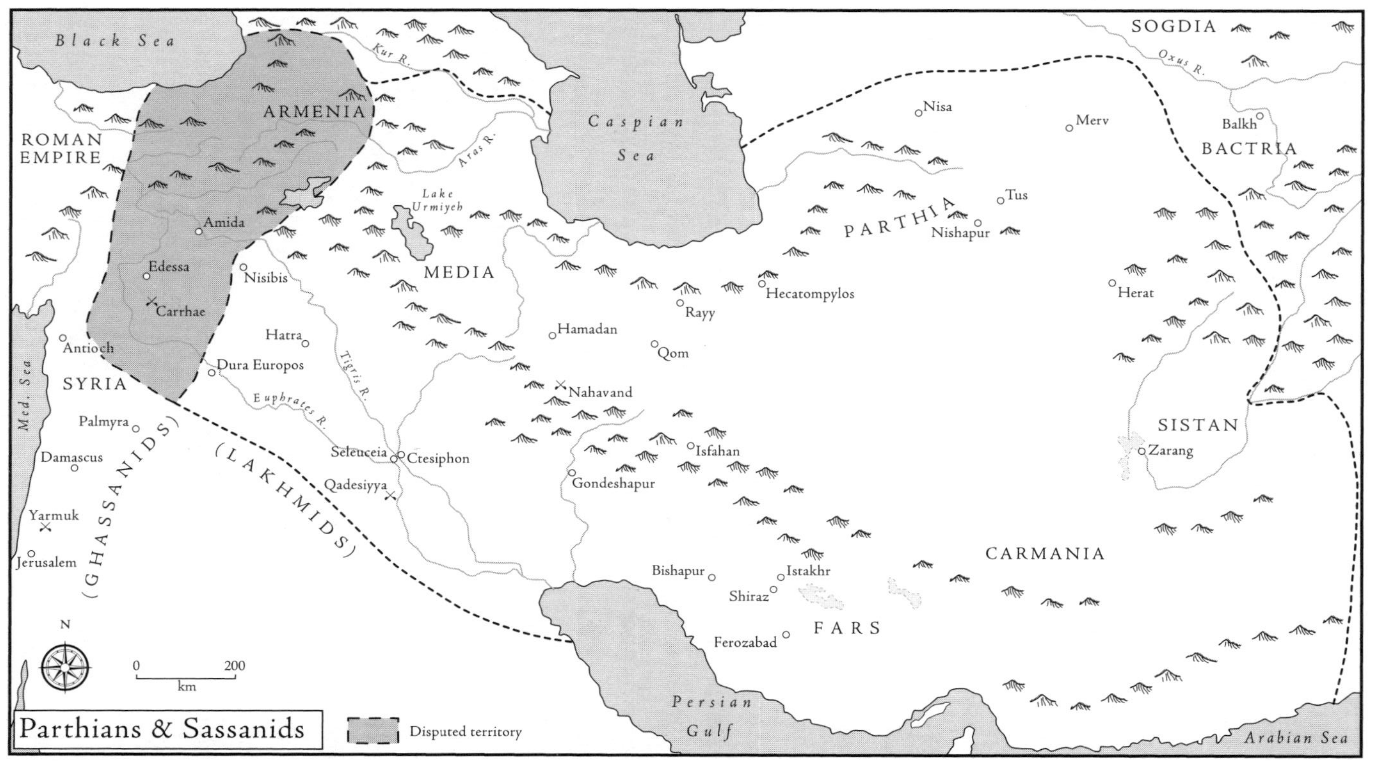
Black Sea
ARMENIA
ROMAN EMPIRE
Kur R.
Aras R.
Caspian Sea
SOGDIA
Oxus R.
Nisa
Merv
Balkh
BACTRIA
Lake Urmiyeh
Tus
PARTHIA
Nishapur
Amida
MEDIA
Edessa
Nisibis
Hecatompylos
Herat
Carrhae
Rayy
Hatra
Hamadan
Antioch
Qom
Dura Europos
Tigris R.
SYRIA
Nahavand
Euphrates R.
Med. Sea
Palmyra
SISTAN
Zarang
Damascus
Seleuceia
Ctesiphon
Isfahan
(LAKHMIDS)
Gondeshapur
Qadesiyya
Yarmuk
(GHASSANIDS)
CARMANIA
Jerusalem
Bishapur
Istakhr
Shiraz
N
FARS
Ferozabad
0
200
km
Persian Gulf
Parthians & Sassanids
Disputed territory
Arabian Sea

leaders who saw conquest and military glory as necessary adjuncts to a successful political career, the Roman republic by the first half of the first century BC had taken over the eastern Mediterranean from its previous Hellenistic overlords and had begun to press even farther eastward. The Romans' main area of conflict with the Parthians was in Armenia, Syria, and northern Mesopotamia.

In 53 BC Marcus Licinius Crassus, a fabulously rich Roman politician who had destroyed the slave revolt of Spartacus in southern Italy in earlier years, became the new governor of Roman Syria. Hoping to make conquests in the east to rival those recently achieved by Caesar in Gaul, Crassus marched an army of some forty thousand men east to Carrhae (modern Harran)—arrogantly rejecting the advice of the king of Armenia to take advantage of his friendship and follow a less exposed northerly route. At Carrhae Crassus's army was met in the open plain by a smaller but fast-moving force of about ten thousand Parthian horsemen, including large numbers of horse archers, supported by a much smaller force of heavily armored cavalrymen on armored horses, each man wielding a long, heavy lance. The Roman force was composed primarily of armored infantry equipped with swords and heavy throwing spears, along with some Gaulish cavalrymen who were either lightly armored or not armored at all.

The Parthians confronted Crassus with a kind of fighting that the Romans had not previously encountered, and against which they had no answer. The Roman infantry advanced, but the Parthian horse archers withdrew before them, circling around to shoot arrows into the flanks of their column. Hour after hour the arrows rained down on the Romans, and despite their heavy armor the powerful Parthian war bows frequently zinged an arrow past the edge of a shield, found a gap at the neck between body armor and helmet, punched through a weak link in chain mail, or wounded a soldier's unprotected hands or feet. The Romans grew tired and thirsty in the heat, and their frustration at not being able to get to grips with the Parthians turned to defeatism, especially when they saw the Parthians resupply themselves with arrows from masses of heavily laden pack camels.

At one point Crassus's son led a detachment, including the Gaulish cavalry, against the Parthians. The Parthians pulled back as if in disorder, but their real intention was to draw the detachment away beyond any possible assistance from the main body. When the Gauls rode ahead to chase off the archers, the Parthian heavy cavalry charged down on them, spearing the lightly armored Gauls and their horses with their long lances. In desperation, the Gauls tried to attack the Parthian horses by dismounting and rolling under them, trying to stab up at their unprotected bellies, but even this desperate tactic could not save them. Then the full strength of the Parthian horse archers turned on the Roman detachment. More and more of them were hit by arrows, while all were disoriented and confused by the clouds of dust thrown up by the Parthians' horses. Crassus's son pulled his men back to a small hill—where they were surrounded and eventually killed, with the exception of about five hundred, who were taken prisoner.

The defeat of the detachment and the jubilation of the Parthians further demoralized the main Roman force. Finally, Crassus attempted to negotiate with the Parthian general, Suren, only to be killed in a scuffle and beheaded. The survivors of the Roman army withdrew in disorder back into Roman Syria. Meanwhile, as many as ten thousand Roman prisoners were marched off by the Parthians to the remote northeast of the empire.

According to the Greek historian Plutarch the head of Crassus was sent to the Parthian king, Orodes, and it arrived while the king was listening to an actor delivering some lines from Euripedes's play *The Bacchae*. To the applause of the court, the actor took the head and spoke the words of Queen Agave of Thebes, who in the play unwittingly killed her own son, King Pentheus, while in a Bacchic trance:

> We've hunted down a lion's whelp today,
> And from the mountains bring a noble prey[4]

Some have suggested that the Parthian general, recorded in the Western sources as Suren, was the warrior-hero later remembered as Rostam and immortalized in the revered tenth-century Persian poet Ferdowsi's *Shahnameh*

(Book of Kings). Like Rostam, Suren hailed from Sistan (originally Sakastan—the land of the Sakae), and like Rostam, he also had a troubled relationship with his king. Orodes was so resentful of Suren's victory that he had him murdered.

The defeat at Carrhae was a great blow to Roman prestige in the east, and after it the Parthians were able to extend their control to include Armenia. But in the fiercely competitive environment of Rome toward the end of the republic, the defeat, humiliation, and death of Crassus were a challenge as much as a warning. To succeed where Crassus had failed—to win a Parthian triumph—became an inviting political prize. Another incentive was the wealth of the silk trade. While the hostile Parthians controlled the central part of the route to China, wealthy Romans were dismayed to see much of the gold they paid to have their wives and daughters clothed in expensive silks going to their most redoubtable enemies.

The next Roman to test the Parthians in a major way was Mark Antony. But between the expeditions of Crassus and Antony, the Parthians and the Romans fought several other campaigns, with mixed outcomes. In 51 BC some Roman survivors from Carrhae ambushed an invading Parthian force near Antioch and destroyed it. But in 40 BC another Parthian force, commanded by Orodes's son Pacorus (with the help of a renegade Roman, Quintus Labienus), broke out of Syria and conquered both Palestine and most of the provinces of Asia Minor. Exploiting the chaos of the civil wars that followed the murder of Julius Caesar in 44 BC, the Parthian invaders received the submission of many towns without a siege. But a year or so later Publius Ventidius, one of Mark Antony's subordinates, rescued the eastern provinces with some of the veteran legions of Caesar's army. He defeated the Parthians in a series of battles in which all the main Parthian commanders were killed, including Pacorus and Labienus. Back in Rome, Ventidius's triumph over the Parthians was considered a rare honor. Seeing his lieutenant so praised, Mark Antony wanted the glory of a victory against the Parthians for himself.

In 36 BC he took an army more than double the size of that of Crassus into the same area of upper Mesopotamia.[5] Antony soon encountered many of the same difficulties that had frustrated Crassus. The Romans found that their best remedy against the Parthian arrows was to form the close formation called the *testudo* (tortoise), in which the soldiers closed up so that their shields made a wall in front, with the ranks behind holding their shields over their heads, overlapping, to make a roof. This made an effective defense but slowed the army's advance to a crawl. The Roman infantry still could not hit back at the Parthian horse archers, whose mobility enabled them to range at will around the marching Romans and attack them at their most vulnerable. The Parthians were also able to attack Antony's supply columns, and the difficulty of finding food and water made the large numbers of the invading force a liability rather than an asset. Having suffered in this way in the south, Antony attempted a more northerly attack on Parthian territory, penetrating into what is now Azerbaijan. But he achieved little, and was forced to retreat through Armenia in the winter cold, losing as many as twenty-four thousand men.

Antony saved some face by a later campaign in Armenia, but the overall message of these Roman encounters with the Parthians was that the styles of warfare of the opponents, and the geography of the region, dictated a stalemate that would be difficult for either side to break. The Parthian cavalry was vulnerable to ambush by Roman infantry in the hilly, less open terrain of the Roman-controlled territories, and lacked the siege equipment necessary to take the Roman towns. At the same time, the Romans were vulnerable to the Parthians in the open Mesopotamian plain and would always find it difficult to protect their supply lines against the more mobile Parthian forces. These factors were more or less permanent.

Perhaps recognizing the intractability of this situation, after Augustus eventually achieved supremacy in the Roman Empire and ended the civil wars by defeating Mark Antony in 31/30 BC, Augustus followed a policy of diplomacy with the Parthians. In this way he was able to retrieve the eagle standards of the legions that had been lost at Carrhae. The Parthians seem to have used the period of peace in the west to create a new Indo-Parthian empire in the Punjab, under a line descended from the Suren family. But the wars in the west began again in the reign of Nero, after the Parthian king

Vologases I (Valkash) had appointed a new king in Armenia, which the Romans regarded as a dependent state of the Roman Empire. The general Gnaeus Domitius Corbulo conquered Armenia in AD 58–60, but the Parthians counterattacked with some success thereafter, capturing a Roman force.[6] It has been suggested that the Roman armor made of overlapping plates (*lorica segmentata*), familiar from films and children's books, was developed as a counter to Parthian arrows around the time of the campaign of Corbulo. The outcome of the Armenian war was that the Romans and Parthians signed a treaty agreeing to the establishment of an independent Arsacid dynasty in Armenia as a buffer state, but with the succession subject to Roman approval.

Vologases I may also be significant in the history of Mazdaism and the beginnings of its transition into the modern religion of Zoroastrianism. Later Zoroastrian texts say that a king Valkash (they do not specify which one—several Arsacid kings took that name) was the first to tell the Magian priests to bring together all the oral and written traditions of their religion and record them systematically. This began the process that, several centuries later, led to the assembly of the texts of the *Avesta* and the other holy scriptures of Zoroastrianism.[7] If indeed it was Vologases I who gave out those instructions (a conjecture supported by the fact that his brother Tiridates was known also for his Mazdaean piety[8]), it would perhaps fit with other decisions and policies during his reign, which seem consistently to have stressed a desire to reassert the Iranian character of the state. Vologases I is believed to have built a new capital named after himself near Seleuceia and Ctesiphon, with the aim of avoiding the Greek character of those places. Some of his coins were struck with lettering in Aramaic script (the script in which the Parthian language was usually written) rather than in Greek, as had been the case before. And there are suggestions also that he was hostile to the Jews, which was atypical in the Arsacid period.[9] Although his immediate successors did not follow through with all of these novelties, they do prefigure the policies of the Sassanids. The gradual erosion of Greek influence and the strengthening of Iranian identity are features of the reigns after Vologases I.

Sol Invictus

Something else taken west by the Roman soldiers from their encounters in the east was a new religion—Mithraism. Having been one of the subordinate deities of Mazdaism in the Achaemenid period, Mithras became the central god of a religion in its own right after his transition westward (in the west he became known as Mithras rather than Mithra). It may be that his significance had grown in a particular context or location in Persia or Asia Minor at an earlier stage, and some have suggested that the cult was a wholly new one that took little from Persia beyond the name.[10] As worshipped in the west, Mithras always remained primarily a god of soldiers (which may point up a connection with the Parthian wars) and was an important bonding element in the lives of military men who might find themselves separated from friends and familiar places again and again in the course of their lives, as they were posted from place to place. Although Mithras was associated with the sun (*sol invictus*—the Invincible Sun), Mithraism seems to have taken on some of the ritualized cult character of Western paganism, losing most of the ethical content of Iranian Mazdaism and becoming a kind of secret society a little like the Freemasons. Its tenets included secret ceremonies (mysteries), initiation rites, and a hierarchy of grades of membership. The underground temples of Mithras are found all over the empire, as far away from Iran as by the Walbrook in London and at Carrawburgh (Roman Brocolitia) on Hadrian's Wall. The period of the cult's early popularity and spread was the first century AD.

Mithraism joins the list of important religious and intellectual influences from the Iranian lands on the West. It is thought to have had an important influence on the early Christian church, as the Christian bishops made converts and tried to make the new religion as acceptable as possible to former pagans (though the rise of Mithraism only narrowly predates the rise of Christianity). Mithras's followers believed he was born on December 25, of a virgin (though some accounts say he was born from a rock), with shepherds as his first worshippers. His rites included a kind of baptism and a sacramental meal. Other aspects of the cult reflected its Mazdaean origins—Mithras was believed to have killed a bull as a sacrifice, and it was from the blood of that bull that all other living things emerged. Mithras was the ally of Ahura Mazda against the evil principle in the world, Ahriman.

In the following century the great soldier-emperor Trajan managed to break the strategic logjam in the East with a new invasion of Mesopotamia, after the Parthian Vologases III had given him a pretext by deposing one ruler of Armenia and appointing another, whom the Romans did not like. Instead of trying to toil south in the heat toward Ctesiphon on foot, under a hail of arrows, in AD 115 Trajan put his men and equipment into boats and ran them downstream through Mesopotamia along the river Tigris. When they reached Ctesiphon and Seleuceia, they drove off the Parthian defenders and applied the most refined techniques of Roman siege engineering. The twin capital fell, and Trajan annexed the provinces of Mesopotamia to the Roman Empire. He marched his men as far as the shore of the Persian Gulf and would have liked to go farther, emulating Alexander. But in 116 he fell ill while besieging Hatra, which his armies had bypassed earlier. A year later, he died.

Trajan's conquests, although impressive enough to win him the title Parthicus, could not destroy the centers of Parthian power further east. In the end, they proved to be little more permanent than the Parthian conquests of Pacorus and Labienus in Palestine and Asia Minor of 40 BC. Before Trajan died, the Romans had been assailed by revolts in Mesopotamia and elsewhere in their eastern provinces. His successor, Hadrian, abandoned Trajan's conquests in Armenia and Mesopotamia and made peace with the Parthian king Osroes (Khosraw) on the basis of the old frontier on the Euphrates River. Nonetheless, Trajan had overcome the ghost of Carrhae and had shown his successors how to crack the strategic problem of Mesopotamia.

It may be that the Trajanic invasion marks the beginning of a decline of the Arsacids, and it is certainly plain that Mesopotamia had ceased to be the secure possession it had been before. Over the next century, Roman armies penetrated to Seleuceia/Ctesiphon twice more—in AD 165 (under Verus) and in 199 (under Septimus Severus). But over the same period the Parthians fought back hard (assisted in 165/166 by the outbreak of a disease among the Romans that may have been smallpox), and made their own incursion into Syria.

In 216, at the instigation of Emperor Caracalla, the Romans again invaded, but got no farther than Arbela (Irbil/Hewler). Caracalla was one of the most brutal of the Roman emperors (in 215 he had massacred thousands of people in Alexandria because the citizens were reported to have ridiculed him). While relieving himself on the side of a road near Carrhae, he was apparently stabbed to death by his own bodyguards. The Parthians under Artabanus (Ardavan) IV then struck back at the Romans under Caracalla's successor, Macrinus, and inflicted a heavy defeat on them at Nisibis. After that, in 218, Macrinus had to yield up a heavy war reparation that cost two hundred million sesterces (according to Dio Cassius) to secure peace.

Whatever the precise effect of the wars on the Arsacid monarchy, they must have been exhausting and damaging—especially in Mesopotamia and the northwest, which would always have been, in good times, some of the wealthiest provinces of the empire. There had always been vicious and protracted succession disputes among the Arsacids, thanks mostly to the nature of court politics and, perhaps, the effect of the involvement of a group of noble families (central to Arsacid rule seems to have been alliances with a small group of wealthy families, including those of the Suren, Karen, and Mehran). But these difficult succession struggles seem also to have grown more frequent and intractable, exacerbating a falling-off of the authority of the monarchy.

The Persian Revival

Early in the third century AD a new power began to arise in the province of Persis—Fars, the province from which the Achaemenids had emerged. A family owing allegiance to the Arsacids came to prominence as local rulers there, but in April 224 the latest head of this family, having broadened his support to include the cities of Kerman and Isfahan, led an army against Artabanus IV and killed him in battle at Hormuzdgan near Shushtar in

Khuzestan. This victor's name was Ardashir, a reference back to the name Artakhshathra (Artaxerxes), the name of several of the Achaemenid kings. Ardashir claimed Achaemenid descent, probably to disguise the more recent, relatively humble origins of his family (who called themselves Sassanids, after a predecessor called Sasan).

Ardashir also made a strong association between his cause and that of the form of Mazdaism followed in Fars (his father, Papak, had been a priest of Anahita at the religious center of Istakhr). The downfall of Artabanus was later celebrated in a dramatic rock-carving at Ferozabad, which showed Ardashir and his followers on galloping chargers, striking the Parthian king and his men from their horses with their lances.

The Arsacid regime did not collapse immediately, and their coins were still minted in Mesopotamia until 228. But in 226 Ardashir had himself crowned King of Kings after taking Ctesiphon, and within a few years he controlled all the territory of the former Parthian Empire. That fact alone suggests that several of the great Parthian families (whose local rulerships are known to have persisted long after 224) cooperated in the change of dynasty.

Ardashir was determined from the beginning that his new dynasty would assert and justify itself in a new way. His coins (and those of his successors) bore inscriptions in Persian script instead of the Greek used on Arsacid coins, and on the reverse showed a Mazdaean fire temple. The Sassanids were to be Iranian, Mazdaean kings before all else. In another massively impressive rock-carving at Naqsh-e Rostam near Persepolis, Ardashir is shown on horseback receiving the symbol of his kingship from Ormuzd (the name of Ahura Mazda in Middle Persian). Artabanus IV is depicted crushed beneath the feet of Ardashir's horse, and Ahriman under the hooves of the horse on which Ormuzd is seated. The message could not be more clear—Ardashir had been chosen by God. His victory over the last Arsacid had been assisted by God, and he had overcome Artabanus in a struggle that paralleled directly that of Ormuzd against Ahriman, the principle of chaos and evil.[11] Coinage inscriptions also declared Ardashir to be of divine descent. This was an innovation with important later resonances.

Paradoxically for this very Iranian monarch, the idea may have originated in the preceding period of Greek influence. The pattern of a new, autocratic ruler from more or less obscure origins, taking power by force after a period of disorder—and claiming the decision of God for his victory and his justification—has been suggested as a recurring theme in Iranian history by Homa Katouzian, and perhaps has its archetypal image in this relief carving.[12] The rebellion of Ardashir also, with its heavy religious overtones, echoes earlier and later religious revolutions in Iran.

This rock-relief at Naqsh-e Rostam also includes the first known inscription referring to Iran, though there are references in the *Avesta* that probably pre-date the Sassanid period, and the word also appears on Ardashir's coins. From other contemporary evidence, the term *Iran* may refer to the territory over which those responsible for the inscriptions considered the Mazdaean religion to be observed. Or it may possibly refer to the territories in which the Iranian family of languages were spoken (though the inclusion of Babylonia and Mesene within Iran makes this doubtful). Or, perhaps, it signified something less clearly defined, about people rather than territory, which partook of both things.

What is more certain is that alongside the concept of Iran was that of a *non-Iran* (*Aniran*)—territories ruled by the Sassanid shah but not regarded as Iranian. These included Syria, Cilicia, and Georgia.[13] Whatever the precise significance of these terms, their use on the rock-carving strongly suggests a sense of Iranian identity, perhaps centered on Fars but with significance much beyond. It also seems unlikely that Ardashir conjured these concepts from thin air. Their utility for him was as an underpinning for his royal authority. To be effective for that purpose, they must have had some resonance with his subjects—a resonance that touched on an older sense of land, people, and political culture.

In later years Ardashir attempted to round off his success in taking over the Parthian Empire by launching attacks on the Romans, along the old front in upper Mesopotamia and Syria. This suggests that he felt the need to justify his access to power by success against the Romans and, by extension, that the Parthians' perceived failures against the Romans had been part of the reason for their downfall. At first impression, the interminable series of wars between the Roman Empire and Persia (both in the Parthian period and again in the Sassanid period) look almost inexplicable. They went on and on, century after century. There was a potential economic gain for both sides—the disputed provinces were rich provinces. But it was evident, certainly by the time of Ardashir, that the wars were very costly, that it would be very difficult indeed for either party to deliver a knockout blow to the other, and that any gains would be difficult for either side to hold permanently. The wars and the disputed provinces had taken on a totemic value—they had become part of the apparatus by which Persian shahs and Roman emperors alike justified their rule. This explains their personal participation in the campaigns, the triumphs in Rome and the rock-reliefs carved on the hillsides of Fars. Upper Mesopotamia, Armenia, and Syria had become an unfortunate playground for princes.

Ardashir was not initially successful in his wars against the Romans, but after some years he was able to retake Nisibis and Carrhae. In his last years he ruled jointly with his son Shapur, who succeeded him after his death in 241. And it was Shapur who achieved some of the most dramatic successes of the long wars with Rome. These began with his defeat of the Romans at Misikoe in 243, during which the Roman Emperor Gordian was killed. In 244, Shapur accepted the submission of Emperor Philip the Arab and the cession of Armenia. In 259/260 the Emperor Valerian led an army against Shapur—but the Persians defeated Valerian west of Edessa and took him prisoner. These events are commemorated by another mural sculpture at Naqsh-e Rostam, which shows Shapur on horseback receiving the submission of both Roman emperors. The inscription claims that Philip paid five hundred thousand denarii in ransom, and that Shapur captured Valerian in battle "Ourselves with Our own hands."[14] There are different accounts of what happened to Valerian thereafter. The more sensational one (from Roman sources) is that after some years of humiliation the former emperor was eventually flayed alive; his skin was then stuffed with straw and exhibited as a reminder of the superiority of Persian arms. Anthony Hecht wrote a poem based on this story, from which the following is an excerpt:

> . . . A hideous life-sized doll, filled out with straw,
> In the skin of the Roman Emperor, Valerian . . .
> Swung in the wind on a rope from the palace flag-pole
> And young girls were brought there by their mothers
> To be told about the male anatomy. . . .[15]

But the inscription at Naqsh-e Rostam says the Roman captives were settled in various places around the empire, and there is evidence of this at Bishapur and Shushtar, where the Romans showed their engineering expertise by building a combined bridge and dam, the remains of which can still be seen (along with other Roman-built bridges elsewhere). It may be that Valerian, rather than surviving only as a stuffed skin to be giggled at, lived out his days as *pontifex maximus* of a Persian city. Given the other evidence of Shapur's generally humane conduct (and the spirit of the Naqsh-e Rostam relief itself, which seems to show magnanimity rather than brutal humiliation of the enemy), it may be that the former story is just a rather gruesome fable, reported by uncritical Roman historians who had no idea what really had become of Valerian after his capture, but were ready to believe the worst of the Persians. Large numbers of ordinary people, including many Christians from Antioch and elsewhere, were brought back and settled in Persia by Shapur after his campaigns. In addition to the wars with Rome, both Ardashir and Shapur campaigned in the east against the Kushans, eventually establishing Sassanid rule over large parts of what are now Central Asia, Afghanistan, and northern India.

Ardashir and Shapur made changes in government that may have paralleled the beginnings of some deeper changes in society. Government became more centralized, the bureaucracy expanded, and from the devolved system of the Parthians (sometimes, probably misleadingly, described as a kind of feudalism) a new pattern evolved.[16] New offices and titles appeared in inscriptions, including *dibir* (scribe), *ganzwar* (treasurer), and *dadwar* (judge). The old Parthian families continued, but were given court offices and may thereby, one may say, have been domesticated (a change reminiscent of the way in which Louis XIV of France tamed the French nobility after the

Fronde civil wars of the mid-seventeenth century). This change in role for the great nobles may in time have helped initiate another phenomenon of social, cultural, and military significance: the emergence of a class of gentry, the *dehqans,* who in later centuries controlled the countryside, its villages, and its peasantry on the shah's behalf, and provided the armored cavalry that were the central battle-winning weapon of the Sassanid armies. (Though in the interim the great noble families retained much of their power in the provinces, and the cavalry were provided in large part by their retainers—as in the time of the Parthians.)

In several other ways the long reign of Shapur continued and fulfilled the policies set in motion by Ardashir. Following the precedent of his father at Ferozabad and elsewhere, Shapur was also a great founder of cities—Bishapur and Nishapur, among others. The establishment of these cities[17] and the growth of old ones, abetted by the expansion of trade within and beyond the large empire (especially along the silk routes as well as, increasingly, by sea to India and China), brought about changes in the Persian economy. Bazaars of the kind familiar later, in the Islamic period, grew up in the cities—a home to merchants and artisans, who formed trade guilds. Agriculture expanded to meet the demand for food from the towns, and nomadic pastoralism receded in significance. The spread of land under cultivation was facilitated by the use of *qanat*—underground irrigation canals that carried water as far as several kilometers, from highland areas to villages. There it could be distributed to fields. Agriculture was also expanded in Mesopotamia, where, if properly irrigated, the rich soils of the great river valley were potentially very productive, capable of yielding several crops a year.

Culturally, the resettlement of Greeks, Syrians, and others from the Roman Empire brought in a renewed burst of interest in Greek learning, and new translations into Pahlavi were carried out (Pahlavi was the Middle Persian language spoken in the Sassanid period, simplified from the more grammatically complex Old Persian spoken in Achaemenid times). Eventually, recognized schools of learning, including those for medicine and other sciences, flourished in cities like Gondeshapur and Nisibis. Inscriptions also record Shapur's pious establishment of fire altars named for various members of his family. Each altar would have involved an endowment to support the priests and their families. These endowments, along with similar ones established by the great nobles, enhanced the economic and political power of the priests (*mobad*).

Dark Prophet

Another phenomenon that emerged in the reign of Shapur was a new religion—Manichaeism, named after its originator, the prophet Mani. Aside from a more or less vague idea of a dualistic division between good and evil, Mani and his doctrines are obscure to most people today. But on closer examination Mani's ideas and his movement turn out to have been enormously influential, especially in medieval Europe.

Mani was born in April 216 in Parthian Mesopotamia, of Iranian parents descended from a branch of the Arsacid royal family, who had moved there from Hamadan/Ecbatana. There is a story that he was born lame, and some have suggested that his pessimism and his disgust at the human body had something to do with that. As with other founders of world religions, Mani was born into a troubled time and place. His parents seem to have been Christians,[18] and he was strongly influenced by gnostic ideas in his formative years. (The gnostics were an important sect of early Christianity, though some believe their ideas pre-date Christianity, incorporating Platonic ideas. Similar movements in Judaism and even, later, Islam have been identified and labelled gnostic. Broadly, they believed in a secret knowledge—*gnosis*—that derived from a personal, direct experience with the divine.) At some point before about 240, Mani claimed to have received a revelation that told him not to eat meat or drink wine or to sleep with women. The doctrine of Mani incorporated Christian elements, but depended heavily on a creation myth (if it can be called that) derived from Mazdaean concepts, particularly the pessimistically and deterministically inclined forms of the branch of Mazdaism called Zurvanism. This had been particularly important in Mesopotamia for several centuries, drawing on indigenous traditions like that of astrology.

Put simply, Manichaeism was based on the idea of a queasy, dystopic creation in which the good—the light—had been overwhelmed and dominated by evil—the demonic—which was itself identified with matter. Through copulation and reproduction (inherently sinful), evil had imprisoned light in matter and had established the dominance of evil on earth. Jesus was able to liberate man from this miserable condition, but only briefly, and the only real hope was the eventual liberation of the spirit in death. This dismal and ugly vision of existence was presented as a religion of liberation from material existence and evil. Mani wrote down a series of religious texts and liturgies, many of which were quite beautiful. After a meeting with Shapur in 243 at which Mani impressed the shah favorably,[19] Mani was allowed to preach the new religion all over the Sassanid Empire. Presumably the king failed to question him too closely—Shapur was distinguished by a tolerant attitude to all religions, including Judaism and Christianity. It is tempting to wish that he had made an exception in Mani's case. Mani accompanied Shapur in some of the campaigning that year against the Romans, which is coincidental because the great Neoplatonist, Plotinus, was apparently accompanying the Roman emperor through the same campaign, on the other side.

The teachings of Mani spread rapidly and widely—beyond Persia into India, Europe, and Central Asia. They survived longest in Central Asia, as an open rather than a persecuted, underground movement, and there yielded most of the authoritative texts from which Manichaeism is understood by academics today. Mani organized teams of scribes to translate and copy his writings into different languages.[20] His followers formed a hierarchy of believers, with an exclusive elect of pharisaic priests at their head. These were the people who followed the purity rules and the rules of abstinence and chastity and other life-hating mumbo jumbo to their fullest extent. But the sect was generally despised and declared heretical—especially by the Mazdaean Magi, but also by the Jews, the Christians, and even by gnostics like the Mandaeans. Eventually, Mani returned from his travels (after Shapur's death) to a less tolerant atmosphere, and the Magi—who hated Mani more than anyone else because of his subversion and distortion of their own beliefs—were able to have him imprisoned. In February 277 Mani was killed by being crushed over a period of twenty-six days by some very heavy chains.

By the time of Mani's death, though, the damage was done. It would be foolish to attribute *all* the evils of religion to Mani, but he does seem to have done a remarkably good job of infecting a range of belief systems with the most damaging and depressing ideas about impurity, the corruption of material existence, and the sinfulness of sexual pleasure. Of course, some of his notions were useful also to those wishing to elaborate metaphysically upon misogynistic impulses, and to those with a deterministic bent. His thinking was a kind of Pandora's box of malignity, the particles from which went fluttering off in all directions on their misshapen wings. As the scholar of Persian religion Alessandro Bausani said, Mani seems to have constructed myths out of a sense of the "monstrosity of existence":

> . . . myths that have the particularly unpleasant characteristic of not being natural and rising from below . . . not based on a wide-ranging religious sociality like the Zoroastrian ones, for they are almost the personal dreams of an exhausted and maniacal intellectual.[21]

But his ideas were complex, varied, and innovative, and not *all* bad. They may later have had some influence on Islam—Mani, like Mohammad in the seventh century, declared himself to be the "seal of the prophets," and there are other parallels.[22] But the central tenets of Islam were intrinsically anti-Manichaean in spirit, and the Prophet Mohammad, speaking of various sects and faiths, was clear that "All will be saved except one: that of the Manichaeans."[23] Despite the condemnation heaped upon Mani's teachings, they seem to have persisted among an underground sect. But the most startling story is that of Mani's influence in the West.

Of all the fathers of the Christian church, probably the most influential was St. Augustine of Hippo. Augustine wrote wonderful books that explained the Christian religion to the uneducated—explained the downfall of the Roman Empire in Christian terms, absolving the Christians of blame (some, like Gibbon, have remained unconvinced); Augustine also explained in touching and humane terms his own life, his own sense of sin, and his own (late) conversion to Christianity ("O Lord, Make me chaste—but not yet"). Augustine's presence in the thought of the church in later centuries was dominant. He also explained the reasons Manichaeism was heretical in a Christian context. But the remarkable fact is, before he converted to Christianity, Augustine himself had been an avowed Manichaean, had converted others to the sect, and may have served as a Manichaean priest. It has been disputed, but the imprint of Manichaeism on Augustine's thinking is obvious and heavy.

Many of the ideas that Augustine's teaching successfully fixed in Catholic Christian doctrine—notably that of original sin (strongly associated by him with sexuality), predestination, the idea of an elect of the saved, and (notoriously) the damnation of unbaptized infants—originated at least partly in debates that had been going on earlier within the Christian church, though those discussions had been influenced by similar gnostic ideas to those which had inspired Mani. But many of these key concepts—especially the central one, original sin—also show a striking congruence with Manichaean doctrine. Surely Augustine could not successfully have foisted upon the Christian church Manichaean ideas that the church had already declared heretical? Yet that seems to have been what happened, and Augustine was accused of doing precisely this by contemporaries—notably by the apostle of free will, Pelagius, who in the early years of the fifth century fought long and hard with Augustine over precisely these theological problems. Pelagius lost, and was himself declared a heretic. It was perhaps the most damaging decision ever made by the Christian church.[24]

As pursued later by the Western Christian church in medieval Europe, the full grim panoply of Manichaean/Augustinian formulae emerged to blight millions of lives, and they are still exerting their sad effect today—the distaste for the human body, the disgust for and guilt about sexuality, the misogyny, the determinism (and the tendency toward irresponsibility that emerges from it), the obsessive idealization of the spirit, the disdain for the material—all distant indeed from the original teachings of Jesus. One could argue that the extreme Manichaean duality of evil materiality versus good spirituality emerged most strongly in heresies like those of the Cathars and the Bogomils that the church pursued most energetically (the same Bogomils from whom the English language acquired the term "bugger"). The great scholar and Persianist Bausani (from whom I have taken much of my account of Manichaean beliefs) doubted the connection with these Western heresies,[25] but many of their beliefs and practices showed a close identity with those of Manichaeism, which is not easily discounted. The ferocity of the medieval church's persecution of the Cathars and others derived really from the dangerous similarity between the heretics' doctrines and the orthodox ones—they had merely carried orthodox doctrine to its logical extreme. The church was trying to destroy its own ugly shadow. The Eastern Orthodox Church, sensibly, never embraced Augustinian theology to the same extent.

The real opponent to Augustinian orthodoxy was Pelagianism—a simple, natural golden thread, sometimes concealed, running through medieval thought, to emerge again in Renaissance humanism. If ever a Christian thinker deserved to be made a saint, then surely Pelagius did. If ever a pair of thinkers deserved Nietzsche's title *Weltverleumder*[26] (world-slanderers), then they were Mani and Augustine.

To return to Persia from this excursion, we should remember that Manichaeism was condemned by the Mazdaean Magi as a heresy at an early stage, and that it is more correct to see it as a distortion of Iranian thinking—or indeed as an outgrowth of Christian gnosticism dressed in Mazdaean trappings—than as representative of anything enduring in Iranian thought.

Renewed War

Shapur's defeats of the Romans had contributed to the near-collapse of the Roman Empire in the third century. For a while after the capture of Valerian in 260 the Romans were in no fit state to strike back, and it seemed as if the whole East was open to Persian conquest. But a new power arose in the vacuum, based on the Syrian city of Palmyra. It was led by Septimius Odenathus, a Romanized Arab, and his wife Zenobia (Zeinab).

Odenathus swept through the Roman provinces of the East, and some Western sources have suggested that he campaigned successfully in the western part of the Sassanid Empire as well, though this has been disputed. Odenathus was assassinated in about 267 and was succeeded by Zenobia, who conquered Egypt in 269 but was defeated by the emperor Aurelian in 273. Aurelian restored the fortunes of Rome in the region. By that time Shapur was dead; he probably died of illness in Bishapur in May 270, though some have put his death in AD 272.[27] In any case, his reign had boosted the prestige of the Sassanid dynasty enormously, and had established the Persian Empire as the equal of Rome in the East.

After Shapur's death several of his sons reigned for short periods in succession, and a Mazdaean priest named Kerdir gradually strengthened his position at court. Kerdir used this position to begin asserting Mazdaean orthodoxy more aggressively, achieving not just the death of Mani and the persecution of his followers, but also the persecution of Jews, Christians, Buddhists, and others. Not for the last time the over-involvement of religious leaders in Iranian politics led to the persecution of minorities (and perhaps too, at length, to the discrediting of the persecutors).

In 283 the Romans invaded Persian territory again, and the outcome of the war was a new settlement, dividing Armenia between the two rival empires and losing some frontier provinces that Shapur had conquered. The Persians made further concessions in 298 after some less-than-successful fighting under Narseh, another of Shapur's sons (who had ascended to the throne in the wake of the Kerdir episode). The peace treaty signed then lasted for many years, and Armenia was confirmed as an Arsacid kingdom under Roman protection. A rock-relief at Naqsh-e Rostam shows Narseh being invested with royalty by Anahita, the traditional patroness of the Sassanids. It has been suggested that this signified a post-Kerdir return to a traditional, more tolerant religious policy.[28]

In 310 a young boy ascended the throne as Shapur II, after some dispute over the succession. He reigned a long time, until 379. One notable aspect of this reign is that it appears to have consolidated the process of revision, collation, and codification that the Mazdaean religion had been undergoing since the accession of Ardashir, and perhaps before. According to a later Zoroastrian tradition, Ardashir had instructed his high priest to reassemble and complete the dispersed fragments of text and oral tradition that had been preserved. Shapur I ordered that these should be augmented by all the knowledge of science, philosophy, and other fields that could be gathered from sources outside Persia—notably from India and Greece. Finally, Shapur II organized an extended discussion and debate between the various disputing sects of Mazdaism in order to establish a single, authorized doctrine. A priest called Adhurpat endured an ordeal by fire to prove the validity of his arguments. Because he emerged safely, he was permitted to make final liturgical additions to the *Avesta*. This seems to have been the decisive moment at which the previous differences were resolved and Zoroastrian religion coalesced from its previous disparate elements into a single, unitary orthodoxy—from which, in turn, modern Zoroastrianism derives. From this point on, and acknowledging the arbitrariness of choosing any particular time to mark what was a gradual transition, it makes sense to speak of Zoroastrianism rather than Mazdaism.[29]

Shortly before Shapur II became shah, Armenia turned Christian, at least officially. During Shapur's reign the Emperor Constantine designated Christianity the official religion of the Roman Empire too, claiming to be the protector of all Christians everywhere. Thus Christians within Persia became suspect as potential spies and traitors, and this tense situation gradually made the previous tolerance of most of the earlier Sassanid kings difficult to sustain. The new orthodoxy of Zoroastrianism, with its political connections and influence, became intolerant of rivals within Persia, and religious strife resulted. Tension also increased because Constantine was keeping at his court one of Shapur's brothers, Hormuzd, as a potential claimant to the Persian throne. After learning the trade of war in campaigns against the Arabs (in which he was successful, resettling some defeated tribes to Khuzestan), Shapur II demanded the restitution of the provinces won by Shapur I in northern Mesopotamia and subsequently lost by his successors. War with Rome broke out again, rolling back and forth between 337 and 359, and the Persians eventually took Amida (modern Diyarbakir in Turkey).

In 363 the Emperor Julian, one of the most interesting of the later Roman emperors—a scholar and a pagan who did his best to overturn Constantine's establishment of Christianity in the empire—launched a campaign to restore Rome's position in Syria, and to put the Persians in their place. Accompanied by the pretender Hormuzd, Julian, who had been a successful military commander in the West, brought an army of some eighty thousand men down the Euphrates as far as Ctesiphon. But he was dissuaded from a siege and, perhaps by accident, burned his boats. Soon the problems of heat, thirst, supply, and demoralization began to bite in a way that Crassus would have found familiar, and the Romans retreated. Eventually Julian was killed in battle and his successor, Jovian, made a peace that was favorable to the Persians. This treaty restored the frontiers as they had been at the end of the reign of Shapur I, with a few additions. Shapur II was also given a free hand in Armenia, which he proceeded to annex, but desultory fighting continued until his death in 379. The achievements of Shapur II's reign are all the more remarkable for the fact that, at several points, he had to switch fronts to the East to deal with attacks from the Chionite Huns, who had established themselves in Transoxiana and Bactria.[30]

Strife, Revolution, and Free Love

Shapur II was a strong, successful king with enormous prestige. But his successors, who inclined to tolerance of religious minorities, a peace-oriented foreign policy, and in some cases measures to uphold justice and protect the poor, had trouble restraining a priesthood and a noble class who were inclined—or maybe even conditioned—to intolerance and war, and who disliked any attempt to mitigate their social supremacy. Ardashir II, Shapur III, and Bahram IV were all murdered or died in suspicious circumstances (Bahram was shot full of arrows by mutinous commanders).[31] Their successor, Yazdegerd I, ruled from 399 and kept a peace with the Romans throughout his reign—so much so that the Roman Emperor of the East, Arcadius, asked him to become the guardian of his son, Theodosius. This gesture neatly symbolized the parity of the two empires, which now entered on a phase of partnership. Shahs and emperors cooperated (albeit warily and at a distance) against the internal and external instabilities that menaced them both. The heroic period of ambition-driven warfare was over, and even when war broke out again between the two empires in the sixth century, it was waged not by glory-hungry emperors, but by their generals.

Yazdegerd I also followed a tolerant religious policy. He was friendly to the Jews (who hailed him as the new Cyrus) and employed Jewish officials. It was during his reign that a distinct Persian Christianity emerged to become what is normally called the Nestorian church, the first synod of which was held in AD 410. This measure would have had the obvious effect of detaching Persian Christians from the taint of being a fifth column for the Romans. But not everyone approved. These religious policies made the shah unpopular with the clergy, and Yazdegerd, like his immediate predecessors, was murdered. The fact that his name was taken up by several later successors suggests that his memory was nonetheless respected in court circles.

The reigns following that of Shapur II are significant because they indicate the emergence of a theory of kingship that went beyond a system of alliance or identification with a particular religion or class, to assert that the shah had a duty to uphold justice for all his subjects. That such a theory existed we know from post-Islamic sources, who advised rulers of later times on the basis of patterns and ideas that had been the standard under the Sassanids. The king ruled on the basis of divine grace (*kvarrah* in Middle Persian/Pahlavi—a concept that goes back to the *Avesta* and the Achaemenid period, evidenced primarily by success in war) and was allowed to raise taxes and keep soldiers, but only on the basis that he ruled justly and not tyrannically. Injustice and tyranny would break the peace that permitted productive agriculture and trade. That in turn would reduce the tax yield, lessen the king's ability to reward soldiers, and threaten the stability of his rule. Justice was the key that turned a vicious circle into a virtuous circle. But in practice, the attempts of a king like Yazdegerd to rule justly, according to *his* judgment, might not accord with the ideas of the Zoroastrian priests. The abstract principle could be used as a weapon by either side.

After some confusion, Yazdegerd was succeeded by his son, Bahram V, also known as Bahram Gur (wild ass) after his enthusiasm for hunting those animals. Bahram became a legendary figure, around whom many popular stories were told. They elaborated on his love of women, music, and poetry, as well as on his generosity and bravery. He had been brought up in Hira by an Arab foster father, and there is evidence that the over-mighty clergy may have disliked this. In war, Bahram Gur was successful at protecting Persian frontiers in the East, re-establishing Persian control of Armenia, and making a treaty with the Romans that provided for religious tolerance in both empires. But his love of hunting was his downfall. He is believed to have disappeared into quicksand after a mishap while pursuing game in marshland in Media in 438/439.

Yazdegerd II, who succeeded Bahram Gur, seems to have been a ruler more to the liking of the Zoroastrian priesthood. He attempted to re-impose Zoroastrianism on Armenia, provoking a civil war there. He seems also to have permitted renewed persecution of Christians and Jews in Persia proper. Touraj Daryaee, an expert on Sassanid Persia, suggests that Yazdegerd II also inclined to the more east Persian kingly mythology, derived from the *Avesta* and its references to the Kayanid kings, rather than to the west Persian sub-Achaemenid version.[32]

Throughout this period the threat from northern and eastern tribal nomads intensified (the Romans came under the same pressure, which is one reason the wars with Rome abated at this time). Yazdegerd II was successful against them for the most part, but in 454 he was forced to retreat. He died three years later. After a dynastic struggle, his son Peroz (Feruz) gained the throne with the help of the people known as the Hephtalite Huns. But the Hephtalites captured him in battle in 469, and Peroz was forced to pay a huge ransom, and to yield territory, in return for his release. This was also a time of hardship, drought, and famine. Peroz renewed the struggle with the Hephtalites in 484 but was killed in battle, and the Persians were utterly defeated. His successor could only fend off his eastern enemies by paying them tribute, and he was eventually deposed.

Kavad I came to the throne in 488 at a time of crisis. The Hephtalites had sliced off a swath of Persia's eastern provinces. Repeated famines, the exactions of the arrogant nobility, and taxes required to make tribute payments had reduced the peasantry to a miserable state. Provinces in the west and southwest were in revolt.

Then, on top of all this, a version of the Manichaean heresy reappeared in a new, revolutionary movement. Its members preached that since wealth and desire for women caused all the trouble in the world, wealth should be distributed equally—and women should be held in common. (The latter is often thought to have been exaggerated by the sect's enemies, but there is evidence that "shrines and inns" were established where people could meet and make love freely.)[33] The movement has been named Mazdakism after its leader, Mazdak, though some have doubted how central to the phenomenon Mazdak actually was. Kavad himself was apparently converted to the new beliefs, having seen an opportunity to humble the nobles and the clergy. Granaries were thrown open to the people, and land was redistributed. But the nobility and clergy managed to overcome Kavad, imprison him, and replace him with his more malleable brother. The country (especially Mesopotamia, but also other parts) was in turmoil. Eventually, Kavad was able to escape from prison and, with the help of the Hephtalites, reimpose his authority.

The Arab historian Al-Tabari wrote that Kavad escaped through the intervention of his daughter, who went to the prison commander and said she would allow him to sleep with her if she could see her father.[34] She stayed with Kavad for one day, then left in the company of a sturdy servant, who was carrying a rolled-up carpet. The commander asked about the carpet, but the girl told him it was the one she had slept on, and since she was having her period, she was going to wash it and bring it back. The commander let the girl go on her way, neglecting to investigate the carpet further "lest he become polluted by it." But once the girl and the servant were out of the prison, Kavad rolled out of the carpet and they all escaped to the Hephtalites. The superstitious taboo about the impurity of menstrual blood was to prove damaging to the nobles and the clergy. There is a kind of cosmic justice to it.

In the remainder of Kavad's reign, and in that of his son and successor Khosraw (531–579), the two kings pushed through a number of important reforms that established the Sassanid Empire in something like its final shape. Both kings exploited the chaos caused by the Mazdakite revolution to diminish the power of the nobility and the clergy (this came across most clearly in Kavad's later years, when Khosraw's succession was in question—the clergy and nobility were forced to support Khosraw for fear that another of Kavad's sons, a pro-Mazdakite, would become shah). Perhaps most importantly, the taxation system was reformed, a poll tax was established, and a survey of taxable land was carried out to ensure the taxation was equitable.[35] The empire was divided into four sectors, each under the command of a military commander (*spahbod*) and supported by a chancery (*diwan*) that kept his troops supplied. In addition, a new clerical office was established—a Protector of the Poor, who reinforced the moral duty of the priesthood to look after the interests of the lowest strata of society (a duty they had presumably neglected before). The reforms created, or certainly greatly strengthened, a new class of *dehqans*—rural gentry who collected tax in the villages and were themselves small landowners. The dehqans also provided the battle-winning Persian cavalry that dominated the shah's armies. From now on, though, they were paid and retained by the shah instead of the great noble families. Identifying closely with the shah's interest, and providing administrators and courtiers as well as soldiers, the dehqan class became the prime means by which the traditions and culture of Sassanid Persia were preserved and transmitted onward after the Islamic conquest.

With these reforms well under way by the 520s, Kavad decided that Mazdak had outlived his usefulness.[36] It seems a debate was organized in order to discredit his doctrines, at which not just the Zoroastrian clergy but also the Christians and Jews spoke out against Mazdak. According to the story told much later by Ferdowsi, Kavad then turned Mazdak and his followers over to Khosraw, who had the charismatic communist's people buried alive—planted head down in a walled orchard, with only their feet showing above the ground. Khosraw then invited Mazdak to view his garden, telling him,

> You will find trees there that no-one has ever seen and no-one ever heard of even from the mouth of the ancient sages . . .

Mazdak went to the garden and opened the gate, but when he saw the kind of trees that were planted in Khosraw's garden he gave a loud cry, and fainted. Khosraw had him strung up by the feet from a gallows, then killed him with volleys of arrows. Ferdowsi concluded,

> If you are wise, do not follow the path of Mazdak. And so the nobles became secure in their possessions, and women, and children, and their rich treasures.[37]

This story may record some aspect of a contemporary memory, and we know that Ferdowsi worked from much earlier accounts of events. We cannot be sure how Mazdak died, but the religious revolution associated with him was an important episode. It did not usher in a new order of shared property (let alone free love). It did weaken the power of the great nobles and bring at least some benefits for the lower classes, though the main beneficiaries were the dehqans. But if we look at it another way, it tells us some important things about the interplay of social and political interests, and the insurrection itself may appear in a different light. Mazdak and his adherents seem, at least initially, to have depended heavily on the authority of the king to get their revolution going. Even if he misjudged the forces that would be released, Kavad handled events cleverly. He was too important to the clergy and the nobles, by the time of his imprisonment, for them to simply kill him. He was the last thing standing between them and utter destruction. The revolution was an overdue reminder to them of the basis of their privileges and the importance of the monarchy in holding society together. Justice, even if not perfect (let alone egalitarian), had to be more than lip-service; and at least the principle of justice gave everyone a legitimate expectation from the system, if not necessarily a right to be heard. The effect of the revolution, like most revolutions, was a broadening of the social bases of political power, releasing new reserves of human energy. The prestige and power of the monarchy were reaffirmed and enhanced, and it now entered what came to be regarded as its golden age.

Khosraw Anushirvan

After his accession in 531, Khosraw continued with his father's reforms, completing the destruction of the Mazdakites.[38] His court became a center for learning, attracting in particular some of the Greek Neoplatonists whose school of philosophy had been closed down in Athens by the emperor

Justinian. But as Gibbon wrote, these were Platonists "whom Plato himself would have blushed to acknowledge":

> The disappointment of the philosophers provoked them to overlook the real virtues of the Persians; and they were scandalized, more deeply perhaps than became their profession, with the plurality of wives and concubines, the incestuous marriages, and the custom of exposing dead bodies to the dogs and vultures, instead of hiding them in the earth, or consuming them with fire. Their repentance was expressed by a precipitate return, and they loudly declared that they had rather die on the border of the empire, than enjoy the wealth and favour of the Barbarian. From this journey, however, they derived a benefit which reflects the purest lustre on the character of Chosroes [Khosraw]. He required, that the seven sages who had visited the court of Persia, should be exempted from the penal laws which Justinian enacted against his pagan subjects; and this privilege, expressly stipulated in a treaty of peace, was guarded by the vigilance of a powerful mediator.[39]

Khosraw encouraged the translation of texts from the Greek, Indian, and Syriac languages, and it was apparently in his reign that the game of chess was introduced from India (and probably somewhat amended). He instigated the compilation of a history of Persia, and an astronomical almanac. He upheld the position of Zoroastrianism in the country, but personally took a more rationalist approach, based on his reading of philosophy and of writings from other religions. Through his reputation for wisdom and justice, Khosraw later acquired the title Anushirvan (Khosraw of the Immortal Soul). In the west he was known—partly through his contact with the Neoplatonists—as the philosopher-king. The Arabs, as they recorded later, knew him as "The Just." He established a magnificent court, and built the palace at Ctesiphon (the great *iwan* arch of which can still be seen today) along with spreading gardens and precincts that have since disappeared. The reign of Khosraw, for its intellectual achievements, for its exemplification of the Sassanid idea of kingship, was the pinnacle of Sassanid rule. In later centuries it became almost the Platonic form of what monarchy should be, even after the Sassanids themselves had long since disappeared.

Khosraw was also successful in war, defeating not just the Hephtalites but also the Turks, who had been instrumental in weakening the Hephtalites at an earlier stage and were now pressing on the empire's northern and northeastern borders. Following up the successes of his father and his father's *spahbod* (commander) Azarethes in defeating the great general Belisarius at Nisibis and Callinicum in 530 and 531, Khosraw also fought a series of wars with the East Romans (hereafter usually called the Byzantines) in which he was generally successful. The Byzantines renewed treaties according to which the Persians, in return for large cash sums, would prevent enemies from invading Asia Minor through the Caucasus. Finally, Khosraw retook the strategic town of Dara in 572 and was able again to send his troops raiding into Syria as far as Antioch. The Byzantines made further truces, buying the Persians off with large sums of gold.[40]

On Khosraw's death in 579, his son Hormuzd IV took the throne. Hormuzd seems to have done his best to maintain the balance established by his father—supporting the dehqans against the nobility and defending the rights of the lower classes, as well as resisting attempts by the clergy to reassert themselves. But he resorted to executions to do so, and was remembered accordingly by the Zoroastrians as a cruel and unjust king. In this situation, one of the generals, Bahram Chubin, who had achieved successes in war in the east, marched on Ctesiphon after being criticized by Hormuzd for a less-than-brilliant performance in war in the west. Bahram Chubin was a descendant of the old Parthian Arsacid line, through the great family of the Mehran. With the help of other nobles, he deposed, blinded, and later killed Hormuzd, putting Hormuzd's son, Khosraw II, in power (in about 589/590).

But then Bahram declared himself king, restoring the Arsacid dynasty. This was too much for the majority of the political class, who held strongly to the dynastic principle and supported the right of Khosraw II to rule. After a reverse that forced him to flee to the west, Khosraw II returned with the support of the Byzantine emperor, Maurice, and ejected Bahram, who fled to the territory of the Turks (Turan) and was murdered there.

Khosraw Parvez

Surviving various further disputes and rebellions among the nobility with Armenian and Byzantine help, Khosraw II was able to establish his supremacy again by 600, and took the title Khosraw *Parvez*—The Victorious. The title was to prove apposite, but Khosraw II did not have the vision or the moral greatness of his namesake, his grandfather. He may even have been implicated in the murder of his father, and his life was studded with incidents of cruelty and vindictiveness, intensifying as he grew older. He did everything to excess. He burdened his subjects with increasingly heavy taxation, accumulating enormous wealth in the process. Although he was remembered afterward for the great story of his love for the Christian girl Shirin, he had an enormous harem of wives, concubines, dancers, musicians, and other entertainers. When he went hunting he did so in a huge park stuffed with game of all kinds. At court he sat on a splendid throne, under a dome across which celestial spheres moved by a hidden mechanism in a planetarium.

But his greatest excess was in war. In 602 Khosraw II's benefactor, the Byzantine emperor Maurice, was murdered and supplanted by a usurper, Phocas—one account says that Maurice was forced to watch the execution of his five sons before he himself was killed. The Byzantine territories subsequently fell into disorder and civil war, made worse by divisions between Christian sects. Phocas sent an army against dissenting Christians in Antioch, perpetrating a massacre there. At Edessa, a local Byzantine general was resisting Phocas's forces. Khosraw used the pretext of Maurice's murder to make war against Phocas in revenge, and relieved Edessa. He was able from there to extend his control over the other Byzantine frontier posts and then, after some preparation, to unleash his armies on the eastern Byzantine Empire. The Byzantines had been concentrating their efforts on their Danube frontier against the Avars, and were relatively weak in the east.

By this time (610) Phocas had been deposed by Heraclius, who was to prove one of the most capable of all Byzantine emperors. Of Armenian descent, Heraclius tried to make peace with the Persians, but Khosraw ignored him. The able Persian generals Shahrvaraz and Shahin led the Sassanid armies through Mesopotamia, Armenia, and Syria into Palestine and Asia Minor. They took Antioch in 611, Damascus in 613, and then Jerusalem in 614 (sending a shock through the whole of the Christian world). At Jerusalem the Christian defenders refused to give up the city, and it was taken by assault after three weeks, and given over to sack. According to Byzantine Christian sources, the Jews of the city and the surrounding region (who had been persecuted and excluded from the city for centuries) joined in a massacre in which sixty thousand Christians died.[41] The Persians carried off the relic of the True Cross to Ctesiphon. Within another four years they had conquered Egypt and were in control of most of Asia Minor, as far as Chalcedon, opposite Constantinople on the shores of the Bosphorus. No shah of Persia since Cyrus had achieved such military successes.

But then Fortune switched her allegiance. Heraclius made careful preparations and crystallized the religious dimension of the conflict into a holy war, devoting himself and his army to God. Later Christian chroniclers included his expedition with the descriptions of the Crusades. In a bold move, in 622 (the same year as the Prophet Mohammad's flight from Mecca to Medina) he took a small band of elite troops by water to the southeastern corner of the Black Sea, bypassing all the Sassanid forces in Asia Minor, and from there burst into Armenia, deliberately devastating the countryside everywhere he went. Heraclius managed to keep Shahrvaraz inactive by sending him letters that suggested Khosraw intended to kill him. With the support of the Turkish Khazars from north of the Caucasus, the Byzantines marched on into Azerbaijan and destroyed one of the most sacred Persian fire temples, at what is today called Takht-e Soleiman (The Throne of Solomon).

The Persians withdrew from Asia Minor, and in 627 suffered a crushing defeat at Nineveh. Early the following year, with Heraclius threatening Ctesiphon, Khosraw II was deposed and his son Kavad II became shah. Kavad sued for peace, offering the restitution of all the previous Persian conquests, and this was agreed to in 629. Khosraw, put on trial, was convicted of a lengthy series of crimes including patricide (his complicity in the murder of

Hormuzd IV), cruelty toward his subjects (especially soldiers and women), ingratitude toward the Byzantines, ruinous avarice, and mistreatment of his own children.[42] But Kavad showed himself scarcely more of a just ruler, murdering all his brothers to eliminate rivals. These killings (which repeated some of the worst cruelties of the Arsacid period) meant a shortage of candidates with obvious legitimacy in the years that followed.

The destruction of the wars had ruined some of the richest provinces of both empires, and the taxation to pay for them had impoverished the rest. Turks were on the loose throughout the eastern provinces of Persia, the Khazars were dominant in the northwest, and the Arabs, with a new determination and cohesion derived from the message of Mohammad, were raiding and beginning to establish themselves in Mesopotamia. Civil wars broke out between rival great nobles, and floods broke the irrigation works in Mesopotamia, turning productive land into swamps. Plague appeared, killing many in the western provinces and carrying off Kavad himself. The internal chaos and infighting brought a succession of short-lived monarchs to the throne (ten in two years), including the former general Shahrvaraz and two queens, Purandokht and Azarmedokht (a daughter of Khosrow II, Purandokht attempted some sensible measures to restore order in the empire, but was removed by another general before she could make much headway). Finally, in 632, Yazdegerd III, a grandson of Khosraw II, was crowned. He was eight years old.

3

Islam and Invasions

The Arabs, Turks, and Mongols—The Iranian Reconquest of Islam, the Sufis, and the Poets

Dusham gozar oftad be viraneh-e Tus
Didam joghdi neshaste jaye tavus
Goftam che khabar dari az in viraneh
Gofta khabar inast ke afsus afsus

Last night I passed by the ruins of Tus
And saw that an owl had taken the place of the peacock.
I asked, "What news from these ruins?"
It answered, "The news is—Alas, Alas."

—Attributed to Shahid Balkhi (d. 937).
The owl is a symbol of death.

One of the recurring questions in the history of Iran is the problem of continuity from pre-Islamic Iran to the Islamic period and to modern times. The great institutions of Persia as the period of Sassanid rule reached its climax were the monarchy and the Zoroastrian religion. Both of these were swept away by the Islamic conquest, and within three centuries there was little apparent remnant of them.

But there are some indisputable facts that point the other way. The first and most important is the language. The Persian language survived, while many other languages in the lands the Arabs conquered went under, to be replaced by Arabic. Persian changed from the Middle Persian, or Pahlavi, of the Parthian and Sassanid periods, acquired a large number of loan words from Arabic, and re-emerged after two obscure centuries as the elegantly simple tongue spoken by Iranians today.[1] Some would say that Persian became a new language, much as English was transformed in the Middle Ages after the Norman conquest. People continued to speak Persian, and Persian came to be written in Arabic script. Modern Persian is remarkably unchanged since the eleventh century. The poetry in particular that has come down from that time is readily understandable by modern Iranians, is studied in school, and is often quoted from memory.

There is another monument to continuity, itself a nexus of language, history, folk-memory, and poetry—the *Shahnameh* (Book of Kings) of Ferdowsi. This is the greatest single body of poetry from the period of transition, containing passages and stories familiar to most Iranians even today. Ferdowsi reworked a traditional canon of stories of the kings and heroes of Iran that is known in fragments from other sources. He wrote deliberately to preserve, as if in a time capsule, as much as he could of the culture of pre-Islamic Iran. The language of the stories itself avoids all but a very few of the Arabic loan words that by Ferdowsi's time had become almost indispensable in everyday usage, especially in written usage. Such is the quality of the poetry that it influenced almost all subsequent Iranian poets. And the characters of the stories—Kay Kavus, Rostam, Sohrab, Siavosh, Khosraw, Shirin—are as familiar to Iranians today as in Ferdowsi's time.

But in discussing Ferdowsi we anticipate events, and to understand him it is necessary to appreciate the significance of Islam and the history of the first three centuries of Muslim rule.

Mohammad

The Arabs of Mohammad's time were not just simple bedouin. Mohammad himself was the son of a merchant (born in Mecca sometime around the year 570), and later he served a rich widow as a guard and leader of her trading caravans. Eventually, he married her and ran the business himself. This was a period of change, both social and economic. Towns like Medina and Mecca had become an important part of life in the Arabian peninsula, and there was tension between austere nomad values and the more sophisticated urban way of life. This was especially true between the traditional polytheism of tribes and the monotheism of urban Jews (there were significant Jewish communities in the Arabian peninsula—notably at Medina but also elsewhere). As in Persia, religious ideas traveled through the peninsula and beyond with the merchants' trade goods. Christian hermits rubbed shoulders with Jews as well as with polytheistic Arabs in the Arabian towns. Arabs had served both the Sassanids and the Romans as mercenaries, and the Ghassanid and Lakhmid Arab kingdoms had served as buffer states between the two empires in the south just as Armenia had in the north. Arabs had settled in the western part of what is now Iraq, and as far north as Syria.

Muslims believe that Mohammad received his first revelations from the Angel Gabriel, which appear in the opening five lines of Sura 96 of the Qor'an, in the hills around Mecca around the year 610. The early revelations gave the pronouncements of a just God, who at the Day of Judgment would decide on the basis of men's actions in life whether they should go to paradise or to hell. They condemned false pride, neglect of the poor, and cruelty to the weak. They emphasized the duty of prayer. Around 613 Mohammad began preaching the revelation he had received in Mecca, and his reception there reflected social divisions and tensions. His early converts were mainly among the poor—among members of weak clans and the younger sons of richer families. But his preaching threatened the proprietors of the existing order in Mecca by creating an alternative pole of social authority, and by condemning the polytheism that among other things gave the ruling families an income from religious visitors.

Eventually the hostility to Mohammad from the ruling families of Mecca made his position there untenable. He fled Mecca, and in 622 was accepted into Medina by a group of prominent citizens. Life in Medina had been marred by feuding between rival clans, and it seems that Mohammad's welcome reflected their need for an arbitrator to prevent further strife. As it turned out, the arrival of Mohammad in Medina signified the acceptance of a new principle of spiritual leadership—one superseding the previous structure based on patriarchal kinship relations. The move to Medina is remembered by Muslims as the Hijra, which means "migration," and has central importance in the early history of Islam. The migration from Mecca and the establishment of the Muslim community in Medina provides the date at which the Muslim calendar begins.

Initially the group around Mohammad was open to Jews and Christians, but it gradually became clear that the revelation was dictating a new religion in its own right, distinct from either Judaism or Christianity (though building on and surpassing the teaching of the prophets of both). Put simply, Mohammad rejected the Trinity and the divinity of Jesus, and the Jews rejected Mohammad's presentation of himself as a prophet after the pattern of the Jewish prophets of the Old Testament.

This was important in Medina because there were three important Jewish tribes there. Early on, Mohammad had given Jerusalem as the direction of prayer and had made other provisions that apparently conciliated Judaism. The earliest, most essential elements of Islam are strikingly congruent with Judaism in content and significance. But the Jews rejected Mohammad's revelation, and relations between them and the Muslims deteriorated. The Jewish tribes were accused of treacherous contacts with the Meccans, and in succession they were ejected from Medina. Their property was confiscated and the males of the last tribe were massacred after they attempted to betray the Medinans at the Battle of the Trench (AD 627).[2] As the remaining inhabitants were converted, Medina became the model of a unified Muslim community—the *umma*.

Islam now took something like its final form, as expressed through the Qor'an. The faith was based on five pillars: the *shahada*—the obligation to acknowledge the existence of one God, with Mohammad as his Prophet; prayer (*salat*); almsgiving (*zakat*); pilgrimage (*hajj*); and the *Ramadan* fast. These five pillars were supplemented by social rulings, regularizing and imposing a rational morality on the previous chaos of clan customs. They established an overarching ethic of commonality and brotherhood while reinforcing some traditions of patriarchy and clan loyalty. The institution of the blood feud was discouraged and regulated, as was divorce. Incest was outlawed, and honesty and fairness in business dealings were encouraged.

The importance of women in the story of Mohammad's life—first Khadija, then his later wives, Aisha and others, and his daughter Fatima[3]—is expressed in the provisions he made for them, which in every case limited the power of men over women while leaving male supremacy intact. The Qor'an urged respect for women within marriage and respect for their modesty and privacy, though it made no specific rules for women's dress or veiling, and some have suggested that the veil originated as an elite practice, copied from the Christian Byzantine court—comparable perhaps with the custom among aristocratic Englishwomen in Victorian times. The Qor'an gave women the right to own property in their own name. It also discouraged the pre-Islamic practice of killing unwanted girl infants (in Sura 81, speaking of the Day of Judgment: "*. . . when the infant girl, buried alive, is asked for what crime she was slain; when the records of men's deeds are laid open, and heaven is stripped bare; when Hell burns fiercely and Paradise is brought near: then each soul shall know what it has done*"). Many have judged that the Qoranic ideal and Mohammad's example were more favorable to women than later Arab and Muslim practice.[4]

The decade after the Hijra was marked by continuing hostility and eventually war with the ruling families of Mecca, and by missionary effort toward the tribes of Arabia as a whole. Gradually Mohammad and his followers made headway, and finally in 630 the Meccans accepted Islam and Mohammad's supremacy. The Ka'ba of Mecca was made the central, holy shrine of Islam. Islam's victory over the Meccans' resistance won over most of the remaining Arab tribes. By the time of the Prophet's death in 632, most of Arabia was unified under the new religion. Vigorous, idealistic, and determined to spread its dominance more widely, Islam had created a powerful religious, political, and military force that was to change the face of the region—and the world.

The Arab Conquest

When Mohammad died, the Muslim umma threatened to fall apart. Different factions had different ideas about the succession, and some tribes sought to regain their independence. Mohammad's friend Abu Bakr was elected as the Prophet's successor, becoming the first caliph (*Khalifa* means successor) and promising to follow Mohammad's example (*sunna*). It was natural that this should include further efforts to spread the message of Islam as Mohammad had done—both by negotiation and by armed force, including raiding into hostile territory. Initially this meant consolidation in the southern and eastern parts of the Arabian peninsula, and then expansion northward into what is now Iraq and Syria. The dynamic of expansion helped to stabilize the rule of the first four caliphs (known by Sunni Muslims as the *Rashidun*, the righteous caliphs), but their rule was nonetheless turbulent and three of them died violently.

The crucial point at which raiding turned into more deliberate wars of conquest was the Battle of Ajnadayn, near Gaza, in 634, where the Muslim Arabs defeated a Byzantine army sent to restore order in Palestine. The burst of confidence inspired by this success prompted further victories—Damascus was taken in 636 and a Byzantine relief force was decisively beaten at the Battle of Yarmuk in the same year, confirming the Muslims in possession of Syria. Their enemies discovered that Islam had given the Arabs an almost invincible cohesion and confidence in battle. This attribute was later described by the great Arab historian Ibn Khaldun as *asabiyah*, roughly translating as "group feeling." In the following year the Muslim armies moved east against the Sassanid Empire.

Persia, like the Byzantine Empire, was weakened by the wars that had raged through the reign of Khosraw II. The Sassanids had repulsed initial moves by Arab raiding parties into Mesopotamia, but the royal army under King Yazdegerd III was defeated at Qadesiyya (near Hilla in modern Iraq) in 637, after which the Arabs took Ctesiphon and the whole of Mesopotamia. Arab generals persuaded the caliph to continue the offensive against the Persians rather than allow Yazdegerd to counterattack, and they defeated him a second time at Nahavand, near Hamadan, in 641. After this, Sassanid resistance effectively collapsed and Yazdegerd fled east, begging local rulers to help him against the Arabs (he was killed at Merv in 651—not by the invaders but by one of his own subjects, like Darius III). The

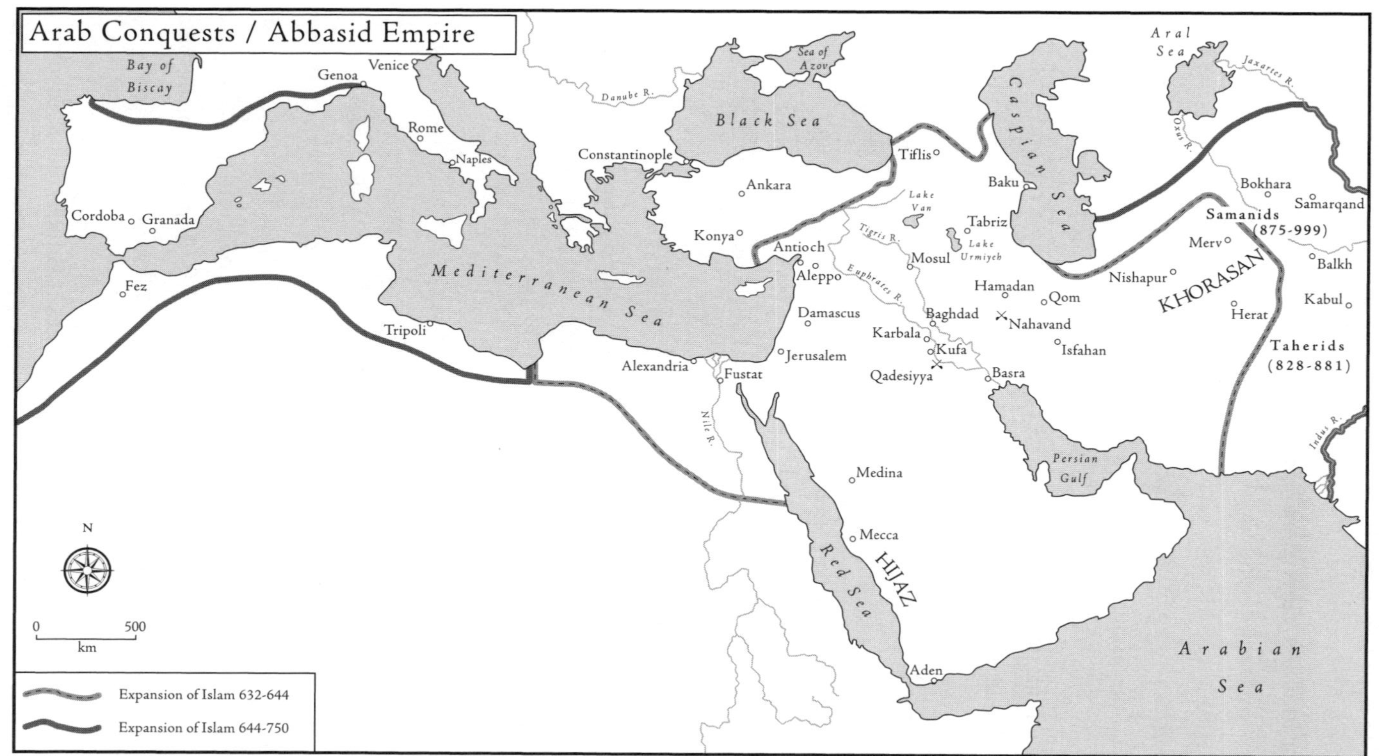

Arab Conquests / Abbasid Empire

Arabs increasingly established their dominion over the Iranian plateau, though towns like Qom and Kashan fought hard before surrendering, and resistance in the Caspian provinces of Tabarestan continued for many years.[5] Khorasan was conquered by 654, and despite resistance in the outlying territories along the southern coast of the Caspian and in the northeast, these were all taken and Balkh captured by 707.

The conquest was not, for the most part, followed by mass murder, forced conversion, or what today we would call ethnic cleansing. Instead the new Arab masters were content, as a matter of policy, simply to replace the ruling elites of the territories they had conquered. The Arab troops set up armed camps in the new lands, on the fringe of existing cities or in the form of new settlements, often on the margin between cultivated land and uncultivated territory that could be used to graze animals. The Arabs generally allowed existing proprietors, peasants, and merchants to go about their business as normal, expropriating only state land, the estates of the Zoroastrian temples, and those of members of the old elites who had fled or had died in the fighting.

Religious policy was marked by the same tolerance and restraint once the conquest was over. Mohammad had specified tolerance for Christians and Jews ("people of the Book") on condition that they paid tribute, which became a special tax for non-Muslims (the *jizya*). But this left Iranian Zoroastrians in a gray area, and many fire temples were destroyed and priests killed before it became normal for Zoroastrians to be treated with similar tolerance, subject to the jizya.[6] The example of the new rulers, and the settlement of Arab soldiers into the new territories, began a slow process of Islamization, made easier by the similarity of many of the precepts of Islam to the familiar features of Mazdaism—righteous thought and action, judgment, heaven and hell, and so on. There was a religious ferment through this period, within which many concepts and formulae might be held in common across different sects. Consider the following:

> . . . at whatever moment he dies eighty maiden angels will come to meet him with flowers . . . and a golden bedstead, and they will speak to him thus: do not

> fear etc. . . . And his fruitful work, in the form of a wondrous divine princess, a virgin, will come before him, immortal . . . and she herself will guide him to heaven.[7]

This remarkable passage links the idea of the *houris* of paradise, familiar from the Qoranic context, with the Mazdaean idea of the daena leading the soul to heaven. But this text is a Manichaean one, in the Iranian Sogdian language, from Central Asia. Bausani has given a series of significant parallels between passages in the Zoroastrian scriptures and passages in the Qor'an.[8] Despite the firm, clear, guiding principle of the Mohammadan revelation, other earlier ideas continued to bubble, sometimes to appear again later in some of the more diverse and eclectic Islamic sects.

The propertied and elite classes of Iran had an interest in converting to Islam, in order to avoid the jizya. They and more modest folk converted and often attached themselves to Arab clans or families as *mawali* (clients), sometimes taking Arabic names. But most inhabitants of Iran remained non-Muslim for several centuries. The restraint of the conquerors is probably another important explanation for the success of the conquest—many of the subjects of the new empire may have been less heavily taxed than previously, and ordinary Iranians probably benefited from the replacement of a strongly hierarchical aristocratic and priestly system by the more egalitarian Islamic arrangements, with their emphasis on the duty of ordinary Muslims to the poor. But as in other epochs, the victors wrote the history; if more contemporary material from the peoples of the conquered lands had survived, the picture of tolerance might be more shaded. There were massacres at Ray and Istakhr, both Mazdaean religious centers that resisted more stubbornly than elsewhere.[9]

Umayyads and Abbasids

Within twenty years of Mohammad's death, his Arab successors had conquered most of the territory we now call the Middle East. After one hundred years, they controlled an area that extended from the Atlantic to the

Indian Ocean. From this point on, *Iran zamin* (the land of Iran) was ruled for the most part by foreign monarchs for nearly a millennium. But conquest and the problems of wealth and power it brought also created new tensions among the victorious Arabs.

The fourth caliph, Ali, was Mohammad's cousin, and had married his daughter Fatima. But despite these close ties to the Prophet and his own pious reputation, Ali's caliphate was marred by civil war with the followers of the previous caliph, Uthman. When Ali was assassinated, a close relative of Uthman, Mu'awiya, declared himself caliph. This was in 661, a date that marks the beginning of the Umayyad dynasty, named after the family from which the dynasty was descended—one of the leading families of Mecca that Mohammad had fought before Mecca's submission to Islam.

Soon the new empire adopted forms of government resembling those of its predecessors, the Romans and the Sassanid Persians. The capital moved to Damascus (at that time, of course, a city formed by centuries of Christian, Roman, and Byzantine rule) and henceforth the caliphate passed mainly from father to son. The Umayyads discriminated strongly in favor of Arabs in the running of the empire, but were criticized among the Arabs for becoming too worldly and making too many compromises. They distanced themselves from their origins, became lax personally in their religious observances, and depended on paid soldiers rather than kinsmen and clan followers. As the empire and their responsibilities expanded, these changes were probably inevitable, as was the response—part of the eternal tension in Islam between piety and political authority.

Throughout this period there was dissent over the right of the Umayyads to rule. One group, the Kharijites, said that the caliph should be chosen by popular assent from among righteous Muslims, and deposed if he acted wrongly. Another group was to prove more important in the long run, and their dissent from orthodox Sunni Islam (named after the *sunna*—the example of the Prophet) eventually created a permanent schism. These Muslims identified with Ali, and the family of the Prophet descended through him. They believed that Ali should have been the first caliph, and that the caliphate should have descended in his line, which (through Ali's wife Fatima) was also the line of the Prophet himself. Ali's second son Hosein attempted a revolt in 680 but was overwhelmed at Karbala by Umayyad troops and killed. This was a crucial event, the full significance of which will be explored in a later chapter. Eventually the attachment to the family of the Prophet—to Ali and his descendants—evolved a theology of its own and a firm belief that the descendants of Ali were the only legitimate authority in Islam, becoming what we now call Shi'ism.

Tension and dissent reached a crescendo in the middle years of the eighth century. In the 740s there was a revolt against the Umayyads in Kufa, and they suffered external defeats by the Turks in Transoxiana and by the Byzantines in Anatolia. Then in the late 740s a Persian convert, Abu Muslim, began a revolt against Umayyad rule in Khorasan, where the creative dynamic between survivors of the old Persian land owning gentry (the *dehqans*) and the new Arab settlers had been particularly powerful, and where much intermarrying and conversion had occurred. There appears to have been a real fusion of cultures, with Arab settlers adopting the Persian language, Persian dress, and even some pre-Islamic Persian festivals.

Abu Muslim led his revolt in the name of the Prophet's family, thereby concealing the movement's final purpose and ensuring a wide appeal. Drawing support from Arab settlers in Khorasan, who resented their taxes and felt betrayed by the Umayyads, Abu Muslim and his followers defeated local opposition and, starting from Merv, led their armies westward under a black banner. They defeated the forces sent against them by the Umayyad caliph in a series of battles in 749–750, and in the latter year proclaimed a new caliph in Kufa—Abu'l Abbas (for whom the Abbasid dynasty was named). Abbas was a descendant not of Ali but of another of Mohammad's cousins. Before long the new caliph, uneasy at the continuing strength of Abu Muslim's support in Khorasan, had him executed (in 755),[10] the effect of which was to endorse orthodox Sunnism and to marginalize once again the followers of Ali, the Kharijites and other disparate groups that had supported the revolt originally. But the revolt of Abu Muslim was another important religious revolution in Iran. He was remembered long afterward by Iranians, and still later by Iranian Shi'ites, as a righteous, brave, and successful revolutionary betrayed by those he put in power.

Instead of Damascus, the new capital of the Abbasid dynasty was established in Baghdad, hard by the old Sassanid capital of Ctesiphon (though the seat of Abbasid government later moved north to Samarra). The center of gravity of the empire had moved east in a deeper sense, too. As time went on, Persian influence at the court of the new dynasty became more and more marked (especially through the Persian Barmakid family of officials), and some historians have represented the Abbasid supremacy as a cultural reconquest of the Arab conquerors by the Persians. The strengthening of Persian influence had begun already under the Umayyads. But now texts recording Sassanid court practice were translated into Arabic and applied by the new bureaucrats. This created a more hierarchical pattern of government. The caliph was screened by officials from contact with petitioners, a departure from earlier Umayyad practice in which the caliph had still taken counsel from tribal leaders in assembly and manipulated their loyalties and allegiances in age-old patriarchal fashion. Now new offices appeared in the government of the Abbasids, including that of vizier, or chief adviser or minister, and the administration was divided into separate departments or ministries called *diwans*. These institutions were taken directly from Sassanid court practice, and were to endure in Islamic rulership for more than a thousand years.

The influence was also apparent in the buildings constructed by the Abbasids, and Persian architects built many of the buildings of Baghdad. Even the circular ground plan of the new city may have been copied from the Sassanian royal city of Ferozabad in Fars. Where the Umayyads had tended to follow Byzantine architectural models, Abbasid styles were based on Sassanid ones. This is apparent in the open spaces enclosed by arcaded walls, in the use of stucco decoration, in the way domes were constructed above straight-walled buildings below, and, above all, in the classic motif of Sassanian architecture, the *iwans*. These were large open arches, often in the middle of one side of a court, often with arcades stretching away on each side, often used as audience halls. As with other cultural inheritances from

Sassanid Iran, these architectural motifs survived for centuries in the Islamic world.[11]

Particularly under the Abbasid caliph Al-Mansur many Persian administrators and scholars came to the court, mainly from Khorasan and Transoxiana (though they still worked there in Arabic, and many had Arabic names). These Persians encountered opposition from some Arabs, who called them *Ajam*, which means the mute ones, or the mumblers—a disparaging reference to their poor Arabic. The Persians defended themselves and their cultural identity from Arab chauvinism through the so-called *shu'ubiyya* movement, the title of which refers to a verse from the forty-ninth Sura of the Qor'an, in which Allah demands mutual respect between different peoples (*shu'ub*). It was primarily a movement among Persian scribes and officials; their opponents (including some Persians) tended to be the scholars and philologians. But the shu'ubiyya sometimes went beyond asserting equality or parity in favor of the superiority of Persian culture, especially literature. Given the religious history of Persia and the lingering attachment of many Persians to Mazdaean or sub-Mazdaean beliefs, shu'ubiyya also implied a challenge to Islam, or at least to the form of Islam practiced by the Arabs. A satirical contemporary recorded the attitude of a typical young scribe, steeped in the texts that recorded the history and the procedures of the Sassanid monarchy:

> ... His first task is to attack the composition of the Qor'an and denounce its inconsistencies.... If anyone in his presence acknowledges the pre-eminence of the Companions of the Prophet he pulls a grimace, and turns his back when their merits are extolled.... And then he straight away interrupts the conversation to speak of the policies of Ardashir Papagan, the administration of Anushirvan, and the admirable way the country was run under the Sasanians ...[12]

In time, the solution to such conflicts proved to be assimilation and synthesis, but the shu'ubiyya gave the Persians in Baghdad a collective self-confidence and helped to ensure the survival of a strong element of pre-Islamic Persian culture as part of that synthesis.[13] Like the religious controversies about free will and the nature of the Qor'an that were going on at the same time, the shu'ubiyya was a sign of conflict, change, and creative energy.

Boosted by the creativity of the Persians the Abbasid regime set a standard and was looked back on later as a golden age. Baghdad grew to be the largest city in the world outside China—by the ninth century it had a population of around four hundred thousand. The Abbasids endeavored to evade the tensions between piety and government and to cement their support among all Muslims by abandoning the Umayyad principle of Arab supremacy and by establishing the principle of equality between all Muslims. This same inclusive spirit extended even to taking Christians, Jews, and descendants of Ali into the government—provided they proved loyal to the regime.

The integration of the huge area of the Arab conquests under the peaceful and orderly rule of the Abbasid caliphate brought new and dynamic patterns of trade, as well as a great release of economic energy. The caliphs encouraged improvements in agriculture, particularly through irrigation, which created new prosperity especially in Mesopotamia, as well as on the Iranian plateau. There the following centuries saw the widespread introduction of rice cultivation, groves of citrus fruits, and other novelties.[14] The region of Khorasan and Transoxiana profited hugely from revitalized trade along the ancient Silk Route to China, from the agricultural improvements, and from the mixing of old and new, Arab and Iranian. Because of these changes, the area entered an economic and intellectual golden age of its own.

The Abbasid system relied first on the local networks of control set up by provincial governors across the vast territories of the empire, and second on the bureaucracy that tied those governors to the center in Baghdad. The governors collected tax locally, deducted for their expenses (including military outlays), and remitted the remainder to the Abbasid court. The hand of central government was relatively light, but these arrangements put considerable power in the hands of the governors, which in the long run was to erode the authority of the caliphate.

The Abbasid court became rich, but it also became very learned. The caliphs, especially caliph al-Ma'mun (813–833, himself the son of a Persian concubine), encouraged and supported scholars who translated ancient texts into Arabic. These were initially translated from Persian, but later also from Syriac and Greek, drawing on writings discovered across the conquered territories. Al-Ma'mun's predecessor al-Mansur (754–775) had founded a new library, the *Beyt al-Hikma* (House of Wisdom), which attempted to assimilate all knowledge in one place and translate it into Arabic. An idea taken directly from the model of the Sassanid royal libraries, the House of Wisdom drew extensively on writings and scholars from Gondeshapur in Khuzestan, the most famous of the Sassanid academies.[15] Gondeshapur had survived up to that point, but it seems thereafter to have been eclipsed by Baghdad. At the same time, the diffusion of scholarship also profited from the introduction of paper manufacturing from China, which replaced the more expensive and awkward papyrus and parchment.

Al-Ma'mun seems to have encouraged a shift in emphasis toward astrology, mathematics, and the translation of Greek texts, under the eye of his chief translator, Hunayn ibn Ishaq. These developments led to what has been called the ninth-century renaissance, as Persian scholars writing in Arabic discovered and applied the lessons especially of Greek philosophy, mathematics, science, medicine, history, and literature. The new scholarship was not merely passive, but creative. It produced new scientific writings, literature, histories, and poetry of great and lasting quality, forming the basis of much later intellectual endeavor—including in Europe—in the centuries that followed.

Through the translations, Aristotelian and Platonic philosophies were especially influential, thanks to prestigious philosophers al-Kindi and al-Farabi. The great historian al-Tabari (838–923) also worked in Baghdad at this time. Medicine made significant advances through properly scientific researches into anatomy, epidemiology, and other disciplines, building on and eventually far surpassing the work of the classical Greek physician Galen. Many of these achievements were later collated and made known in the West through the writings of another Persian, the great Avicenna (born Ibn Sina, 980–1037). Avicenna's writings were important in both East and West for his presentation of Aristotelian philosophical method and especially logic. Disputations along Aristotelian lines became central to teaching at the higher level in eastern *madresehs* from the time of Avicenna onward.

It was a period of great intellectual energy, excitement, and discovery, and as the Abbasid court became a model for succeeding generations in government and in other ways, so too it became a model in the intellectual and cultural sphere. The translations into Arabic done by Persians in Baghdad in the eleventh century were later put into Latin for Western readers by translators like Gerard of Cremona, working in Toledo in Spain in the twelfth century. Access to these writings gave a new vitality to Western scholarship. Avicenna and Averroes—the latter an Arab and an Aristotelian like Avicenna—became familiar names in the new universities of Europe, and after the time of Thomas Aquinas the philosophy of Aristotle, following their model, dominated European learning for two hundred years or more.

But at the same time there developed a separate tradition of Islamic scholarship across the towns and cities of the empire. This learning, independent of the authority of the caliph, was based instead on the authority of the Qor'an and the *hadith* (the huge body of traditions of the Prophet's life and sayings, and related material, collated with varying degrees of reliability in the centuries after his death). The *ulema*—scholars practiced in the study and interpretation of those religious texts—tended to be hostile to the sophistication and magnificence of the court. This was particularly the case in the time of al-Ma'mun and his immediate successors, when the caliph and the court inclined toward the religious thinking of the group called the Mu'tazilis, who favored ideas of free will, a doctrine of the created nature of the Qor'an, and (partly under the influence of Greek philosophy) the legitimacy of interpretation of religious texts based on reason.

In contrast, many of the ulema outside court circles tended to favor more deterministic positions and a strict traditionalism that insisted on the sufficiency of the texts on their own. They also disapproved of extra-Islamic influences. The parallel cultures of the Abbasid court and the ulema expressed the continuing tension between political authority and religion under Islam. In the end, the traditionalist tendency was the one that prevailed—with variations and some compromises—in the four schools or *mazhabs* of Sunnism: the Hanbali, Shafi'i, Maliki, and Hanafi.

But aspects of Mu'tazili thinking endured more strongly in the separate Shi'a tradition. The great Arab historian and social theorist Ibn Khaldun recognized in the fourteenth century that most of the hadith scholars and theologians were Persians working in Arabic (two of the four Sunni mazhabs were founded by Persians). So too were the philologists who established the grammar of the Arabic language and recorded it formally.[16] In the Iranian lands, the usages of the ulema were a major conduit for bringing Arabic words into Persian, and to this day the Persian of the mullahs tends to be the most Arabized.

On a more popular level, religious sects and groups proliferated in the towns and villages of Iran including sects that were regarded as heretical by both Muslims and Zoroastrians. These groups, often encompassing sub-Mazdakite ideas, were labelled Khorramites,[17] a term that may derive from a word meaning ribald or joyous. Some such groups were involved in the initial revolt of Abu Muslim, but also in other revolts, including those of Sonbad the Magian (756), Ustad-sis (767–768), al-Muqanna (780)—all mainly centered on Khorasan—and again in the revolt of Papak in what is now Kurdistan and Azerbaijan in 817–838. Several of these revolts showed millenarian and other features (including an anti-Muslim celebration of wine and women), drawing in part on Mazdaism—features that were to resurface later in Shi'ism, and Sufism. On women, for example, a contemporary said that some of the Khorramites:

> . . . believe in communal access to women, provided that the women agree, and in free access to everything in which the self takes pleasure and to which nature inclines, as long as no-one is harmed thereby

And another:

> They say that a woman is like a flower, no matter who smells it, nothing is detracted from it. [18]

As early as the caliphate of Harun al-Rashid (786–809), the processes of dislocation and separation that were to split the united empire of the Abbasids became manifest. Provincial governors, valued for their local authority and retained in place for that reason, began to pass on their governorships to their sons, creating local dynasties. The latter acquired courts of their own, new poles of culture, and authority. As they did so their expenses became greater, and less tax revenue was sent to the center. They quickly became effectively independent, though most of them still deferred to the caliphate as the continuing central authority in Islam.

It is in the nature of the history of empires that their story gets told in terms of their decline and fall. Historians are always looking for explanations, causes, and the origins of things. When it comes to empires, this tends to mean that their end casts a long shadow backward in time. This could make the system and institutions of the Abbasid empire, for example, look flawed and faulty almost from the very beginning. That would be misleading. The Abbasid period was a time of enormous human achievement, in political terms as well as in terms of civilization, art, architecture, science, and literature. The release of new ideas and the exchange of old ones within a huge area, held together by a generally benign and tolerant government, brought about a dynamic and hugely influential civilization, way ahead of what was going on in Europe at the time.

The first of the regional dynasties to establish itself as a real rival to central authority was that of the Taherids of Khorasan (821–873), followed by the Saffarids of Sistan (861–1003) and the Samanids of Bokhara (875–999)—all dynasties of Iranian origin. The Samanids were based on Bokhara and the region around Balkh, claiming descent from the Sassanid prince Bahram Chubin. Each of these dynasties (especially the Samanids) and those that followed (notably the Ghaznavids and Buyids) tended to set up courts adorned with Persian bureaucrats, scholars, astrologers, and poets. Imitating in this way the great caliphal court of Baghdad, these provincial courts enhanced their own dynasties' prestige and also disguised their tenure of power, which otherwise might have appeared as more nakedly dependent on brute military force. The patronage of these courts, working on the intellectual and religious ferment of the eastern Iranian lands at a time when the potential of the new form of the Persian language was ready to be explored, produced the beginnings of a great outpouring of wonderful poetic literature, including some of the most sublime poetry ever created. The poetry is so unfamiliar to most Western readers, so fresh and surprising in its content, and so important in its effect on later Iranian and Persianate culture across the region that it warrants more detailed attention.

Drunk with Love: The Poets and the Sufis, the Turks and the Mongols

From the very beginning, the grand theme of Persian poetry is love. But it is a whole teeming continent of love—sexual love, divine love, homoerotic love, unrequited love, hopeless love, and hopeful love. It is love aspiring to oblivion, love aspiring to union, and love as solace and resignation. Often it may be two or more of these at the same time, intermingled and ambiguously hinted at through metaphor. Other times love may not even be mentioned, but will be present nonetheless through other metaphors—notably through another great poetic theme, wine.

It is possible that the Persian poetry of this period inherited ideas and patterns from a lost tradition of Sassanid court poetry—love poetry and heroic poetry—just as Ferdowsi's *Shahnameh* emerged from a known tradition of stories about the kings of Persia. But most of the verse forms, along with the immediate precedents of themes of love, derive from previous Arabic poetic traditions and reflect the exchange of linguistic and other cultural materials between Iranians and Arabs in the years after the conquest. While there are fragments of poetry known from earlier times, the first more substantial verses from known poets come from the period of the Taherids. But the first great figure was a poet at the Samanid court—Rudaki:

Del sir nagardadat ze bidadgari
Cheshm ab nagardadat cho dar man nagari
In torfe ke dusttar ze janat daram
Ba anke ze sad hezar doshman batari

Your heart never has its fill of cruelty
Your eyes do not soften with tears when you look at me
It is strange that I love you more than my own soul,
Because you are worse than a hundred thousand enemies.[19]

Rudaki (who died around 940), along with other poets like Shahid Balkhi and Daqiqi Tusi, benefited from the deliberate Persianizing policy of the Samanid court. The Samanids gave the poets their patronage and generally encouraged the use of Persian rather than Arabic. Abolqasem Ferdowsi (c. 935–c. 1020) was less fortunate. He was born in the period of Samanid rule, but later, when the Samanid regime crumbled, he came under the rule of the Ghaznavids, a dynasty of Turkic origin. His *Shahnameh* (which continued and completed a project begun for the Samanids by Daqiqi) can be seen as the logical fulfillment of Samanid cultural policy—avoiding Arabic words, eulogizing the pre-Islamic Persian kings, and going beyond a non-Islamic position to an explicitly pro-Mazdaean one. Some of the concluding lines of the *Shahnameh*, speaking as if from just before the defeat at Qadesiyya and the coming of Islam, echo the earliest Mazdaean inscriptions of Darius at Bisitun. This is shocking in an eleventh-century Islamic context (the *minbar*, mentioned in the first line, is the raised platform, rather like a church pulpit, from which prayers are led in the mosque):

They'll set the minbar level with the throne,
And name their children Omar and Osman.
Then will our heavy labours come to ruin.
O, from this height a long descent begins. . .

. . .

Then men will break their compact with the Truth
And crookedness and Lies will be held dear.[20]

It's no surprise then that Ferdowsi's great work, when finished, got a less-than-enthusiastic welcome from the ruling Ghaznavid prince, whose views were more orthodox. Many of the stories passed down through the centuries about the lives of the poets are unreliable, but some of them may at least reflect some aspects of real events. One story about the *Shahnameh* says that the Ghaznavid sultan, having expected a shorter work of different character, sent only a small reward to Ferdowsi in return. The poet, disgusted, split the money between his local wine seller and a bath attendant. The sultan eventually read a particularly brilliant passage from the *Shahnameh*, realized its greatness, and sent Ferdowsi a generous gift, but too late—as the pack animals bearing Ferdowsi's treasure entered his town through one gate, his body was carried out for burial through another.

The great themes of the *Shahnameh* are the exploits of proud heroes on horseback with lance and bow, their conflicts of loyalty between their consciences and their kings, their affairs with feisty women who are as slim as cypresses and radiant as the moon, and royal courts full of fighting and feasting—*razm o bazm*. It is not difficult to read into this the nostalgia of a class of bureaucrats and scholars descended from the small gentry landowners (the dehqans) who had provided the proud cavalry of the Sassanid armies. Reduced now from the sword to the pen, they watch Arabs and Turks play the great games of war and politics.

Tahamtan chinin pasokh avord baz
Ke hastam ze Kavus Key bi niaz
Mara takht zin bashad o taj targ
Qaba joshan o del nahade bemarg

The brave Rostam replied to them in turn,
"I have no need of Kay Kavus.
This saddle is my throne, this helm my crown.
My robe is chain mail; my heart's prepared for death"[21]

The *Shahnameh* has had a significance in Persian culture comparable to that of Shakespeare in English or the Lutheran Bible in German, only perhaps more so—it has been a central text in education and in many homes, second only to the Qor'an and the great fourteenth-century poet Hafez. It has helped to fix and unify the language, to supply models of morality and conduct, and to uphold a sense of Iranian identity—reaching back beyond the Islamic conquest—that might otherwise have faded with the Sassanids.

The poetry of the *Shahnameh*, and its themes of heroism on horseback, love, loyalty, and betrayal, has much in common with the romances of medieval Europe, and it is thought-provoking that it first attained fame a few decades before the First Crusade brought an increased level of contact between western Europe and the lands at the eastern end of the Mediterranean. There is also a theory that the troubadour tradition, and thus the immensely fruitful medieval European trope of courtly love, originated at least in part with the Sufis of Arab Spain.[22] But it may just be a case of parallel development.

The Ghaznavids did not reverse the Samanid pattern of patronage and continued to encourage poets writing in Persian. But the later poets were less strict about linguistic purity and more content to use commonplace Arabic loan words. Further west the Buyid dynasty, originating among Shi'a Muslims in Tabarestan, had expanded to absorb Mesopotamia and take Baghdad (in 945), ending the independent rule of the Abbasid caliphs and ruling from then on in their name. But the great literary revival continued to be centered in the east.

Naser-e Khosraw, born near Balkh in 1003, is believed to have written perhaps thirty thousand lines of verse in his lifetime, of which about eleven thousand have survived. He was brought up as a Shi'a, made the pilgrimage to Mecca in 1050, and later became an Ismaili before returning to Badakhshan to write. Most of his poetry is philosophical and religious:

Know yourself; for if you know yourself
You will also know the difference between good and evil.
First become intimate with your own inner being,
Then commander of the whole company.
When you know yourself, you know everything;
When you know that, you have escaped from all evil

Be wakeful for once: how long have you been sleeping?
Look at yourself: you are something wonderful enough.[23]

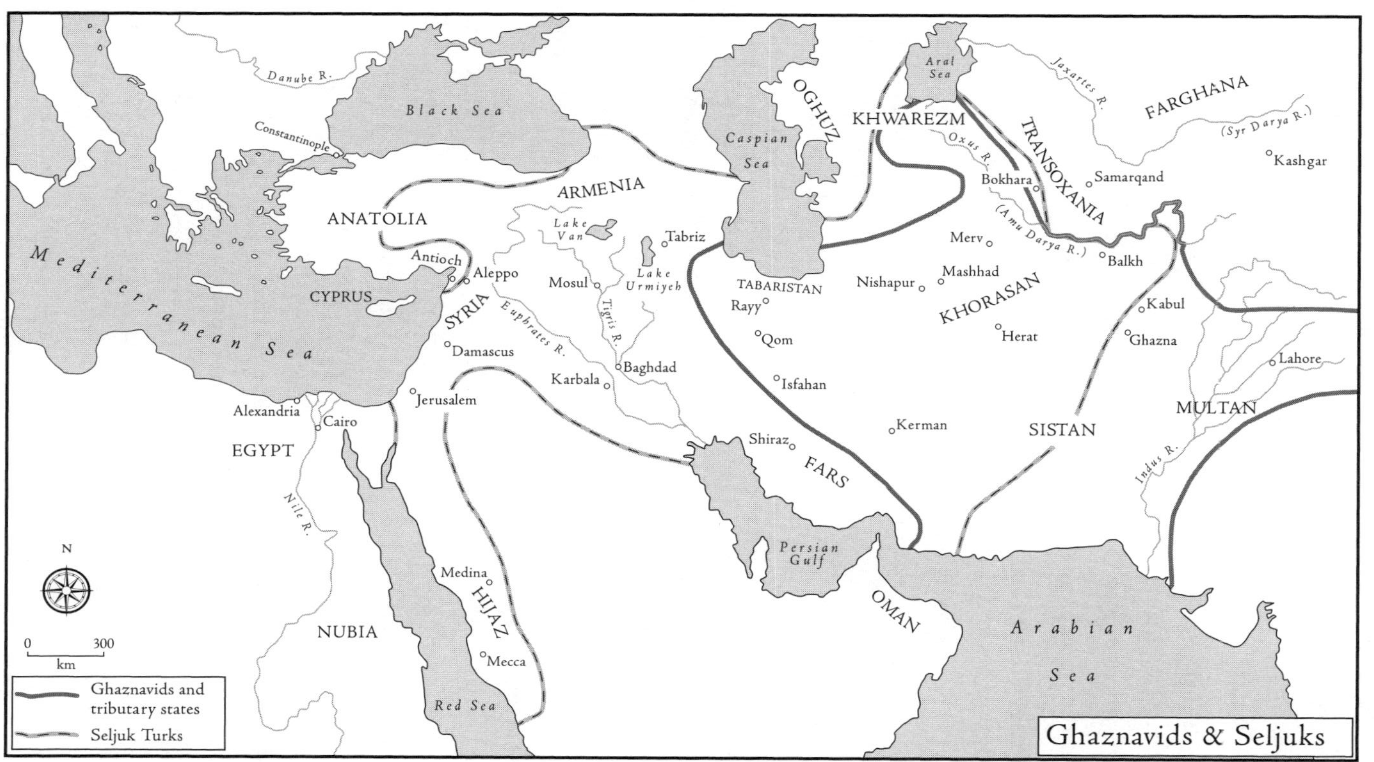
Black Sea
Danube R.
Constantinople
ANATOLIA
ARMENIA
Caspian Sea
OGHUZ
KHWAREZM
Aral Sea
Jaxartes R.
FARGHANA
(Syr Darya R.)
Kashgar
Oxus R.
TRANSOXANIA
Bokhara
Samarqand
(Amu Darya R.)
Balkh
Merv
Mashhad
Nishapur
KHORASAN
Herat
Kabul
Ghazna
Lahore
Tabriz
Lake Van
Lake Urmiyeh
Mosul
Tigris R.
Baghdad
Karbala
Euphrates R.
Antioch
Aleppo
SYRIA
Damascus
Jerusalem
Mediterranean Sea
CYPRUS
Alexandria
Cairo
EGYPT
Nile R.
NUBIA
Medina
HIJAZ
Mecca
Red Sea
TABARISTAN
Rayy
Qom
Isfahan
Kerman
SISTAN
MULTAN
Indus R.
Shiraz
FARS
Persian Gulf
OMAN
Arabian Sea
N
0
300
km
Ghaznavids and tributary states
Seljuk Turks
Ghaznavids & Seljuks

For many years the Abbasid caliphs and the other dynasties had employed Turkish mercenaries, taken as slaves from Central Asia, to fight their wars and police their territories. Turks had in turn become important in the politics of the empire, and on occasion had threatened to take control—the Ghaznavids had succeeded in doing so in the eastern part of the empire. But in the middle of the eleventh century a confederation of Turkic tribes under the leadership of the Seljuk Turks went farther. Defeating the Ghaznavids in the northeast, they broke into the heartlands of the empire and took Baghdad before fighting their way farther west. In 1071 they defeated the Byzantines and occupied most of the interior of Asia Minor.

Centuries of contact with the Abbasid regime and its successors had Islamized the Turks and had made them relatively assimilable. The second Seljuk sultan, Alp Arslan, had as his chief vizier a Persian, Hasan Tusi Nizam ol-Mulk (1018–1092), and before long the dynasty was ruling according to the Persianate Abbasid model like the others before it. Nizam ol-Mulk wrote a book of guidance for Alp Arslan's successor. Called the *Siyasat-Nameh,* which translates as The Book of Government, it (along with the slightly earlier *Qabus-name*) was for centuries the model for the Mirror-of-Princes genre of literature, providing manuals of guidance for rulers. It also influenced European versions of the same kind of thing, down to the time of Machiavelli and his *Principe*.

Nizam ol-Mulk was a friend of Omar Khayyam (c. 1048–c. 1124/1129) and there are some famous stories of dubious veracity about the friendship.[24] But it is probably true that when Nizam ol-Mulk became vizier he gave some financial help to Omar Khayyam, and possibly some protection, too. Among Iranians it is commonplace to say that Omar Khayyam was a more distinguished mathematician and astronomer than a poet. To assess the validity of this is like trying to compare apples with billiard balls. He did work on Euclidean geometry, cubic equations, binomial expansion, and quadratic equations that experts in mathematics regard as influential and important. He developed a new calendar for the Seljuk sultan, based on highly accurate observations of the sun, that was at least as accurate as the Gregorian calendar ordained in sixteenth-century Europe by the Catholic church.[25] And it seems he was probably the first to demonstrate the theory that the nightly progression of the constellations through the sky was due to the earth spinning around its axis, rather than the movement of the skies around a fixed earth as had previously been assumed.

Omar Khayyam's dry skepticism in his poetry makes his voice unique among the other Persian poets, but also reflects a self-confidence drawn perhaps from his preeminent position in his other studies—his knowledge that in them he had surpassed what was known before. His name is famous in the West through the translations of Edward Fitzgerald, which were taken by readers to represent a spirit of eat, drink, and be merry hedonism. This is not quite right. Fitzgerald's are free translations, and his nineteenth-century idiom (fine though his verses are), with its dashes and exclamation marks, ohs and ahs, to a degree misrepresents the sober force of the originals. Here, for example, is Fitzgerald:

"How sweet is mortal Sovranty!"—think some:
Others—"How blest the Paradise to come!"
Ah, take the cash in hand and waive the Rest;
Oh, the brave Music of a distant Drum!

Here is the original:

Guyand kasan behesht ba hur khosh ast
Man miguyam ke ab-e angur khosh ast
In naqd begir o dast az an nesye bedar
K'avaz-e dohol shenidan az dur khosh ast

And here a more literal translation:

It is said that paradise, with its houris, is well.
I say, the juice of the grape is well.
Take this cash and let go that credit
Because hearing the sound of the drums, from afar, is well.[26]

Translating poetry is notoriously difficult, and some would say that it is a vain endeavor entirely. For example, the word *khosh* has a wide range of related meanings and is found in a series of compound words in Persian so that, with those, it takes up several pages in any dictionary. It means delicious, delightful, sweet, happy, cheerful, pleasant, good, and prosperous. One can see different shades of these meanings in each of the three lines in which it appears in this poem. The form of the poem is the quatrain, or *ruba'i*—the plural is *rubaiyat*. Other Persian verse forms include the *ghazal*, the *masnavi*, and the *qasida*.

Most of Omar Khayyam's surviving poetry is in the ruba'i form, but there has been much doubt as to which of the thousand or more rubaiyat attributed to him were actually his work. It seems likely that the poems of others—poems that were of a skeptical or irreligious tendency and might therefore have attracted disapproval—were attributed to him in order to have the grace accorded his great name. At the same time, it may be that he set down doubts in his poems that were only part of his thinking about the deity. But one can read in his poems a rugged humanism in the face of the harsh realities of life, and an impatience with easy, consoling answers, that anticipates existentialism: a recognition of the complexity of existence, the intractability of its problems, and a principled acceptance. His philosophical writing largely revolved around questions of free will, determinism, existence, and essence.[27]

Niki o badi ke dar nahad-e bashar ast,
Shadi o ghami ke dar qaza o qadar ast
Ba charkh makon havale k'andar rah-e aql
Charkh az tu hezar bar bicharetar ast

Good and evil, which are in the nature of mankind,
Joy and sadness, which are in chance and fate
Do not attribute them to the machinery of the heavens, because in reason
That machine is a thousand times more helpless than you[28]

There are dozens of quatrains that one could bring forward to illustrate the subtlety and intellectual power of this great man, but this cannot be a book about just Omar Khayyam. The following poem belongs to a collection from an early manuscript attributed to Omar Khayyam by the British scholar Arberry, which since Arberry's time has been considered doubtful. But it is known from other manuscripts, too, and many scholars still include this poem with Omar Khayyam's best. If it is not by him, it nonetheless presents a defiant personal manifesto close to the spirit he expressed elsewhere:

Gar man ze mey-e moghaneh mastam, hastam
Var asheq o rend o botparastam, hastam
Har kas be khiyal-e khod gamane darad
Man khod danam, har anche hastam, hastam.

If I am drunk on forbidden wine, I am.
And if a worshipper of love, and roguery, and false gods, then I am.
Everyone has their own doubts.
I know myself; whatever I am, I am.[29]

The eleventh century saw the first great upsurge in the unique mystical movement that is Sufism,[30] and in this poem, as elsewhere, Omar Khayyam uses terms that were commonplace in Sufi poetry and were used as key concepts, often metaphorically. *Mey-e moghaneh,* for example, means Magian wine—forbidden wine bought from the Zoroastrians. *Rend* means a wild young man, a rogue or rake. *Kharabat* is the house of ruin, the tavern; and the *saqi* is the young boy who serves the wine and is the object of homoerotic longing. But although some commentators have claimed Omar Khayyam as a Sufi, and notwithstanding he may have had some sympathy for the Sufis, his voice is too much his own, too unique to be set in any religious category. And his skepticism is too strong.

Sufism is a huge and complex phenomenon, with very different aspects at different times and in different places, from eleventh-century Asia Minor to North Africa to modern Pakistan and beyond. Its origins are unclear, but Islam sustained a mystical element from the very beginning—as is shown, some would say, by the revelation of the Qor'an to Mohammad himself, in the wilderness outside Mecca. The essence of Sufism was a seeking after precisely this kind of personal spiritual encounter, and an abandonment of self and all kinds of worldly egotism in the presence of the divine.

But in practices and imagery it also partook of the religious turbulence of the centuries after the Islamic conquest, reflecting popular pre-Islamic ideas and influences, including the mystically inclined movements of Neoplatonism and gnosticism. These influences, along with a deliberate anarchic and antinomian tendency, set it up from the start in tension with the text-based, scholarly, urban tradition of the ulema and the urban preachers who solemnly read and re-read the Qor'an and hadith to assert anew the correct definition of shari'a (Islamic law). There was tension and conflict, and a number of Sufis or mystically inclined thinkers—like al-Hallaj and Sohravardi, for example—were condemned as heretics by the ulema, and were executed (in 922 and 1191, respectively). It may be that the renewed rise of Sufism in the eleventh and twelfth centuries had something to do with a reaction to the increasing concentration of Islamic practice and Islamic study in the madresehs, directly under the eye of the ulema, that was taking place at this time.

The significance of Sufism within the Islamic lands in this period has sometimes been neglected, but in reality it was all-pervasive. In Persia its cultural influence is indicated by its effect on Persian poetry, but everywhere in the land there were Sufi *khanaqas*—lodging houses for wandering Sufis that also served local people for religious gatherings. In the larger towns there might be khanaqas for different Sufi orders, as well as bazaar guilds and other associations that often had Sufi connections. Even small villages might have khanaqas. There are parallels here with the friaries set up for the mendicant orders in Europe in the Middle Ages. Like the friars, the Sufis were intimately involved in the religious lives of ordinary people and were responsible for missionary activity in the countryside and beyond Persia. Given the low level of literacy at the time, and the fact that the population lived overwhelmingly in the countryside, it becomes plain that the Sufis were central to the diffusion of Islam outside the towns and cities. The center of their activity was in Persia, and especially in Khorasan, but they probably were the prime means by which Persianate culture spread and consolidated its popular influence from the Bosphorus to Delhi and beyond.[31]

Many Sufis, in particular many of the Sufi poets, openly scorned what they saw as the self-important egotism of the ulema. The Sufis provoked and attacked them for their obsession with rules and their vain pride in observing them, which forgot the selflessness necessary for true spirituality. It is not difficult to see why some orthodox Muslims (especially Wahhabis and their sympathizers since the eighteenth century) have anathematized and persecuted Sufism. But in the period we are dealing with here, the missionary activity of traveling Sufis (known also as dervishes) was important, probably crucial, in the conversion of new Muslims. This was true in the remoter rural parts like Tabarestan, where orthodox Islam had been slow to penetrate, but especially in newly conquered territories like Anatolia, and among the Turks in their Central Asian homelands in the far northeast.

The first great theorist of Sufism was al-Ghazali (1058–1111), a native of Tus in Khorasan (though there were major Sufi figures much earlier, Junayd, for example, who died around 910). The relationship between orthodox Sunnism and Sufism was not one of simple opposition, and al-Ghazali was primarily an orthodox Sunni of the Shafi'i mazhhab, who wrote works attacking the Mu'tazilis, Avicenna, and the introduction of ideas from Greek philosophy. But he also wrote an influential Sufi work called *Kimiya-ye sa'adat*—The Alchemy of Happiness. In general he tried to remove the obstacles between orthodoxy and Sufism, presenting the latter as a legitimate aspect of the former. In the early centuries of Sufism, Shi'a Muslims tended to be more hostile to the Sufi dervishes than the Sunnis.[32]

Sana'i was the first great poet with a clear Sufi allegiance, and some have compared his literary style with that of al-Ghazali. Sana'i's long poem *Hadiqat al-haqiqa* (*The Garden of Truth*, completed in 1131) is a classic of Sufi poetry, but he wrote a large body of poems beyond that, and in them it is easy to see the fusion of the traditions of love poetry with the impulses of mysticism:

Since my heart was caught in the snare of love,
Since my soul became wine in the cup of love,
Ah, the pains I have known through loverhood
Since like a hawk I fell in the snare of love!
Trapped in time, I am turned to a drunken sot
By the exciting, dreg-draining cup of love.
Dreading the fierce affliction of loverhood,
I dare not utter the very name of love;
And the more amazing is this, since I see
Every creature on earth is at peace with love.[33]

Here, too, wine has become a metaphor for love, taking the imagery into another dimension of complexity. Where an orthodox Muslim might favor abstinence (*zohd*) in accordance with religious law, Sana'i says that in going beyond law into infidelity (*kofr*)—leaving behind his venal, carnal soul (*nafs*)—the Sufi can find another way to God. The point is that both love and wine can be ways in which a man may forget himself. They are familiar experiences in which the sense of self is changed or obliterated. Such an experience can give a taste of (and therefore provide a metaphor for) the loss of self experienced by the mystic in the face of God—the loss of self that is necessary for genuine religious experience, that is yearned for as the lover longs for the beloved.

The Seljuk period produced a profusion of poets, and it is not possible to do justice to them all, but Nizami Ganjavi, who composed his *Khosraw va Shirin* in 1180 and *Layla va Majnoun* in 1188, is too important to be overlooked. Though he wrote many others, both these long poems retold much older stories—the former a tale from the Sassanid court and the latter of Arab origin. Both are love stories that became hugely popular, but they have deeper resonances, reflecting Nizami's religious beliefs. Layla and Majnoun fall in love, but then are separated, and Majnoun goes mad (*Majnoun* means "mad") and wanders in the wilderness. He becomes a poet, writing to Layla through a third party:

> Oh my love, with your breasts like jasmine! Loving you, my life fades, my lips wither, my eyes are full of tears. You cannot imagine how much I am "Majnoun." For you, I have lost myself. But that path can only be taken by those who forget themselves. In love, the faithful have to pay with the blood of their hearts; otherwise their love is not worth a grain of rye. So you are leading me, revealing the true faith of love, even if your faith should remain hidden forever.[34]

Without hope in his love (Layla's father will not let them marry), Majnoun spiritualizes it. In going into the desert, losing his selfhood in madness, stepping outside all ordinary conventions, and writing poetry, he has effectively become a Sufi.[35] So even this overtly profane story has a spiritual dimension that is not immediately apparent. But to have psychological force, the metaphor and the spiritual message first require our sympathy with the lovers' predicament. The poem is not simply about the Sufi's approach to God. It is that, but also a love story—and therein lies its human appeal. It has been translated into almost every language in the Islamic world, as well as many others beyond it.

Farid al-Din Attar, who lived in Nishapur from around 1158 to around 1221 or 1229, wrote more than forty-five thousand lines of verse in his lifetime. Establishing the elements of a "religion of love," Attar strongly influenced all subsequent Sufi poets. He developed the idea of the *qalandar*, the wild man, the outcast, whose only guide is the ethic of that religion:

> *Har ke ra dar 'eshq mohkam shod qadam*
> *Dar-gozasht az kofr va az islam ham*
>
> *Whoever sets foot firmly forward in love*
> *Will go beyond both Islam and unbelief* [36]

The classic of Attar's poetry is the *Mantiq al-tayr* (*The Conference of the Birds*), one of the best-known Persian poems of all. Embedded within the charming story of the birds questing for the mysterious phoenix—the *simorgh*—is the story of Shaykh San'an, which brings out the full meaning of Sufism in its logical extreme. Deliberately provocative and shocking in the Islamic context, the story was important and influential in the later development of Sufism.

Shaykh San'an is a learned, well-respected holy man who has always done the right thing. He has made the pilgrimage to Mecca fifty times, has fasted and prayed, and has taught four hundred pupils. He argues fine points of religious law and is admired by everyone. But he has a recurring dream, in which he lives in *Rum* (by which was probably meant the Christian part of Anatolia, or possibly Constantinople, rather than Rome itself) and worships in a Christian church there. This is disturbing, and he concludes that to resolve the problem he must go to the Christian territory. He sets off, but just short of his goal he sees a Christian girl—"*In beauty's mansion she was like a sun. . . .*"

Her eyes spoke promises to those in love,
Their fine brows arched coquettishly above—
Those brows sent glancing messages that seemed
To offer everything her lovers dreamed.

And, as sometimes happens, the old man falls in love:

"I have no faith" he cried. "The heart I gave
Is useless now; I am the Christian's slave."

His companions try to get Shaykh San'an to see reason, but he answers them in terms even more shocking and subversive. They tell him to pray, and he agrees—but instead of toward Mecca, as a Muslim should, he asks to know where her face is, that he may pray in her direction. Another asks him whether he does not regret turning away from Islam, and he answers that he only regrets his previous folly, and that he had not fallen in love before. Another says he has lost his wits, and he says he has, and also his fame—but fraud and fear along with them. Another urges him to confess his shame before God, and he replies, "*God Himself has lit this flame.*"

The shaykh lives for a month with the dogs in the dust of the street in front of his beloved's house, finally falling ill. He begs her to show him some pity, a little affection, but she laughs and mocks him, saying that he is old—he should be looking for a shroud, not for love. He begs again, and she says he must do four things to win her trust—burn the Qor'an, drink wine, *seal up faith's eye*, and bow down to images. The shaykh hesitates, but then agrees. Invited in, he takes wine and gets drunk:

He drank, oblivion overwhelmed his soul.
Wine mingled with his love—her laughter seemed
To challenge him to take the bliss he dreamed.

He agrees to everything the girl demands, but it is not enough—she wants gold and silver, and he is poor. Eventually she takes pity on him. She will overlook the gold and silver—if he will look after some pigs for a year as a swineherd. He agrees.

From this extreme point, the story takes a more conventional turn, as was necessary if the book was not to be banned and destroyed. A vision of the Prophet intervenes, the shaykh returns to the faith, the girl repents her treatment of the shaykh, becomes a Muslim, and dies. But this cannot draw the sting of the first part of the story—the message that conventional piety is not enough, that it may in fact lead down the wrong path, and that the peeling away of conventional trappings and the loss of self in love is the only way to attain a higher spirituality. As Attar wrote at the beginning, when he introduced the story:

When neither Blasphemy nor faith remain,
The body and the Self have both been slain;
Then the fierce fortitude the Way will ask
Is yours, and you are worthy of our task.
Begin the journey without fear; be calm;
Forget what is and what is not Islam . . .

Taken as a whole, the story appears ambiguous, but it contains a startling challenge to the religious conventions of the time.[37]

Attar, the apostle of love, died at some point in the 1220s—massacred along with most of the population of Nishapur when the Mongols invaded Khorasan and Persia. The Mongol invasions were an unparalleled cataclysm for the lands of Iran. Where the Arabs and Turks had been relatively familiar and restrained conquerors, the Mongols were both alien and wantonly cruel.

The Seljuk Empire had been split toward the end of the twelfth century by the rise of a subject tribe from Khwarezm, whose leaders established themselves as the rulers of the eastern part of the empire. They were known as the Khwarezmshahs. In the early years of the thirteenth century, the ruling Khwarezmshah, Sultan Mohammad, became dimly aware that a new power was rising in the steppe lands beyond Transoxiana. There were impossible rumors—true, as it turned out—that the Chinese empire had been conquered. There may have been some attempts at diplomatic contact, but these were bungled, resulting in the deaths of some Mongol merchants and ambassadors. Contrary to popular perception, the Mongols were not just a ravening mob of uncivilized, semi-human killers. Their armies were tightly controlled, well disciplined, and ruthlessly efficient. They were not wantonly destructive.[38] But their ultimate foundation was the prestige of their warlord, Genghis Khan, and an insult could not be overlooked. After the killing of the Mongol emissaries, what came next in Transoxiana and Khorasan was particularly dreadful because of the Mongols' vengeful purpose. There followed a series of Mongol invasions, aimed initially at punishing Sultan Mohammad—who, veering from tragedy toward comedy, fled westward to Ray, pursued by a Mongol flying column, and then north until he died on an island off the Caspian coast. These invasions later developed into conquest and occupation. What this meant for the hapless Iranians can be illustrated by what happened at Merv, after the Mongols had already conquered and destroyed the cities of Transoxiana:

> . . . on the next day, 25 February 1221, the Mongols arrived before the gates of Merv. Tolui in person [the son of Genghiz Khan], with an escort of five hundred

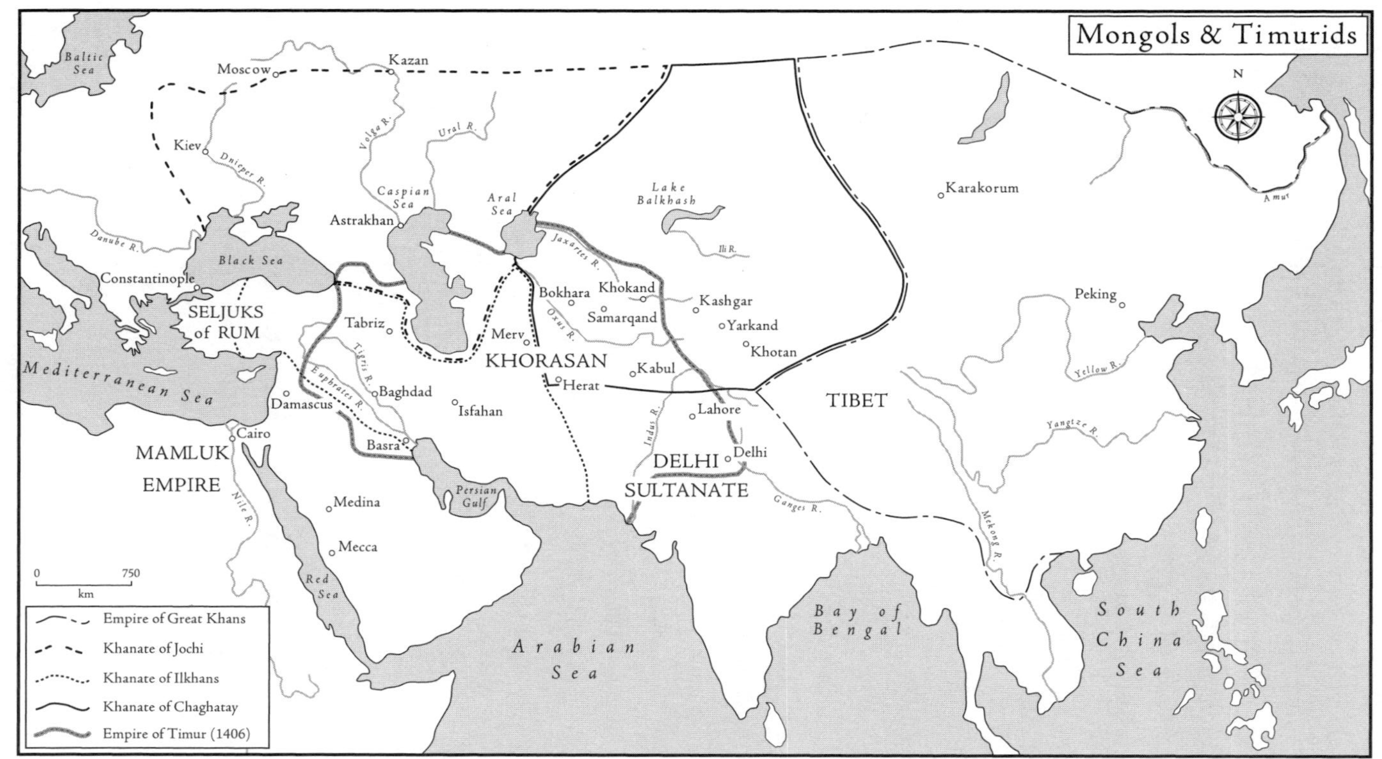
Mongols & Timurids
N
Baltic Sea
Moscow
Kazan
Kiev
Dnieper R.
Volga R.
Ural R.
Caspian Sea
Aral Sea
Lake Balkhash
Ili R.
Karakorum
Amur
Astrakhan
Danube R.
Black Sea
Constantinople
SELJUKS of RUM
Jaxartes R.
Bokhara
Khokand
Samarqand
Kashgar
Yarkand
Khotan
Oxus R.
Tabriz
Merv
KHORASAN
Kabul
Herat
Tigris R.
Euphrates R.
Baghdad
Isfahan
Damascus
Mediterranean Sea
Lahore
TIBET
Peking
Yellow R.
Yangtze R.
Indus R.
Cairo
MAMLUK EMPIRE
Basra
DELHI SULTANATE
Delhi
Persian Gulf
Ganges R.
Nile R.
Medina
Mecca
Mekong R.
Red Sea
0 750 km
Arabian Sea
Bay of Bengal
South China Sea
Empire of Great Khans
Khanate of Jochi
Khanate of Ilkhans
Khanate of Chaghatay
Empire of Timur (1406)

> horsemen, rode the whole distance around the walls, and for six days the Mongols continued to inspect the defences, reaching the conclusion that they were in good repair and would withstand a lengthy siege. On the seventh day the Mongols launched a general assault. The townspeople made two sallies from different gates, being in both cases at once driven back by the Mongol forces. They seem then to have lost all will to resist. The next day the governor surrendered the town, having been reassured by promises that were not in fact to be kept. The whole population was now driven out into the open country, and for four days and nights the people continued to pour out of the town. Four hundred artisans and a number of children were selected to be carried off as slaves, and it was commanded that the whole of the remaining population, men, women, children, should be put to the sword. They were distributed, for this purpose, among the troops, and to each individual soldier was allotted the execution of three to four hundred persons. These troops included levies from the captured towns, and Juvaini records that the people of Sarakhs, who had a feud with the people of Merv, exceeded the ferocity of the heathen Mongols in the slaughter of their fellow-Muslims. Even now the ordeal of Merv was not yet over. When the Mongols withdrew, those who had escaped death by concealing themselves in holes and cavities emerged from their hiding places. They amounted in all to some five thousand people. A detachment of Mongols, part of the rearguard, now arrived before the town. Wishing to have their share of the slaughter they called upon these unfortunate wretches to come out into the open country, each carrying a skirtful of grain. And having them thus at their mercy they massacred these last feeble remnants of one of the greatest cities of Islam. . . .[39]

Contemporary eyewitnesses at Merv gave estimates for the numbers killed ranging between 700,000 and 1.3 million. These figures are huge but credible, representing a high proportion of the population of northern Khorasan and Transoxiana at the time. The numbers were probably greater than normal because country people and refugees from tens and hundreds of miles around fled there before the siege began. When we talk of the magnitude of twentieth-century massacres and genocides as if they were unparalleled, we sometimes forget what enormities were perpetrated in earlier centuries with the cold blade alone. *A skirtful of grain.* The Nishapur of Omar Khayyam, Tus, Herat, and other cities in Khorasan suffered the same fate. The only option for the citizens other than massacre was immediate capitulation as soon as the Mongol columns hove into sight.

Some places, encouraged by rumors of resistance by Sultan Mohammad's son, Jalal al-Din, tried to hold their towns against the invaders, and suffered terribly as a result. But by the end of 1231, despite having achieved a string of brilliant victories against the Mongols and others, and a legend of *razm o bazm* to rival the heroes of Ferdowsi, Jalal al-Din was dead. It might have been better for the people of Iran, at this critical time, if the Khwarezmshah had been a wiser man with less panache.

Khorasan suffered terribly again as the Mongols moved in to punish those who continued to resist, and to set up their occupation regime. In Tus, which they made their base, the Mongols initially found only fifty houses still standing.[40] The golden age of Khorasan was over, and in some parts of the region agriculture never really recovered. Where there had been towns and irrigated fields, the war horses of the conquerors and their confederates now were turned out to graze. Wide expanses of Iran reverted to nomad pastoralism, but these nomads were more dangerous, ruthless mounted warriors of a different kind. Peasants were subjected to taxes that were ruinously high and were collected after the fashion of a military campaign. Many fled the land or were forced into slavery, while those artisan city dwellers who had survived the massacres were forced to labor in workhouses for their conquerors. Minorities suffered, too. In the 1280s a Jew was appointed as vizier by the Mongols, but his appointment grew unpopular, he fell from office, and Jews were attacked by Muslims in the cities, establishing a dismal pattern for later centuries: "[They] *fell upon the Jews in every city of the empire, to wreak their vengeance upon them for the degradation which they had suffered from the Mongols.*"[41] It was a grim time indeed. Khorasan was more affected than other parts, but the general collapse of the economy hit the entire region.

The Mongols, who made Tabriz their capital, spent the next few decades consolidating their conquests and destroying the Ismaili Assassins in the

Alborz mountains, just as the Seljuks had tried and failed to do for many years before 1220. Some smaller rulers who had submitted to the Mongols were allowed to continue as vassals, and in the west the rump of the Seljuk Empire survived in Anatolia on the same basis as the Sultanate of Rum. In 1258 the Mongols took Baghdad. They killed the last Abbasid caliph by wrapping him in a carpet and trampling him to death with horses.

Yet within a few decades, astoundingly, or perhaps predictably, the Persian class of scholars and administrators had pulled off their trick of conquering the conquerors—for the third time. Before long they made themselves indispensable. A Shi'a astrologer, Naser od-Din Tusi, captured by the Mongols at the end of the campaign against the Ismailis, had taken service with the Mongol prince Hulagu, and served as his adviser in the campaign against Baghdad. Naser od-Din Tusi then set up an astronomical observatory for Hulagu in Azerbaijan. One member of the Persian Juvayni family became governor of Baghdad and wrote the history of the Mongols; another became the vizier of a later Mongol Il-Khan, or king. Within a couple of generations Persian officials were as firmly in place at the court of the Il-Khans as they had been with the Seljuks, the Ghaznavids, and earlier dynasties. The Mongols initially retained their paganism, but in 1295 their Buddhist ruler converted to Islam along with his army. In 1316 his son Oljeitu died and was buried in a mausoleum that still stands in Soltaniyeh—one of the grandest monuments of Iranian Islamic architecture and a monument also to the resilience and assimilating power of Iranian culture.

Another important invasion took place a little earlier than the Mongol invasion of Khorasan—the invasion and conquest of India by Muslim Persians and Turks, establishing what became known as the Delhi Sultanate. We have seen already that the Parthians and Sassanids at different times invaded northern India and established dynasties that ruled there. The Ghaznavids and their provincial governors also raided into northern India, and one such governor, Mohammad Ghuri, took that practice a step further in the latter part of the twelfth century, conquering Multan, Sind, Lahore, and Delhi. A series of dynasties followed thereafter, expanding the reach of the Delhi Sultanate east into Bengal and south to the Deccan, creating a unique Indo-Islamic culture that fused Persian, Hindustani, Arabic, and Turkic elements, and—in the northwest—the Urdu language. Northern India came under strong Islamic influence. Sufi missionaries set to work, and it became an important region for the development of Persianate culture in the following centuries.

Culmination: Rumi, Iraqi, Sa'di, and Hafez

The reassertion of Persian influence over the conquerors is not the only extraordinary feature of the period following the Mongol conquest. One might have thought that the poetry would come to a halt, or at least a hiatus, in the grim, blackened aftermath of the Mongol conquest. But three of the very greatest Persian poets flourished at this time, to be followed by the fourth a little later. Rumi was born in 1207, Iraqi in 1211, Sa'di some time in the same decade, and Hafez a century later. Iranians themselves normally consider Rumi, Hafez, and Sa'di to be (with Ferdowsi) the greatest of their poets, and it is not possible in a small space to do more than give a sense of who they were and the merest taste of what they wrote. Iraqi is likewise an important figure, especially in Sufism. Together these poets represent the culmination of literary development in Persian since the Arab conquest.

Jalal al-Din Molavi Rumi (normally called Mawlana by Iranians) was born in Balkh in 1207. It was not a good time or place. His father, like others fearing the approach of the Mongols, left Balkh in 1219, initially for Mecca on the hajj, later to Konya in Anatolia. Rumi spent most of the rest of his life in Konya. Initially he lived, as had his father, as an orthodox member of the ulema, preaching and studying according to the Hanafi school. He also learned about Sufism, but around 1244 he turned to it entirely under the influence of another Sufi mystic and poet, Shams-e Tabrizi, with whom Rumi had an intense emotional friendship (at least). Then, three or four years later, Shams disappeared, perhaps murdered. Between that time and his own death in 1273, Rumi wrote about sixty-five thousand lines of poetry. His poetry is a world of its own—a highly complex mystical world that has become popular in the United States in recent years. Some say Rumi is the most popular poet in the United States today, at least in the sense that his books sell better than those of other poets. Some of Rumi's most famous lines, which come from the opening of his *masnavi*, express the longing of the soul for union with God:

Now listen to this reed-flute's deep lament
About the heartache being apart has meant:
Since from the reed-bed they uprooted me
My song's expressed each human's agony,
A breast which separation's split in two
Is what I seek, to share this pain with you:
When kept from their origin, all yearn
For union on the day they can return . . .

. . .

The reed consoles those forced to be apart,
Its notes will lift the veil upon your heart,
Where's antidote or poison like its song
Or confidant, or one who's pined so long?
This reed relates a tortuous path ahead,
Recalls the love with which Majnoun's heart bled:
The few who hear the truths the reed has sung
Have lost their wits so they can speak this tongue . . .[42]

And this is the simple idea at the core of Rumi's thought—the unity of God, the unity of the human spirit with God, and the yearning for reunion with God (Plato puts a similar idea into the mouth of Aristophanes in the *Symposium*). Rumi expresses the same idea in a different way in the following ruba'i (the Beloved was a common Sufi term signifying God):

Ma'shuq chu aftab taban gardad
'Asheq bemesal-e zarre gardan gardad
Chun bad-e bahar-e eshq jonban gardad
Har shakh ke khoshk nist raqsan gardad

The Beloved starts shining like the sun,
And the lover begins to whirl like a dust-mote.

When the spring wind of love begins to move,
Any branch that is not withered starts to dance[43]

Many of Rumi's poems contain overt or concealed references to Shams-e Tabrizi: *shams* in Arabic means sun, and the reference is obvious. But this does not mean that the Beloved is simply Shams; the Beloved is also God, the sun, and in a sense Rumi himself.

Fakhroddin al-Iraqi, despite his name, was an Iranian born near Hamadan in 1211. At the time that western province was known as Iraq-e Ajam—the Iraq of the *Ajam,* the non-Arabs—in other words, the Persians. Hence the name al-Iraqi. The stories about Iraqi's life give us a vivid idea of his personality, which was unashamedly eccentric. This fits with and adds to the sense of his personality as conveyed by his poems. Iraqi showed an early facility for learning and scholarship, but his head was turned in his teens by the arrival in Hamadan of some Sufi *qalandar*—wild men. Iraqi joined them without hesitation:

We've moved our bedrolls from the mosque to the tavern of ruin [kharabat]
We've scribbled all over the page of asceticism and erased all miracles of piety.
Now we sit with the lovers in the lane of the Magians
And drink a cup from the hands of the dissolute people of the tavern.
If the heart should tweak the ear of respectability now, why not?[44]

In another poem he says:

All fear of God, all self-denial I deny; bring wine, nothing but wine
For in all sincerity I repent my worship which is but hypocrisy.
Yes, bring me wine, for I have renounced all renunciation
And all my vaunted self-righteousness seems to me but swagger and self-display.[45]

Iraqi went traveling with the other beggars. He wrote many poems about the beauty of young men and boys, and the homoerotic strain in Persian poetry is especially plain in his work. But his contemporary defenders claimed that he only admired the boys longingly from afar. Eventually, he came under the influence of a follower of the Sufi philosopher Ibn Arabi, perhaps the greatest thinker of Islamic mysticism, who had died in 1240.

Ibn Arabi's thought—steeped primarily in the Qor'an and the traditions of the hadith, but influenced also by Neoplatonism and the thinking of earlier Sufis—elaborated what appears very like a version of Plato's theory of forms: that phenomena in the material world are manifestations of original, essential truths in a higher sphere (itself an idea possibly derived from Iranian Mazdaism, as we saw earlier). Therefore true reality lay paradoxically in the spiritual, metaphysical world beyond, of which the physical world was a mere shadow. Central also to Ibn Arabi's thinking were ideas of the oneness of God's creation (*wahdat al-wujud*) and of the imagination (*khiyal*).

Another very significant concept that Ibn Arabi developed from the formulae of earlier thinkers was the idea of the Perfect Man (*al-insan al-kamil*). According to this notion the sphere of existence that is not God is divided between the macrocosm, the world beyond Man, and the microcosm, the inner world of Man. These two worlds reflect each other, and through religious contemplation and self-development, Man can "polish his soul" until the two worlds are congruent. Man can improve and perfect himself until he takes on the form of the divine, becoming the Perfect Man.[46] He can then become a conduit for the will of God in the world. This state is achieved by religious discipline and mystical devotion, an idea that was to have great significance in later Islamic thinking. Ayatollah Ruhollah Khomeini was fascinated by these ideas and wrote one of his earliest books about a later commentary on the *Fusus al-Hikam* (Seals of Wisdom) of Ibn Arabi.

Consider also the following extract, about the possibility of a mystic being able to visit the alternative Earth of True Reality:

> Then he meets those Forms who stand and keep watch at the entrances to the ways of approach, God having especially assigned them this task. One of them hastens towards the newcomer, clothes him in a robe suitable to his rank, takes him by the hand, and walks with him over that Earth and they do in it

> as they will. He lingers to look at the divine works of art; every stone, every tree, every village, every single thing he comes across, he may speak with, if he wishes, as a man converses with a companion. . . . When he has attained his object and thinks of returning to his dwelling place, his companion goes with him and takes him back to the place at which he entered. There she says goodbye to him; she takes off the robe in which she had clothed him and departs from him . . .[47]

The idea that the world of experience was a mere shadow of the real world of forms beyond had great potential for metaphor in spiritual poetry, and traces of this idea can be seen in many of the Persian poets. They reached their apotheosis with Shabestari, who in his *Gulshan-e raz* put forward a full-fledged aesthetic according to which eyebrows, curls, or the down on the beloved's upper lip might represent heavenly or metaphysical concepts.

Iraqi was devoted to the ideas of Ibn Arabi for the rest of his life. He wrote his *Divine Flashes* in exposition of them, and when he died in 1289 he was buried next to Ibn Arabi in Damascus. But he never settled down to a conventional life. One story says that when he arrived in Cairo on his travels, the sultan honored him by setting him on his own horse and giving him some splendid clothes; but as he rode through the streets accompanied by many other scholars and dignitaries on foot, Iraqi suddenly snatched off his turban and put it on the saddle in front of him. Seeing him traveling in such splendor, but bareheaded, the people watching laughed. When the sultan heard about it he was displeased, because it made him look ridiculous. Iraqi explained that he had removed the turban to avoid sin. As he rode along it occurred to him that no one had ever been so honored, and as he felt his ego rise up he had deliberately humbled himself.[48]

Some commentators feel that Iraqi's poetry was better and livelier before his encounter with the thought of Ibn Arabi—that it became overburdened metaphysically afterward. But there is something especially touching about Iraqi and his poetry, especially his early work. It shows perhaps more clearly than any other Sufi poetry the urge to dispense with the self-regarding piety and the holier-than-thou observance of mere rules pursued by the orthodox.

It also shocks and provokes the orthodox by blatant flouting of their rules. In this, the impulse driving the Sufis is very close to the teachings of Jesus against the Pharisees ("*Woe to you, scribes and Pharisees, hypocrites!*"). Jesus is revered by many Iranian Muslims (not just Sufis) for this trait—for speaking from the heart of spirituality and avoiding getting caught up in its trappings.

With Sa'di and Hafez we begin to run out of superlatives. Both have had a profound influence on the thinking of ordinary Iranians, and phrases from their poems are common sayings. Teachers of the Persian language used to use Sa'di's *Golestan* (*Garden of Roses*) to teach their pupils, having them memorize excerpts in order to help them absorb vocabulary and remember grammar and patterns of usage. His works were some of the first to be translated into European languages in the eighteenth century. One passage from the *Golestan* appears above the entrance to the United Nations in New York:

Bani-Adam a'za-ye yek-digarand
Ke dar afarinesh ze yek gawharand
Chu 'ozvi be dard avarad ruzegar
Digar ozvha ra numanat qarar

All men are fellow-members of one body
For they were created from one essence
When fate afflicts one limb with pain
The other limbs may not stay unmoved

And it continues:

Tu kaz mehnat-e digaran dighami
Nashayad ke namat nahand adami

You who are without sorrow for the suffering of others
You do not deserve to be called human

Sa'di was born in Shiraz (a city saved from Mongol destruction by the wise decision of its ruler to submit to them early), probably sometime between 1213 and 1219. In his poems there are many stories about his travels, some of which are dubious. He was back in Shiraz by around 1256, and died there in 1292. He was familiar with Sufism but was not openly a devotee. His *Bustan* (*The Orchard*) is an extended poem of moral tales, not only encouraging wisdom and virtue, humility and kindness, but also common sense and pragmatism. Some of these features emerge in the following story of Omar and the beggar (Omar was the second caliph, after Abu Bakr—one of the four Righteous Caliphs of Sunni Islam):

I've heard there was a beggar in a narrow place,
On whose foot Omar placed his own;
The hapless pauper, knowing not who he was
(For in anger one knows not enemy from friend),
Flew at him, saying "Are you blind, then?"
At which the just commander, Omar, said to him:
"Blind I am not, but I did slip
Unwittingly; pray, remit my sin."
How even-handed were the great ones of the Faith
To deal thus with subordinates.
Much will be made tomorrow of those who cultivate humility,
While the heads of mighty men hang low for embarrassment;
If you're afraid of the Day of Judgement,
Remit the slips of those afraid of you;
Oppress not your subordinates with impunity,
For over your hand lies a hand likewise[49]

Some have thought that Sa'di's pragmatism strayed too far in the direction of relativism and amorality, citing for example the well-known dictum from the first story in the *Golestan* that *"an expedient falsehood is preferable to a mischievous truth."*[50] But Sa'di is not the only literary figure to have made such a suggestion—one could draw a similar moral from playwright Henrik Ibsen's

Wild Duck without concluding that Ibsen was an amoral relativist. Sa'di's views are diverse and sometimes appear contradictory, but that is a reflection of the complexities he addressed. It is right that Sa'di became known for his epigrams because he had a gift for communicating pithy thoughts in vivid language:

Ananke pari-ruy o shekar goftarand
Hayfast ke ru-ye khub penhan darand
Fi'l-jomle neqab niz bifayede nist
Ta zesht bepushand o niku bogzarand

Those nymph-faced, sugar-speaking ones,
What a pity they should hide their fair faces.
But the veil is not worthless either;
The ugly should put it on, and the beautiful, off.[51]

And:

Ya ru-ye bekonj-e khalvat avar shab o ruz
Ya atash-e 'eshq bar kon o khaneh besuz
Masturi o 'asheqi beham nayad rast
Gar pardeh nakhahi ke darad dideh beduz

Either choose a corner of seclusion day and night
Or light love's fire and let the house burn.
Concealment and love do not get on well.
If you do not want the veil torn, seal up your eyes[52]

Hafez too was born in Shiraz, but a century later—about 1315. "Hafez" is a pen name, signifying that he had learned the Qor'an by heart; his real name was Shams al-Din Mohammad Shirazi. Little is known of his life. He died around 1390, when the impact of Timur (Tamerlane) was beginning to be felt—another round of invasions, warfare, and mass killings to rival that of the Mongols in ferocity and misery. The scholar A. J. Arberry believed that one of Hafez's last *ghazals* was prompted by these new disasters:

Again the times are out of joint; and again
For wine and the Beloved's languid glance I am fain.
The wheel of fortune is a marvellous thing:
What next proud head to the lowly dust will it bring?

'Tis a famous tale, the deceitfulness of earth;
The night is pregnant: what will dawn bring to birth?
Tumult and bloody battle rage in the plain:
Bring blood-red wine, and fill the cup again.[53]

But before the skies darkened again with the smoke of war and massacre, Hafez took the previous patterns of Persian poetry and elevated them to new, unsurpassed heights of expression. In the following ghazal the familiar images of wine and the Beloved ripple, interfere, overlap, reflect each other, and thereby transcend the immediate eroticism, pointing beyond desire to the world of the spirit. It is saying that if love is offered, it must be taken; and if taken, it must be drunk to the dregs because love demands full commitment. Only then can its true significance be grasped—that love is the essential gift, the essence of life, given to us before time:

Her hair was still tangled, her mouth still drunk
And laughing, her shoulders sweaty, the blouse
Torn open, singing love songs, her wine cup full.
Her eyes were looking for a fight, her lips
Ready for jibes. She sat down
Last night at midnight on my bed.
She put her lips close to my ear and said
In a whisper these words: 'What is this?
Aren't you my old lover—Are you asleep?'

The friend of wisdom who receives
This wine that steals sleep is a traitor to love
If he doesn't worship that same wine.
Oh you prudes, go away. Stop arguing with those
Who drink the bitter dregs, because it was precisely
This gift the divine ones gave us before Eternity.
Whatever God poured into our cup
We drank, whether it was the wine
Of heaven or the wine of drunkenness.
The laughter of the wine, and the dishevelled curls of the Beloved
Oh, how many nights of repentance—like those of Hafez
Have been broken by moments like this?[54]

Poems like this unsettle many Iranians even today.[55] Some religious Iranians will say directly that these poems are not really about wine or erotic love at all—that the meaning is entirely on a spiritual level, and that the poets themselves never touched wine. Whether or not that is true (and personally I doubt it), the fact is that the poems only work if the eroticism and the alcoholic intoxication are real. Rather, they work *because* they are real, because they ring true and speak directly to our own experience as only great literature can. They seem to remind us of something we had always known but had somehow forgotten. Otherwise the metaphors would be just a device, the rebellion against convention no more than a pose. This poetry has more bite, more impact than that. Hafez wrote the following in a period of officious imposition of religious orthodoxy (and some have pointed up its relevance in contemporary Iran):

Bovad aya ke dar-e maykadeha bogshayand
Gereh az kar-e forubaste-ye ma bogshayand
Agar az bahr-e del-e zahed-e khodbin bastand
Del qavi dar ke az bahr-e khoda bogshayand

Might they open the doors of the wine shops
And loosen their hold on our knotted lives?

If shut to satisfy the ego of the puritan
Take heart, for they will reopen to satisfy God.[56]

In later times Hafez was appreciated and translated by Goethe, whose enthusiasm for this poetry reflected that of many other Europeans. As for the Persians, they so revered Hafez that his *Divan* (the conventional term for a book collecting a poet's work in one volume) was used as an oracle, and sometimes is still. People wanting to know their fortune open it at random in the hope of texts that can be interpreted as optimistic predictions. The only other book used in that way is the Qor'an.

Ay bad, hadis-e man nahanash migu
Serr-e del-e man be sad zabanash migu
Migu na bedansan ke malalash girad
Migu sokhani o dar miyanash migu

O wind, tell her my story secretly.
Tell her my heart's secret in a hundred tongues.
Tell her, but not in a way that may offend her.
Speak to her and between the words tell her my story.[57]

Persians did not stop writing poetry in the fifteenth century. There were many important poets after Hafez—notably Jami, and later Bidel. By that time a body of literature of unparalleled importance had been created. It is literature of almost inconceivable quantity, great diversity, and sublime quality. One could compare this body of literature to a human brain and think of it in the way that some theorists now consider human consciousness—that consciousness is not located in any one part of the brain, but is instead the consequence of the impossibly complex interaction of millions of different cells and their sparking synapses. Somehow, out of this poetry and the combinations and interactions of the ideas and metaphors contained within them emerged the Iranian soul.

Every hundred years or so, the reading public in the West discovers another of these Persian poets. In 1800 it was Hafez, in 1900 Omar Khayyam, in 2000 it is Rumi. The choice depends not so much on the merits or true nature of the poets or their poetry, but more on their capacity to be interpreted in accordance with passing Western literary and cultural fashions. So Hafez was interpreted to fit with the mood of Romanticism, Omar Khayyam with the aesthetic movement, and it has been Rumi's misfortune to be befriended by numb-brained New Agery. Of course, an attentive and imaginative reader can avoid the solipsistic trap, especially if he or she can read even a little Persian. But the mirror of language and translation means that the reader may see only a hazy but consoling reflection of himself and his times, rather than looking into the true depths of the poetry—which might be more unsettling.

On the surface, the religion of love of these Sufi poets from eight hundred years ago might seem rather distant and archaic. That is belied less by the burgeoning popularity of Rumi and Attar than by the deeper message of these poets. Darwinists who, like Richard Dawkins, believe Darwinism ineluctably entails atheism might be upset by the idea, but what could be more appropriate to an intellectual world that has abandoned creationism for evolution theory than a religion of love? Darwinism and evolutionary theory have demonstrated the intense focus of all life on the act of reproduction, the act of love. The spirit of that act and the drive behind it are the spirit of life itself. What could be more fitting than a religion that uses the emotional drive behind that act as a metaphor for a higher spirituality, and its longing as a longing for union with the Godhead—"*This gift the divine ones gave us before Eternity.*"

Timur

After about 1300 (notably under the ruler Ghazan Khan) the Mongol Il-Khans, becoming Islamized and Persianized, reversed their extractive, destructive, slash-and-burn style of rule. They began trying to reconstruct cities they had destroyed, trying to resurrect systems of irrigation and agriculture that had been abandoned. They had some success, and the new capital Tabriz certainly prospered. Azerbaijan, with its wetter climate, was favored generally by the conquering horsemen for the better pasture it offered. The great historian Rashid al-Din (a converted Jew) enjoyed the patronage of the Il-Khans and, building on the earlier works of Juvaini and others, wrote a huge and definitive history. The cultural flow was not all one way—Persian miniature painting was permanently influenced by an imported Chinese aesthetic, and there were other examples. But Iran under the Il-Khans, for all the signs of regeneration, was a poorer, harsher place than before. The empire of the Il-Khans began to fragment with an almost deterministic inevitability. Local vassal rulers slowly made themselves independent of the center, as had happened before under the Seljuks and the Abbasids.

In the mid-fourteenth century in Khorasan, around Sabzavar, a rebel movement called the *sarbedari* (heads-in-noose) arose. It displayed egalitarian tendencies and co-opted Shi'a and Sufi elements.[58] Like some later and earlier movements, the sarbedari show the eclectic nature of popular, provincial religion in Iran at this time. Elsewhere, the Shi'a and the Sufis tended to be in opposition, but the sarbedari seem to have had little difficulty fusing the apparently contradictory tenets of the different beliefs involved, and this creative ferment of popular religion was to prove important later, too. The sarbedari are also significant in another way—they represent again a spirit of popular resistance to the invaders, independent of contingent dynastic leadership. This same spirit was there after the Arab invasion, at the beginning of the Mongol period,[59] and it appears again later in Iranian history. This might prompt questions about nationalism that could easily absorb the rest of this book.[60] What we call nationalism today is in my view too specifically a constructed phenomenon of the nineteenth and twentieth centuries to be considered without anachronism in the fourteenth century or other earlier periods. But we have seen that there was a sense of Iranianness, beyond local or dynastic loyalty, in the time of the Sassanids and before; it was part of what later inspired the shu'ubiyya, the Samanids, and Ferdowsi. Nationalism is the wrong word, but to deny any Iranian identity in this era requires some serious contortions of evidence and logic.

From 1380, the hopeful vassal dynasty builders, the resurgent cities and peasants, and the bold sarbedari were all alike submerged by the next invading surge of steppe nomads under Timur (*Timur-e lang*—Timur the Lame—Tamerlane or, in Marlowe, Tamburlaine). Timur was the son of a minor Turkic vassal in Transoxiana, who set up a following of warriors and built a tightly disciplined army explicitly on the model of the great Mongol, Genghis Khan. He married a princess from the great Khan family and called himself Güregen (which means son-in-law) to draw on the prestige of his predecessor. He also took Mongol precedent as a precedent for terror.

Timur established himself first in the cities of Transoxiana, with a base at Samarkand, and then invaded Persia. Cities were razed, their citizens massacred, and the plunder sent with any valuable survivors back to Samarkand, to adorn a new paradise of gardens and grand buildings. To intimidate his enemies, Timur raised up pillars of human heads as he marched through the Persian provinces—outside Isfahan alone (where the people had been foolish enough to attack the Timurid garrison) he lopped off seventy thousand heads, which were then set in 120 pillars. In his bloody wake the desert again encroached on abandoned farmlands and irrigation works. Unlike the Mongols, Timur conquered in the name of orthodox Sunni Islam, but this in no way moderated his conduct of war. After taking Persia and defeating the Mongols of the Golden Horde in the steppe lands around Moscow, he moved into India and took Delhi. Then he turned west again, where he conquered Baghdad (another ninety thousand heads), defeated the Ottoman sultan, captured him, and returned to Samarkand. He died in 1405 in the midst of preparations for an attack on China.

There is a story that Timur met Hafez, but it is probably apocryphal. But Timur did meet the Arab historian and thinker Ibn Khaldun. No historian looking at the history of the Islamic world in the period covered by this chapter could avoid noticing the cyclical pattern of dynastic rise, decline, and nomad invasion. But Ibn Khaldun came up with a theory to explain it.[61] His theory began with the *asabiyya*, the strong solidarity or group feeling of nomad warriors, fostered by the interdependence that was necessary in mobile tribal life in the harsh conditions of desert, mountains, and the margins of the steppes. This was the cohesive spirit that made the nomads such formidable warriors, that enabled them to invade and dominate areas of sedentary settlement, and conquer cities. But having done so, their leaders had to consolidate their support. They had to protect themselves against being supplanted by other members of the tribe, and therefore gave patronage to other groups—city dwellers, bureaucratic officials, and the ulema. They also used building projects and a magnificent court to impress their subjects with their prestige, and employed mercenaries as soldiers, because they were more reliable. So the original asabiyya of the conquerors was diluted and lost. Eventually the ruling dynasty came to believe its own myth and spent increasingly on vain display, weakening its strength outside the capital city and within it. The ulema and ordinary citizens, disillusioned with the dynasty's decadence, became ready to welcome another wave of conquering nomads, who would start up a new dynasty and set the cycle off all over again.

The theory—of which the above is a greatly simplified version—does not address all the elements of the cycle of invasions as they affected Iran. We have seen how the prosperity of the Silk Route encouraged plundering invasions as well as trade, and how the vulnerability of Iran (and particularly Khorasan) flowed from its central geographical position, just as geography gave it great economic and cultural advantages. The Abbasids and their successors were weakened repeatedly by the measures they used to try to overcome the difficulty of gathering taxes. Officials tended to become corrupt and siphon off tax revenue, so the rulers gave the responsibility to tax farmers instead; they then tended to plunder the peasant farmers, quickly running down the productivity of agriculture. The rulers could grant land holdings (*iqta, soyurgal*) to soldiers in return for military service, but this tended to mean in time that the soldiers came to think of themselves as farmers or landowners rather than soldiers. Or they could do a similar thing on a grander scale and grant whole provinces to trusted families in return for fiscal tribute and military support. But as we have seen, the likelihood then was that the provincial governors would grow powerful enough to become independent and even take over the state themselves.

Ibn Khaldun's theory does not fully explain the history of this period on its own, and it may apply better to the Islamic states of North Africa, where the historian lived for most of his life. But it is a useful model nonetheless, and it also accounts for some deep attitudes among the people themselves. Ibn Khaldun did not invent those attitudes, he observed them. The nomads often were regarded (especially by themselves, of course) as having a primitive martial virtue. The court was regarded as a decadent place that tended to corrupt its members. The ulema might often be regarded as authoritative arbitrators in a crisis. These were mental, social, and cultural structures that in themselves helped to influence events.

For our purposes, the most important thing to emphasize is the resilience and intellectual power of the small class of Persian scholar-bureaucrats. Nostalgic for their heroic Sassanid ancestors, escaping from official duplicity and courtiership into either dreams of love and gardens, religious mysticism, the design of splendid palaces and mosques, or the complexities of mathematics, astronomy, and medicine, they bounced back from crisis after crisis, accommodated to their conquerors, made themselves indispensable again, and eventually reasserted something like control over them. In the process, they ensured (whether based in Baghdad, Balkh, Tabriz, or Herat) the survival of their language, their culture, and an unrivaled intellectual heritage. It is one of the most remarkable phenomena in world history. Behind the history described in this chapter, the Arab conquest and the succession of empires—Abbasid, Ghaznavid, Seljuk, Mongol, Timurid—lies the story of what ultimately proved to be a more important empire: the Iranian Empire of the Mind.

After Timur, the process followed its usual pattern. The conquerors took on the characteristics of the conquered. Timur's son Shahrokh ruled from Herat and patronized the beginnings of another Persianate cultural flowering that continued under his successors and produced great architecture, manuscript illustrations, and painted miniatures, prefiguring later cultural developments in the Moghul and Safavid empires. As others before, the Timurid Empire gradually fragmented into a patchwork of dynastic successor-states. In the latter part of the fifteenth century, two of them—two great confederations of Mongolized Turkic tribes, the *Aq-Qoyunlu* and the *Qara-Qoyunlu* (White Sheep and Black Sheep Turks, respectively)—slugged it out for hegemony over the war-ravaged Iranian plateau. The White Sheep came out on top, but were then overwhelmed by a new dynasty from Turkic Anatolia, the Safavids. But to understand the Safavids it is necessary first to go right back to the seventh century again for a deeper understanding of the history and development of Shi'ism.

4

SHI'ISM AND THE SAFAVIDS

Men wiser and more learned than I have discerned in history a plot, a rhythm, a predetermined pattern. These harmonies are concealed from me. I can see only one emergency following upon another as wave follows upon wave, only one great fact with respect to which, since it is unique, there can be no generalisations, only one safe rule for the historian: that he should recognise in the development of human destinies the play of the contingent and the unforeseen. This is not a doctrine of cynicism and despair. The fact of progress is written plain and large on the page of history; but progress is not a law of nature. The ground gained by one generation may be lost by the next. The thoughts of men may flow into the channels which lead to disaster and barbarism.

—H. A. L. Fisher

THE ORIGINS OF SHI'ISM

Early in October AD 680[1] a group of less than one hundred armed men, accompanied by their families, approached the town of Kufa, south of the present-day site of Baghdad, on the river Euphrates. They had come from Mecca, hundreds of miles away across the Arabian Desert. As the travelers and their leader, Hosein, drew near the town, they were intercepted by a thousand mounted troops. The travelers agreed to move on to the north, away from Kufa, escorted by the troops. The following day a further four thousand men arrived with orders to make Hosein swear allegiance to the caliph Yazid. Hosein refused. By now his people were running out of water, and the soldiers blocked their way to the river.

After several days a new order arrived: Hosein and his followers should be compelled to submit by force. The soldiers formed up in battle order and bore down on Hosein's smaller group. He tried to persuade his people to save themselves and let him face their enemies alone, but they would not leave him. He spoke to the troops confronting him, reproaching them. But his enemies were obdurate and soon after began to shoot arrows into Hosein's camp. Completely outnumbered, Hosein's men were killed one by one as the arrows rained down among the tents and tethered animals. Some of them fought back against their tormentors, charging in ones and twos into the serried ranks that surrounded them, but they were soon killed. At last Hosein was the only one left alive, holding the body of his infant son, who had taken an arrow through the throat. The soldiers surrounded Hosein, who fought hard until at last he was struck to the ground and one of them finished him off.

Of Hosein's male relatives only one of his sons survived (having lain ill in the camp through the fighting). In Kufa, Hosein's head was brought before Yazid's deputy, who struck the dead man's face. A bystander reproached him for striking the lips that the Prophet of God had once kissed.

Hosein was the grandson of the Prophet Mohammad, through the Prophet's daughter Fatima and his cousin Ali. This account of the massacre at Karbala of the Prophet's closest family has been passed down by generations of Shi'a Muslims. As always, there must have been another side to the story. From another perspective the Umayyad caliphs might look less wicked, more like pragmatists struggling to hold a disparate empire together, and Hosein, Ali, and their partisans more like incompetent idealists. But the important thing is to understand how the Shi'a themselves later understood the story. Karbala was the central, defining event in the early history of Shi'a Islam. The shrine of Hosein at Karbala, on the site where it happened, is one of the most important Shi'a holy places. Each year the anniversary (Ashura) is still marked with deep mourning, by mass religious demonstrations and outpourings of pious grief. Ever since Karbala, Shi'a Muslims have brooded over the martyrdom of Hosein and its symbolism, and have nursed a sense of grievance, betrayal, and shame.

The great schisms of the Christian church, between East and West, and later between Catholic and Protestant, came centuries after the time of Christ. But the great schism in Islam that still divides Muslims today, between Sunni and Shi'a, originated in the earliest days of the faith—even before Karbala, in the time of the Prophet Mohammad himself. Comparisons with the Christian schisms do not really work. A more apposite analogy, as noted by the historian Richard N. Frye and others,[2] can be drawn between, on the one hand, the emphasis on law and tradition in Sunni Islam and Judaism and, on the other hand, the emphasis on humility, sacrifice, and the religious hierarchy in Christianity and Shi'ism. The public grief of Ashura is similar in spirit to that which one can still see on Good Friday in some Catholic countries. The purpose in making comparisons between Shi'ism and various aspects of Christianity is not to suggest that they are somehow the same (they are not), nor to encourage some kind of happy joining-hands ecumenism (naïve), but rather to try to illuminate something that initially looks unfamiliar, and to suggest by analogy that it may not be so strange or unfamiliar after all. Or at least, that it is no more strange than Christian Catholicism.

The term *Shi'a* signifies Shi'a Ali—the party of Ali. Ali was the Prophet's cousin, and one of Mohammad's earliest converts. The Shi'a (sometimes called Alids at this early phase) were simply those who favored rule by both the blood descendants of Ali and the Prophet. Other characteristics and doctrines only developed later.

From the beginning, Mohammad's followers, the earliest Muslims, had run into conflict with temporal authority. Mohammad, Ali, and the others had been forced to flee from Mecca to Medina when their relationship with the rulers of Mecca deteriorated into open hostility. This situation recurs again and again in Islamic history—particularly in the history of Shi'ism. Mohammad challenged the Meccans' way of life, calling for more moral and pious forms of conduct based on the revelation of God's will in the Qor'an. The Meccan authorities responded with derision and persecution. The conflict between arrogant, worldly, corrupt authority and earnest, pious austerity was established as a cultural model for centuries, down to the Iranian revolution of 1979, and to the present day.

Shi'a Muslims believe that Mohammad nominated Ali as his successor, as caliph, after his death, but that the rightful succession was usurped by others. By the time Ali became the fourth caliph, in AD 656, the rulers of Islam had conquered huge territories, from Egypt to Persia, as we saw in the previous chapter. This meant great new power for some of the leading families of the Arab tribes (notably for some members of the Quraysh family, many of whom had opposed Mohammad himself before Mecca submitted and converted), but also required the Arab conquerors to adopt new patterns of rule and power relationships.

Many Muslims did not approve of the changes, political deals, and pragmatic compromises involved. Ali, for example, held himself aloof, maintaining a pious life of austerity and prayer. He became a natural focus for dissent and was in turn resented by those around the caliph, bringing forth the authority/piety conflict within Islam itself for the first time. When Ali became caliph, this mutual hostility led to civil war (*fitna*). Then when Ali tried to make peace in 661, some of his more radical Kharijite supporters felt betrayed and murdered him, whereupon the leader of his former opponents—Mu'awiya—took power as the first Umayyad caliph. In time, Mu'awiya died and was succeeded by his son—the caliph Yazid that was Hosein's enemy at the time of Karbala in 680.

Hosein's rebellion in defiance of Yazid's authority was, as Shi'a believe, a bid to purify Islam and return it to its original principles. It drew force from Hosein's own blood link to the Prophet, but also from the perceived impiety of Yazid and his court, where wine drinking was common and some of the forms of pre-Islamic Byzantine and Persian practices had taken hold. Hosein hoped for support from Kufa, but Yazid's troops got there first and bullied the Kufans into passivity. Some Shi'a historians believe that Hosein went to his death at Karbala knowingly and willingly, in the belief that only by sacrificing himself could he bring about the renewal he desired (another point at which some have drawn comparisons with Christianity). The failure of Hosein's Kufan supporters to help him added a strong sense of guilt to the Shi'a memory of Karbala.

After Karbala, the Umayyad dynasty of Yazid and his successors continued to rule at the head of Islam, and the conquest of new territory continued. To give an idea of the sense of shame and grievance felt by the Shi'a, one might try to imagine how Christians would have felt if the leadership of the church after the death of Christ had fallen to Judas Iscariot, Pontius Pilate, and their successors. The Shi'a saw themselves as the underdogs, the dispossessed, those always betrayed and humiliated by the powerful and the unrighteous (notwithstanding that powerful Shi'a dynasties arose later, dominating extensive territories). A deep inclination to sympathy and compassion for the oppressed—and a tendency to see them as naturally more righteous than the rich and powerful—has persisted in popular Shi'ism right through to the present day. The early Shi'a regarded the Umayyad caliphs as illegitimate usurpers and hoped for a revolt that would bring to power the descendants of Mohammad, Ali, and Hosein. These descendants were the Shi'a Emams, the sidelined but legitimate leaders of Islam, an alternative line of descent to rival that of the Umayyad and Abbasid caliphs. Shi'a Muslims saw themselves as a more or less persecuted minority within states run by and for Sunni Muslims.

Despite the schism, in the early centuries there was a fairly free interchange of ideas, a considerable pluralism of belief, and considerable diversity of opinion among the Alids or Shi'a themselves. Overall, Shi'a theology and law tended to be looser than in Sunni Islam, more open to the application of reason in theology, more inclined to a free will position than a determinist one, and more open to some of the more heterodox ideas circulating in the Islamic world. This was partly the result of a broader hadith tradition, which included the sayings and doings of the Shi'a Emams. Shi'a theology also differed because it addressed problems that were specific to the Shi'a, such as conduct under persecution.

The sixth Shi'a Emam, Ja'far al-Sadiq, developed a strategy for the evasion of persecution that was to prove controversial. The doctrine of *taqiyeh*, or dissimulation, permitted Shi'a Muslims to deny their faith if necessary to avoid persecution—a special dispensation that has striking similarities with the doctrine of "mental reservation" granted for similar reasons by the Catholic church in the period of the Counter-Reformation, and associated with the Jesuits (though it originated before their time). Just as the Jesuits acquired a reputation for deviousness and terminological trickery among Protestants (whence in English we have the adjective "Jesuitical"), so the doctrine of taqiyeh earned the Shi'a a similar reputation among some Sunni Muslims.

Some commentators argue that the doctrines of Ja'far al-Sadiq reflected a period of Shi'a quietism—a retreat from politics, from confrontation, and from efforts to overturn the caliphate. This quietism, with its disposition to modesty and unpretentious virtue, was one thread of Shi'ism in the following centuries (and still is). But there were Shi'a movements that emphatically did not follow this pattern, including several major Shi'a revolts in Ja'far's lifetime—the significant Shi'a participation in the revolt of Abu Muslim that founded the Abbasid caliphate, for example. After Ja'far al-Sadiq's death (in 765) there was a further schism. One group of Shi'a supported Ja'far's son Musa, while another group acclaimed his other son Ismail as the seventh Emam, giving rise to the Ismaili or "Sevener" branch of Shi'ism espoused by the later Fatimid rulers of Egypt. The Ismaili sect also spawned the notorious movement known as the Assassins, a shadowy organization whose doings were much distorted by Western chroniclers. The Assassins established themselves as a power in the Alborz mountains in the twelfth and thirteenth centuries, and they were especially important in the period just before and after the Mongol invasions of the 1220s.

In the ninth century a further period of confusion followed the death of the eleventh Emam (it was the dome of the shrine of the eleventh Emam, at

Samarra in Iraq, that was blown up by Sunni extremists in February 2006, precipitating a new phase of serious Sunni/Shi'a intercommunal violence) because it seemed he had no living heir. The main, non-Ismaili strand of Shi'ism divided into many different sects with different theological solutions to this problem. Eventually the faith coalesced again around the explanation that the eleventh Emam had had an heir, a son, but that this boy had been concealed or "occluded" shortly after the death of his father, in order to avoid persecution. At the right time, a time of chaos and crisis, this hidden twelfth Emam would reappear to reestablish the righteous rule of God on earth. The parallels with the Christian doctrine of the apocalypse and the second coming of Christ are obvious (in fact, many Shi'a believe that Jesus will accompany the Hidden Emam on his return). But the doctrine also compares with the Zoroastrian belief in a Messiah to come—the Saoshyant.

This development added a further, messianic, millenarian element to Shi'ism. But it also added a new instability, a self doubt, a kind of permanent question mark to the problem of the relation of Shi'a Muslims to both secular and religious authority. If the Emam was the only legitimate authority, then what of a world without the active presence of the Emam? Shi'ism already had a problem with temporal power, but now it had a further problem about authority within Shi'ism itself.

The Hidden Emam was the twelfth and last in succession to Ali, and those who awaited his return were called Twelver Shi'as. The largest Shi'a community, the Twelver Shi'as, were a scattered sect, perhaps better regarded as a tendency, with elements in southern Mesopotamia, in central Iran around Qom, in northeastern Iran and Central Asia, in Lebanon, along the southern shore of the Persian Gulf, and elsewhere (today there are Shi'a in Afghanistan, Pakistan, and India also). But after a phase of powerful Ismaili and other Shi'a dynasties like the Fatimids, Buyids, Qarmatians, and others from the tenth century, Sunni Muslim rulers predominated. Following the Mongol invasions the staunchly orthodox Sunni Ottomans rose inexorably to control the western part of the Islamic world.

The Safavids

By the end of the fifteenth century a militant brotherhood from northwest Iran and eastern Anatolia, made up of Turkic horsemen and based initially at Ardebil, had grown to military and political importance, and had begun to look to expansion on a grander scale. Eastern Anatolia and Azerbaijan at this time contained many such brotherhoods, more or less militant, more or less exaggerated or extreme (*ghuluww*) in their beliefs (as perceived by their neighbors), often incorporating elements of Sufism, millenarianism, Shi'ism, and saint-worship. The beliefs of these brotherhoods have been traced back to pre-Islamic, Mazdaean roots, through the Khorramites of the eighth and ninth centuries.[3] They attracted the flotsam and jetsam of warrior society after the destruction and dislocation of the Mongol and Timurid invasions—the dispossessed, the fugitives, the opponents of powerful tribal chiefs, and others. They created an alternative center of power, comparable in that way to the rebel sarbedari in Khorasan under the Mongol Il-Khans. Further west, in the fourteenth century, a not dissimilar group of Turkish warriors had established the beginnings of the Ottoman Empire through the prestige of successful fighting against the Byzantines.

The brotherhood in Ardebil were the Safavids, named after one of their early leaders, Shaykh Safi (1252–1334), a Sunni and a Sufi, who had preached a purified and restored Islam and a new religious order on earth. It is possible that he was of Kurdish descent. The early history of the Safavids is an uncertain and complex subject, but it seems his successor Sadr al-Din (1334–1391) organized the movement and created a hierarchy and the arrangements for it to own property. This turned it from a loose association into a more disciplined organization, one that started to create a wider network of tribal alliances through favors and marriages. Under the later Safavid shaykhs new groupings or tribes (*oymaq*) coalesced, held together by these alliances, and by religious fervor[4] (in which devotion to the spiritual and military example of the Emam Ali was also an element). Under the leadership of Shaykh Junayd (1447–1460), the Safavids and their followers allied themselves with the Aq-Qoyunlu (White Sheep Turks, referred to in the preceding chapter), then the dominant power in the ancient territories of Iran. The Safavids made successful raids into Christian Georgian territory and developed into a significant military force, later fighting other local Muslim tribal groups.

After the account of Sufism and Sufi poetry in the previous chapter, the appearance of fervently warlike Sufis, intent on conquest, might be hard to reconcile. But Sufism was an extensive, diverse, and multifaceted phenomenon, and the school of love was only one manifestation of it. Some Sufi shaykhs were learned hermits, wedded to poverty and contemplation. But others were less contemplative and more proselytizing, more *ghuluww* (extreme), more inclined to the realization of divine purposes in the world through worldly acts, and more ambivalent about violence. The obedience of the Sufi postulant to his Sufi Master (*pir*) was an institution common to most Sufi brotherhoods, but it had an obvious military value in the more militant ones—like, for example, the Safavids. The military strength of the Safavids lay in the fighting prowess of the Turkic warriors they led, known collectively as the *Qezelbash*, after the red hats they wore (Qezelbash means "red heads"). Some of the Qezelbash went into battle on horseback without armor, believing that their faith made them invulnerable. The Sufism of most of the Qezelbash would have been unsophisticated, centering on some group rituals and a collective mutual loyalty—just as their Shi'ism may initially have amounted to little more than a reverence for Ali as the archetype of a holy warrior. But it created a powerful group cohesion—*asabiyah*.

It is uncertain just when the Safavids turned Shi'a; in the religious context of that time and place, the question is somewhat artificial. Shi'a notions were just one part of an eclectic mix. By the end of the fifteenth century a new Safavid leader, Esma'il, was able to expand Safavid influence at the expense of the Aq-Qoyunlu, who had been weakened by disputes over the dynastic succession. Esma'il was himself the grandson of Uzun Hasan, the great Aq-Qoyunlu chief of the 1460s and 1470s, and may have emulated some of his grandfather's charismatic and messianic leadership style. In 1501 Esma'il and his Qezelbash followers conquered Tabriz (the old Seljuk capital) in northwestern Iran, and Esma'il declared himself shah. He was only fourteen years old. A contemporary Italian visitor described him as fair and handsome, not very tall, stout and strong with broad shoulders and reddish hair. He had long moustaches (a Qezelbash characteristic, prominent in many contemporary illustrations), was left-handed, and was skilled with the bow.[5]

At the time of his conquest of Tabriz, Esma'il proclaimed Twelver Shi'ism as the new religion of his territories. Esma'il's Shi'ism took an extreme form, which required the faithful to curse the memory of the first three caliphs that had preceded Ali. This was very offensive to Sunni Muslims, who venerated those caliphs, along with Ali, as the *Rashidun* or righteous caliphs. Esma'il's demand intensified the division between the Safavids and their enemies, especially the staunchly Sunni Ottomans to the west. Recent scholarship suggests that even if there was a pro-Shi'a tendency among the Qezelbash earlier, Esma'il's declaration of Shi'ism in 1501 was a deliberate political act.

Within a further ten years Esma'il conquered the rest of Iran and all the territories of the old Sassanid Empire, including Mesopotamia and the old Abbasid capital of Baghdad. He defeated the remnants of the Aq-Qoyunlu, as well as the Uzbeks in the northeast and various rebels. Two followers of one rebel leader were captured in 1504, taken to Isfahan, and roasted on spits as kebabs. Esma'il ordered his companions to eat the kebab to show their loyalty (this is not the only example of cannibalism as a kind of extreme fetish among the Qezelbash).[6]

Esma'il attempted to consolidate his control by asserting Shi'ism throughout his new domains (though the conventional view that this was achieved in a short time and that the import of Shi'a scholars from outside Iran was significant in the process has been put into doubt[7]). He also did his best to suppress rival Sufi orders. It is important to stress that although there had been strong Shi'a elements in Iran for centuries before 1501, and important Shi'a shrines like Qom and Mashhad, Iran had been predominantly Sunni, like most of the rest of the Islamic world. The center of Shi'ism had been the shrine cities of southern Iraq.[8]

Esma'il wrote some poetry (mostly in the Turkic dialect of Azerbaijan, which became the language of the Safavid court), and it is likely that his followers recited and sang his compositions as well as other religious songs. The following poem of Esma'il's gives a flavor of the religious intensity and militant confidence of the Qezelbash:

My name is Shah Esma'il.
I am on God's side: I am the leader of these warriors.
My mother is Fatima, my father Ali:
I too am one of the twelve Emams.
I took back my father's blood from Yazid.
Know for certain that I am the true coin of Haydar [i.e., Ali]
Ever-living Khezr, Jesus son of Mary
I am the Alexander of the people of this age[9]

In addition to these great figures of the past, Esma'il identified himself also with Abu Muslim, who had led the revolt that had overturned the rule of the Umayyads in 750 and established the Abbasid caliphate.

But Esma'il's hopes of westward expansion, aiming to take advantage of the Shi'a orientation of many more Turkic tribes in eastern Anatolia, were destroyed when the élan of the Qezelbash was blown away by Ottoman cannon at the Battle of Chaldiran, northwest of Tabriz, in 1514. A legend says that Esma'il vented his frustration by slashing at a cannon with his sword, leaving a deep gash in the barrel.

After this defeat Esma'il could no longer sustain the loyalty of the Qezelbash at its previous high pitch, nor their belief in his divine mission. He went into mourning and took to drink. Wars between the Sunni Ottomans and the Shi'a Safavids continued for many years, made more bitter by the religious schism. Tabriz, Baghdad, and the shrine towns of Iraq changed hands several times. Shi'a were persecuted and killed within the Ottoman territories, particularly in eastern Anatolia where they were regarded as actual or potential traitors. The Safavids turned Iran into the predominantly Shi'a state it is today, and there were spasmodic episodes of persecution there too, especially of Zoroastrians, Christians, and Jews—despite the ostensible protected status of at least the latter two groups as "People of the

Book." One could make a parallel with the way that religious persecution intensified either side of the Roman/Persian border in the fourth century AD, in the reign of Shapur II, after Constantine made Christianity the state religion of the Roman Empire.

The Safavid monarchs also turned against the Sufis, despite the Safavids' Sufi heritage. The Sufis were persecuted to the point that the only surviving Sufi order was the Safavid one, and the others disappeared or went underground. In the long term, the main beneficiary of this were the Shi'a ulema. This was important because the Sufis had previously had a dominant or almost dominant position in the religious life of Iran, especially in the countryside.

The empire established by Esma'il also created a series of problems for itself. Prime among these was the unruly militancy of the Qezelbash, the suspicion between Turks and Tajiks (the latter being a disparaging Turkic term for a Persian), and the division between the Sufi-inclined, eclectic Qezelbash and the shari'a tradition of the urban Shi'a ulema. Gradually all of these were resolved in favor of the Persians and the ulema, as Ibn Khaldun would have predicted. Esma'il's successor, Tahmasp (r. 1524–1576), lived through several years of civil war as a minor, losing territory over his reign to both the Ottomans in the west (including Baghdad in 1534) and to the Uzbeks in the east. He moved the capital from Tabriz to Qazvin, making it more secure, but after his death there was civil war again, and a troubled period that saw two shahs in succession—before Abbas, cleverly manipulating alliances with chosen Qezelbash tribes, took the throne in 1587.

Abbas the Great

Abbas's achievements as shah ranged from military success to institutional reform to the building of spectacular architectural monuments—for all of which he is usually referred to as Abbas the Great. He was a talented administrator and military leader, and a ruthless autocrat. His reign was the outstanding creative period of the Safavid era. But the civil wars and troubles of his childhood (when many of his relatives were murdered) left him with a dark twist of suspicion and brutality at the center of his personality.

Most of Abbas's innovations and reforms centered on the military. He deliberately sidelined the Qezelbash tribes, establishing instead the core of a new standing army based in the new capital, Isfahan. The new army was largely organized around the introduction—on a significant scale for the first time—of gunpowder weapons, including up-to-date cannon and a corps of musketeers. Many features of it echoed Ottoman practice—the musketeers were designed to be the equals of the redoubtable Ottoman janissaries. Troops were recruited from among the Qezelbash and from the Persian population of the towns and villages. But Georgians, Armenians, and others were also brought to Isfahan for the army in large numbers—at least nominally as slaves, or *ghulams*—and the loyalty of such soldiers, far from home and in a more or less alien environment, wholly dependent on the shah, was much more reliable. Many Georgian and Armenian ghulams also served as commanders, bureaucrats, and regional governors. But despite the improvements, when the shah went to war the central core of the army was augmented by provincial Qezelbash troops, who were usually in a majority in the field.[10]

As with any pre-industrial state, policy on land and taxation was closely tied to military necessities. The Qezelbash tribal leaders lost out here, too. Abbas took over many of the lands they had previously enjoyed and either gave them over to be administered centrally by his bureaucrats or distributed them as *tuyul*—lands apportioned not to individuals but to state offices, from which office holders drew an income as long as they held the office. Usually the income was only a proportion of the total yield of the land holding. The idea was to maximize the loyalty of the office holders to the state and to minimize the likelihood that land would be permanently alienated away from the crown to ambitious magnates. State revenue was also boosted by the tightening of the government's grip on trade, especially the silk trade, based on silk production in Gilan. Most Persian trade in this period went east, to India, but some silk was exported west to Europe, especially by Armenian merchants. To the same end, Abbas used the English East India Company (that acquired the right to trade in Persia in 1616) to take back control of the Strait of Hormuz from the Portuguese, and to reestablish the Persian presence in the Persian Gulf.[11]

A weaker monarch would not have lasted long with the Qezelbash if he had attempted these reforms. But Abbas cunningly played the tribes against one another, and his success in war gave him huge prestige, making almost everything possible. With his new army he defeated the Uzbeks in the east—restoring the border on the Oxus river—and the Ottomans in the west. He took Baghdad twice. To consolidate his victories, especially in the northeast, he sent large numbers of Kurds, along with Qezelbash tribesmen like the Qajars and Afshars, to serve as protectors of the new borders. This resettlement policy served also to reinforce his authority over the tribes, while weakening their independent power by fragmenting them. He moved provincial governors from post to new post regularly to prevent any of them from creating regional power bases for themselves. He also resettled many Armenians from the northwest to a suburb south of Isfahan, New Julfa, where Christian Armenians and their bishop still live today.

The new capital, Isfahan, had been a significant place even in the time of the Sassanids, containing important monuments and mosques from later periods. But today it stands as perhaps the most splendid and impressive gallery of Islamic architecture in the world, and it is substantially a creation of the Safavid period. The central structures, the soaring blue iwans of the shah mosque, the beautiful Allahvardi Khan bridge, the Ali Qapu and Chehel Sotoun palaces, the Shaykh Lotfallah mosque, and the great Meidan-e Shah—all were built or at least begun in the time of Shah Abbas, though others were added later. The buildings assert Safavid power and prestige and their identification with Shi'a Islam, resulting in a magnificence that has rarely been surpassed.

One of Abbas's great successes was simply surviving and ruling long enough for his various enterprises to bear fruit. But in the process he created a problem—the succession. Succession was a common difficulty for many monarchs. In Europe, the problem was that every so often a ruler could not produce a son. This could create all sorts of difficulties—attempts at divorce (Henry VIII, for example), attempts to secure recognition for the succession of a daughter or more distant relative, disputes over succession resulting in war. In the Islamic world, the problem was different. Polygamy meant that kings did not normally have a problem producing a son, but they might, on the contrary, have too many sons. This could mean fierce fighting among potential heirs and their supporters when the father died. In the Ottoman Empire such battles were institutionalized—rival sons who had served their father as provincial governors would, on hearing of his death, race for the capital to claim the throne. The winner would get the support of the janissaries, and would then have the other sons put to death. Later, the Ottomans adopted a more dignified arrangement, keeping the possible heirs in the Sultan's harem palace until their father died. But this meant they would have little understanding of or aptitude for government, and the new practice helped to increase the power of the chief minister, the vizier, so that the vizier ruled effectively as viceroy. It was a conundrum.

Many fathers have disagreements and clashes with their sons, and history is full of feuds between kings and their crown princes. Abbas was no exception; he had come to power himself by deposing his father. Following the Ottoman precedent again, he imprisoned his sons in the harem for fear that they would attempt to dethrone him. But he still feared that they might plot against him, so he had them blinded, and he had one of them killed. Eventually, he was succeeded by one of his grandsons. The unhappy practice of keeping royal heirs in the harem was kept up thereafter by the Safavid monarchs.

Although Abbas showed reverence for the shrines of his Sufi ancestors in Ardebil, his deliberate weakening of the Qezelbash was matched, after signs of opposition from the Nuqtavi Sufis, by executions and other punishments that broke them too. Abbas favored instead the ulema and the endowments (*awqaf*) that supported them—especially in the shrine cities of Mashhad and Qom. On one occasion he spent twenty-eight days walking as a pilgrim across the desert from Isfahan to Mashhad—to show his devotion and to set an example. Since the continuing hostilities with the Ottomans made access to the shrines of southern Iraq difficult and uncertain, the shah's example helped to swing ordinary Persian Shi'as toward the Persian shrine cities. More endowments followed the pilgrims, and the grateful ulema aligned themselves ever more closely with the Safavid regime. These developments were also significant for the future. Abbas had been astute in his construction of a governmental system that protected state revenue, and his was more successful than most previous dynasties had been. But over the century that followed, more and more land was given over to religious endowments, sometimes merely as a kind of tax dodge, since religious property was exempt from tax.[12]

Under Shah Abbas the Safavid dynasty achieved a more sophisticated, more powerful, and more enduring governmental system than the traditional lands of Iran had seen for many centuries.[13] The Safavid state, its administration, and its institutionalizing of Shi'ism set the parameters for the modern shape of Iran. In its material culture—in metalwork, textiles, carpet making, miniature painting, ceramics, and above all in its architecture—the period was one of surpassing creativity in the making of beautiful things. The dominance of Shi'ism and the Shi'a ulema was also accompanied by a period of creativity in Shi'a thought—notably among the thinkers who have been called the School of Isfahan (Mir Damad, Mir Fendereski, and Shaykh Baha'i), and the religious philosophy of the great Molla Sadra.

Molla Sadra was born in Shiraz in 1571 or 1572. He studied in Qazvin and Isfahan as a young man, being interested in philosophy and the usual religious studies as well as Sufism. He was taught by two great thinkers of the age, Mir Damad and Shaykh Baha'i, and spent some time living near Qom and traveling before finally settling as a teacher in Shiraz again. His ideas (most notably expressed in the book known as *al-Afsar al-arba'a*—Four Journeys) drew upon the philosophy of Avicenna and Neoplatonism, but also on traditional Shi'a thought and on the Sufism of Sohravardi (Illuminationism), and Ibn Arabi. Molla Sadra's thought was controversial at the time for its leaning toward mysticism, which the ulema had traditionally opposed. But in explaining a way that philosophical rationalism and personal mystical insight should be combined in a program of individual reflection and study,[14] Molla Sadra was able to domesticate mysticism and, calling it *erfan*, make it acceptable to the madreseh tradition.[15] His thinking has been central in Islamic philosophy in the centuries since his time.

Persian cultural influence in the eastern part of the Islamic world was still strong, and it was in these centuries that it flowered outside Persia with the greatest brilliance—in Ottoman Turkey (where Persian was used for diplomatic correspondence, and Turkish poetry followed Persian forms), in the Khanates of Central Asia, and above all in Moghul India, where Persian was the language of the court and a whole new Persianate culture of poetry, music, and religious thought flourished. Some have called the poetry of this period Safavid poetry; others, reflecting the fact that much of it, even if written in Persian, was composed in India, have labelled it the Indian period. Opinion has also divided over its quality; the great Iranian critic Bahar disliked it, and the general view from the mid-nineteenth century was negative—the poetry was held to have been insipid, making use of rather stale imagery and lacking in real insight. To a degree, this view reflected the more favorable judgment of the same critics on the movement of poetry that supplanted the Safavid style from the 1760s onward (in Persia, though not elsewhere), and others have found more merit in the Safavid poets.

Whatever the judgments of taste, it is nonetheless true that there was a Persianate literary culture at this time that maintained itself from Istanbul to Delhi and Samarkand. This in turn had a strong impact on contemporary and later poetic compositions in Turkish and Urdu, reflecting the wider intellectual, religious, and court influences. But in some ways this Persianate culture was weakest in the Persian capital, where the court language was Turkic and mullahs tended to be more in favor than poets.[16] Many poets and other Persians emigrated to the fabulously wealthy Moghul court.

As a consequence of political instability and the existence of competing polities within the cultural space of Persianate influence, there had been by accident conditions in Persia in previous centuries that permitted considerable (albeit erratic) pluralism of religion and relative freedom of thought. Over the period of strong Safavid rule, the central territorial core of the Iranian plateau was kept safe from invasion, which after the trauma of the preceding centuries must have seemed an invaluable blessing. But some previous freedoms wilted and narrowed.

The Shi'ism of the Safavids and the ulema under their rule had from the beginning more than a streak of extremism and intolerance within it, and this tendency was intensified by the religious conflict with the Ottomans. The Safavids from the outset tended to be more earnestly religious than many previous Sunni rulers had been. This is a delicate subject, but it is important to look at it squarely. The Sufis were increasingly out of favor, and intellectual life was channeled into the madresehs. There were always hangers-on and pseudo-mullahs who could attract a following among the *luti* (unruly youths) of the towns by being more extreme than their more reflective, educated rivals; and the perceived history of persecution suffered by the Shi'a did not always prompt a sensitivity to the vulnerability of other minorities once the Shi'a became the dominant sect. Notions of the religious impurity (*najes*) of unbelievers, especially Jews, contributed to a general worsening in the condition of minorities, and after 1642 there was a particularly grim period of persecution and forced conversions. Orders were issued that Jews should wear distinguishing red patches on their clothing to identify themselves, that their word at law was near worthless, that they must not wear matching shoes, fine clothes, or waist sashes, that they must not walk in the middle of the street or walk past a Muslim, that they must not enter a shop and touch things, that their weddings must be held in secret, that if they were cursed by a Muslim they must stay silent, and so on.[17] Many of these would-be rules (running directly contrary to the spirit of proper tolerance accorded to People of the Book in Islam, and reminiscent of similar ugly rulings imposed in Christian Europe in the Middle Ages and at other times) probably reflect the aspirations of a few extremist mullahs rather than the reality as lived. Conditions would have varied greatly from town to town and changed over time, but they were still indicative of the attitudes of some and appeared to legitimize the actions of others. As authority figures in villages and towns, humane, educated mullahs were often the most important protectors of the Jews, Christians, and Zoroastrians.[18] But other, lesser mullahs frequently agitated against these vulnerable groups.

Some have suggested that even among the ulema the close relationship between the Safavid state and the Shi'a clergy was not a healthy phenomenon. The over-close relationship led some mullahs to overlook the strong distrust of politics, kingship, and secular authority that is deeply entrenched in Shi'ism (and is perhaps one of its most attractive characteristics) in their scramble for the good things that the Safavid shahs had on offer—appointments, endowments, and a chance to wield some political authority.[19] As is often the case with unchecked processes that involve greed, this one brought some of the senior Shi'a clergy to shipwreck at the end of the Safavid period.

After the death of Abbas the Great in 1629, the Safavid dynasty endured for almost a century. But except for an interlude in the reign of Shah Abbas II (1642–1666) it was a period of stagnation. Baghdad was lost to the Ottomans again in 1638, and the Treaty of Zohab in 1639 fixed the Ottoman/Persian boundary in its present-day position between Iran and Iraq. Abbas II took Kandahar from the Moghuls in 1648, but thereafter there was peace in the east also.

Militarily, the Safavid state probably reached its apogee under Shah Abbas the Great and Abbas II. But despite its classification with Ottoman Turkey and Moghul India as one of the Gunpowder Empires (by Marshall G. S. Hodgson), there is good reason to judge that the practices and structures of the Safavid Empire were transformed less by the introduction of gunpowder weapons than those other empires were. Cannon and muskets were present in Persian armies, but as add-ons to previous patterns of warfare rather than elements transforming the *conduct* of war, as they were elsewhere. The mounted tradition of Persian lance-and-bow warfare, harking back culturally to Ferdowsi, was resistant to the introduction of awkward and noisy firearms. Their cavalry usually outclassed that of their enemies, but Persians did not take to heavy cannon and the greater technical demands of siege warfare as the Ottomans and Moghuls did. The great distances, lack of navigable rivers, rugged terrain, and poor roads of the Iranian plateau did not favor the transport of heavy cannon. Most Iranian cities were either unwalled or were protected by crumbling walls that were centuries old—this at a time when huge, sophisticated, and highly expensive fortifications were being constructed in Europe and elsewhere to deal with the challenge of heavy cannon. Persia's military revolution was left incomplete.[20]

Alcohol seems to have played a significant part in the poor showing of the later Safavid monarchs. From the time of Shah Esma'il and before, drinking sessions had been a part of the group rituals of the Qezelbash, building probably on the ancient practices of the Mongols and the Turkic tribes in Central Asia, but also on ghuluww Sufi practice and the Persian tradition of razm o bazm—fighting and feasting. There is a story that Esma'il drank wine in a boat on the Tigris while watching the execution of his defeated foes after his conquest of Baghdad in 1508,[21] and his drinking accelerated after his defeat at the Battle of Chaldiran. Some accounts even suggest that alcohol was instrumental in his early death in 1524. Within the wider Islamic culture that was hostile to alcohol, it seems that in court circles wine had all the added allure of the forbidden. One could draw a parallel with the way in which binge drinking is a feature of British and other traditionally Protestant societies whose religious authorities tended in the past to frown on alcohol consumption. Shah Tahmasp appears to have stopped drinking in 1532/1533, maintaining his pledge until his death in 1576, but alcohol was blamed by contemporaries as a cause or a contributory factor in the deaths of his successor Shah Esma'il II, of Shah Safi (reigned 1629–1642), and of Shah Abbas II (1642–1666).[22]

Some of this can perhaps be attributed to a moralizing judgment on rulers who were thought to have failed more generally. For writers who disapproved of alcohol, drinking wine was a sufficient explanation for (or at least a sign of) incompetence, indolence, or general moral weakness and bad character. (Shah Abbas I drank too, without damaging his reputation.) But there is too much evidence for the drinking to be dismissed as the invention of chroniclers. The reign of Shah Soleiman represents the apotheosis of the phenomenon.

Soleiman came to the throne in 1666 and reigned for the next twenty-eight years. A contemporary reported,

> He was tall, strong, and active, a little too effeminate for a monarch—with a Roman nose, very well proportioned to other parts, very large blue eyes and a middling mouth, a beard dyed black, shaved round and well turned back, even to his ears. His manner was affable but nevertheless majestic. He had a masculine and agreeable voice, a gentle way of speaking and was so very engaging that, when you had bowed to him he seemed in some measure to return it by a courteous inclination of his head, and this he always did smiling.[23]

Soleiman's reign was for the most part quiet. Some fine mosques and palaces were built, but one could take those as material symbols of the growing diversion of economic resources into religious endowments, and of the blinkered, inward-looking tendency of the monarch and his court. Both of these were to prove damaging in the long run. Soleiman showed little interest in governing, leaving state business to his officials.

Sometimes he would amuse himself by forcing them (especially the most pious ones) to drink to the dregs an especially huge goblet of wine (called the *hazar pishah*). Sometimes they collapsed and had to be carried out. If they stayed on their feet, the shah might, for a joke, order them to explain their views of important matters of government.[24]

Shah Soleiman himself drank heavily, despite occasional outbreaks of temperance induced by health worries and religious conscience.[25] His pleasure-loving insouciance was the natural outcome of his upbringing in the harem. He had little sense of the world beyond the court and little interest in it. He merely wanted to continue the lazy life he had enjoyed before, augmented by the luxuries he had formerly been denied. But some contemporary accounts say that when drunk he could turn nasty, that on one occasion he had his brother blinded, and that at other times he ordered executions.

It is a testament to the strength and sophistication of the Safavid state and its bureaucracy that it continued to function despite the lack of a strong monarch. In other Islamic states this situation often permitted the emergence of a vizier or chief minister as the effective ruler. In Isfahan it seems that the influence of other important office holders (as well as that of Maryam Begum, the shah's great aunt, who came to dominate the harem) was enough to prevent any single personality achieving dominance. But as time went on the officials acted more and more in their own private and factional interests, against the interests of their rivals, and less and less in the interest of the state. Bureaucracies are not of themselves virtuous institutions—they need firm masters and periodic reform to reinforce an ethic of service if they are not to go wrong. And if the officials see their masters acting irresponsibly, they will imitate their vices.

The influence of the politically inclined ulema at court strengthened as the shah's involvement in business slumped, and one leading cleric, Mohammad Baqer Majlesi, has been associated with a deliberate policy of targeting minorities for persecution (at least in the case of Hindu Indian merchants) to appeal to the worst instincts among the people and thereby enhance the popularity of the regime.[26] Persecution was episodic and unpredictable, sometimes concentrating on the Indians or Jews, sometimes on the Armenians, sometimes on the Sufis, or the Zoroastrians, or Sunni Muslims in the provinces. In general, minorities—even Jews and Christians, who should have enjoyed protection as People of the Book—were disadvantaged at law, subject to everyday humiliations, and vulnerable to the ambitions of rabble-rousing preachers who might seek greater fame for themselves by inciting urban mobs against them. The cleric Majlesi's personal responsibility for a worsening of the situation from the reign of Shah Soleiman onward has been disputed (for example, his treatise *Lightning Bolts Against the Jews* turns out on examination to be rather more moderate in setting out the provisions of Islamic law on the minorities than its title might suggest[27]), but he was an influential figure and was briefly to become dominant in the succeeding reign. His voluminous writings also included strong blasts against Sunnis and Sufis. The movement was broader than just Majlesi (whom it may have suited to appear radical to one constituency and moderate to another), but it is important to remember that it represented only one strand of Shi'ism at the time; other Shi'a ulema were critical of Majlesi's repressive policy.[28]

As Shah Soleiman's reign drew to a close, the Safavid regime looked strong but had been seriously weakened. Its monuments looked splendid, but the intellectual world of Persia, once distinguished for its tolerance and vision, was now led by narrower, smaller minds.

5

The Fall of the Safavids, Nader Shah, the Eighteenth-Century Interregnum, and the Early Years of the Qajar Dynasty

Morghi didam neshaste bar bareh-e Tus
Dar pish nahade kalleh-e Kay Kavus
Ba kalleh hami goft ke afsus afsus
Ku bang-e jarasha o koja shod naleh-e kus

I saw a bird on the walls of Tus
That had before it the skull of Kay Kavus.
The bird was saying to the skull "Alas, alas"
Where now the warlike bells? And where the moan of the kettledrums?

—attributed to Omar Khayyam

According to a story that was widely repeated, when Shah Soleiman lay dying in July 1694, he left it undecided which of his sons should succeed him. Calling his courtiers and officials, he told them—"If you desire ease, elevate

Hosein Mirza. If the glory of your country be the object of your wishes, raise Abbas Mirza to the throne."[1] Once Soleiman was dead, the eunuch officials who supervised the harem decided for Hosein because they judged he would be easier for them to control. Hosein was also the favorite of his great aunt, Maryam Begum, the dominant personality in the harem, so Hosein duly became shah.

Such stories present historians with a problem. Their anecdotal quality, though vivid, does not fit the style of modern historical writing, and even their wide contemporary currency cannot overcome a reluctance to accept them at face value. The deathbed speech, the neat characterization of the two princes, and the cynical choice of the bureaucrats—it is all too pat. But to dismiss it out of hand would be as wrong as to accept it at face value. It is more sensible to accept the story as a reflection of the overall nature of motivations and events, even if the actual words reported were never said. The story reflects the impression of casual negligence, even irresponsible mischief, that we know of Shah Soleiman from other sources. As the consequences will show, it also gives an accurate picture of the character of Shah Sultan Hosein, and the motivation of his courtiers. It is quite credible that Shah Soleiman left the succession open and that over-powerful officials chose the prince they thought would be most malleable.

Initially, Shah Sultan Hosein appeared to be as pious and orthodox as Mohammed Baqer Majlesi, the pre-eminent cleric at court, could have wished. Under the latter's influence the bottles from the royal wine cellar were brought out into the *meidan* in front of the royal palace and publicly smashed. Instead of allowing a Sufi the honor of buckling on his sword at his coronation, as had been traditional (reflecting the Sufi origins of the Safavid dynasty), the new shah had Majlesi do it instead. Within the year orders went out for taverns, coffee houses, and brothels to be closed, and for prostitution, opium, "colorful herbs," sodomy, public music, dancing, and gambling to be banned—along with more innocent amusements like kite flying. Women were to stay at home, to behave modestly, and were forbidden to mix with men who were not relatives. Islamic dress was to be worn. The new laws were applied despite the protests of treasury officials, who warned that there would be a huge drop in revenue, equivalent to 50 kg of gold *per day*, because the state had made so much money from the taxation of prostitution and other forms of entertainment. To make sure the new order was widely publicized, it was read out in the mosques, and in some it was carved in stone over the door. A later order stipulated that Majlesi, as *Shaykh ol-eslam* (the title given to the senior cleric in Isfahan), should be obeyed by all viziers, governors, and other secular officials across the empire. Anyone who broke the rules, or had done so in the past, was to be punished.[2] It was a kind of Islamic revolution.

Yet within a few months of his taking the throne, Shah Sultan Hosein was drinking as much as his father had, and his great aunt, Maryam Begum (perhaps affronted among other things at Majlesi's attack on women's freedoms), had reasserted her dominance at court. The Sufis were eclipsed but not wholly suppressed. The decrees did not achieve temperance at court and were probably widely flouted, but they contributed to an atmosphere of renewed intolerance and repression of minorities. This was to prove especially damaging in the frontier provinces, where Sunnis were in the majority in many areas—notably in Baluchistan, Herat, Kandahar, and Shirvan. Such was Majlesi's achievement by the time of his death in 1699. Other clerics at court followed in his spirit thereafter.

Shah Sultan Hosein was a mild-tempered, well-meaning man. He had no streak of cruelty in his character, and there is no record of his having ordered any executions over the period of his reign (which, like that of his father, also lasted twenty-eight years). His sequestered upbringing and indolent nature meant that he disliked being disturbed or bothered with problems. The indications are that he was what we would call institutionalized, and as a result was lacking in confidence with the world outside the palace or with people he did not know. He enjoyed wine and eating, but otherwise was pious and humane, putting his energies into a new complex of gardens and pavilions at Farahabad, southwest of Isfahan. His courtiers and officials encouraged him to leave state business to them. His other main interest was sex. His emissaries collected pretty girls from all over his domains (from any group or religion except the Jews), brought them to

Isfahan, and delivered them to the shah's harem for his enjoyment. After a time, if they became pregnant, they would be taken away again, well furnished with money and presents. Some were married off to prominent nobles, so that when male children were born, they became the heirs of those nobles.[3]

One could make an argument that the world would have been a better place if there had been more monarchs like Shah Soleiman and Shah Sultan Hosein—pacific, passive, interested in little more than building pleasure pavilions, making garden improvements, drinking, and silken dalliance. But war and politics, like nature, abhor a vacuum. Persia in 1700 was, as states go, well placed: it had strong, natural frontiers, and its traditional enemies were either as passive as itself or distracted by more pressing troubles. The state of the economy has been debated, but it now seems that what were once taken as signs of economic decline were in fact signs mainly of the failure of the state to adapt to economic change.[4] The expansion of European trade to dominance, subordinating and damaging the economies of Asia, had yet to happen. Persian architects still produced beautiful buildings—the Madar-e Shah madreseh in Isfahan shows the loveliness of Safavid style in this last phase. The state administration continued to function despite the shah's negligence and was still capable of raising taxation (albeit less than it should have raised) and powerful armies. But the Safavid state had a soft center, and the wider world was no less harsh and competitive than in the days of the Mongols and their successors. The story of the end of the Safavids is a powerful reminder that the prime concern of a state is always (or should always be) security—what Machiavelli called *mantenere lo stato* (to maintain the state). The rest—the palaces, the sophisticated court, the religious endowments, the parks and gardens, the fine clothes, paintings, jewelry, and so on, however delightful—were mere froth.

The Afghan Revolt

The prime agent of the Safavid dynasty's destruction was an Afghan of the Ghilzai tribe, from Kandahar, Mir Veis. He was wealthy and well connected and also had a reputation for generosity to the poor and to his friends; this made him popular among the Afghans, who valued rugged austerity and piety and disliked ostentation. The oppressive Safavid governor of Kandahar—doubly unpopular because he was a Georgian asserting Shi'a supremacy—worried that Mir Veis had enough influence to organize a rebellion and made the mistake of sending him to Isfahan. There Mir Veis soon summed up the debility of the regime.

Like most Pashtun-speaking Afghans, Mir Veis was a Sunni Muslim. While in Isfahan he secured permission from the shah to go on the *hajj* to Mecca, where he obtained a fatwa legitimizing a revolt against Safavid rule. After his return to Kandahar (he charmed Shah Sultan Hosein and easily convinced him of his loyalty) Mir Veis coordinated a successful revolt and killed the Georgian governor in 1709. A succession of armies were sent from Isfahan to crush the rebels, and there is evidence that at least one vizier made serious attempts to galvanize the state—among other things reestablishing the artillery corps that had ceased to exist in the time of Shah Soleiman. But the expeditions failed, and their failure encouraged the Abdali Afghans of Herat to revolt, too. Maneuvers by jealous courtiers in Isfahan impeded active officials or removed them from office, and the shah failed to intervene. As the prestige of the state wilted, Safavid subjects in other territories revolted or seceded—in Baluchistan, Khorasan, Shirvan, and the island of Bahrain. Maryam Begum tried to prod the shah into more determined action to restore order, but little was done and (mercifully for her) she seems to have been dead by 1721.

Mir Veis died in 1715, but in 1719 his young son, Mahmud, raided onto the Iranian plateau as far as Kerman, capturing the city and doing terrible damage there. Encouraged by this success, Mahmud returned in 1721 with an army of Afghans, Baluchis, and other adventurers. Mahmud was an unstable character, and paradoxically he might not have succeeded but for his instability. He encountered difficulties at Kerman and Yazd, but rather than turning back as a more cautious leader might have done, he boldly pressed on toward the Safavid capital. The Safavid vizier mobilized an army against the Afghans that probably outnumbered them by more than two to one, but on the day of battle at Golnabad on March 8, 1722, the Persian commanders were divided by court faction and failed to support one another in the fighting. Shah Sultan Hosein stayed behind in Isfahan (something Shah Abbas would never have done). His Georgian guards were surrounded on the battlefield and massacred while the vizier's troops stood by and watched. The Persian cannon were overrun before they could fire more than a few shots, and the rest of the Safavid troops fled for the capital.

The Afghans, perhaps barely able to believe their luck, blockaded Isfahan—their numbers were insufficient for a successful assault and they had no heavy artillery to breach the walls. From March to October the capital endured a terrible siege that slowly starved the inhabitants until they were eating shoe leather and bark from the trees. There were also reports of cannibalism. Opportunities to bring in supplies or to coordinate relieving forces from outside were missed, but Tahmasp, one of the shah's sons, escaped, and began rather ineffectually to collect supporters in the northern part of Persia. Finally, on October 23, the shah rode out of the city on a borrowed horse to his former pleasure gardens at Farahabad and surrendered the city and the throne to Mahmud Ghilzai.

After the Afghan occupation of Isfahan, the Ottoman Turks took the opportunity to conquer the western provinces of Iran, including Tabriz, Kermanshah, and Hamadan (though not without fierce resistance by many of the inhabitants). Peter the Great of Russia, unwilling to see Ottoman power in the region expand unopposed, moved south on his last campaign to occupy the southern coast of the Caspian Sea. With these occupations completed, and in the absence of any obvious focus for resistance, it looked as though the Iranian state established by the Safavids in the early sixteenth century was gone for good. In Isfahan, isolated from the base of his support in Kandahar and in control of only a relatively small part of the previous Safavid realm, Mahmud grew increasingly unhinged and paranoid. In February 1725 he personally massacred almost all the surviving male members of the Safavid royal family in one of the courts of the palace, ceasing the slaughter only when the former Shah Sultan Hosein physically intervened. Shortly afterward Mahmud, by now raving, either died of illness or was murdered and was replaced as shah by his cousin Ashraf. Ashraf initially made promises to protect the abdicated Shah Sultan Hosein but eventually had him beheaded to forestall an Ottoman attempt to restore him to the throne.

The 1720s were a miserable decade for many Persians. In the territories occupied by the Ottomans, some people were initially carried off as slaves (it was permissible to enslave Shi'as because the Sunni Ottomans regarded them as heretics). In the area controlled by the Afghans, Persian townspeople and peasants were frequently attacked and plundered, and Ashraf issued an edict ordering that the Persians should be treated the worst of a hierarchy of groups—worse than Christians, Zoroastrians, or even Jews.[5] Fighting continued between the various occupiers and those who still resisted them, and the economy was badly disrupted, causing further impoverishment, hardship, and suffering.

The Slave of Tahmasp

By this time a young warlord called Nader Qoli, from the old Afshar Qezelbash tribe, had risen from obscure beginnings through the chaos and disorder of the times to become a local power in the province of Khorasan in the northeast. Contemporaries described him as tall and handsome, with intelligent dark eyes. He was ruthless with his enemies but magnanimous to those who submitted and capable of charming those he needed to impress. A fine horseman who loved horses, he was energetic and always happiest in the saddle. He had a prodigiously loud voice; he was once credited with putting an army of rebels to flight by the sound of his voice alone—until the rebels heard him giving orders for the attack, they believed they were only confronting a subordinate.[6] The Safavid cause regained some impetus in the autumn of 1726 when this stentorian commander joined forces with Tahmasp (the son of Shah Sultan Hosein, who had been named shah by his supporters and had been chased up and down northern Iran by the Afghans and Ottomans) and reconquered Mashhad, the capital of Khorasan. In recognition of his services, Tahmasp gave Nader the name Tahmasp Qoli Khan, which means "the slave of Tahmasp." It was an honor to be given the name of royalty in this way, but Tahmasp Qoli Khan was to prove an over-mighty servant. By contrast with Nader, Tahmasp combined the faults of his father and grandfather—he was an ineffectual, lazy, vindictive alcoholic. The usual upbringing had taken its usual effect. One of Tahmasp's courtiers commented that he would never make a success of his reign because he was always drunk and no one was in a position to correct him.[7]

After consolidating his position by making a punitive campaign to cow the Abdali Afghans of Herat, and having established his dominance at Tahmasp's court, Nader by the autumn of 1729 was finally ready to attack the Afghan forces that were occupying Isfahan. An eyewitness account from this time, from the Greek merchant and traveler Basile Vatatzes, gives a vivid impression of the daily exercises Nader had imposed on the army to prepare them for battle. We know that he made these routine for his troops throughout his career, but no other source describes the exercises in such detail.

Vatatzes wrote that Nader, entering the exercise area on his horse, would nod in greeting to his officers. He would then halt his horse and sit silently for some time, examining the assembled troops. Finally, he would turn to the officers and ask what battle formations or weapons the troops would practice with that day. Then the exercises would begin:

> And they would attack from various positions, and they would do wheels and counter-wheels, and close up formation, and charges, and disperse formation, and then close up again on the same spot; and flights; and in these flights they would make counter-attacks, quickly rallying together the dispersed troops. . . . And they exercised all sorts of military manoeuvres on horseback, and they would use real weapons, but with great care so as not to wound their companions.

As well as practicing movement in formation, the horsemen also showed their skill with individual weapons—lance, sword, shield, and bow. As a target for their arrows, a glass ball was put at the top of a pole, and the men would ride toward it at the gallop, and try to hit it. Few could, but when

Nader performed the exercise he would gallop along, opening and closing his arms like wings as he handled the bow and the quiver, and hit the target two or three times in three or four attempts, looking "like an eagle." The cavalry exercises lasted three hours. The infantry also exercised together:

> . . . the infantry—I mean those that carried muskets—would get together in their own units and they would shoot their guns at a target and exercise continuously. If [Nader] saw an ordinary soldier consistently on top form he would promote him to be a leader of 100 men or a leader of 50 men. He encouraged all the soldiers toward bravery, ability and experience, and in simple words he himself gave an example of strong character and military virtue.[8]

Vatatzes's description dwells on cavalry maneuvers and the display of individual weapon skills because these were dramatic. But his description of infantry training and the expenditure of costly powder and ball in exercises is significant because it shows Nader's concern to maximize the firepower of his troops, which was to prove crucial. This passage also makes plain the care he took with the selection of good officers, and their promotion by merit. For the army to act quickly, intelligently, and flexibly under his orders, it was essential to have good officers to transmit them. Three hours a day of maneuvers, over time, brought Nader's men to a high standard of control and discipline, so that on the battlefield they moved and fought almost as extensions of his own mind. Vatatzes shows the way Nader impressed on the men what they had to do by personal example—a principle he followed in battle, too. Training, firepower, discipline, control, and personal example were part of the key to his success in war. Nader's transformation of the army was already well advanced.

By the end of 1729 Nader's army had defeated the Afghans in three battles and had retaken Isfahan. Tahmasp was reinstalled in the old capital as shah. But before Nader agreed to pursue the defeated Afghans, he forced Tahmasp to concede the right to collect taxes to support the army. The right to levy taxes enabled Nader to establish a state within the state, based on the army.

Nader duly finished off the remnants of the Afghan occupying force. He went on to throw the Ottoman Turks out of western Persia before turning rapidly east to conquer Herat. In all these campaigns his modernized forces, strong in gunpowder weapons, outclassed their opponents and showed themselves able to overcome the ferocity of the Afghan cavalry charges and the attacks of the provincial Ottoman troops. But while he was in Herat, he learned that in his absence Tahmasp had renewed the war with the Ottomans, allowed himself to be defeated, and concluded a humiliating peace with the Ottomans. Nader issued a manifesto repudiating the treaty, and marched west. It is striking that he declared himself publicly and sought popular support for his action—a modern moment that argues against those who deny the existence of any but local and dynastic loyalties in this period.

Arriving in Isfahan in the late summer of 1732—and having prepared what was to come with typical care—Nader fooled Tahmasp into a false sense of security and got him drunk. He then displayed the Safavid shah in this disreputable state to the Shi'a courtiers and army officers. The assembled notables, prompted by Nader, declared Tahmasp unfit to rule, and elevated his infant son Abbas to the throne instead. Nader continued as generalissimo to this infant, announcing at the coronation his intention to "throw reins around the necks of the rulers of Kandahar, Bokhara, Delhi, and Istanbul" on his behalf. Those present may have thought this to be vain boasting, but events were to prove them wrong.

Nader's first priority was to attack the Ottomans again and restore the traditional frontiers of Persia in the west and north. In his first campaign in Ottoman Iraq he met a setback: a powerful army including some of the best troops held centrally by the Ottoman state marched east to relieve Baghdad, led by an experienced commander. This was warfare of a different order to that Nader had experienced up to that time. Overconfident, he divided his army outside Baghdad—attempting to prevent supplies getting through to the besieged city—and suffered a serious defeat. But within a few months, after replacing lost men and equipment with a ruthless efficiency that caused much suffering among the hapless peasants and townspeople who had to pay for it, Nader renewed the Turkish war, this time defeating the Ottoman forces near Kirkuk. Moving north, he then inflicted a devastating defeat on a new Ottoman army near Yerevan. This was in June 1735. A truce was negotiated on the basis of the old frontiers that had existed before 1722, and the Ottomans withdrew. The Russians—Nader's allies against the Ottomans—had already withdrawn from the Persian lands along the Caspian coast, their regiments having lost many men to disease in the humid climate of Gilan.

Nader Shah

With the exception of Kandahar, Nader had now restored control over all the traditional territories of Safavid Persia. He decided the time was right to make himself shah, and he did so by means of an acclamation by all the great nobles, tribal chiefs, and senior clerics of Persia at an assembly on the Moghan plain. There was little dissent, but the chief mullah was overheard speaking privately in favor of the continuation of Safavid rule, and was strangled. The infant Abbas was deposed, and the rule of the Safavid dynasty at last came to an end. It is noteworthy that despite Nader's later reputation for tyrannical cruelty, and with the exception of the unfortunate chief mullah (whose execution carried its own political message), he achieved his rise to power almost without the use of political violence. He brought about the deposition of Tahmasp and the coronation at the Moghan not by assassination, but by careful preparation, propaganda, cunning maneuvering, and the presence of overbearing military force—and above all by the prestige of his military successes.

Some other significant events occurred at the Moghan. Nader made it a condition of his acceptance of the throne that the Persian people accepted the cessation of Shi'a practices offensive to Sunni Muslims (especially the ritual cursing of the first three caliphs). This new religious policy served a variety of purposes. The reorientation toward Sunnism helped to reinforce the loyalty of the large Sunni contingent in Nader's army, which he had built up in order to avoid too great a dependence on the traditionalist Shi'a element, who

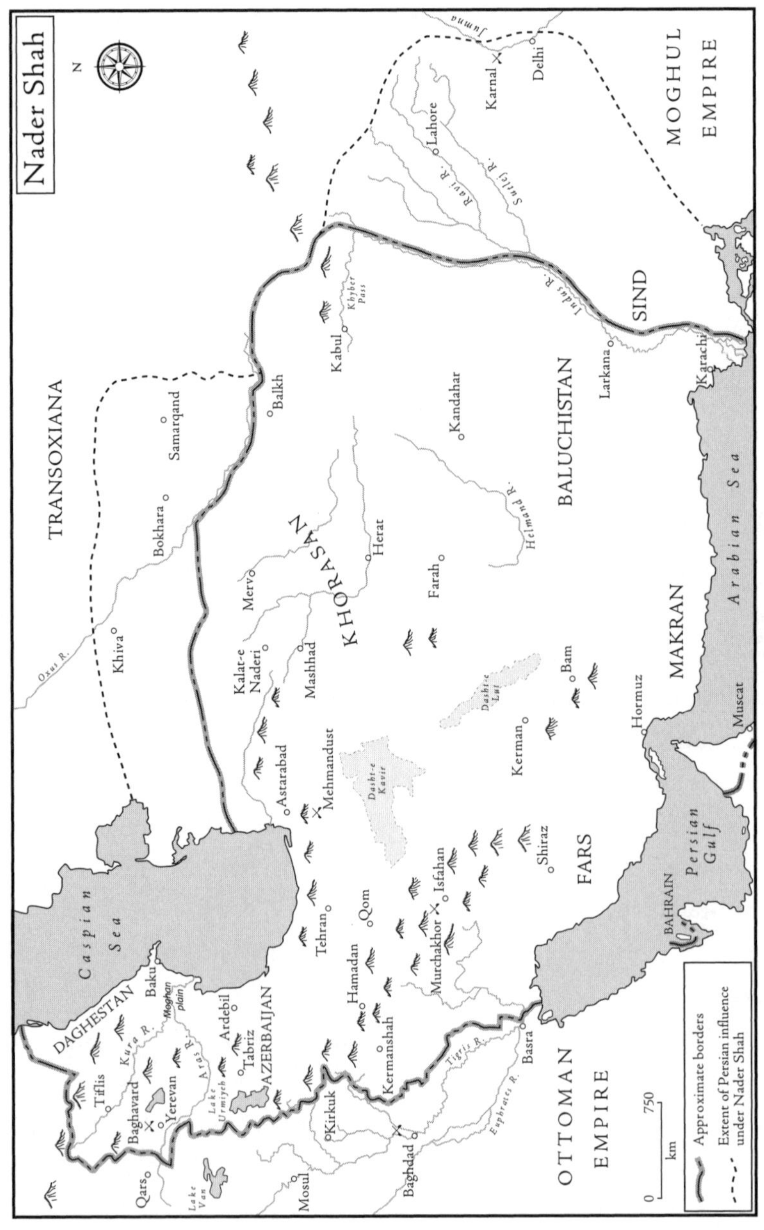
Nader Shah
N
TRANSOXIANA
Samarqand
Bokhara
Khiva
Oxus R.
Merv
Balkh
Kabul
Khyber Pass
Lahore
Karnal
Delhi
Jumna
Ravi R.
Sutlej R.
Indus R.
SIND
MOGHUL EMPIRE
Kandahar
Larkana
Karachi
BALUCHISTAN
Helmand R.
Herat
Farah
KHORASAN
Kalat-e Naderi
Mashhad
MAKRAN
Arabian Sea
Hormuz
Muscat
Bam
Dasht-e Lut
Kerman
Mehmandust
Astarabad
Dasht-e Kavir
Shiraz
FARS
Persian Gulf
BAHRAIN
Isfahan
Murchakhor
Qom
Tehran
Hamadan
Kermanshah
Caspian Sea
Baku
Moghan plain
DAGHESTAN
Kura R.
Ardebil
Tabriz
AZERBAIJAN
Aras R.
Tiflis
Baghavard
Yerevan
Lake Urmiyeh
Kirkuk
Qars
Lake Van
Mosul
Baghdad
Tigris R.
Euphrates R.
Basra
OTTOMAN EMPIRE
0
750
km
Approximate borders
Extent of Persian influence under Nader Shah

tended to be pro-Safavid. But also the new policy was not aggressively dogmatic. Religious minorities were treated with greater tolerance. Nader was generous to the Armenians, and his reign was regarded later by the Jews as one of relief from persecution (though minorities suffered as much as anyone else from his violent oppression and heavy taxation, especially in later years).[9] The religious policy made it easier for Nader to make a grab for the endowments of Shi'a mosques and shrines, an important extra source of cash to pay his troops. Within Persia, Nader sought only to amend religious practices—not to impose Sunnism wholesale. But outside Persia he presented himself and the country as converts to Sunnism[10]—which enabled Nader to set himself up as a potential rival to the Ottoman sultan for supremacy over Islam as a whole, something that would have been impossible if he and his state had remained orthodox Shi'a.

The religious policy also served to distinguish Nader's regime and its principles from those of the Safavids. He did this in other ways, too, notably with his policy toward minorities, and by giving his sons governorships rather than penning them up in the harem. He also showed moderation in the size of his harem and issued decrees forbidding the abduction of women. This change was probably directed, at least in part, at pointing up the contrast between his rule and that of the last Safavids.

Crowned shah, with his western frontiers secure and in undisputed control of the central lands of Persia, Nader set off eastward to conquer Kandahar. The exactions to pay for this new campaign caused great suffering and in many parts of the country brought the economy almost to a standstill. Nader took Kandahar after a long siege, but he did not stop there. Using the excuse that the Moghul authorities had given refuge to Afghan fugitives, Nader crossed the old frontier between the Persian and Moghul empires, took Kabul, and marched on toward Delhi. North of Delhi, at Karnal, the Persian army encountered the army of the Moghul emperor, Mohammad Shah. The Persians were much inferior in number to the Moghul forces, yet thanks to the better training and firepower of his soldiers, and rivalry and disunity among the Moghul commanders, Nader defeated them. He was helped by the fact that the Moghul commanders were mounted on elephants, which besides proving vulnerable to firearms were liable to run wild—to the dismay of their distinguished riders and anyone who happened to be in their path.

From the battlefield of Karnal, Nader went on to Delhi, where he arrived in March 1739. Shortly after his arrival there, rioting broke out and some Persian soldiers were killed. So far from home, and with the wealth of the Moghul Empire at stake, Nader could not afford to lose control. He ordered a ruthless massacre in which an estimated thirty thousand people died, mostly innocent civilians. Prior to this point, Nader had generally (at least away from the battlefield) achieved his ends without excessive bloodshed. But after Delhi, he may have decided that his previous scruples had become redundant.

With a characteristic blend of threat and diplomacy, Nader stripped the Moghul emperor of a vast treasure of jewels, gold, and silver, and accepted the gift of all the Moghul territories west of the Indus River. The treasure was worth as much as perhaps 700 million rupees. To put this sum in some kind of context, it has been calculated that the total cost to the French government of the Seven Years' War (1756–1763), including subsidies paid to the Austrian government as well as all the costs of the fighting on land and sea, was about 1.8 billion *livres tournois* (the standard unit of account in prerevolutionary France). This was equivalent to about £90 million sterling at the time—close to the rough estimate of £87.5 million sterling for the value of Nader's haul from Delhi. Some of the jewels he took away—the largest, most impressive ones, like the *Kuh-e Nur*, the *Darya-ye Nur*, and the *Taj-e Mah*—had a complex and often bloody history of their own in the following decades.

Nader did not attempt to annex the Moghul Empire outright. His purpose in conquering Delhi had been to secure the cash necessary to continue his wars of conquest in the west, for which the wealth of Persia alone had, by the time of his coronation, begun to prove inadequate.

Nader's campaigns are a reminder of the centrality of Persia to events in the region, in ways that have parallels today. A list of some of Nader's sieges—Baghdad, Basra, Kirkuk, Mosul, Kandahar, Herat, Kabul—has a familiar ring to it after the events of the first years of the twenty-first century. It is worth recalling that Persians were not strangers in any of the lands in which Nader campaigned. Although he and his Safavid predecessors were of Turkic origin and spoke a Turkic language at court, the cultural influence of Persian was such that the language of the court and administration in Delhi and across northern India was Persian, and diplomatic correspondence from the Ottoman court in Istanbul was normally in Persian, too. Persian hegemony from Delhi to Istanbul would, in some ways, have seemed natural to many of the inhabitants of the region, echoing as it did the Persian character of earlier empires and the pervasive influence of Persian literary, religious, and artistic culture.

Nader's annexation of Moghul territory west of the Indus, removing the geographical barrier of the Afghan mountains, was one indicator that his regime, had it endured, might have expanded further into India. Other indications include his construction of a fleet in the Persian Gulf, which would have greatly facilitated communications between the different parts of such an empire, and his adoption of a new currency designed to be interchangeable with the rupee. If this had happened—especially if the trade route through to Basra, Baghdad, and beyond had been opened up—and if it had been managed wisely, Nader could have seen a release of trade and economic energy comparable to that under the Abbasids a thousand years earlier. But that was not to happen.

On his return from India, Nader discovered that his son, Reza Qoli, who had been made viceroy in his absence, had executed the former Safavid shahs Tahmasp and Abbas. Nader's displeasure at this was increased by his dislike of the magnificent entourage Reza Qoli had built up while Nader had been in India. In response, Nader took away his son's viceroyship and humiliated him. From this point, their relationship deteriorated, and Nader came to believe that Reza Qoli was plotting to supplant him.

From India, Nader made a successful campaign in Turkestan. Then he went on to subdue the rebellious Lezges of Daghestan, but there he was unlucky. The Lezges avoided open battle and carried out a guerrilla war of ambush and attacks on supply convoys. Nader's troops suffered from lack of food, and Nader himself was troubled by illness, probably liver disease caused originally by malaria and exacerbated by heavy drinking. The sickness, which grew worse after his return from India, was accompanied by great rages that became more ungovernable as time went on. While he was in Daghestan in the summer of 1742, he was told that Reza Qoli had instigated an assassination attempt against him. Reza Qoli denied his guilt. But Nader did not believe him and had him blinded to prevent his ever taking the throne.

Nader's failure in Daghestan, his illness, and above all his terrible remorse over the blinding of his son brought about a crisis, a kind of breakdown, from which he never recovered. Perhaps because of the poverty and humiliations of his childhood, Nader's family were of central importance to him, and loyalty within the family had up to that time been unquestioned. It had been one of the fixed points on which he had constructed his regime. Now with that foundation given way, Nader's actions no longer showed his former energy and drive to succeed, and he underwent a drastic mental and physical decline. Withdrawing from Daghestan without having subdued the Lezges tribes, he called new forces together—according to plans laid months and years before—for another campaign in Ottoman Iraq.

When they gathered, his army numbered some 375,000 men—larger than the combined forces of Austria and Prussia, the main protagonists in the European theater of the Seven Years' War when that conflict began thirteen years later.[11] This was the most powerful single military force in the world at that time. It was also, in the long term, an insupportable number of troops for a state the size of Persia (no Iranian army would reach that size again until the Iran/Iraq war of 1980–1988). It has been estimated that whereas there were around thirty million people in the Ottoman territories in the eighteenth century, and perhaps one hundred fifty million in the Moghul Empire, Persia's population was perhaps as low as six million, having fallen from nine million before the Afghan revolt. Over the same period the economy collapsed, as a result of invasion, war, and exactions to pay for war.[12]

The army, and the taxation to pay for it, are recurring themes in Nader's story. Was this army a nomad host, or a modern military force? This points to the wider question of whether Nader's style of rule looked backward or forward. It is an extreme mixture. Nader repeatedly compared himself with Timur, stressing his Turkic origin and Timurid precedents in many of his public statements. He named his grandson Shahrokh after Timur's son and successor. At one point he even removed Timur's tombstone from Samarkand for his own mausoleum, only to return it later (unfortunately, it was broken in half in the process). On several occasions he described himself as the instrument of God's wrath on a sinful people, after the manner of earlier Asiatic conquerors, and his brutal conduct of government—particularly after his return from India—has as much in common with the actions of a nomad warlord as with those of a modern statesman.

But he was not in any simple sense a tribal leader, and in many ways he remained an outsider throughout his life. He was not born into the leadership of the Afshar tribe to which he belonged, and some of his most determined enemies throughout his career were fellow Afshars. From the beginning his followers were diverse, including especially Kurds and Jalayir tribesmen. Later he repudiated his Shi'a heritage, turned Sunni (at least for public consumption), and depended most heavily on his Afghan troops. Like other Persian leaders (as well as Napoleon), he was close to his immediate family and promoted them politically; but in his wider connections he was an opportunist, and the term *Afsharid* that is applied to him and his dynasty is misleading. The name Nader means "rarity" or "prodigy," and both are appropriate. He was *sui generis*, a parvenu.

Nader used government cleverly, began an important and thorough reform of taxation, and had a strong administrative grip. His religious policy was novel and tolerant in spirit. One should not overstate it, but some contemporaries remarked upon his unusually considerate treatment of women. In military matters he was wholly modern. He established the beginnings of a navy and it now seems plain that something very like the beginnings of a military revolution, as described in the European context by Geoffrey Parker, was brought about in Persia by Nader Shah. It was under Nader that the majority of troops in the army were equipped with firearms for the first time, necessitating a greater emphasis on drill and training—characteristic of developments that had taken place in Europe in the previous century. Under Nader the army increased greatly in size and cost, and he was forced to make improvements in his capability for siege warfare. He began to reshape state administration to make structures more efficient. These are all elements that have been shown to be typical of the military revolution in Europe.

If Nader had reigned longer and more wisely, and had passed on his rule to a competent successor, the drive to pay for his successful army could have transformed the Persian state administration and ultimately the economy, as happened in Europe. It could have brought about in Iran a modernizing state capable of resisting colonial intervention in the following century. If that had happened, Nader might today be remembered in the history of Iran and the Middle East as a figure comparable with Peter the Great in Russia: as a ruthless, militaristic reformer who set his country on a new path. In the early 1740s he seemed set for great things—contemporaries held their breath to see whether he could succeed in taking Ottoman Iraq and establishing his supremacy through the Islamic world as a whole. He had already achieved a large part of that task. Unfortunately, Nader's derangement in the last five years of his life meant that the expense of his military innovations turned Persia into a desert rather than developing the country. His insatiable demands for cash brought about his downfall and the downfall of his dynasty.

Nader's troops invaded Ottoman Iraq in 1743 and rapidly overran most of the province, except the major cities. Baghdad and Basra were blockaded. Nader brought up a new array of siege cannon and mortars to bombard Kirkuk, which quickly surrendered, but the defense of Mosul was conducted more resolutely. Nader's new siege artillery pounded the walls and devastated the interior of the city, but a lot of his men were killed in unsuccessful assaults, and he no longer had the will or patience to sustain a long siege. When he withdrew, he sent peace proposals to the Ottomans. Mosul marked the end of his ambition to subdue the Ottoman sultan and demonstrate his preeminence in the Islamic world. It was another important turning point.

The latest round of forced contributions and requisitioning, to make good the losses in Daghestan and provide for the campaign of 1743, had caused great distress and resentment across Persia. Revolts broke out in Astarabad (led by Mohammad Hasan Khan Qajar, whose son was to found the Qajar dynasty later in the century), Shiraz, and elsewhere. Early in 1744, Nader withdrew to a camp near Hamadan, in order to be closer to the troubles and coordinate action against them. The insurrections were put down with great severity. Shiraz and Astarabad were devastated, and in each place two white towers were erected, studded with niches that held the heads of hundreds of executed men.

At length Nader realized that the Ottomans were not going to accept his peace proposals—new Ottoman armies were advancing toward his frontiers. Nader's son Nasrollah defeated one of these forces, while Nader achieved victory over the other—near Yerevan, in the summer of 1745. This was his last great victory, and it was followed by a treaty with the Ottomans in the following year. But by this time, new revolts had broken out, driven by Nader's oppressive practices: each place he visited was ransacked by his troops and tax collectors, as if they were plundering enemies. His demands for money reached insane levels, and cruel beatings, mutilations, and killings became commonplace. His illness recurred and furthered his mental instability. By the winter of 1746–1747 his crazy demands for money extended even to his inner circle of family and close advisers, and no one could feel safe. His nephew, Ali Qoli, joined a revolt in Sistan and refused to return to obedience. Unlike previous rebels, Ali Qoli and his companions had contacts among Nader's closest attendants. In June 1747 Nader was assassinated by officers of his own bodyguard near Mashhad. They burst into his tent in the harem while he was sleeping. One of the assassins cut off his arm as he raised his sword to defend himself, and then another sliced off his head.[13]

The short-lived nature of Nader's achievements is one explanation for his not being better known outside Iran, but it is not a sufficient one. With a few exceptions Nader, having excited much interest and writing in Europe among his eighteenth-century contemporaries, was largely ignored in the nineteenth. Why should this have been so?

Without overstating the case, it seems plausible that it was because Nader's vigor and his successes fit badly with the crude Victorian view of the

Orient as incorrigibly decadent and corrupt, ripe for and in need of colonization. From a purely British perspective, his military successes might then have been thought to detract from the later victories of Clive and Wellington in India, and to have conflicted with the myth of the supposedly inherent superiority of European arms (an important element in the edifice of British imperialism). By the latter part of the twentieth century the Great Men of History—as Carlyle described them—could no longer be regarded with the same hero worship they had enjoyed before, and the oblivion to which Nader had been consigned was perhaps deepened by a general distaste for conquerors.

But Nader's historian, Mirza Mahdi Astarabadi, far from showing distaste, celebrated Nader's victories as a sign of the favor of God—and of God's will that Nader should reign. In this as well as in other respects, Mirza Mahdi's account serves as a conduit for Nader's own attitudes. Writing as Nader's official historian in Nader's own lifetime, Mirza Mahdi was never likely to show any radical independence of thought. An independent observer who met him described him as "wise, humble, polite, attentive, and respectable. . . ." His history is painstakingly accurate about dates and places, with only occasional lapses. Having accompanied Nader on his campaigns from the earliest days, he was in an almost unique position to know the facts of what happened, but he tended to put a favorable gloss on events. On occasion he even omitted mention of actions that would have reflected badly on Nader.

By far the greatest single omission in Mirza Mahdi's narrative was his failure to include the blinding of Reza Qoli Mirza in 1742. It is generally agreed that Mirza Mahdi's history was for the most part written as a chronicle while Nader was alive. But some years later he added a section dealing with the last months of Nader's life, and the aftermath of his assassination. In this section the criticism he had been forced to suppress in Nader's lifetime flooded out. He described how Nader's cruelties, instead of calming him, only made him more frenzied; and how many of his people were driven by his oppression to abandon their houses and towns and take to the deserts and mountains, or to emigrate. The words that Mirza Mahdi used to introduce this last section of his history serve well to summarize Nader's career. He wrote,

> From the beginning of Nader Shah's reign until his return from Khwarezm and his march into Daghestan, he was entirely occupied with the care of his empire and the administration of justice, in such a manner that the people of Iran would have given their lives for his preservation; but after this time he changed his conduct entirely. At the instigation of some hostile spirit, this unhappy monarch listened to ill-intentioned spies, and had the eyes of Reza Qoli, the best and the dearest of his sons, torn out. Remorse quickly followed this rash cruelty, and Nader Shah became like a madman. The reports of bad news that he received in succession thereafter of troubles in various parts of his dominion increased his rage.[14]

New Maps of Hell

The story of the decades after Nader's death is one of chaos, destruction, violence, and misery. Anyone looking to restore their faith in the innate goodness of human nature would do well to skip the next few pages. After Nader's assassination his nephew Ali Qoli made himself shah, renamed himself Adel Shah (which means The Just Shah—a misnomer), and sent troops to Nader's stronghold at Kalat-e Naderi in Khorasan. There they murdered all but one of Nader's sons and grandsons, and even cut open the bellies of pregnant women in the harem to finish off heirs as yet unborn.

The army Nader had assembled, within which he had encouraged competition between commanders and ethnic groups, could not hold together once he was gone. Like that of Alexander after his death, the army split, following charismatic generals. The commander of the Afghans, Ahmad Khan Abdali—whom Nader had released from prison in Kandahar in 1738—fought Nader's assassins in the camp and then left for home. Along the way he and his men captured a quantity of treasure, including the fabulous *Kuh-e Nur* diamond that Nader had taken from Delhi. On his arrival in Kandahar, Ahmad was elected to be the first shah of the Durrani dynasty, founding a state based on Kandahar, Herat, and Kabul that was to become modern Afghanistan. In this sense one could say that Afghanistan was founded in the muster lists of Nader Shah. Another of Nader's commanders, the Georgian Erekle, who had accompanied him to Delhi, went home and established an independent kingdom in Georgia. Most of the other ethnic and tribal groups Nader had assembled in Khorasan returned home also, including the small Zand tribe, originally from Lorestan (though perhaps ultimately of Kurdish origin), under one of their leaders, Karim Khan, and the Bakhtiari, under Ali Mardan Khan.

Adel Shah, who was unable to maintain control in an impoverished country swarming with unemployed soldiers, was deposed after little more than a year by his brother, Ebrahim. Other rulers followed, only to be deposed in turn: Nader's surviving grandson, Shahrokh; then a Safavid descendant of Shah Soleiman; then Shahrokh again (though he had been blinded in the interim). Shahrokh remained in place from 1750 until 1796, seemingly with the consent and even the protection of Ahmad Shah Durrani, who respected him as the descendant of Nader. But from the early 1750s the regime in Mashhad could exert little influence beyond Khorasan.[15]

Adel Shah's brother Ebrahim had initially controlled Isfahan, but after he moved east Karim Khan Zand and Ali Mardan Khan Bakhtiari took over the western provinces, coming to an agreement with each other and ruling in the name of another Safavid prince, Esma'il III. Step-by-step Karim Khan removed his rivals, killing Ali Mardan Khan in 1754 and deposing Esma'il in 1759. Karim Khan stabilized his regime by fighting off external rivals as well: Azad Khan, another of Nader Shah's Afghan commanders, who controlled Azerbaijan; and Mohammad Hasan Khan Qajar, who had his power base in Mazanderan. Karim Khan also fought the Ottomans and conquered Basra, something Nader Shah had never achieved.

The rule of Karim Khan Zand created an island of relative calm and peace in an otherwise bloody and destructive period. In the years of the Afghan revolt and the reign of Nader Shah, many cities in Iran were devastated by war and repression (some, like Kerman, more than once—in 1719 and 1747—and it was to suffer terribly again in 1794). By mid-century most of the built-up area of Isfahan, the former capital, was deserted and inhabited only by owls and wild animals. In the last years of the Safavids it had been a thriving city of 550,000 people, one of the world's largest cities—similar in size to London at the time, or even bigger.[16] By the end of the siege of 1722 only 100,000 people were left. Although many citizens later returned, the number fell yet further during the Afghan occupation and beyond. By 1736 there were only 50,000 left.[17] It has been estimated that the overall total population of Persia fell from around nine million at the beginning of the century to perhaps six million or less by mid-century—through war, disease, and emigration. Population levels did not begin to rise significantly again until after 1800[18] (by contrast, the population of England rose from around six million in 1700 to around nine million in 1800). Trade fell to one-fifth of its previous level.[19]

But despite the pitiful state into which the country had descended, the major outside powers, Russia and the Ottoman Empire, did not intervene as they had in 1722–1725. It was partly that they were busy elsewhere, and surely also that the outcome of their previous attempts had not encouraged them to repeat the experiment.

The eighteenth century has been portrayed as a period of tribal resurgence, and the names of the main parties contending for supremacy for much of the century—Afshar, Zand, and Qajar—alone point in that direction.[20] Many of the troops that fought in the civil wars, most of them horsemen, were recruited from the nomadic tribes who still would have comprised between one-third and one-half of the population. The makeup of the tribes was complex and far from static—here were many different terms to express different kinds of clans, tribal subdivisions, tribes, and tribal confederations, and alliances between tribes occasionally formed, broke, and reformed in new combinations. In the best of times—for centuries if not millennia—the tribes lived in uneasy tension with the more settled people of the towns and villages. The tribes and the townspeople were usually divided by ethnicity, language, or religion, or by a combination of all three. The tribesmen, living in more rugged mountain and arid territory, had rugged attitudes to go with their more marginal existence. They raised livestock and traded their surplus to supply the towns and villages with wool and meat. In return they received goods they could not make for themselves—some foodstuffs as well as weapons. But in addition to this more open form of exchange, there was often an exchange on the basis of security, one that was more or less disguised. Peasants might pay tribute to a local tribal leader to have their crops left alone at harvest time, or to avoid raids that might otherwise result in their being carried off as slaves (especially in the northeast). On the other hand, the local tribal leader might have been co-opted to serve as the regional governor, in which case he would collect tax instead of protection money. But in general, the tribes and their leaders tended to have the upper hand, which they exploited politically. Their position of supremacy was only decisively overturned when the twentieth century was quite well advanced.

Karim Khan Zand did not have Nader's insatiable love of war or his lust for conquest, and his governmental system was less highly geared. After removing Esma'il, Karim Khan refused to make himself shah, ruling instead as *vakil-e ra'aya* (deputy or regent of the people)—a modern-sounding title that probably reflected his awareness of the weariness of the Iranian people and their longing for peace. He restored traditional Shi'ism as the religion in his territories, dropping Nader's experiment with Sunnism. Karim Khan chose Shiraz as his capital, and built mosques, elegant gardens, and palaces that still stand—erasing the scars of the revolt of 1744 and beautifying the city that had been the home of Sa'di and Hafez. Karim Khan ruled there until his death in 1779. He was a ruthless, tough leader, as was necessary in those harsh times, but he also acquired an enduring reputation for modesty, compassion, pragmatism, and good government, unlike most of his rivals. His reputation shone the brighter for the surrounding ugliness and violence of his times.

Renewed War

After Karim Khan's death, Persia lapsed again into the misery of civil war. This time the struggle was between various Zand princes on the one side and the Qajars, based in Mazanderan, on the other. The Qajars were united by Agha Mohammad Khan (son of Mohammad Hasan Khan Qajar), who had fallen into the hands of Adel Shah in 1747 or 1748 and had been castrated at Adel Shah's orders when he was only five or six years old. After that Agha Mohammad was kept as a hostage by Karim Khan but was treated kindly.[21] Agha Mohammad grew up to be a fiercely intelligent, pragmatic man, but also grim and bitter, with a bad temper and a vicious cruel streak that grew worse as he got older. He was never able to overcome the loss of his manhood. Contemporary illustrations depicted him as looking drawn and beardless as a sign of it.

When Karim Khan died, Agha Mohammad escaped to the north, where he successfully conciliated other branches of the Qajar tribe that had previously feuded with his family. But he had to fight his own brothers to establish his dominance. Agha Mohammad's rise was much more firmly based on his lineage and on the Qajar tribe than that of Nader Shah had been based on the Afshars. Once his supremacy within the tribe was achieved, Agha Mohammad ejected Zand forces from Mazanderan and began campaigning south of the Alborz mountains, with the help of the Yomut Turkmen allies that had long supported his family. But when he arrived outside Tehran, the gates were closed against him. The citizens politely told him that the Zands were in charge in Isfahan. That meant that the people of Tehran had to obey the Zands, but it also implied that if Agha Mohammad Khan could take Isfahan, they would obey him, too. Agha Mohammad marched on to Isfahan, taking it in the early part of 1785. He was then duly accepted into Tehran in March 1786, after other successful campaigning in the west. From then on it became clear that he intended to establish himself as ruler of the whole country, and Tehran has been the capital since that time.

There was to be much more fighting before Agha Mohammad could rule supreme, and he was still far from secure in the south. Isfahan changed hands several times. But the Zands could not deliver a knockout blow either, and in January 1789 their leader (Ja'far Khan) was assassinated. The ruling family of the Zands then fought among themselves for the leadership, until Lotf Ali Khan Zand, a young grand-nephew of Karim Khan, entered Shiraz in May 1789, establishing his control.

Lotf Ali Khan was young and charismatic and a natural focus for the hopes of those who remembered the prestige of his great uncle, but militarily he was at a disadvantage from the start. He fought off an attack by Agha Mohammad in June 1789, but when he made a move on Isfahan in 1791 Shiraz revolted against him behind his back. He returned but was blocked from re-entering his former capital and was forced to lay siege to the city. The Shirazis sent for help to Agha Mohammad—and sent Lotf Ali Khan's family as prisoners to him too. Lotf Ali Khan was able to defeat a combined force of Qajars and troops from Shiraz, but the city still held out. Then in 1792 Agha Mohammad himself marched south with a large army. By this time Agha Mohammad was showing some of the fierce anger and vicious cruelty for which he later became notorious. At one point he saw a coin minted in Lotf Ali's name and became so enraged that he gave orders for the Zand's son to be castrated.

Lotf Ali Khan now nearly brought off a coup that could have won him the war. As Agha Mohammad approached Shiraz, he camped with his Qajar troops near the ancient sites of Persepolis and Istakhr. After night fell, Lotf Ali approached the camp with a smaller force and attacked from several directions in the dark. Chaos erupted. Lotf Ali sent thirty or forty men right into the camp, penetrating as far as Agha Mohammad's private compound, which was defended against them by a few musketeers. At this point one of Agha Mohammad's courtiers went to Lotf Ali and told him that Agha Mohammad had fled. The battle appeared to be over and Lotf Ali was persuaded that further fighting would only risk his own troops killing one another in the dark. He ordered his men to sheathe their sabres. Many of them dispersed, plundered the parts of the camp they were in control of, and left the scene with the booty. But when dawn came Lotf Ali discovered to his horror that Agha Mohammad was still there. He had not fled, and the Qajar troops were regrouping around him. With only one thousand of his own men still with him, Lotf Ali Khan was surrounded and outnumbered. He quickly withdrew, fleeing eastward.[22]

From this point on Lotf Ali Khan's support began to dwindle away. He captured Kerman, but Agha Mohammad Khan moved against the city and besieged it. The Qajars broke into the city by treachery in October 1794 and Lotf Ali Khan fled to Bam. Agha Mohammad ordered that the women and children of Kerman be given over to his soldiers as slaves; the surviving men were to be blinded. To ensure that his orders were followed, he demanded that the men's eyeballs be cut out, brought to him in baskets, and poured out on the floor. There were twenty thousand of them. Sir John Malcolm recorded that these blinded victims were later to be found begging across Persia, telling the story of the disaster that had befallen their city.[23]

Lotf Ali Khan was betrayed in Bam and was taken in chains to Agha Mohammad, who ordered his Turkmen slaves to do to him "what had been done by the people of Lot." After the gang rape, Lotf Ali Khan was blinded and sent to Tehran, where he was tortured to death.[24]

Agha Mohammad Khan was now the undisputed master of the Iranian plateau. He turned to the northwest, where he marched into Georgia and reasserted Persian sovereignty. In September 1795 he conquered Tbilisi after a furious battle in which the Georgians seemed to be winning at several points, despite their inferior numbers. Thousands were massacred in Tbilisi, and fifteen thousand women and children were taken away as slaves. But the king of Georgia had put himself under Russian protection in 1783, and the destruction of Tbilisi caused anger in St Petersburg. Later on, it was to bring humiliation for Persia in the Caucasus.

In the spring of 1796 Agha Mohammad had himself crowned on the Moghan plain, where Nader Shah had assumed the same dignity exactly sixty years earlier. At the coronation Agha Mohammad wore armbands on which were mounted the *Darya-ye Nur* and the *Taj-e Mah* jewels taken from Lotf Ali Khan, which had previously belonged to Nader Shah. Agha Mohammad Khan liked jewels. After the coronation he marched east to Khorasan, where he accepted the submission of Shahrokh, Nader Shah's grandson. He had Shahrokh tortured until he gave up more jewels, also from the treasure Nader had brought away from Delhi. Shahrokh died of the treatment shortly afterward, in Damghan.

Agha Mohammad Shah had now resumed control of the main territories of Safavid Persia, with the exception of the Afghan provinces. But he did not enjoy them, or his jewels, for long. In June 1797, while campaigning in what is now Nagorno-Karabakh, he was stabbed to death by two of his servants, whom he had sentenced to be executed but unwisely left alive and at liberty overnight.

Religious Change: Seeds of Revolution

Eighteenth-century Persia was not just a place of massacre and misery. Many if not most places away from the major towns and cities probably continued in relative tranquillity for most of the period. And other developments were at work—changes in Shi'a theology and in the religious-social structure of Shi'ism—that were to have crucial importance in the longer term. The old argument between tradition and reason, which had rolled back and forth in a Sunni context between the Mu'tazilis and their opponents in the time of the Abbasids, resurfaced in the sixteenth and seventeenth centuries in a different form. This dispute, between what came to be called the Akhbari and Usuli schools, was not to be resolved until the nineteenth century.

The Akhbaris asserted that ordinary Muslims should read and interpret the holy texts for themselves, without the need for intermediaries. The traditions (hadith)—especially the traditions of the Shi'a Emams—were the best guide. The Usulis rejected this doctrine, saying that authoritative interpretation (*ijtihad*) on the basis of reason was necessary and required extended scholarly training, which could only be achieved by specially talented scholars among the ulema, called *mojtaheds*. Almost all areas of human conduct were open to *ijtihad* (the Akhbaris had taken the view that disputes that could not be resolved by precedents in the holy texts would have to be referred to the secular powers).

The Usulis eventually won the argument, thanks largely to the leadership of the great mojtahed Aqa Mohammad Baqer Behbehani (1706–1790). But the Akhbaris, whose views were closer to the orthodoxy of Sunnism, had a moment of near-triumph during the reign of Nader Shah, supported by Nader's ambiguous but broadly pro-Sunni policy.[25] The dispute was not fully resolved until the early Qajar period, by which time a theory of interpretation and a hierarchy had developed on this basis: each Shi'a Muslim had to have a *marja-e taqlid,* an "object of emulation" or religious role model. This had to be a living person, a mojtahed, which in practice meant only one or two of just a few mojtaheds in each generation. As some were thus elevated, a hierarchy of mojtaheds came to be created. The senior, more authoritative among them became known as *hojjatoleslam* (proof of Islam), ayatollah (sign of God), or, later, grand ayatollah. Just as in other contexts, competition for the titles produced a kind of inflation:[26] as more people acquired the original titles, new, more exalted ones had to be invented.

In this way, a religion that—in the absence of the hidden Emam—formally still asserted the illegitimacy of all authority on earth paradoxically came to give a few religious scholars great potential power. This power eventually came to flex its muscles not just in religion but also in politics. The position of the ulema was further strengthened by the fact that the leading marjas often lived in Najaf or Karbala in Ottoman Iraq, beyond the reach of the Persian authorities. Shi'ism acquired a hierarchical structure, comparable to those of the Christian churches, but markedly different from the less hierarchical arrangements of Judaism and Sunni Islam. The combination of beliefs—in the illegitimacy of secular authority, in the righteousness of the oppressed, and in the legitimacy of an organized hierarchy of clerics—looks with the benefit of hindsight like a recipe for eventual religious revolution.

There was—is—a further important element in this religious culture: the various manifestations of popular Shi'ism, including most importantly the Ashura processions and the *ta'zieh*. Every year, on the anniversary of the martyrdom of the Emam Hosein at Karbala, Shi'a Muslims in Iran and elsewhere take part in processions through towns and villages to commemorate the bitter events of that day. The best way to think of these is as reenacted funeral processions, in which devotion to and identification with the martyrs of Karbala is as vivid and strong as the feeling for the dead at a real funeral. Bazaar guilds and strongmen from the *zur-khaneh* (the house of strength—traditional associations of men who gather to build their fitness through juggling heavy clubs, wrestling, and other sweaty pursuits, but often with religious overtones) compete to display their devotion and grief. Some carry large symbolic coffins representing the coffin of Hosein, or huge multi-pointed symbolic banners representing his war standard. Others beat themselves with chains. Some also cut their heads with swords, but this is an excess that has been increasingly frowned upon by the religious authorities. The Ashura demonstrations build a collective sense of grief, bitterness, injustice, and guilt (the last from the failure of the Kufans to save Hosein), reliving emotionally the grim events of Karbala. Western news media find images of these processions irresistible when they need to illustrate accounts of Shi'a religious fanaticism, but the emotions of grief and guilt and the symbolic representations of suffering (even the blood in some cases) are—as mentioned earlier—strikingly similar to those in traditional Good Friday processions in many Catholic countries in Europe and elsewhere. It would be possible to interleave film sequences of both in such a way that the gloom, tears, and intensity of the participants would be almost indistinguishable.

The ta'zieh is a form of religious street theater, unique in the Islamic world but similar in spirit and function to the religious mystery plays of medieval Europe. Again, the usual theme is Karbala, but the performance may focus on different aspects of the drama. The performers recite familiar lines describing the action and the audience may join in. Those watching experience and show tears and intense emotion. The ta'zieh normally occurs in the month of Moharram and Ashura, but *rowzeh-khans* (preachers) used to recite impromptu versions at any time of the year. Through the nineteenth century many eminent Iranians erected buildings, as acts of piety, to house the ta'zieh performances. Previously they had taken place in tents or on street corners.[27]

All these manifestations have served to remind Shi'a Muslims of the central events of their religion. But they have also reinforced a commitment to collective religious feeling based on the sense of injustice that many oppressed and downtrodden communities of Shi'as have felt at different times and places. The emotions and the custom of street processions may serve as a kind of precedent, or template, for collective action and collective solidarity, as has appeared at several points in Iranian history.

But to characterize the grief of Ashura as a kind of training ground or launch pad for street demonstrations or even mob violence (notwithstanding that such have happened, in exceptional circumstances) would be a gross distortion. The more normal association in Shi'ism is with passive melancholy, modesty, a belief in the righteousness of humble self sacrifice, and in the virtue of quietly doing good in adverse circumstances.

The eighteenth century in the Islamic world (the concept itself is questionable—in Islamic terms we are talking mainly about the twelfth century, though the centuries do not exactly correspond in the two calendars) has often been depicted as a period of decline and decadence. It is easy to see why that was the case—the Ottoman Empire lost territory, the Safavid monarchy collapsed, and so did the Moghul dynasty, ushering in the period of European colonial dominance. These are facts that cannot be denied. But there were important signs of change, development, and vigor in the Islamic world that have often been overlooked. Some of them were significant in their own right, while others contained the seeds of major future developments. We have already looked at the importance of the reign of Nader Shah, though its significance emerges more fully in the light of the Persian/Russian wars of 1804–1828. Also, the Akhbari/Usuli dispute and its outcome were important for the future development of the Shi'a ulema in Iran, and the Iranian revolutions of the twentieth century cannot be properly understood without them.

But there were other significant developments in the Islamic world in this period—notably the rise of Wahhabism in Arabia. According to some accounts the movement's founder, Abd al-Wahhab, studied for a time in Isfahan, though this seems doubtful.[28] His was a truly fundamentalist movement within Sunnism, one deeply hostile to Sufism, Shi'ism, any real or apparent kind of departure from monotheism, and any form of what it called "innovation"—all of which it considered heretical. Wahhabism insisted on a return to what its exponents considered to be the earliest principles of Islam, as exemplified by Mohammad and his earliest converts. In alliance with the Al-Saud family, devotees of Wahhabism made progress in Arabia until the early nineteenth century, destroying shrines and tombs in their fervor, and sacking Karbala itself in 1802. That was a deep shock and a great insult to Shi'a Muslims. By 1818 Ottoman forces had defeated the Al-Saud and reasserted their control of the Arabian peninsula and the holy places. But the Al-Saud and the Wahhabis returned to take control of most of the Arabian peninsula in the twentieth century.

Fath Ali Shah

After the death of Agha Mohammad Shah, Persia could again have slid into chaos and civil war, as had happened after the death of Karim Khan Zand. That this did not occur was largely due to the foresight of Agha Mohammad Shah in the 1780s and after, as he resolved feuds within the Qajar tribe and prepared the succession for his nephew Fath Ali Khan, and for Fath Ali Khan's son Abbas Mirza.[29] There were some disturbances in Azerbaijan, and Fath Ali Khan marched to assert his authority. He defeated his enemies near Qazvin, and went on to punish the old shah's murderers and have Agha Mohammad's body buried in Najaf. He then had himself crowned, on March 21, 1798, at the feast of Noruz, the New Year.

Fath Ali Shah has some prominence in the history of Iran for a variety of contingent and unrelated reasons. One is that it was during his reign that Europeans suddenly began traveling to and reporting back from Persia in larger numbers, both as tourists and as state representatives operating out of diplomatic missions. This was because Fath Ali Shah's reign coincided with the revolutionary and Napoleonic Wars, and the European powers were reaching out in competition with one another to find new allies. Another reason is that Fath Ali Shah encouraged a new wave of portrait painting, the favorite subject of which was himself, resplendent with waist-long black beard and spangled with jewels from belt to arms to crown. So a wealth of arresting images of him have survived to the present day. Unlike his uncle and other predecessors like Karim Khan Zand and Nader Shah, Fath Ali Shah loved magnificence. A further claim to fame was his prodigious fathering of children—it has been calculated that he had by the end of his reign a total of 260 sons by 158 wives. Finally, he reigned for a relatively long time—thirty-seven years—and from that fact alone he later symbolized an era.

Some of these factors have combined to give a broadly negative impression of Fath Ali Shah that may not be wholly justified. Many of the Europeans who reported back about Persia at his time made invidious and sometimes ignorant and prejudiced comparisons between Persia and Europe. Many of them did not fully realize the degree of the trauma and destruction Persia had suffered over the previous century, nor the very different nature of state and government in Persia. The other inescapable fact was that Persia lost large swathes of valuable territory in the Caucasus to the Russians during the reign of Fath Ali Shah, and the performance of his armies in the wars against Russia was for the most part poor.

But from another perspective Fath Ali Shah's reign looks more successful. Building on his uncle's achievements, he avoided serious civil war (no small thing in itself), and his reign saw a modest renewal of economic activity and prosperity. Persia lost territory but preserved her independence, and kept the bulk of her lands free from warfare in a dangerous and destructive period of international conflict. It could have been worse. Sir John Malcolm, probably the most knowledgeable and balanced foreign observer of Persia at this time, wrote in 1814,

> Fortunately Persia is at present happier and more tranquil than it has been for a long period; and its reigning monarch, who has already occupied the throne seventeen years, by the comparative mildness and justice of his rule has already entitled himself to a high rank among the Kings of Persia.[30]

Encounter with the West: Diplomacy and War

The story of Persia's dealings with the Western powers in the reign of Fath Ali Shah would be almost comical if the consequences, both short and long term, had not proved so damaging. From the perspectives of the individual European states themselves, their conduct was logical, if shortsighted, given wartime necessity. From a Persian perspective, it looks fickle and crass.

But it began well: the first European mission successfully to agree to a treaty was from the English East India Company (EIC), and they knew how to handle things. In 1800 the company sent a very able young man, the future historian John Malcolm, with a retinue of some five hundred men, including a military escort of one hundred Indian cavalry. The almost royal progress of this caravan made a strong impression, as did the lavish gifts the company could afford to send with it. The government of India and its counterpart in London had been shocked by Napoleon's invasion of Egypt in 1798, and alarmed by a French mission to Tehran in 1796. They were determined to make an alliance with Persia to secure the western approaches to India. The alliance could also be used against the danger of Afghan incursion into northern India. In January 1801 political and commercial treaties were signed, according to which the French were to be excluded from Persia, and Fath Ali Shah agreed to attack the Afghans if the Afghans made any incursion in India. The British agreed to send "cannon and warlike stores" if the Afghans or the French were to attack Persia. The company's commercial privileges in Persia were confirmed and enhanced, and a solid Anglo-Persian alliance seemed to be taking shape.[31]

But the big question mark over the treaties was Russia, which was a more immediate concern for the Persians than France. After Agha Mohammad's massacre at Tbilisi in 1795, the Russians established a protectorate in Georgia, stationed troops there in 1799, and later abolished the Georgian monarchy after the death of its king—effectively annexing the territory. Fath Ali Shah continued to declare Persia's sovereignty over Georgia, to no avail, and Russian generals speculated about pushing the Russian frontier farther south, to the Araxes. In 1804, led by a brutal general called Tsitsianov, the Russians set about it in earnest, taking Ganja and massacring as many as three thousand people there (including five hundred Muslims who had taken sanctuary in a mosque). They fought an inconclusive battle against Fath Ali Shah's son Abbas Mirza outside Yerevan. But as Nader Shah had discovered to his cost, and as many later Russian military men including Tolstoy and Lermontov were to confirm, the Caucasus was an awkward place to go soldiering. The war proved more difficult than Tsitsianov had anticipated, and a little later the Persians succeeded in killing him by a trick. The Russians suggested some negotiations with the Persian governor of

Baku, but the Persian governor, suspecting bad faith, made preparations for an assassination. Tsitsianov and the governor both went to the appointed meeting place with just three attendants each, but when they arrived the governor's nephew shot Tsitsianov through the chest.[32]

In the meantime, British interest in Persia had faded. It was complicated: after a short peace between Britain and France, hostilities reopened between them, and whereas before 1801 the British had suspected Russia of wanting to cooperate with the French against India, they now secured an alliance with Russia against Napoleon. Fath Ali Shah invoked the Treaty of 1801 and asked the British for help against Russia in the Caucasus, but the British valued their northern ally more than their Persian one. They ignored the request.

Seeing an opportunity, the French made overtures to the Persians and in May 1807 Fath Ali Shah agreed to sign the Treaty of Finckenstein with them (the treaty was signed in East Prussia, as Napoleon's army recovered from the bloody Battle of Eylau and prepared for a renewed attack on the Russians). This was a mirror image of the previous treaty with the British: the Persians agreed to expel the British and to attack India; Napoleon recognized Persian sovereignty over Georgia and promised military assistance against the Russians; and a mission under the Frenchman Claude Matthieu, Count Gardane, set out for Tehran to fulfill those terms. But before Gardane could get there Napoleon defeated the Russians decisively at Friedland in June 1807, and signed a treaty of alliance with the Russian tsar at Tilsit the next month. The diplomatic dance swung around, and the partners changed again.

With a French military mission in Tehran training up a Persian army to invade India, the British were impressed once more with the urgency of an alliance with Fath Ali Shah. But because the government in London and the East India Company government in India could not agree on which should take precedence in policy on Persia, they sent two competing missions—one from London under Sir Harford Jones, and one from Bombay again headed by John Malcolm. Malcolm got to Persia first but was allowed no farther than Bushire, because of Fath Ali Shah's commitments to the French; Malcolm sailed back to Bombay in July 1808 after three fruitless months. Meanwhile, Count Gardane was in an impossible position, training Persians whose only real interest was in the continuing war with Russia and the re-conquest of Georgia. And Russia was now France's ally. Harford Jones succeeded where Malcolm had failed, reaching Tehran in March 1809. Gardane, by now discredited, flitted out of the country a month later, abandoning France's commitments to Persia.

Jones and the Persians signed a Treaty of Friendship and Alliance that went further than the Treaty of 1801 and gave the Persians more watertight guarantees. The Persians were to receive help against any invading European power, even if Britain had made a separate peace with that power, provided Persia was not the aggressor. The help was to be in the form of British troops, or failing that, subsidies, cannon, muskets, and British officers. For his part, the shah undertook not to do anything to endanger British interests in India, and to give military assistance in case of an attack by the Afghans.

But although the British encouraged Fath Ali Shah to continue the costly war with the Russians, when Napoleon attacked Russia in 1812 Britain and Russia again became allies, and Britain's enthusiasm for helping Persia against the Russians evaporated. The war in the Caucasus was now, for Britain, an embarrassment that needed tidying up. Although the Persians fought hard with some successes under Fath Ali's son Abbas Mirza, their failures were more damaging, culminating in October 1812 in a heavy defeat at Aslanduz on the Araxes. Britain served as a mediator for a peace signed at Golestan in October 1813. The treaty was a terrible humiliation. Persia kept Yerevan and Nakhichevan, but lost everything else north of the Araxes, including Daghestan, Shirvan, and Georgia, and cities that had been part of the Persian Empire for centuries—Darband, Baku, Tblisi, and Ganja among them.[33] It also included provisions that only the Russians could maintain warships on the Caspian Sea, and that Russia would recognize and support the legitimate heir to the throne of Persia. This last point gave the Russians a locus for meddling in the royal succession, which was to prove seriously damaging. When the terms of the treaty became known, they caused anger in Persia and calls for renewed jihad against the Russians, led by bellicose mullahs in the towns. Abbas Mirza regarded the treaty only as a truce, and redoubled his efforts to turn the army he controlled in Azerbaijan into a modernized force that could fight the Russians on equal terms.

It didn't work. War was renewed with Russia in 1826, after a period in which Abbas Mirza drew further help from the British (who with the final defeat of Napoleon in 1815 grew more anti-Russian again), and another aggressive Russian general, Yermolov, did his best to alienate the new subject populations—over-interpreting the terms of the Golestan treaty and further irritating the Persians. Yermolov proved more belligerent in peace than in war, and the Persians made some initial gains, marching toward Tbilisi and up the Caspian coast. Many local leaders went over to the Persian side, and Yermolov abandoned Ganja. But soon Russian reinforcements arrived under more active commanders. Once war was begun, the British refused further help, pointing to the clause in the Treaty of 1809 that exempted them from doing so if Persia were the aggressor. Before the year was out the armies of Abbas Mirza and his brother Mohammad Mirza were defeated in separate battles, Ganja was retaken, and the Persians were back where they had started. In 1827 the Russians advanced farther, taking Yerevan at the beginning of October and Tabriz later in the month.

The mountains and forests of the Caucasus were ideal country for guerrilla warfare, and if, especially in this second war, when the local tribes were ill-disposed toward the Russians, the Persians had fought in that way, they might have been more successful. The Lezges had fought off Nader Shah with guerrilla tactics in the 1740s, and they (with the Chechens) would give the Russians enormous difficulties in the long wars they fought in the decades after 1830. But the Persians had seen themselves as equals of the Russians, and had aspired to fight them in the open field. They disdained to fight the hit-and-run war of the ragged Sunni tribesmen of the Caucasus, whose overlords they had been for centuries. That was their mistake; they were not flexible enough, and misjudged the measure of Russian military superiority.

Peace was concluded at Turkmanchai in February 1828, with even more humiliating terms than those of Golestan. Persia lost Yerevan, and the border was set at the river Araxes. Persia had to pay Russia twenty million rubles as reparations and all captives had to be returned to Russian territory—even if they had been taken twenty or more years before. According to commercial agreements made at the same time, Russian merchants were to be allowed to operate freely in Persia, and (these provisions were aptly named capitulations) were effectively exempt from Persian jurisdiction.[34]

The treaty had a violent and undiplomatic postscript. A distinguished literary man and friend of Pushkin, Alexander Griboyedov, arrived in Tehran as Russian Minister Plenipotentiary and set about enforcing the terms of the treaty, being particularly exercised about the provisions over the return of captives. He set about extricating from Persian families women who had been taken captive as Christians but who had subsequently converted. Some of these women were less than keen to be rescued, and the Russians' interference in private Persian households gave great offense, which was whipped up further by radical mullahs. A mob gathered outside the Russian embassy on January 30, 1829. One account says a Cossack on the roof shot a boy in the crowd.[35] The mob broke in and found and murdered an Armenian eunuch who had previously served the shah. Two women were also dragged away, and several of the crowd were killed in the fighting as the Cossacks who served as guards tried to protect the building. The bodies were carried away to the mosques, but later the mob returned, broke in again, and massacred all the Russians except one, who escaped dressed as a Persian. Griboyedov was apparently convinced that the shah himself was behind the attacks. It seems his last words were *Fath Ali Shah! Je m'en fous!*[36]

Fath Ali Shah could perhaps have tried harder to control the situation that led to the killings, but it is most unlikely that he was in any serious way to blame (some Russians have blamed the British ambassador also, for inciting the mob, which illustrates the rivalry between the two powers in Persia by this time, but has no basis in fact). Fath Ali Shah had to send a mission to St. Petersburg to present his apologies and smooth things over.

The Persian/Russian wars and their consequences illustrated a number of important realities about the state of Fath Ali Shah's realm. Militarily and economically, it was no match for the European powers. The army Abbas Mirza led into the Caucasus in 1826 was thirty-five thousand strong, which

was large by comparison with those that had fought the civil wars forty years earlier, but the Russians had lost a larger number of men as casualties in a single day when they fought Napoleon at Borodino in 1812. The Russians had some difficulties getting troops to the Caucasus and in supplying them once there, but their reserves of manpower and war materials were impossible for the Persians to equal—even if the Persians could have come up to the Russian standard of drill, training, and staff work.

The point was not that the Persians were bad soldiers, nor really that they had fallen behind technologically (not yet). It was just that the Qajar state was not the same kind of state, nor was it trying to be.[37] It controlled its territory loosely, through proxies and alliances with local tribes. The state bureaucracy was small, revolving around the court much as it had in the days of the Safavids. It has been estimated that between a half and a third of the population were still nomadic or semi-nomadic pastoralists.[38] Provincial governors were often tribal leaders. They ruled independently, with little interference from the capital, and sent there what tax revenue was left after they had deducted their own expenses, which was not usually very much (Abbas Mirza's army was largely recruited and paid for from the province of Azerbaijan in which he was governor). To raise money for the wars, Fath Ali Shah had alienated crown lands, increasing the devolved tendency. Nader Shah would have handled matters differently, but the apparent lesson of his reign was that ambition, greater integration, centralization, militarism, and higher taxation went together—they alienated important supporters, created opposition and revolt, and led to civil war. All Persian rulers after Nader, from Karim Khan Zand onward (even Agha Mohammad Shah), seemed to have absorbed that lesson. They rejected Nader's model and accepted a more devolved state as the price of stability and popular consent to their rule.

The other side of the story is that most Iranians at the time probably preferred it this way. In the smaller towns and villages of the country (where most still lived), the wars in Armenia and Shirvan were a long way off, and there would have been only sporadic (and inaccurate) news of them. The civil wars between the Qajars and the Zands, let alone the earlier revolts in the time of Nader Shah and the Afghans, had affected many more Iranians either directly or indirectly through economic dislocation. Those terrible events were still within living memory, and most Iranians would have been grateful to have been spared them. Under Fath Ali Shah some moderate prosperity returned to these traditional communities.

But the popular agitation for war and the murder of Griboyedov showed the influence of the mullahs, and the closeness of some of them to at least one important strand of popular feeling in the towns (as always, one should be wary of assuming all the mullahs thought the same way—they did not). In later decades, as other European powers demanded, secured, and exploited the same privileges as those accorded the Russians at Turkmanchai, popular feeling became more and more bitter at the apparent inability of the Qajar monarchy to uphold Persian sovereignty and dignity.

6

The Crisis of the Qajar Monarchy, the Revolution of 1905–1911, and the Accession of the Pahlavi Dynasty

Whatever happens will be for the worse, and therefore it is in our interest that as little should happen as possible.

—Lord Salisbury, writing about Persian affairs in December 1879

[Aya] ma ra az mum sakhta-and?
Are we made of wax?

—Naser od-Din Shah, March 1855[1]

Fath Ali Shah died in 1834, shortly after the death of his son, Abbas Mirza, who had been his designated heir. This meant that another son, Mohammad, took the throne. Mohammad Shah's accession was supported by both the Russians and the British and was achieved peacefully—they judged, correctly, that he would uphold the treaties that gave them their privileges within Persia. But his reign brought few benefits for the Persian people. He made little real effort to develop the country or defend its essential interests, despite the increasingly manifest developmental gap between Persia and Europe. His first prime minister was a reformer, but the shah had him strangled in 1835. Persian merchants began to protest the fact that cheap European products, especially textiles, were coming onto Persian markets with low or no tariffs and were undercutting domestic craftsmen, destroying their livelihoods. Predictably, the merchants who made a profit from handling the imports kept quiet.

Perhaps partly in reaction to the defeat in war, the humiliating treaty of Turkmanchai, and the increasing and unwelcome presence of foreigners and foreign influences, there were attacks on minorities in the 1830s—especially the Jews. These tended to be led, as at other times, by preachers or mullahs of marginal status who disregarded the established, humane, and dignified precepts of their faith for the temporary popularity that could accrue from extremism and hatred. A serious attack by a mob in Tabriz in 1830 seems to have resulted in the death or flight of most of the previous Jewish population there. It may have begun (like similar cases in medieval Europe) with a false allegation that a Muslim child had been murdered by a Jew.[2] Other such attacks followed elsewhere in Azerbaijan, prompting Jews to begin avoiding the whole province. There were also forced conversions of Jews in Shiraz and other places: in Mashhad in 1839 a riot broke out and many Jews were killed before moderate Shi'a clergy intervened. The Jews were then forced to convert or flee.[3] For many years the converts, called *jadidi*, kept to themselves in their own communities; many such converts still observed Jewish rites in private, and some eventually reverted to Judaism, risking being accused of apostasy if they did. Later in the century there were similar outbreaks at Babol on the Caspian Sea (in 1866) and in Hamadan (1892).[4] Jewish and other travelers recorded that the Jews they saw were generally living in poor ghettoes and were subject to daily low-level intimidation and humiliation, though their position may have improved toward the end of the century, in some places at least. There was persecution elsewhere in the Islamic world at the same time, and some have suggested that the impact of European anti-Semitic writings was a factor.[5] No doubt only a small minority of Muslims were actively involved in attacks, and there is evidence that some ulema and others did what they could to prevent or limit them. But as in other times and other places, it could not have happened at all without the majority preferring to look away. The Armenians seem generally to have avoided this degree of persecution in this period.

Despite their agreement on the succession, in the time of Mohammad Shah the British and Russians were still rivals in Persia, Afghanistan, and Central Asia. This rivalry came to be called The Great Game. Before the war of 1826–1828, the British had supported the Persians against the Russians; now the Russians encouraged Mohammad Shah to take compensation for Persia's loss of territory in that war by grabbing back the former territories of Herat and Kandahar in the east. Mohammad Shah sent troops to Herat in 1837, besieging the place for a few months.[6] But the British, who disliked the prospect of any encroachment in Afghanistan that might threaten India or make Russian access to India any easier, occupied Kharg Island in the Persian Gulf and demanded that Mohammed Shah quit Afghanistan. He withdrew in 1838 and made further trading concessions to Britain in a new treaty in 1841.

Hajji Mirza Aqasi, Mohammad Shah's second prime minister (who had been instrumental in the removal and killing of the first), was pro-Sufi and encouraged the shah to follow his example. Fath Ali Shah had always been careful to conciliate the ulema, but Mohammad Shah's Sufi inclinations made him deeply unpopular with them, bringing forward again the ever-latent Shi'a antagonism toward secular authority.

The Babi Movement, Naser od-Din Shah, and Amir Kabir

Another development during the reign of Mohammad Shah was the appearance in Iran of the Babi movement, which eventually gave rise to the Baha'i religion. This originated around the year 1844, which was 1260 in the

Muslim calendar—a year that had been long awaited as the one-thousandth anniversary of the disappearance of the twelfth Emam. Since the eighteenth century, followers of a branch of Shi'ism called Shaykhism had speculated that there must be a gate ("Bab") through which the Hidden Emam could communicate with the faithful. This Bab was expected to take the form of a person, and as the year 1260 approached, some Shaykhis grew increasingly excited that the Bab might be revealed in that year. When the time finally came, some people identified a particular pious young man from Shiraz, Seyyed Ali Mohammad, as the Bab. In May 1844 he declared that he was indeed the Bab and began preaching against the shortcomings of the ulema. He advocated better treatment of women (thereby attracting many female followers), recommended that the Islamic ban on interest be lifted, argued that judicial punishments should be made less harsh, and urged that children should be better treated. From one perspective his teaching looks progressive; from another it appears as little more than the conventional teaching of the milder strand of orthodox Shi'ism. But in 1848 the Bab and his followers began preaching that the Bab was in fact the Hidden Emam himself, and that their faith was a new belief—one superseding the previous revelation of Islam. This changed the position, putting the Babis and the ulema in direct conflict. The Bab was soon taken into custody.

One of the most remarkable and radical of the Bab's followers was a woman from Qazvin, Qorrat al-Ain, who discarded the veil as a sign that shari'a law had been set aside. She was a poet, debated theology with the ulema, and preached the emancipation of women. She was sent into exile in Iraq at one point, but later returned. Like the Bab, she was arrested. But unlike him, she was still able to speak to her followers while under house arrest.

When Mohammad Shah died in 1848 his seventeen-year-old son Naser od-Din took the throne, again with the support of the Russians and the British. The boy was thoughtful and intelligent in appearance, with large dark eyes and a dreamy tendency; he could lose himself for hours in books of Persian folk tales.[7]

But after the accession of the new shah, there were revolts involving Babis in Fars, Mazanderan, and in Zanjan, which were crushed by the government with great severity. Following these disturbances, which have been linked to social upheavals elsewhere in the world at this time, the Bab was executed in Tabriz in 1850. The story is that the firing squad had to shoot twice, because the first time the bullets only cut the ropes binding him, setting him free. Animosity between the Babis and the monarchy escalated rapidly. In August 1852 three Babis tried to assassinate the new shah. Although they failed, there was a harsh backlash. Later that same year Qorrat al-Ain was killed by her captors, along with most of the other leaders of the movement, and the Bab's followers were viciously persecuted as heretics and apostates. The new faith appeared to be a challenge to both the secular and the religious authorities, and as such stood little chance, despite converting quite large numbers. Many thousands of Babis died, and others left the country.

The movement continued to grow in exile. In the 1860s it split, with a new leader, Baha'ullah, announcing himself as the new prophet ("He Whom God Shall Make Manifest") predicted by the Bab. Most Babis followed Baha'ullah, and since that time his movement has been known as the Baha'i faith. Within Iran, Baha'is have been persecuted and killed in almost every decade since that time.

The story of Qorrat al-Ain and her advocacy of women's emancipation is an important point in the history of women in Persia, and therefore for the story of Iranian society as a whole. There are some surprises here. From our viewpoint in the early twenty-first century, with the Islamic regime in power in Iran and with what is often perceived (not entirely accurately) as a traditional role for women reimposed since the revolution of 1979, one might assume that before the twentieth century all Iranian women were closeted at home and never went out except when heavily veiled. But this is not at all the case. Before the social changes brought by industrialization and urbanization, the structure of society was very different. Before 1900, up to half the population were nomadic or semi-nomadic, and in such societies, tightly integrated and often living at both the geographical and economic margins, women's roles were of necessity more equal and less restricted. Broadly speaking, women oversaw the domestic arrangements while men ranged widely looking after the flocks. But with the men away, the women had to make important decisions, often as a group, and bear responsibility. When time came to move, everyone had to take an active part.[8] Traditional tribal costumes vary enormously across Iran even today, and are often colorful and eye-catching, with no veil in sight.

Of the remainder of the population, the majority were peasant farmers and laborers. But among these people, too, women had an essential economic role and some independence (insofar as anyone in the poorer classes could properly be thought of as independent). Women had to work hard in the fields and probably did the majority of the routine work—of all but the heaviest sort. Again, a veil of the enveloping *chador* kind was normally quite incompatible with that sort of activity.

Even in the towns and cities, the majority of people were relatively poor, and in those households most women would have had to work outside the home. And there were significant numbers of prostitutes, to whom the rules of respectability certainly did not apply. So the setup we might think of as typical—of heavily veiled women seldom leaving the home and even in the home kept apart from males who were not relatives—was in fact atypical before 1900. When it did occur, it was limited to middle- or high-class families in towns (precisely the class that looms large historically, being the book-writing, book-reading class—perhaps only four percent or less of families overall). But that arrangement was, or became, an aspiration for many men who could not afford to make it a reality. One could think of the heavy veil as a kind of elite fetish, similar to some of the fashions of nineteenth-century Europe that immobilized women, being wholly impractical and incompatible with work of any kind. For a man's wife to be out of the house and out of his control, especially in the towns, perhaps partly because of the presence of prostitutes in the towns, potentially exposed him to derision and ridicule. But for her to be kept at home and to emerge only veiled was expensive and a sign of the man's status. It would be easy to overlook or underestimate the significance and implications of this trope among men in Iranian society and elsewhere. Rather than being an outgrowth of traditional religion and society—there is little justification for it in the Qor'an or the earliest hadith, which originated in different social circumstances—it may largely underpin them. Possession of material goods had its patterns and its social consequences, but so also did the possession of women.

As the population later became steadily more urban and in some ways at least more prosperous, more women were more restricted, stayed in the home more, and wore the heavy veil. But we should not think of those arrangements as typical of pre-industrial Iran; one could accurately say that for the majority of Iranian women, they were a twentieth-century innovation.

The conflict with the Babis around the time of Naser od-Din's accession was only one of the problems he had to deal with. There was a serious revolt in Khorasan that took two years to overcome, an army mutiny in Tehran, and serious infighting between officials at court in which the Russian and British ambassadors both meddled, anxious that each might outdo the other. In this confused and dangerous situation, the shah's first minister, Amir Kabir, attempted to steer the government in a reforming direction, urging the shah to take a personal interest in the details of government. Kabir's influence over the young shah stemmed from the time he had spent with him as Naser od-Din's right-hand man, when Naser od-Din had been crown prince and governor of Azerbaijan. Kabir was disliked by the Russians because they thought him to be pro-British, but the British were none too keen on him either.[9]

An able and intelligent man, Amir Kabir was dedicated to the interests of the monarchy and the country. He made a review of finances and enforced a retrenchment in state expenditures, especially on payments and pensions to courtiers. This inevitably made him unpopular with some members of the court. He set up a state-funded school or polytechnic along western lines—the Dar al-Funun, which in later years collaborated to publish translations of Western technical books and literature—and organized a thoroughgoing reform of the army to bring it properly up-to-date. He set about some improvements in agriculture, and even tried to build some factories for manufactured products. All this was achieved within three years, showing what was possible and promising greater things for the future. But the thickets of court politics proved too much for Amir Kabir. He made the mistake of trying to intercede with Naser od-Din on behalf of the shah's half-brother, an effort that offended both the shah and the shah's mother, who had significant influence at court. In time, Amir Kabir's critics succeeded in eroding the shah's confidence in him, without which he was powerless. In November 1851 Amir Kabir was dismissed as prime minister and sent to Kashan. At the beginning of 1852 Naser od-Din, influenced by his courtiers and relatives and following the precedent set by his grandfather and father before him, had his former first minister murdered. When Amir Kabir died, so did hope for any kind of serious push for development in Persia, at a time when elsewhere in the world, not just in Europe, the motors of industrialization and major structural change were accelerating.

Ugly Sisters: Russia, Britain, and the Concessions

A new first minister, Mirza Agha Khan Nuri, took Amir Kabir's place and proved more to the liking of the court: he was as corrupt and reactionary as they could have wished, and no further reform went forward. Later in the decade the Russians gained influence, and another Persian army set out to reconquer Herat. This time they succeeded in taking the city (in October 1856), but they also precipitated war with Britain. British troops landed at Bushire and defeated Persian troops there, and again the Persians were obliged to make peace. The Peace of Paris, signed in March 1857, stipulated that Persia must abandon all claim to Afghan territory. In 1858, Nuri fell from office, and from that time Naser od-Din Shah ruled as his own first minister, but he never found fully satisfactory arrangements for doing so.[10]

Throughout this period and the decades that followed, the British and Russians interfered so insistently in Persian government that in some respects the shah's independence appeared merely nominal. That this was not made more obvious was only due to the shah's unwillingness to pursue projects that might displease the European powers. He was willing to offend one of them at any time—if he had the support of the other—but could not afford to alienate both together. Thus, for example, at a time when railways—rightly seen as the very embodiment of progress—were spreading all over the globe, yielding benefits for communications and commerce that could have been highly valuable for Persia too, particularly so given the huge distances and impossible roads of the Iranian plateau, no railways were built. The British and Russians disliked the idea for strategic reasons; railways could have delivered hostile armies more rapidly to their respective borders. By the end of Naser od-Din's reign in 1896 there was still only one railway in Persia. It was a narrow-gauge line built by the Belgians, running out of Tehran to a little shrine town five miles away—the shrine of Shah Abd ol-Azim—which was to prove a fateful backdrop to several important events over the next few years.[11]

What were the real interests of Britain and Russia in Persia at this time? How damaging was their involvement? There are a number of different elements to these questions. Britain and Russia stood for different things in the nineteenth century, and for different aspects of the European model. Britain stood for, or appeared to stand for, progress, liberalism, science, commerce, and improvement. In contrast, Russia stood for the traditional order in Europe—for the adaptation of modern tools to maintain the status quo of the old dynastic monarchies, for the Orthodox Christian church, and against political radicalism. Both had their attractions for different interests and groups in Persia. But both states, whatever impression they might have given, were primarily concerned with their own strategic interests, in which the interests of the Persians had little part. Both had other, greater priorities. And both loomed much larger to Persians than did Persia in the calculations of either. Each power would edge ahead of the other, if it could, but was normally content to reach a *modus vivendi* with the other over Persia—which meant stasis and avoiding surprises. This rivalry was good in one way: it made it difficult for either power to take Persia as a colony. One could claim that Britain prevented Russia from overwhelming Persia altogether in the nineteenth century, and vice versa. But the negative was that both powers were suspicious of change or of vigorous Persian reformers who might shake things up or give an advantage to their rival. As time went on, the shah was more and more suspicious of change and reform, too. The result was stagnation.

After a decade of personal rule, in 1871 the shah appointed a first minister again. This was Mirza Hosein Khan, who had served the shah overseas as a diplomat, notably in Istanbul, where he had seen the effects of some of the Tanzimat reforms in the Ottoman Empire. Convinced that similar change needed to happen in Persia, he encouraged Naser od-Din Shah to travel so that he could see for himself some of the developments taking place in other countries. In 1872 Mirza Hosein Khan succeeded in persuading the shah to agree to what was called the Reuter concession. This was a remarkable initiative, a blueprint for development of the most sweeping kind, including a railway from the Caspian to the south, mining rights, and all kinds of industrial and other economic improvements. It could have brought benefits, but the trade-off was that it abandoned a huge swath of sovereign rights to the foreigner putting up the money for those improvements: the Baron de Reuter, a British Jew born in Germany and the founder of the Reuters news agency. In return for the concession, the shah received £40,000 as an advance.

Over the previous decades, the Iranian economy had changed and shifted in response to an increasing penetration of markets by foreigners. Many Iranian products proved unable to compete with cheap imports, while agriculture began producing more for export (cotton and opium, for example). The reduced capacity for domestic food production contributed to a number of severe famines, especially in 1870–1871, in which it has been estimated that up to one-tenth of the population perished.[12] The changes left many people angry and contributed to the opposition to the Reuter concession. The shah returned from a visit to Europe in 1873 to powerful demands for the removal of Mirza Hosein Khan, and he duly went.

The Reuter concession was also strongly disliked by the Russians, and the shah had discovered while in Europe that the British were no better than lukewarm about it. Along with the domestic opposition, this was enough for the shah to find an excuse to cancel it in the same year. But there followed an extended dispute over the advance, which the shah held on to. Eventually, in 1889, Baron de Reuter was given another concession in compensation—he was allowed to set up the Imperial Bank of Persia, with the exclusive right to print paper currency. Up to that time, the British were able to use the Reuter dispute to prevent Russian proposals for a railway from going ahead. But in 1879 the Russians helped the shah set up the Iranian Cossack Brigade, which was led by Russian officers. This became the most modern, best-disciplined armed force in the country, and was loyal to the shah—but it was also an instrument of Russian influence.

For a period in the 1870s, the British government considered a more positive attitude toward Persia, which could have resulted in Persia becoming a genuine ally rather than a dupe and a cat's-paw.[13] This episode was prompted by Russian conquests in Central Asia—notably the surrender to them of Khiva in 1873—but also by the deterioration of British influence in Afghanistan. In 1879 the foreign secretary Lord Salisbury, briefly setting aside the policy of "masterly inactivity" governing Britain's attitude to the borders of India, considered a plan that would have given Herat to Naser od-Din Shah, along with a subsidy from the British government and help with internal reforms. Persia would have become a partner and an ally, an essential element in Britain's colonial defenses rather than a theater for spoiling actions to prevent the Russians gaining influence. It would have been in Britain's interests to help build up Persia, rather than keeping Persia down. Talks went on between the British and the Persians in London, led on the Persian side by Malkom Khan, head of the Persian diplomatic mission there. But in the end Naser od-Din Shah broke off the negotiations. The British believed that this was because the Russians had intervened to block them. The liberal government that followed was not inclined to take up the talks again, and the opportunity was lost, but the episode shows that the realpolitik pursued by Britain vis-à-vis Persia was not necessarily the inevitable and logical corollary to their imperial position. A cynical policy, or a policy of realpolitik as its proponents would call it, may sometimes be pursued out of laziness and lack of imagination rather than anything else. The cynical policy maker cannot predict the future any more than the moralist can, but he knows that at least he cannot be accused of starry-eyed idealism. Sometimes that edge is all it takes to allow the cynic to dominate. Truly farsighted politicians sometimes insist that if you get the principles right, then the small change of policy will look after itself. But often the principles get lost along the way, and cynicism and short-termism prevail. The cynicism of British policy in Persia was to do great damage in the longer term.

Malkom Khan was a significant figure in the latter part of the nineteenth century. He was born in 1833, the son of an Armenian father who had converted to Islam, and who had so admired Sir John Malcolm that he named his son after him. Malkom Khan was educated in Paris, and on his return to Persia taught at the Dar al-Funun. But the shah became suspicious of his reforming ideas and his influence, and his later service as a diplomat outside Iran had something of the character of exile. Eventually, at the end of the 1880s, Malkom Khan fell from favor altogether. He stayed on in London to produce the newspaper *Qanun*, which pressed for an end to arbitrary government and for the establishment of the rule of law, based on a constitution. This paper was distributed in Iran and was widely read among the educated elite. After Naser od-Din's death, Malkom Khan was reconciled to the government. He died in 1908.

Reform-minded officials continued to come and go in Persia through the 1880s, but without the full support of the shah they were unable to get any traction. The shah continued to negotiate concessions to foreigners, but in 1890 he went too far with a tobacco concession, granting monopoly rights to a British company that enabled them to buy, sell, and export tobacco without competition. This drew opposition from a formidable alliance of opponents: landlords and tobacco growers, who found themselves forced to sell at a fixed price; bazaar traders, who saw themselves once more frozen out of a lucrative sector of the economy; the readership of new reform- and nationalist-oriented newspapers operating from overseas; and the ulema, who were closely aligned to the bazaar traders and disliked the foreign presence in the country. This combination of interests became the classic pattern, repeated in later movements. Coordinated largely through the network of connections between the mullahs across the country (making use of the new telegraph system), mass protests against the concession took place in most of the major cities in 1891. They culminated in something like a revolt in Tabriz and a demonstration in Tehran that was fired on by troops, leading to further demonstrations. One of the most important mojtaheds, Hajji Mirza Hasan Shirazi, issued a fatwa in December 1891 calling for a nation-wide boycott, and this was so widely obeyed that even the shah's wives stopped smoking. Early in 1892 the government was forced to cancel the concession, incurring a large debt.

Naser od-Din was bruised by the furor over the tobacco concession. From around this time onward, the Russian interest tended to predominate at court, and the shah followed a more repressive policy, restricting contacts with Europe, banning the Persian-language newspapers imported from overseas, limiting the expansion of education that he had earlier championed, and again favoring reactionary, anti-reform ministers. Some contemporary observers apparently said the shah now preferred courtiers who did not know whether Brussels was a place or a vegetable.[14]

Jamal al-Din al-Afghani

By the latter part of the nineteenth century some thinkers in Iran, and in the Middle East more generally, had gone from an initial response to the West of bafflement, reactionary resentment, or uncritical admiration to adaptation, resistance, or reform. Notable among these was Jamal al-Din al-Afghani, who despite his name was probably born in Iran and brought up as a Shi'a in the 1830s and 1840s. Later he traveled widely, including in India, Afghanistan, Europe, and Egypt, and he lived in Egypt for some years in the 1870s. It is thought that he adopted the name al-Afghani in order to be accepted more easily in a Sunni milieu. In all these places he attracted a following for his strong resistance to European influences. Al-Afghani was energetic and charismatic, with a talent for getting access to powerful people in a variety of countries. But he also tended to be bumptious and seems to have disliked women.

More specifically, al-Afghani opposed British influence, whether in Afghanistan, Egypt, Sudan, or Iran. He was more ambivalent about the Russians. He wanted to see a revival in the Islamic world and believed that the message of Islam had to be revised in the light of reason, to adapt to different conditions in different times. He asserted that there was nothing inconsistent between Islam and reform, or Islam and science. The scientific and technological achievements of the West could be equaled or surpassed by a science based on Islam. But al-Afghani's attitude even to Islam was ambivalent, and his message was different for different audiences at different times. There are undercurrents of Shaykhism and mysticism in his thinking that probably reflect his traditional education. Yet he was a politician and a pragmatist rather than an ascetic or religious dogmatist, and he did not have a reputation for personal holiness. His flirtations with various contemporary governments in Islamic countries usually ended badly, but he became a major influence on later thinkers of Islamism—especially in Egypt and in Iran—though his ideas were too boldly innovative to be accepted by the classically trained ulema, whether Shi'a or Sunni.[15]

Al-Afghani returned to Iran in the 1880s at the invitation of the shah, but when they met there was no meeting of minds. Al-Afghani's ideas were too strongly anti-British for the shah, at least at that stage. Al-Afghani left again and returned again, but was eventually forced out of the country—to Iraq, in 1891—after pamphlets appeared, apparently under his influence, attacking concessions to foreigners.

From Iraq, al-Afghani was an influence in the campaign against the tobacco concession, corresponding in particular with the mojtahed Hajji Mirza Hasan Shirazi before the cleric ordered the tobacco boycott. Al-Afghani was active thereafter with the two main Persian newspapers printed overseas, *Qanun* and *Akhtar*, published in London and Istanbul, respectively. While he was in Istanbul in 1895, he was visited by a Persian ex-prisoner called Mirza Reza Kermani. They discussed future plans, and Kermani later returned to Iran. On May 1, 1896, Kermani shot and killed Naser od-Din Shah, having approached him with a petition while the shah was visiting the shrine of Shah Abd ol-Azim. Naser od-Din was buried there shortly afterward. Kermani was executed by public hanging the following August, and Al-Afghani died of cancer in 1897.

One aspect of the assassination illustrates the complexity of attitudes toward Jews in Iran. Apparently in his interrogation Kermani said that he had

had an earlier opportunity to kill the shah, while he was walking in a park, and had not done so—despite the fact that he could easily have escaped because he knew that a number of Jews had been in the park that day and that they would be blamed for the killing. Kermani did not want the assassination to be blamed on the Jews and did not want to be responsible for the riots and attacks on Jews that might follow.[16] For every anti-Semitic preacher or rabble-rouser, there were many educated, humane Iranians—clerics and others—for whom it was a matter of conscience to do what they could to help the Jews and other minorities, irrespective of the radicalism that might characterize their other beliefs.

The sudden death of the shah could have brought disorder and confusion. But for a time courtiers were able to conceal what had happened, and the Cossack Brigade kept order in Tehran until Naser od-Din's appointed successor, his son Mozaffar od-Din, could arrive from Tabriz and assume the throne.

The Slide to Revolution

Mozaffar od-Din was sick when he became shah and was surrounded by a gaggle of greedy courtiers and hangers-on. They had waited a long time with him in Tabriz for their chance to take over in Tehran, and the shah did not have the energy or force of personality to keep them in check. Initially he had a reforming prime minister, Amin od-Dowleh, who was especially active in improving education. He opened many new schools, including schools for girls. Censorship was lifted, and the shah permitted the formation of cultural and educational associations. Most of this new activity was independent of the state and had little financial cost to the government. But this shah had to pay more for the court than his father had, in addition to his own frequent and expensive trips to Europe for medical treatment. With the exception of the debt incurred after the cancellation of the tobacco concession, Naser od-Din had succeeded in keeping the state finances in order. But state debt accumulated under Mozaffar od-Din Shah, necessitating new loans from the Russians and the granting of new monopolistic concessions.

One of Prime Minister Amin od-Dowleh's money-raising innovations was the introduction of Belgian customs administrators, but in 1898 the shah dismissed him after he failed to secure a British loan. A new prime minister, Amin ol-Sultan, came in and set up Joseph Naus, a Belgian, as customs minister. As time went on Naus effectively became finance minister.[17]

The new customs arrangements were unpopular with many bazaar merchants, who seemed to be paying more than before—and also more than foreign traders. Not only that, they were paying the money to foreigners. The Russian loans were unpopular. The ulema disliked the new schools, which weakened their traditional grip on education. They also took a dim view of the shah's trips to Europe. The lifting of censorship and the freedom to form associations made criticism of the government easier and more public. This gratified the inclinations of a new intelligentsia, a diverse mix of liberal, nationalist, socialist, and Islamic reformist elements, all of whom tended to be hostile to the monarchy for different or overlapping reasons. It was a time of change and ferment, but also resentment and unease.

Among other concessions granted around this time, for fisheries and other rights, was one in 1901 to another British entrepreneur, William Knox D'Arcy. This concession was to prove much more important than was apparent initially: he was allowed to explore the southern part of the country for oil.

The British, feeling their loss of the latest round in The Great Game, decided in 1902/1903 to liaise with some members of the ulema, notably Ayatollah Abdollah Behbehani, to oppose the customs arrangements, including the Belgian administrators and the Russian loans. Money changed hands. There was agitation by the ulema in several cities, but it turned against foreigners and non-Muslims in general. Riots in Isfahan and Yazd in the summer of 1903 led to the killing of several Baha'is, and there were attacks on Jews and Christian minorities, too.

The following year the harvest was bad. Next, the outbreak of the Russo-Japanese war, followed by the 1905 revolution in Russia, interrupted imports from the north and made them more expensive. The significance of the outcome of the war, in which the Japanese inflicted a humiliating defeat on the

Russians (with the help of British-built battleships), was eagerly taken in by Iranian intellectuals, for whom it demonstrated that the dominance of the imperialist Europeans was not unshakeable. Meanwhile, the disruption of commerce meant that in northern cities like Tabriz and Tehran wheat prices in the early months of 1905 went up by ninety percent, and sugar prices went up by thirty-three percent. The government was hit hard, fiscally, because its customs revenues went down. The shah tried to secure another Russian loan and was offered £350,000, but the condition was that he should accept Russian commanders to lead all of his military units. Rejecting these terms, the shah instead raised internal tariffs and postponed payments to local creditors, increasing yet further the pressure on the bazaar merchants.[18] The government's financial problems also meant that the salaries of some ulema went unpaid.

In Tehran in June 1905 there was a demonstration in the mourning month of Moharram that fused economic and religious elements in a way that was to become typical. Two hundred shopkeepers and moneylenders closed their businesses and walked to the shrine of Shah Abd ol-Azim, protesting against the latest damaging government measures and demanding the removal of Monsieur Naus, the Belgian customs chief. The demonstrators passed around offensive pictures of Naus dressed as a mullah at a fancy-dress party. The shah, still sick and suffering, talked to the protestors and promised to satisfy their demands when he came back from his imminent trip to Europe. But this did not happen, and a more serious protest broke out in December 1905 after two sugar merchants from the Tehran bazaar were given beatings on the feet at the orders of the governor of Tehran; their offense had been charging too much for sugar. One of the men was a revered elder of the bazaar who had paid to repair the bazaar and three mosques. His protests—that he was not profiteering and that the prices were high because of the situation in Russia—availed him nothing.

Again the bazaar closed, and this time two thousand or more merchants, religious students, ulema, and others went—led by the mojtaheds Behbehani and Seyyed Mohammad Tabataba'i—to the shrine of Shah Abd ol-Azim and took sanctuary there.

From the shrine they issued their demands: removal of the governor who had ordered the beatings, enforcement of shari'a law, dismissal of Naus, and the establishment of a representative assembly or *adalatkhaneh* (House of Justice). Initially the government was defiant. But the bazaar stayed closed, and after a month the shah dismissed the governor and accepted the protestors' demands.

But there was no attempt to convene the House of Justice in the following months. Further street protests occurred in the summer of 1906, after the government had tried to take action against some radical preachers, and one of them—a *seyyed*, someone believed to be descended from the Prophet Mohammad—was shot dead by the police. This killing created a huge uproar. Ayatollahs Behbehani and Tabataba'i, accompanied by two thousand ulema and their students, left Tehran for Qom (then as now the main center for theological study in the country), and a larger group of merchants, mullahs, and others took sanctuary at the grounds of the summer residence of the British legation at Golhak, then north of Tehran. The British *chargé d'affaires* respected the Persian tradition of sanctuary, or *bast*, and the numbers there eventually reached fourteen thousand. Their accommodation and other needs were organized by the bazaar merchants' guilds. This meant that both the ulema and the bazaar were on strike, which effectively brought the capital to a standstill. Meanwhile, the Golhak compound became a hotbed of political discussion and speculation, with liberal and nationalist intellectuals joining in and addressing the assembled crowds. Many of these began to speak of the need to limit the powers of the shah by establishing a constitution (*mashruteh*), and the demand for a House of Justice became more specific, shifting to a call for a properly representative national assembly. Coordinated by the ulema, similar groups from the provinces sent many telegrams to the shah in support of these demands.

Mashruteh

On August 5, 1906, nearly a month after the first protestors took refuge in Golhak—and menaced by a potential mutiny among the Cossack Brigade, whom the shah had been unable to pay—Mozaffar od-Din Shah gave in and signed an order for the convening of a national assembly, or *Majles*. It convened for the first time in October 1906 and rapidly set about drafting a constitution, the central structure of which took the form of what were called the Fundamental Laws. They were ratified by Mozaffar od-Din Shah on December 30, and he died only five days later. The creation of a constitution was a major event, not just in Iranian history but also in regional and world history. In the 1870s in Turkey, a movement often called the Young Ottomans had established a kind of national assembly in an attempt to recast the Ottoman Empire as a constitutional monarchy, but the experiment had only lasted for a couple of years. The constitutional movement in Iran had a more enduring effect, and even though its revolution is often described as a failure, the Majles survived, and the movement's achievements influenced events throughout the rest of the twentieth century. And the initial success of the revolution was achieved by peaceful, dignified protest—almost wholly without bloodshed.

The Majles was elected on the basis of partial suffrage, on a two-stage system, and represented primarily the middle and upper classes that had headed the protests in the first place. The electors were landowners (only above a middling size), ulema and theological students, and merchants and bazaar-guild members with businesses of average size or above. In each region, these electors chose delegates to regional assemblies, and those delegates nominated the 156 Majles members (except in Tehran where they were elected directly). Numerically, the Majles was dominated by the bazaar merchants and guild elders, and it divided roughly into liberal, moderate, and royalist groupings—of which the moderates were the most numerous by a large margin. Ayatollahs Behbehani and Tabataba'i supported the moderates but were not themselves Majles members. Outside the Majles, both in the capital and in the regional centers, the elections stimulated the creation of further political societies (*anjoman*), some of which grew powerful and influenced the deliberations of the Majles itself. Some of these societies represented occupations, others regions like Azerbaijan, and still others ethnic or religious groups like the Jews and Armenians. There were political societies for women for the first time. A great upsurge in political activity and debate took place across the country, resulting in an expansion of the number of newspapers—from just six before the revolution to more than one hundred.[19] This upsurge was disturbing to the more tradition minded, especially the more conservative members of the ulema.

The Majles expected to govern, and to govern on new principles. The constitution (which remained formally in force until 1979, and was based on the Belgian constitution) stated explicitly that the shah's sovereignty derived from the people, as a power given to him in trust, not as a right bestowed directly by God. The power of the ulema, and their frame of thought, was also manifest in the constitution. Shi'ism was declared to be the state religion, shari'a law was recognized, clerical courts were given a significant role, and there was to be a five-man committee of senior ulema to scrutinize legislation passed by the Majles, to confirm its spiritual legitimacy (that is, until the reappearance of the Hidden Emam, whose proper responsibility this was). But the civil rights of non-Shi'a minorities were also protected, reflecting the involvement of many Jews, Babis, Armenians, and others in the constitutional project. Jews and Armenians had their own protected seats for their representatives in the Majles (though the first Jewish representative withdrew after encountering anti-Semitism from other members of the Majles, and the Jews thereafter chose Behbehani to represent them—another important example of a mojtahed sympathetic to the Jewish minority[20]).

All revolutions are about movement and change—that is obvious. They are also about leadership. The Constitutional Revolution marked the effective end of the Qajar era of government, and promised to usher in a period of government under more regular, legitimate, modern principles. Instead, for a variety of reasons, many of which had nothing to do with the revolution itself, it inaugurated a period of conflict and uncertainty. It was still a major change, a watershed. But in addition to that kind of change, most revolutions bring their own dynamic of change *within* the human groupings and systems of values involved in the revolution. The players in the revolution find their expectations, assumptions, and illusions challenged and, in some cases, subverted or overturned by the progress of the revolution itself. As with other revolutions, notably the French, the Constitutional Revolution in Iran provided a playground for the law of unintended consequences.

The prime revolutionary classes were the ulema and the bazaari merchants, whose motivations, if not their mode of expressing them, were at root conservative. They wanted the removal of foreign interference and a restoration of traditional patterns of commerce and religious authority. In the earliest phase of the revolution, the ulema were in charge. It was their authority that gave the protests authority, and it was their hierarchy and their system of relationships that organized and coordinated the protest. But once the protesters were installed in the British legation, it was a question of "where next," and the ulema had no clear answer. The simple removal of ministers and objectionable Qajar initiatives was plainly not enough; the shah's good faith could not be relied upon, and previous protests had failed to secure future good behavior. The call for a constitution was not just for a vague construct, the pet project of Westernizers; it was manifest that the country needed to commit itself to a permanent change of direction more definitive than anything tried before. The constitution really was an idea whose time had arrived—even the leaders of the ulema initially embraced it, despite its being clearly a Western-inspired idea. But their acceptance, whether or not they realized it straightaway, effectively handed over the initiative, and therefore the leadership, to the owners of the constitutional idea: the liberals and nationalists whose models were secular and Western. Many of these men were members of the state bureaucracy and were spiritual heirs of Amir Kabir. They were eager for reform of the state along Western lines, especially the state's finances, but also its education and justice systems. One could think of them as a new intelligentsia, suddenly grown into importance to rival the traditional intelligentsia, the ulema. They were to be found disproportionally among the Majles delegates from Azerbaijan and Tabriz, and one of their most prominent leaders, Seyyed Hasan Taqizadeh, was from that region. Their agenda extended beyond just a constitution. It soon became increasingly clear to many ulema that the revolution was taking a direction they had neither anticipated nor wanted.

Mozaffar od-Din Shah's successor was his son Mohammad Ali Shah, whose instincts were more autocratic than those of his father. Although he took an oath of loyalty to the constitution, he was resolved from the start to overturn it and restore the previous form of untrammeled monarchy. Through 1907 and the first half of 1908 the Majles passed measures for the reform of taxation and finance, as well as education and judicial matters. The latter were particularly disturbing to the ulema, because they saw their traditional role encroached upon.

The figure of Shaykh Fazlollah Nuri symbolized the change of mind among many of the ulema and their followers at this time. Nuri had been a prominent Tehrani mojtahed in 1905, supporting the protests of 1905–1906. But by 1907 he was arguing that the Majles and its plans were leading away from the initial aims of the protesters—that it was unacceptable that sacred law should be tampered with. It was also unacceptable that other religious groups be treated equally with Muslims before the law, and that the constitutionalists were importing "the customs and practices of the abode of unbelief" (i.e., the West). At one point Nuri led a group of supporters into bast at the shrine of Shah Abd ol-Azim. From there his attacks on the constitutionalists grew stronger, and he expressed open support for the monarchy against the Majles, which he denounced as illegitimate. He also railed against Jews, Bahais, and Zoroastrians, exaggerating their part in the constitutionalist movement. A group of clerics sent telegrams supporting him from the theological center in Najaf.[21] Other mojtaheds, like Tabataba'i, were more willing to accept Western ideas into the framework of political structures that were to govern human affairs in the absence of the Hidden Emam. But it is probably also fair to say that Nuri understood better than many of the ulema the direction that constitutionalism was leading, and from his perspective, the dangers of it. The general ferment of ideas precipitated by the revolution and the years of dissent before it had affected the ulema too. The ulema had never been a united bloc of opinion (no more than any group of intellectuals ever is). Eventually, another leading cleric, Khorasani, attacked Nuri from Najaf, declaring him to be a non-Muslim.

Just as the fighting around Troy in the *Iliad* is paralleled by the disputes of the gods on Mount Olympus, so the struggle between radicals and conservatives in Tehran was paralleled by a struggle between the mojtaheds in Najaf. Before 1906, the most eminent of these—the marja, or religious role model, for many Shi'a Muslims—was Mohammad Kazem Khorasani, who had supported the constitution and the line taken by Tabataba'i when the revolution came. But the ferment caused among the ulema by the revolution was such that as Nuri came to prominence in Tehran, Khorasani lost ground to a more conservative rival, Seyyed Mohammad Kazem Yazdi. This shift took concrete form at prayer: followers sat behind their chosen marja, and one account says that when the struggle was at its height only thirty or so still prayed behind Khorasani, while several thousand took their place behind Yazdi. Later on there was rioting in Najaf between the supporters of the different factions.[22]

In June 1908 the shah, deciding that feeling had moved far enough in his direction for him to act, launched the Cossack Brigade in an attack against the Majles. The troops fired shells at the building until the delegates gave in, and the assembly was closed. Many leading members were arrested and executed, while others, like Taqizadeh, escaped overseas. The shah's coup was successful in Tehran, but not in all the provinces. In Tabriz, delegates from the constitutionalist regional assembly and their supporters (notably the charismatic ex-brigand Sattar Khan) successfully held the city against the royal governor and his forces.

In 1907, newly allied to each other and to France, and concerned at Germany's burgeoning overseas presence, Britain and Russia had finally compounded their mutual suspicions and reached a treaty over their interests in Persia. The treaty showed no respect for the new conditions of popular sovereignty in the country, showing that the apparent British protection of the revolutionaries in their legation in 1906 had had little real significance. This new treaty divided Persia into three zones: a zone of Russian influence in the north, including Tabriz, Tehran, Mashhad, and Isfahan—most of the major cities; a British zone in the southeast, adjacent to the border with British India; and a neutral zone in the middle.

One consequence of the treaty was that the Russians, intolerant as ever of any form of popular movement, felt obliged to send in troops to restore Qajar rule in Tabriz after the shah's coup of June 1908. But some of the revolutionaries were able to escape to Gilan and continue their resistance with other locals there. In July 1909 they made a move on Tehran, coordinated with a move from the south, where revolutionaries in Isfahan had allied themselves with the Bakhtiari tribe and successfully taken over that city. Mohammad Ali Shah fled to the Russian legation, was deposed, and went into exile in Russia. He was replaced by his young son, Ahmad, though Ahmad was not crowned until July 1914.

The constitutionalists were back in control once more, but the revolution had entered a new, more dangerous phase. A new Majles came in (on a new electoral law, which yielded a more conservative assembly), but the divisions between the radicals and the conservatives had deepened. The violence that had reinstated the revolution also had its effect—many of the armed groups that had retaken the capital stayed on there. Several prominent Bakhtiaris took office in the government. The ulema were divided and many sided with the royalists, effectively rejecting the whole project of constitutionalism. But within a few days the leader of the conservative ulema, Nuri, was arrested, tried, and hanged for his alleged connections with the coup of June 1908. There were a series of assassinations carried out by both wings of political opinion—Behbehani was killed, and later Sattar Khan. The radicals—the democratic party in the Majles—found themselves denounced by bazaar crowds as heretics and traitors, and some of them, including Taqizadeh, were forced into exile. Rumors ran around that there was a Babi conspiracy behind the democrats, and there were attacks on the Jews—in Kermanshah in 1909, and Shiraz in 1910, instigated as usual by preachers and marginal mullahs. A later, serious riot against the Jews in Tehran in 1922 was put down by Reza Khan.[23] There was disorder in many provinces. It became impossible to collect taxation, tribal leaders took over in some areas, and brigands became commonplace. To try to address this, and to redress the influence of the Russian-officered Cossack Brigade, the Majles set up a *gendarmerie* trained by Swedish officers.

Prince Charming

Pushing forward despite these storms, the government appointed a young American, Morgan Schuster, as financial adviser. Schuster presented clear-sighted, wide-ranging proposals that addressed law and order and the government's control of the provinces, as well as more narrowly financial matters, and he began to put them into effect. Fulfilling Iranian (or at least some Iranian) aspirations in ways that British realpolitik had disappointed them, the United States in this phase looked like the partner Iran had long hoped to find in the West—antifeudal, anticolonial, modern, but not imperialist—a truly benevolent foreign power that would, for once, treat Iran with respect, as an agent in her own right, not as an instrument. People have suggested that there are only a limited number of stories in literature and folklore—that all the great variety ever told can be reduced to just a handful of archetypal plots. If that is so, and if we think of the British and the Russians in the nineteenth century as the ugly sisters, then at this time Morgan Schuster and his United States looked like Prince Charming. But the story was not to have a happy ending.

The Russians objected to Schuster's appointment of a British officer to head up a new gendarmerie, for tax collection, on the basis that it should not have been made within their sphere of influence without their consent, and the British acquiesced with their uglier sister. Schuster assessed, probably correctly, that the deeper Russian motive was to keep the Persian government's affairs in a state of financial bankruptcy, and thus in a position of relative weakness (as supplicant for Russian loans), the better to manipulate them. Any determined effort to put the government of Persia on a sound financial footing, as Schuster's reforms threatened to do, was a threat to Russian interests. The Russians presented an ultimatum: Schuster had to go. A group of women surged into the Majles to demand that the ultimatum be rejected, and the Majles agreed with them, insisting that the American should stay. But the Russians sent troops to Tehran and as they drew near, the Bakhtiaris and conservatives in the cabinet enacted what has been called a coup, and dismissed both Schuster and the Majles in December 1911.[24]

Schuster later wrote a book about his time in Iran called *The Strangling of Persia*, in which, despite what today reads sometimes with a rather prosy, evangelical style, he expressed his admiration for the moral courage and determination of the people he worked with in the period of the Constitutional Revolution. The book explains much about the revolution, and about Persia at the time. But it also illuminates Schuster's attitudes about the country and the reasons he and, by extension, the United States were so highly regarded by Iranians. He wrote of the Majles that it

> . . . more truly represented the best aspirations of the Persians than any other body that had ever existed in that country. It was as representative as it could be under the difficult circumstances which surround the institution of the Constitutional Government. It was loyally supported by the great mass of the Persians, and that alone was sufficient justification for its existence. The Russian and British Governments, however, were constantly instructing their Ministers at Teheran to obtain this concession or to block that one, failing utterly to recognise that the days had passed in which the affairs, lives and interests of twelve millions of people were entirely in the hands of an easily intimidated and willingly bribed despot.[25]

It would be incorrect to put all the blame for the outcome of the Constitutional Revolution onto the foreigners. The revolution had brought forward violence and rancor between the groups represented in the Majles, and the divisions contributed to the events of December 1911. One could speculate, not least on the basis of the use of terror by other revolutionaries in other revolutions, that if the revolution had not been cut off at that point, the violence might well have gotten a great deal worse, possibly with very damaging long-term effects. But that is to speculate too far. We do not know how it would have turned out. Revolutions may have family resemblances, but they have no timetable and no blueprint, and the Constitutional Revolution arose out of distinctive and unique political and social circumstances. There were, on the other hand, many positive elements in the situation as it was before December 1911 above all that at last, as Schuster pointed out, the country had a truly popular government, and that it was addressing as a priority the fundamental problem of the fiscal structures. Revolutionaries and people showed a strong solidarity against external meddling, a powerful enthusiasm for constitutional government, and for their elected Majles. This enthusiasm had been strong enough to overturn one coup already, and was strong enough to sustain the principles of constitutionalism later, too, notably in 1919–1920. It gives the lie to those who condescendingly suggest that Iran, or Middle Eastern countries in general, are somehow culturally unsuited to constitutional, representative, or (later) democratic government. When those forms of government were offered, Iranians grabbed them with both hands, as other peoples invariably have in other times and places.

Persia, Oil, Battleships, and the First World War

Through this period, even before the British legation had been used for sanctuary by the protesters in 1906, new developments had been at work to reshape Britain's attitude to Iran. Since at least the turn of the century, Britain's traditional rivalries with France and Russia had been replaced by an awareness of the danger of the growing power and belligerence of Germany. France and Russia allied with each other (by implication, against Germany) in 1894; Britain and France allied in 1904; and Britain, France, and Russia allied all together in 1907 (the Triple Entente). Particularly sharp for Britain was the German program of naval shipbuilding over this period. Since the Battle of Trafalgar in 1805, Britain had maintained an unrivaled dominance of the world's oceans—an essential support to her world empire. But under Emperor Wilhelm II the Germans began building modern warships at a rapid rate, threatening the Royal Navy's dominance. British shipyards began to turn out ships to match the German program. In 1906 the British launched HMS *Dreadnought,* which was said to have rendered all previous warships obsolete by its combination of speed and the coordinated firepower of its simplified armament. In 1912 the British navy switched from coal to oil as fuel; oil burned more efficiently and was less bulky. But whereas

Britain had huge domestic reserves of coal, oil had to be sought elsewhere. Under the terms of the D'Arcy concession, large quantities of oil had been discovered—the first oil to be found in the Middle East—in 1908 near Ahwaz in Khuzestan, in southwest Iran.

Persia had for decades been of importance to Britain for the sake of the northwest frontier of India, perhaps of declining importance, especially after the Triple Entente. But now the oil reserves of Khuzestan became vital for the security of the whole British Empire. Britain's sphere of influence according to the agreement with Russia was quickly extended westward to include the rest of the Persian Gulf coast and the oil fields. The Anglo-Persian Oil Company was formed to exploit the oil, and in 1914 the British government bought up a majority share in it.

Partly because of the oil, but also because Britain's rivals fell away one by one over the following years, Britain gradually became the dominant external power in Iran in the decade that followed 1911. It was a period of deepening chaos, poverty, and suffering. The Russians fired on revolutionaries in several of the cities in their northern zone in the aftermath of the coup of December 1911, notably in Mashhad. There protesters took sanctuary in the shrine of the Emam Reza, only for the Russian artillery to shell the shrine itself—an act of sacrilege and humiliation that was deeply felt throughout the country. The British Embassy reported in 1914 that the central government had little influence on events outside Tehran.[26] The British and the Russians exercised a degree of control in their respective zones, but their grip was far from absolute. This was shown by the success of the *Jangali* movement in Gilan (*Jangal* means forest, an allusion to the dense forests of the Caspian coast) under the charismatic leader Kuchek Khan, which continued to sustain some of the spirit of independence that had inspired the revolution.

The revolution is usually said to have ended in 1911, but this date is rather artificial. The constitution established by the revolution was not overturned, and a new Majles convened in December 1914. The spirit of the revolution and the ideals and expectations of the constitutionalists were not crushed. They resurfaced again and again in the events that followed. The revolution was a watershed in the history of Iran, as the episode in which previously more or less inchoate strands of thinking and opinion came together in concrete political form, shifted, changed, and acquired permanent significance. It also had, with the focus of popular debate in Tehran and the role of regional assemblies in sending delegates to the Majles, a centralizing and unifying effect, strengthening the nationalist sympathies of many of those delegates. The revolts in Gilan, and later Azerbaijan, had national, not separatist aims. There could be no going back to the pre-1906 state of things.

During the First World War, despite the government's declaration that Persia was neutral, the country was divided up by the different players that maintained troops in different sectors. There were the Russians in the north, but also the Jangalis. In Tehran there were the troops controlled, at least nominally, by the government—the Cossack Brigade and the Swedish gendarmerie. Set against the Russians were the Ottomans and their allies, the Germans. The Ottomans made an incursion into the country in the west and north. For the most part none of these armed elements was strong enough to control large areas of territory or to establish overall supremacy. Most of the fighting was low in intensity and indecisive. But in the northwest the Ottomans and the Russians fought each other more aggressively, doing much damage to the villages and the local population. A revived rump of the constitutionalist movement was set up under Ottoman and German protection in Kermanshah, and for a period in 1915 prospects for this movement looked good. The Ottomans were doing well in the north, and the Germans, who were allied with the Qashqai and others in the south, also made considerable progress. The British pulled out of their consulates in Hamadan, Isfahan, Yazd, and Kerman.

But in the south the British set up a force called the South Persia Rifles in the spring of 1916, primarily to protect the oil fields. They also had a close relationship with the Bakhtiari, as well as with some of the Arab tribes of Khuzestan and those of the Khamseh confederation. Despite the skillful guerrilla war masterminded by the brilliant German adventurer Wilhelm Wassmuss, who has been compared to Lawrence of Arabia, the

British slowly regained the upper hand, and the situation in Iran, as in the wider war, turned against the Germans and the Ottomans. This was despite the Russians and their troops being removed from the equation after the October revolution of 1917. By the time of the armistice in November 1918, Wassmuss was captured near Isfahan, and the British were resurgent in Persia.

At the end of the war, the country was in a terrible state. There had been a severe famine in the years 1917 and 1918, partly as a result of the dislocation of trade and agricultural production caused by the war. The effect of the Russian Revolution on trade was devastating. Before 1914, sixty-five percent of foreign trade had been with Russia, but this fell to five percent by the end of the First World War. The famine was followed by a serious visitation of the global influenza epidemic in 1918–1919, and typhus killed many as well. Brigands were common. Although there were British troops in several parts of the country, many tribal groups had taken up arms, and the Jangalis were still in control of most of Gilan. Having begun as pro-constitutionalist, the Jangalis came under Russian Bolshevik influence. In the summer of 1918, with the help of some Bolsheviks, they had forced a British force under General Lionel Dunsterville to retreat from a confrontation in Gilan. By this time Dunsterville had learned rather more about the Jangalis than he had known in January 1918, before he took up his duties in Persia, when he wrote in his diary,

> I get a wire to say that Enzeli, my destination on the Caspian Sea, has been seized by some horrid fellows called Jangalis (a very suggestive name) who are intensely anti-British and are in the pay of [the] Germans.[27]

But the political dislocation (if not the economic distress) was less grave than it might appear. The devolved rule of local tribal leaders had, after all, been pretty much the normal state of affairs under the Qajars. Some accounts of the period suggest that there was a disillusionment with constitutionalism and a yearning for strong government. But it is not fully clear that either was a general mood, nor that the two necessarily went together.[28]

In the aftermath of the First World War, Britain was juggling a series of complex and weighty problems over the territory of the Middle East, the resolution of which would be fateful for the future in several different contexts. The size and shape of postwar Turkey had to be resolved, as well as the nature and borders of the post-Ottoman states in Palestine, Syria, and Iraq. The British were concerned also to contain, or if possible overturn, the new communist regime in Russia. All of this came at a time of greatly reduced financial means, as a result of the crippling debt incurred during the war, and with the United States under Woodrow Wilson preaching a new philosophy of international relations—essentially a democratic principle of self-determination—that appeared to undermine the very foundation of British imperialism. Iranian nationalists welcomed Wilson's principles, and again were encouraged to think of the United States as Iran's great hope among the great powers. But like other Middle Eastern states, notably Egypt, representatives of the Iranian government were refused access to the peace negotiations at Versailles.

Anglo-Persian Non-Agreement and Reza Khan

So Britain, having won the war and having achieved supremacy in Persia, was overstretched—too many calls on too scarce means, and with important distractions elsewhere. The British foreign secretary at the time, Lord Curzon, knew Persia well and had written a thoughtful, magisterial book, *Persia and the Persian Question,* on the basis of his travels in 1889–1890. But although that book was sympathetic to the people of Iran in many respects, Curzon seems to have overlooked some of its guiding principles, and to have failed to absorb the significance of the constitutionalist period.[29] In 1919 he proposed—or, rather, he attempted to force through—an Anglo-Persian Agreement that would have reduced Persia to the status of a protectorate (parallel with the mandate arrangements being set up at the same time for Iraq and Palestine), with the military and fiscal responsibilities of government given over to the British. The agreement was rather like earlier concession agreements writ large: security guarantees, promises of infrastructure development for the Persians, and a dollop of cash (a loan of two million pounds sterling—much of which would have been absorbed by the salaries of various British officers, officials, and advisers).

The government of the young Ahmad Shah obligingly accepted the agreement (it was signed in August 1919), but when its details became known it was thoroughly unpopular, over the whole range of opinion from democrats to the ulema. Although the agreement might have yielded some benefits for the development of the country, it was further discredited by the plentiful bribes with which the British were rumored to be smoothing its passage. All sectors of opinion condemned the agreement, from socialists and nationalist former members of the Majles to leading mojtaheds blasting it by telegram from Karbala. A revolt broke out in Azerbaijan, asserting democrat constitutionalist principles and renaming the province Azadistan ("freedom land"); it was not put down until September. The shah's government sent five leading members of the Majles into internal exile, but gradually even the government signatories of the agreement began to recognize the opprobrium heaped on it from all sides, and avoided convening a Majles to ratify it—without which it could not, under the constitution, be legally applied. The British tried to apply the provisions of the agreement willy-nilly, bringing in British officers to command army units, but succeeded only in hastening the collapse of the government and the resignation of the first minister in June 1920.[30]

In London, Lord Curzon still expected to be able to force through the Anglo-Persian Agreement. But local British commanders on the ground thought differently—to them and everyone else in Iran, the agreement looked like a dead duck. The British forces that had been commanded by Dunsterville—forces which had been resisted successfully by the Jangalis and their Bolshevik allies—were commanded from October 1920 by General Ironside. Both men embodied certain Edwardian virtues, and both had literary connections: Dunsterville was the model for Kipling's Stalky, and it has been suggested that Ironside inspired John Buchan's hero Richard Hannay.

The British troops (now based in Qazvin) were unpopular with the Persians and, after their retreat from Gilan, were somewhat discredited—a dangerous combination not calculated to overawe nationalist dislike. Ironside was an intelligent, tough, decisive career soldier and had been given the responsibility of helping reequip the Cossack Brigade, now grown to division strength, which had also recently withdrawn from the Caspian coast to a position near Qazvin. He decided almost as he took up his appointment to exceed his orders. With the reluctant agreement of the shah, he dismissed the remaining Russian officers of the Cossack corps, judging that although the Persian troops were good, sound soldiers, the Russian officers were demoralized, anti-British, and susceptible to Bolshevik infiltration. When Curzon found out, he did not approve, but by then it was too late. Ironside reassured the Persian Cossacks that he had no intention of imposing British officers on them, and Persian officers were appointed. Acting through his second-in-command, Lieutenant Colonel Smyth, Ironside then selected a former sergeant, Reza Khan, as the most effective soldier, and arranged matters so that Reza Khan became the de facto commander. Ironside was worried that, as time went on, the position of the British would deteriorate. The Bolsheviks might move on Tehran, and if that happened, the Persian Cossacks might side with them. He thought that perhaps it would be better to let the Cossacks take over while the British were still in a strong position. The British troops could then make a peaceful withdrawal. Shortly afterward, in January 1921, Ironside wrote in his diary,

> Personally, I am of opinion that we ought to let these people go before I disappear. . . . In fact, a military dictatorship would solve our troubles and let us out of the country without any trouble at all.[31]

The whole question of Britain's role at this point is controversial, but there is no direct evidence of a plot as such. The idea that the world of politics revolves only through the agency of plots and conspiracies is dangerously misleading. Ironside knew what he wanted—he wanted British troops out of Persia (he was personally due to leave in April, but his departure date was brought forward to February 18)—and he had a lighter touch. All he really had to do was let the Cossacks understand that the British would not intervene if they acted against their government. He felt no pressing need to consult London or the British minister in Tehran. Ironside had an eye for an able soldier; events were to show that he also had a canny political sense, and his choice of Reza Khan showed that, too. Reza Khan also proved to have a sharper political sense than expected, or than ordinary soldiers are usually credited with.

On February 16, 1921, Reza Khan marched twenty-five hundred of his Cossacks from their camp near Qazvin toward Tehran. On February 21, he was able to take them into the capital without opposition, and the shah allowed him to set up a new government headed by a nationalist journalist, Seyyed Zia Tabataba'i—not to be confused with the mojtahed Seyyed Mohammad Tabataba'i, who had died in 1918. Reza Khan became Sardar-e Sepah, commander of the army. A few months later Tabataba'i fell from power, having alienated both the shah, by reducing the court, and Reza Khan, by proposing the appointment of British officers to the army. Reza Khan had managed in the interim to make new friends and broaden his support. Now he enhanced his position and became Minister for War.

Later in the same year Reza Khan moved against the Jangalis in Gilan and quickly overcame them, their Soviet allies having departed under the terms of a new treaty with the Persian government. Their leader, Kuchek Khan, took refuge in the mountains but died in the snow; when his body was found his head was brought to Tehran. After this important early success, Reza Khan's priorities turned to regularizing state revenue, strengthening the armed forces, and enforcing government control over the whole territory of Persia. This last task meant tough action against tribes like the Bakhtiari and the Lors, and later the Shahsevan in Azerbaijan and the Turkmen in the northeast. He also acted against one of the Arab tribes allied with the British in the southwest, and was again successful. These actions were popular with most Persians because the tribes had so often facilitated foreign interventions. Also there was the ancient, uneasy hostility between tribesmen on the one hand, and the peasants and townspeople on the other.

The fourth Majles convened in 1921, and Reza Khan was able to keep them broadly supportive of his reform programs by allying with conservative elements. In 1923 he made himself prime minister, and the shah went on what was to prove an extended holiday in Europe. At the end of the year, a fifth Majles convened, later approving a controversial initiative to introduce conscription, after the ulema had been conciliated with an exemption for religious students. In 1924, Reza Khan (inspired by the example of Atatürk's reforms in Turkey) encouraged a movement to create a republic, and acquired four Rolls-Royce armored cars to help him keep order in Tehran. But he misjudged the mood of the country and had to stage a resignation for a time, abandoning the republican project. In 1925, Reza Khan consolidated his support by visiting Najaf on pilgrimage, temporarily concealing his Westernizing intentions. He also took the name Pahlavi, which resonated with nationalists as the name of the Middle Persian language of pre-Islamic times. The Majles deposed Ahmad Shah and the Qajar dynasty in October, after Ahmad Shah had let it be known that he intended to return to the country. Shortly before the end of the year, a constituent assembly agreed to a changeover from the Qajar to the Pahlavi dynasty, and Reza was crowned shah early in 1926. Ahmad Shah never did return and died in Paris in 1930.

Reza Khan's rise to power was facilitated in 1921 by local British commanders for their own reasons, but it is incorrect to see his success as a success for British foreign policy, or him as a British stooge. On the contrary, Ironside supported an action by Reza Khan precisely because he perceived current British policy to have failed. Reza Khan took advantage of Ironside's willingness to give him his chance, but made no commitment to future pro-British alignment, and there is no indication that Ironside expected or asked for any such guarantees. The coup of 1921 and its aftermath came about as a result of a temporary coincidence of interests.

As for the people of Iran, it is not entirely correct to see Reza Khan's success as the outcome of the desire of the people for a strong man on a white horse to overcome political chaos, after a failed democratic experiment. The period 1921–1926 has been compared with the period of regency leading up to Nader Shah's coronation in 1736, in which he too prepared the way with military successes; but the comparison, though attractive, is not entirely apposite. The Constitutional Revolution had aimed, among other things, at modernization, centralization, strong government, and an end to foreign meddling in the country. Reza Khan became shah in 1925–1926 with the connivance of the Majles, because they judged he would fulfill those purposes, where earlier attempts by others had failed. He largely justified their confidence in him. But his reforming success was achieved at the expense of liberal, representative government. He was to an extent the nemesis of the Constitutional Revolution, but he was also the child of it.[32]

7

The Pahlavis and the Revolution of 1979

Is it not passing brave to be a king
And ride in triumph through Persepolis?

—Christopher Marlowe

Reza Khan was about forty-two when he became Sardar-e Sepah after the coup in 1921. Although there was much supposition and mythmaking after he became shah, little is known for sure of his origins beyond that he was born in the village of Alasht in the thickly wooded Savad Kuh region of Mazanderan. Some have suggested that his family had Turkic origins, others Pashtun. It seems his father died when he was still an infant, and his mother brought him to Tehran, where he grew up in her brother's household. Through the uncle's connections with the Cossack Brigade, the young Reza was able to enlist with them when he was fifteen. He grew up to be tall and tough, with a grim expression and a heavy jaw. Some of the better-educated technocrats that he appointed to fulfill his modernization program found his manner and speech embarrassingly crude, and some sneered at his lack of culture. But none would have done so to his face, and most found his presence daunting.[1]

Man of Action

Reza Khan's attitudes and motivations emerge above all from his actions. He came to power not just to be shah or to preside, as the Qajars had done—he disdained their ineffectual style of rule. The Pahlavi monarchy was an odd kind of monarchy, with no real roots in tradition. It was established only after Reza Khan had failed to set up a republic. To him, being shah was a means to an end, not an end in itself. And his underlying purpose was to control the country, to make the country strong, to develop it so that it could be truly independent, to modernize it so that it could deal with the great powers on an equal basis, to have a strong army to resist foreign interventions, and to impose order internally so that, as in other modern countries, the state enjoyed sole control. These aims, and the autocratic methods used to realize them, reflected his military background and the Russian influence he had lived with in the Cossack Brigade. Initially he had to compromise with the Majles, but time would show that he was no friend to free political expression. In addition, he had a model, Kemal Atatürk, who after a successful military career had established himself as the supreme authority in Turkey on secular, nationalist principles, backed by a strong army. With great determination, Atatürk had set about a plan for state-directed industrialization and economic development. Much has been made of Reza Shah's connections with fascism, but this was the age of dictators, whether fascist, communist, or otherwise. Reza Shah had little need to look further afield than Turkey—not in the 1920s, at least.

In 1926 Iran was still a country of peasant villages, tribes, and small towns (in that order), with little industry and an overall population of only twelve million people, the overwhelming majority of whom were illiterate. Patterns of trade and the economic life in the bazaars had adapted to the wider world economy; in Tehran and other major cities, there were some of the superficial trappings of modernity—streetlights, motor vehicles, and paving. But in the great expanses beyond, little had changed since the time of Nader Shah.

Among the transformations imposed by Reza Shah, the first and most central was the expansion of the army. The army was the shah's highest priority and greatest interest, and most of the other developments he imposed can be explained in terms of the support they gave to the goal of making the army strong, efficient, and modern. The plan for an army of five divisions, with ten thousand men per division, was announced in January 1922, but problems with conscription, finance, and equipment persisted, and the force was still twenty percent understrength in 1926. Despite approval of the conscription law in June 1925, there was great opposition to its implementation, especially among tribal groups. The measure was not properly applied until 1930, and not imposed properly on the tribes until the mid-1930s or later. But by the late 1930s the army stood at more than one hundred thousand men, with reserves theoretically taking potential strength up to four hundred thousand.[2]

Despite these figures, the efficiency of the forces (outside Tehran, where the standard of the central division was rather higher) was not impressive. For local actions against the tribes, provincial commanders still recruited tribal contingents on an ad hoc basis, as had been done for centuries. Morale of the ordinary conscripts was low. They were not well paid—most of the large sums spent on the army went to buy equipment, including tanks (from the Skoda works in Czechoslovakia), artillery (from Sweden), and aircraft (an air force of 154 airplanes by 1936), as well as rifles and other material. Forty percent of government expenditure went to the army, even in the 1920s. Later it received almost all of the growing income from oil, though the overall proportion of state revenue spent on defense fell as the size of the total budget rose.[3] From 1922 to 1927, state finances were organized by another American, Arthur Millspaugh (after negotiations in which the Iranians had tried to get Schuster to return). But although their relationship was initially good, and the American had public approval to a degree no Briton or other foreigner could have expected, the shah eventually grew resentful at the restrictions Millspaugh placed on his military spending. They argued, and Reza Pahlavi declared: "There can't be two shahs in this country."[4] Millspaugh's position became impossible, and he resigned in 1927.

A second major effort by the new regime was in the improvement of transport infrastructure. In 1927 there were an estimated thirty-one hundred miles of roads fit for motor transport, nearly a third of which had been built by foreign troops during the First World War; by 1938 there were some fifteen thousand miles of roads. Whereas in 1925 Iran had only about one hundred fifty miles of railways, by 1938 there were a little more than one thousand. But by that time, the less expensive highway transport was tending to supplant rail.

Reza Shah invested in industry a similar amount to that invested in railways. This was especially true of industries aimed at substituting domestic production for imports—textiles, tobacco, sugar, and other food and drink products. Over half of the investment came from private capital.[5] It was not a huge transformation by comparison with what was being achieved in Turkey—let alone Stalin's Russia. But it was impressive, nonetheless, especially given the low base point from which Reza Shah had started, and the failures of the past.

More impressive, and in the long run probably more important, was the expansion of education. Total school attendance went from 55,131 in 1922 to 457,236 in 1938. In 1924 there were 3,300 pupils in secondary schools; by 1940 the number had risen to 28,200. The school system was far from universal, and it neglected almost all the rural population (though there was a small but successful initiative for schools in tribal areas). The system has been criticized for being overly narrow and mechanical, teaching through rote learning and lacking in intellectual stimulation. But this reflected its main purpose: to educate efficient and unimaginative army officers and bureaucrats. Reza Shah did not want to educate a new generation of free thinkers who would oppose his rule and encourage others to do so. But as elsewhere, education proved a slippery thing, and many educated in this way nonetheless went on to dispute Reza Shah's supremacy in just the way he had sought to avoid. Through the 1930s, a small but significant elite were sent on government-funded scholarships to study at universities abroad (especially in France), and in 1935 the foundation was laid for a university in Tehran. In 1940 there were 411 graduates, and in 1941 the university awarded its first doctorates.[6]

From the point at which he became shah, Reza inexorably strengthened his own position and the autocratic nature of his regime. Although he came to power with the agreement of the Majles, opponents like Mohammad Mossadeq (a future prime minister) and Seyyed Hasan Modarres (the leading representative of the ulema in the Majles) had predicted that he would erode the liberal elements of the constitution. Mossadeq held firm to his position and was later imprisoned. But after Reza Shah's coronation, Modarres and others attempted to make a compromise with him that would leave some space for the Majles, and for constitutional government. Constitutionalists took office as ministers, including, later, Hasan Taqizadeh, who had been prominent in 1906–1911. But few of them had happy careers in office. A series of ministers were sacked, imprisoned, or banished, sometimes for no clear reason other than the shah's suspicions—or his need to assert his personal authority. Modarres himself did not accept office, but his compromise failed, he was arrested in 1928, sent in custody to Khorasan, and was murdered there at prayer in 1938. Loyal ministers such as Teymurtash, Firuz, and Davar were arrested and murdered in prison or induced to commit suicide. Taqizadeh was fortunate to be sent overseas in semi-banishment instead.

Writers and poets also suffered, as censorship was tightened and freedom of expression curtailed, strangling the burst of literary output that had emerged in the early decades of the century.

Sadeq Hedayat was one of the most distinguished writers of the twentieth century in Iran. Born in 1903 in Tehran, he studied in France in the 1920s. As a young man, he became an enthusiast for a romantic Iranian nationalism that laid much of the blame for Iran's problems on the Arab conquest of the seventh century. His short stories and novellas—*Talab-e Amorzesh* (*Seeking Absolution*), *Sag-e Velgard* (*Stray Dog*), and his best-known, *Buf-e Kur* (*The Blind Owl*)—combined the every day, the fantastic, and the satirical. Hedayat's work rejected religion, superstition, and Arabic influence in Iranian life (sometimes in unpleasantly vivid terms) but in an innovative, modernist style that through its relentlessly honest observation of everyday life reaches the highest standards of world literature. He translated Kafka, Chekhov, and Sartre into Persian and was also an enthusiast for the poetry of Omar Khayyam. Hedayat committed suicide in Paris in 1951; his works were banned in their entirety by the Ahmadinejad government in 2006.[7]

Another literary figure to die in 1951 was Mohammad Taqi Bahar, himself a poet but also the great critic of Persian poetry. Putting forward a theoretical structure for the literary history of Persia, Bahar identified in particular a revival (*bazgasht*) in the latter part of the eighteenth century, in which poets deliberately rejected the Safavid style in favor of a return to the style of the tenth and eleventh centuries. In Bahar's own lifetime another new wave of poetic style came in, linked like the innovative prose of Hedayat to the change in attitudes in the period of the Constitutional Revolution. The first great exemplar of this change was Nima Yushij, who lived from 1895 to 1959. Nima wrote in a new way, breaking many of the rules of classical Persian poetic form. He used new vocabulary and new images drawn from direct observation of nature. For many years his freer style of poetry was resisted by the more tradition minded. But later it found acceptance, becoming the model for younger poets—notably Forugh Farrokhzad (1935–1967).[8]

Reza Shah visited Atatürk in Turkey in 1934, and the visit symbolized the parallels between the two regimes. The nationalist, modernizing, secularizing, Westernizing features shared by both were obvious. Reza Shah's education policy supported the founding of girls' schools, and he banned the veil. He wanted Iran and the Iranians to look Western and modern—men, too, had to wear Western dress, and at one point he decreed that all should wear Western headgear, with the result that the streets were suddenly awash with fedoras and bowler hats.[9] As in Turkey, the shah set up a language reform to remove words not of Persian origin, and to replace them with Persian words. Then, in order to differentiate his regime from the decadent style and national humiliations of the Qajar period, in 1935 he ordered that foreign governments should drop the name "Persia" in official communications and use instead the name "Iran"—the ancient name that had always been used by Iranians themselves. In 1927/1928 he ended the capitulations, according to which, since the treaty of Turkmanchai, foreigners had enjoyed extraterritorial privilege in Iran, being free from the jurisdiction of the Iranian authorities.

But Reza Shah did not pursue the Westernizing agenda as far as Atatürk. For example, despite the language reform, there was no change of alphabet to the Roman script, as was done in Turkey. And although he achieved the removal of some of the worst abuses of foreign interference in Iran, he eventually had to accept the continuation of British exploitation of oil in the south—a deal that brought a poor return (sixteen percent of profits) in proportion to the real value of such an important national resource. In 1928, the court minister Teymurtash—the shah's closest adviser at the time—wrote to the Anglo-Persian Oil Company, announcing that the terms of the original D'Arcy oil concession had to be renegotiated. The negotiations swung back and forth over the next few years, and in 1932 the shah intervened, unilaterally canceling the concession. The British sent additional ships to the Persian Gulf, and took the case to the International Court of Justice in The Hague. Shortly afterward the shah, frustrated by the failure of the negotiations, sacked Teymurtash, imprisoned him, and in October 1933 had him murdered there. Eventually a deal with Britain was patched up, only modestly increasing the Iranian government's share of the profits to twenty percent. The duration of the concession was extended to 1993.[10]

Atatürk's Turkey was not subject to any such foreign exploitation. And whereas Atatürk retained his personal popularity to the end, by the end of the 1930s Reza Shah had alienated almost all of the support he had been given when he took power. The ulema had seen much of what they had most feared in the Constitutional Revolution—especially in education and the law—enacted without their being able to prevent it. By the end of the 1930s, their prestigious and lucrative role as judges and notaries had been reformed away. They hated the rulings on Western dress and the veil, and a protest against these developments in 1935 had led to a massacre in the shrine precincts of the Emam Reza at Mashhad: several hundred people were machine-gunned by the shah's troops, further deepening the regime's unpopularity.[11] The bazaar merchants disliked the state monopolies on various items that the shah had brought in to boost state revenue. Liberals and intellectuals were alienated by the repression, censorship, and the closure of newspapers, let alone the murders in prison of popular politicians. There was even dissent within the army. So when a new war brought a new crisis, Reza Shah had few friends left.[12]

New Masks, Same Old Ugly Sisters

It is usually said that the British and the Russians took over in Iran in 1941 because Reza Shah had shown himself to be pro-German and pro-Nazi, and the Allies feared that if they did not move in, then the Germans would. But the situation was more complex than that. At the time of the Anglo-Soviet intervention of 1941, no German armed forces were threatening Iran directly. The German push to take Baku and the Caucasus oil fields only came later, in the summer of 1942. The shah himself, despite having encouraged the Germans earlier to a certain extent, had been resisting German influence within the country.

But when Britain and the Soviet Union were thrown into alliance in 1941 by Hitler's invasion of Russia (in June), Britain's position in the Middle East was looking uncertain. The crucial interests for Britain were the Suez Canal and the Iranian oil fields. Having defeated an Italian effort to break into Egypt from Libya in 1940, British forces in North Africa were put on the defensive by the arrival of Rommel and the German Afrika Korps. In the spring of 1941 they had to retreat back toward Alexandria, leaving a garrison to be surrounded in Tobruk. At about the same time, in April, there was an anti-British revolt in Iraq, encouraged by the Germans and assisted by Luftwaffe aircraft. This necessitated an intervention by British troops, who completed their occupation of the country by the end of May. In June, rattled by these developments, Britain sent British and Free French troops into Lebanon and Syria to unseat the Nazi-aligned Vichy French governments there.

Seen in that context, the British and Soviet takeover of Iran in August 1941 looks more like part of a rounding-out of strategic policy in the region, at a particularly dangerous and uncertain moment for the Allies—part of the inexorable totalizing logic of the war itself. But Iran did have major significance in another aspect. Hitler's successes—from Norway to Denmark to Poland to France to Yugoslavia to Greece, in 1940 and the early part of 1941—meant that the avenues for Britain and the Soviet Union to support each other were restricted to the hazardous Arctic route to Murmansk in the north, or some southern alternative. And once Hitler's *Barbarossa* offensive had swept all before it in Byelorussia and the Ukraine, the Soviets urgently needed supplies from the West to help equip the new armies to replace the Soviet troops that had been herded off into German camps or slave-labor factories as prisoners of war. The route from the Persian Gulf to the Caspian, arduous and long though it was, appeared to be an answer. By the end of the war, more than five million tons had been taken to Russia through Iran, by both road and rail—though this was a relatively small part of the overall effort.

Reza Shah had flirted with the Nazi regime in the 1930s, and German diplomats had encouraged what they saw as the shah's Aryanization of the language. Through the 1930s more German technicians and engineers arrived in Iran—the shah favored them as an alternative to the British, who were disliked and suspected by many Iranians. But the shah was as hostile to possible German meddling in Iran as he was to foreign meddling of any other kind. He also had a strong dislike for any nascent political movements—fascist *or* communist—that might oppose his government. A small group of apparently pro-fascist students were arrested in 1937, and their leader was later murdered in prison. In 1940 the police shot a prominent Zoroastrian in the street because his son had made pro-Nazi broadcasts in Germany. A group of Marxists were also arrested in 1937; most of them were given harsh prison sentences, and later went on to form the pro-Communist Tudeh party.[13] These developments reflected the bitter polarization of politics between fascism and communism in Europe at the time. Some of these radicals were from that small elite who had been educated at European universities at the government's expense. An upsurge of ugly anti-Semitic journalism contributed to a period of increased anxiety for Iranian Jews in the 1930s—and may have contributed to an increase in Jewish emigration to Palestine—but the notion of a rising tide of pro-Nazi and pro-German feeling among people and government before August 1941 has sometimes been overstated. The historian Ervand Abrahamian has suggested that the Allied intervention may have been not so much to remove a pro-Nazi shah as to forestall a pro-German coup *against* the shah, as had happened in Iraq.[14]

The Allied demand that Iran should expel German nationals was nonetheless the immediate *casus belli*. After the demand was refused, the Allied invasion of Iran in August 1941 met only token opposition from the army on which Reza Shah had spent so much attention and money (this is where a comparison with Nader Shah finally breaks down), and after three days he ordered his troops to cease further resistance. British and Soviet forces met in central Iran and entered Tehran on September 17, 1941.

The shah abdicated in favor of his son, Mohammad Reza, and the Allies maintained their control over the country until after the end of the war in 1945. It seems that Reza Shah's relationship with his son had been something like that between a senior officer and a subordinate. Mohammad Reza Pahlavi was educated in Switzerland in the 1930s, which did not bring him any closer to his parents or to the people he was going to rule. Mohammad Reza had a sharp mind but was socially shy and diffident—a legacy from his education and his relationship with his harsh father.

The Allies were the immediate cause of Reza Shah's abdication, but his removal was welcomed by most Iranians, and some have suggested that his unpopularity would have made it impossible for the Allies to rule with him still on the throne—even if he had accepted that arrangement.[15] Reza went into exile in South Africa (where he died in July 1944).

In December 1941 the United States joined the Allies against Germany and Japan, and in 1942 American troops joined the British and Russian forces occupying Iran. At the end of 1943 Tehran hosted the first great conference of the leaders of the three Allied powers. Among the arrangements that Churchill, Stalin, and Roosevelt agreed upon for the conduct of the war—including opening a second front in western Europe in 1944—was the commitment to withdraw from Iran within six months of the war's end.

Ripples from the terrible events of the Holocaust also reached the country. In 1942 a group of orphaned children—refugees from the Jewish ghettoes and *shtetls* of Poland who had escaped into Russia only to be interned in Siberia and then sent by train southward—arrived in Iran on the Caspian coast, after many bitter hardships. They were brought to Tehran, where they were given help by the Iranian Jewish community and by Zionist organizations. Having recovered from the poor condition in which they arrived, 848 children eventually made their way to Palestine.[16]

At the same time, a descendant of the Qajar royal family—Abdol-Hosein Sardari Qajar, who has been called the Iranian Schindler—was looking after the Iranian Embassy building in Paris after the embassy's main functions had moved to Vichy. Sardari was left a supply of blank passports, and when Jews in Paris began to be rounded up by the Nazis in 1942, he began issuing them to Iranian Jews, many of whom had lived in Paris for some years. He also secured an assurance from the German authorities in Paris that Iranian citizens would not be detained or harmed. But as the measures against Jews in Paris intensified, French Jews with no Iranian connections began to come to him too, desperate for help. Becoming aware of the enormity of the crime being perpetrated by the Nazis, Sardari gave his passports —more than five hundred of them—to those Jews as well. After the war, Sardari's government charged him with misconduct over these passports, but he was given a personal pardon by Mohammad Reza Shah. When asked later about what he had done for the Jews in Paris, Sardari apparently said it had been his duty to help Iranian citizens. When asked about the Jews who had not been Iranians, he said, "That was my duty as a human being."[17] Sardari died in 1981 and, in 2004, was posthumously given an award by the Simon Wiesenthal Center.

While the war continued, Allied troops maintained their control in Iran, and the powers of the Pahlavi government were severely limited. But Mohammad Reza Shah had confirmed at his coronation that he would rule as a constitutional monarch, and in 1944 elections were held for the first genuinely representative Majles since the 1920s. Many familiar figures from the constitutionalist period reappeared—notably Seyyed Zia Tabataba'i and Mohammad Mossadeq, as well as some of the same nationalist landowners and officials who had been active in politics before Reza Khan became shah. They had just grown older.

The humiliation of the invasion, the presence of the Allies, the food shortages, the economic disruption caused by the war, the weakness of the government—all of it helped to stimulate another upsurge in political activity, especially nationalistic feeling. One focus of this was again the unequal distribution of the Anglo-Iranian Oil Company's (AIOC) profits (the company had changed its name from Anglo-Persian in recognition of the Shah's request that the country be known as Iran). The Iranian-based industry was the biggest and best developed in the Middle East at the time. But through taxation of the AIOC in the United Kingdom, the British government garnered more profit from the Iranian oil industry than the Iranian government did (nearly double over the period 1932–1950[18]). The Allied occupation was unpopular, but the British and Russians were more unpopular than the Americans. A sign of this was that another figure from the past, Arthur Millspaugh, returned in November 1942 to his old job of running Iranian state finances. Although Millspaugh set to work with his usual diligence, he showed a lack of sensitivity to the political and social conditions of Iran at the time. His attempts to end food subsidies and to privatize state institutions eventually made him unpopular, and led to his resignation two years later.

The shah tried to appeal to pro-American feeling, and to the United States for support. He made a speech drawing a comparison between Iranian nationalism and Iran's struggle for independence, and American nationalism and America's struggle for independence—from the British Empire, of course. In the heightened intensity of political debate under the Allied occupation, the young shah felt the need to appeal to popular opinion. As during the constitutionalist period, new newspapers—and this time, new political parties—proliferated. By 1943, there were forty-seven newspapers in Tehran (there would be *seven hundred* by 1951).[19] Of the new parties, the most significant was the founding in 1941 of the pro-Communist Tudeh, which reoriented the intelligentsia in a pro-Tudeh, Marxist-leaning direction.[20] Radio ownership was also expanding rapidly, exercising a further integrating influence and focusing the attention even of isolated villagers on national events and discussions.

As the war came to an end, doubts began to arise over whether or not the Soviet troops would depart from Azerbaijan. Making use of the social democratic tradition in the region and the strong position of the Tudeh party there, the Russians pursued an imperialistic policy that prefigured and helped bring on the confrontation of the Cold War. They encouraged pro-Soviet secessionist movements in Azerbaijan—Kurdish as well as Azeri (there was more serious enthusiasm for secession among the Kurds than among the Azeris), with the aim of re-creating there something like the old

Russian sphere of influence of 1907–1914. By the beginning of January 1946 British and American troops had left Iran, but the Soviets were still there in Azerbaijan, posing as protectors for Tudeh and the secessionists (there had been some attacks on Tudeh offices elsewhere in the country) and confronting the Iranian army on the margins of the province. Nationalist feeling in Tehran about the situation in the northwest was intense. Respected intellectuals like Ahmad Kasravi wrote of the danger that the country could split up entirely.

Kasravi, born in Tabriz in 1890, was initially trained in a seminary and was involved in the dramatic events of the Constitutional Revolution in Azerbaijan. But he rejected his religious training when he learned that the comet he saw in 1910 had been predicted by European astronomers as the return of Halley's comet, last seen in 1835: "I was pleased and happy that in Europe, knowledge had fallen into such a lucid path." Kasravi turned from a clerical postulant into a wickedly intelligent critic of the ulema—but also a critic of many other aspects of contemporary Iranian society. His pamphlet *What Is the Religion of the Hajjis with Warehouses?* attacked the pious posturing of merchants who shamelessly pursued the sharpest of practices in their commercial dealings. Another, entitled *Hasan Is Burning His Book of Hafez,* attacked the disposition, as he saw it, of many Iranians to substitute quotations from the great poets for genuine thought. Devoted to the principles of constitutionalism and secular government, Kasravi was a nationalist who attacked the linguistic and other divisions that divided Iranians and, in his opinion, had made them weak. He worked for many years in the Ministry of Education and as a journalist and writer. In 1946 he was assassinated by a group of Islamic extremists, followers of a man who had chosen to call himself Navvab Safavi.[21]

Kasravi is significant for a number of reasons. He stands for a certain strand of thinking in Iran, typical of the Pahlavi period in some ways, that became important again in the 1960s and 1970s, which rejected the backwardness of Shi'ism and blamed it for many of the weaknesses and failures of the country. His thinking was influential among the middle classes who benefited from the opportunities that arose under the Pahlavis.

His disapproval of the cult of Persian poetry is interesting because it again shows the cultural centrality of the great Persian poets—and points to the ambiguity in Iranian culture that they expressed and perhaps sustained. Roy Mottahedeh wrote:

> In fact, Persian poetry came to be the emotional home in which the ambiguity that was at the heart of Iranian culture lived most freely and openly. What Persian poetry expressed was not an enigma to be solved but an enigma that was unsolvable. In Persian poetry of any worth nothing was merely something else; the inner space of the spirit in which Persian poetry underwent its thousand transformations was ultimately a place where this ambiguous language reached a private emotional value that had to remain private, because to decode it as mere allegory, to reexpress it in any form of explanatory paraphrase would be to place it back in the public domain and, therefore, in the realm in which it was intended to remain ambiguous.[22]

Eventually, after a tense period of negotiations and pressure from the United States and Britain, the Soviets announced their intention to withdraw from Iran. By the end of May 1946, their forces were gone. Iranian troops then marched in and reimposed central government control—with some brutality. The episode discredited the Soviet Union for many Iranians, but not so the members of Tudeh. The party grew in influence, took places in the government cabinet and helped to bring forward new labor laws, set maximum working hours, and established a minimum wage. But in 1949 Tudeh members were accused of instigating an assassination attempt against the young shah. After that the party was banned, and could only make its influence felt through underground activity or through sympathetic writers and journalists. The United States, profiting from the Russians' unpopularity, increased its presence by bringing in advisers and technicians and by supplying training assistance to the army, as well as other aid. Nationalist feeling was gratified by the restoration of Iranian territorial integrity in Azerbaijan, and attention turned back to other grievances—especially to the question of oil.

Mossadeq

The assassination attempt of 1949 against the Shah precipitated an extended period of crisis, demonstrations, and martial law. In 1950 the shah appointed a new prime minister, Ali Razmara, but Razmara was not popular; he was suspected of pro-British sympathies, and his military background encouraged concern that the shah intended a return to the militaristic, autocratic style of government his father had favored in the 1930s. Over the same period, Mohammad Mossadeq assembled a broad coalition of Majles deputies that came to be called the National Front. It was organized around a central demand for oil nationalization, and Mossadeq was also widely believed to have reached an accommodation with Tudeh. The shah's government attempted to negotiate with the AIOC for a revision of the terms of the oil concession, but the AIOC were slow to accept the fifty-fifty split of profits that had become the norm in oil agreements elsewhere in the world. The National Front and its demand for oil nationalization were greatly strengthened in Majles elections in 1950, and in March 1951 Razmara was assassinated by the same extremist Islamic group that had murdered Kasravi. It was inevitable that Mossadeq, as the most popular politician in the country, would become prime minister.

Mossadeq was nearly seventy in 1951. He had Qajar ancestry and had studied in Paris and Switzerland, taking a doctorate in law. Having left the country in protest at the Anglo-Persian Agreement of 1919, he had opposed Reza Shah's accession to power and had been imprisoned for it, before returning to prominence in the 1940s. His whole life had been dedicated to the cause of Iranian national integrity and constitutional government. Under his leadership, the Majles voted on March 15, 1951, to nationalize Iranian oil. On April 28 they named Mossadeq prime minister.

But nationalization created an impasse, as British technicians left the oil installations in Khuzestan and the British government imposed a blockade. No oil could be exported. Instead of contributing to the national revenue, the maintenance of oil installations and the salaries of oil workers became a drain on finances, gradually creating a large debt and wider economic problems.

Mossadeq traveled to the United States in hopes of getting a loan, but he was refused. U.S. oil companies joined a boycott of Iranian oil, and the U.S. government was increasingly concerned at the apparent involvement of communists in the oil nationalization movement (Tudeh had led strikes and demonstrations). In hindsight, the U.S. position seems strange, given the plain fact that nationalization enjoyed broad support across most classes and shades of opinion. But the movement was vocally anti-British, and some voices anti-Western. In the atmosphere of the times, especially after the advent of the Eisenhower administration and of Senator Joe McCarthy, the involvement of an underground communist movement with Soviet support was enough to damn the whole phenomenon in U.S. eyes.

Despite deepening economic difficulties and the disappointing realization that he could expect no help from the United States in his confrontation with the British, Mossadeq continued as prime minister, enjoying massive support both in Majles and in the country itself. But tensions between different elements of the National Front coalition increased, as did the apparent strength of Tudeh, and there were more demonstrations. The government brought in new reforms, including measures that changed the relationship between landlords and peasants in favor of the latter, and Mossadeq used his support to pursue an older agenda of limiting the power of the monarchy. But in the summer of 1952 when Mossadeq demanded the right to appoint the minister of war to deal with the increasing unrest, the shah refused, and Mossadeq resigned. His successor immediately announced negotiations with the British to resolve the oil dispute, and the country erupted in demonstrations of disapproval in which Tudeh took a prominent role. The shah quickly caved in and reappointed Mossadeq, who broke diplomatic relations with Britain altogether at the end of the year. By this time the British were encouraging the United States to cooperate in engineering a coup to get rid of Mossadeq.

Finally, in August 1953, the plan went ahead: Mossadeq was to be removed as prime minister and replaced with General Zahedi, a fervent monarchist. But the plot misfired. Mossadeq found out about the coup, probably through Tudeh, and was able to forestall it. The shah fled the country and anti-royalist rioting broke out. Mossadeq sent in police and troops to control the riots, and they succeeded, but they also alienated many of Mossadeq's own supporters, as well as Tudeh. So when a new demonstration appeared two days later on August 19, this time against Mossadeq, his supporters stayed away. This demonstration included supporters of Ayatollah Abol-Ghasem Kashani—previously loyal to the National Front, but now on the other side—from the bazaar, and people paid to participate by the CIA, which had given the coup the code name Operation Ajax. Many members of the murky south Tehran underworld took part, including gang leaders like Sha'ban Ja'fari Bimokh (Sha'ban the Brainless).[23] In the wake of this demonstration Mossadeq was arrested, the army and Zahedi were in control, and the shah returned. Mossadeq was tried and convicted of treason by a military court but was allowed to live under house arrest until he died in 1967.

The coup could perhaps not have happened without mistakes of Mossadeq's own making—and in fact it nearly failed. But it certainly would not have happened without the intervention of the British SIS and the American CIA.[24] Although the story of the coup did not emerge for many years and perhaps has not done so fully even now, Iranians blamed these two agencies at the time and have done so bitterly ever since. The idea that everything that happened in Iranian politics was manipulated by a hidden foreign hand was again reinforced, fathering dozens of improbable conspiracy theories in later years. Mossadeq became a national hero across most ideological, class, and religious boundaries.

The coup also had significance in a number of other ways. It established the United States in Iran as the prime ally and protector of the Pahlavi regime, and it achieved the aim of eclipsing Soviet communist influence. But it also took away much of the enchantment the United States had previously enjoyed popularly as a virtuous alternative to the older powers. The significance of the event took some time to sink in. For a while some Iranians still believed, or hoped, that the Americans had been duped by the British, and that fundamental U.S. values would reassert themselves. But the United States was Prince Charming no more. One could draw a parallel with British decisions in the 1870s and at other times, which appeared to serve immediate short-term British interests but treated Iran as an instrument to other ends rather than with the respect due a partner. In the long run, as with British actions in the previous century, the removal of Mossadeq damaged U.S. interests in a much more serious way than could have been imagined at the time.

The events of 1951–1953 also alienated many Iranians from the young shah, making popular support for him in subsequent decades equivocal at best. Beyond Iran, the significance of the struggle to nationalize Iranian oil was widely felt in the Middle East. It is generally accepted, for example, that the episode played an important part in the thinking of Egypt's Jamal Abd al-Nasser (Nasser), who in July 1956 followed the example of Mossadeq and nationalized the Suez Canal. It would not be the last time that Iran, for better or worse, would indicate in advance the way events would unfold in the region more widely.

But the Mossadeq era disillusioned many young Iranians about politics and the chances for change. One such was Jalal Al-e Ahmad, a complex man who was against many things, and only ambiguously in favor of a few. He had been born into an ulema family in Tehran in 1923, but turned against a religious career (having read Kasravi) and later became a Marxist under the influence of Khalil Maleki, one of the group arrested by Reza Shah in 1937. But in the long run Ahmad was too critical and too individualistic to be a conventional Marxist. Like Maleki, he disliked the way Tudeh had to toe the Soviet line after World War II. He actively supported Mossadeq, but after his fall renounced politics dramatically and publicly. Like Kasravi, he had an aversion to the traditions of classical Persian literature, favoring a lean style of writing that echoed the colloquial Persian of ordinary people. The most influential of his ideas was that of *gharbzadegi*—often translated as "Westoxication" or "West-strickenness"—which he put forward in talks and a book with that title in 1962. This attacked the uncritical way in which Western ideas had been accepted, advocated, and taught in schools. The result, said Al-e Ahmad, was the creation of a people and a culture that were neither genuinely Iranian nor properly Western. Following a story by Mawlana

Rumi, he compared it to a crow that one day saw the elegant way a partridge walked. The crow tried to imitate the partridge and failed, but kept trying, with the result that he forgot how to walk like a crow—but never succeeded in walking like a partridge.

As time went on, Al-e Ahmad was increasingly drawn back to religion (having initially followed the scornful, satirical example of Hedayat), but he always disliked the superstition and empty traditionalism of many of the ulema—"satisfied to be the gatekeeper at the graveyard." Later, he drew attention to the way oil wealth was spent on imported absurdities that earlier generations of Iranians could never have imagined they could want, and to the artificial, invented historical heritage presented by Mohammad Reza Shah as the backdrop to the Pahlavi monarchy. Al-e Ahmad brought some of the jaded anomie of Western modernism to Iranian literature, while keeping a strongly Iranian voice. He translated Sartre and Camus into Persian, but his firm attachment to intellectual honesty and his search for an authentic way to live did not borrow from anyone. He died young in 1969, and his status as a modernist hero was only slightly weakened by his wife Simin Daneshvar's later revelations of his grumpy selfishness in their married life. He was a strong influence on a whole generation of Iranian intellectuals who were his contemporaries, and on those who came after him.[25]

The Rule of Mohammad Reza Shah and the White Revolution

The Mossadeq coup ended the period of pluralism that had begun with the fall of Reza Shah in 1941, and inaugurated an extended period in which Mohammad Reza Shah ruled personally with few constitutional limitations. The oil dispute was resolved with an arrangement that gave the Iranian government fifty percent of the profits, out of a consortium in which the U.S. companies had a forty percent stake, now equal to that held by the AIOC (renamed British Petroleum in 1954—BP). The increased oil revenue, which grew as the industry developed, permitted a big expansion of government expenditure. Much of this, as in the time of Reza Shah, was spent on military equipment—augmented by $500 million of U.S. military aid between 1953 and 1963. Many in government circles felt that too much money was being spent on the military budget, and in 1959 that dispute contributed to the resignation of Abol-Hassan Ebtehaj, head of the Planning and Budget Organization.[26] In return the shah aligned himself unequivocally with the West, and diplomatic relations with Britain were restored in 1954. But from 1953 onward it was plain to all that the United States was now the dominant external power in Iran.

After the coup, the shah's government kept a tight grip on politics. Candidates for the elections to the eighteenth Majles in 1954 were selected by the regime, and the assembly proved duly obedient. In 1955 the shah dismissed Zahedi and effectively took control into his own hands. Mossadeq's National Front was disbanded, and Tudeh sympathizers were relentlessly pursued by a security agency (known from 1957 as SAVAK) that grew increasingly efficient, with help from the CIA and the Israeli secret service, Mossad. It also grew increasingly brutal. Two puppet political parties were set up for the Majles, controlled by the shah's supporters—*Melliyun* (National Party) and *Mardom* (People's Party)—satirized as the "Yes" party and the "Yes sir" party.[27] Important members of the ulema like Kashani, and the prime marja-e taqlid Ayatollah Borujerdi, had supported the coup of 1953 because they disliked what they saw as Mossadeq's secularizing tendency and the influence of Tudeh. Thereafter, they continued to support the shah, and relations between the shah and Borujerdi in particular were cordial. But many other clerics grew more uneasy and hostile as time went on.

The population of Iran had expanded from around 12 million at the beginning of the century to 15 million in 1938, and 19.3 million in 1950; it would jump to 27.3 million by 1968 and 33.7 million in 1976. Though the regime invested heavily in industry and education, the rural areas still lagged behind. There was also substantial private investment, and between 1954 and 1969 the economy grew on average by seven or eight percent a year.[28] As well as military expenditure, a lot of government money was spent on big, showy engineering projects, like dams—dams that sometimes never linked up to the irrigation networks that had been their justification. As in any other time of major change, the new often looked crass against the dignity of the old that was being pushed aside, and the benefits of change were distributed unequally. But there was a general improvement in material standards of living. The new, educated middle class expanded, encompassing entrepreneurs, engineers, and managers as well as the older professions—lawyers, doctors, and teachers.

In 1957 a British diplomat with more than ordinary perspicacity wrote the following of Tehran, prefiguring the tensions that came into higher relief in the 1960s and 1970s—and making an early differentiation between the character of the Westernized north of the city, and that of the more traditional, poorer south:

> Here the mullahs preach every evening to packed audiences. Most of the sermons are revivalist stuff of a high emotional and low intellectual standard. But certain well known preachers attract the intelligentsia of the town with reasoned historical exposés of considerable merit. . . . The Tehran that we saw on the tenth of Moharram [i.e. Ashura] is a different world, centuries and civilisations apart from the gawdy superficial botch of cadillacs, hotels, antique shops, villas, tourists and diplomats, where we run our daily round . . . but it is not only poverty, ignorance and dirt that distinguish the old south from the parvenu north. The slums have a compact self-conscious unity and communal sense that is totally lacking in the smart districts of chlorinated water, macadamed roads and (fitful) street lighting. The bourgeois does not know his neighbour: the slum-dweller is intensely conscious of his. And in the slums the spurious blessings of Pepsi Cola civilisation have not yet destroyed the old way of life, where every man's comfort and security depend on the spontaneous, un-policed observation of a traditional code. Down in the southern part of the city manners and morals are better and stricter than in the villas of Tajrish: an injury to a neighbour, a pass at another man's wife, a brutality to a child evoke spontaneous retribution without benefit of bar or bench.[29]

In 1960 the shah put forward a proposal for land reform, but by this time the economy was slowing down, and the U.S. government (after January 1961 the Kennedy administration) was putting some pressure on the shah to liberalize. Many of the senior ulema disliked the land reform measure (their extensive land holdings from endowments appeared to be threatened, and many considered the infringement of property rights to be un-Islamic), and Borujerdi declared a fatwa against it. The measure stalled. Prompted by the U.S., the lhah lifted the ban on the National Front, and their criticisms, along with the economic problems, led to strikes and demonstrations. At the beginning of 1963 the shah regained the initiative with a package of reforms announced as the White Revolution. This included a renewed policy of land reform, privatization of state factories, female suffrage, and a literacy corps of young educated people to address the problem of illiteracy in the countryside. Despite a boycott by the National Front (which insisted that such a measure should have been presented and applied by a constitutionally elected Majles), the program received huge support in a referendum—5.5 million out of 6.1 million eligible voters supporting it.[30] The program went ahead, augmenting and broadening the changes in the country that were already afoot.

But early in 1963 a cleric little known outside ulema circles, Ayatollah Ruhollah Khomeini, began to preach in Qom against the shah's government. He attacked its corruption, its neglect of the poor, and its failure to uphold Iran's sovereignty in its relationship with the United States—and he also disliked the shah's sale of oil to Israel. Khomeini made this move at a time when, following the death of Ayatollah Borujerdi in 1961, many Iranian Shi'a were unclear whom to follow as marja-e taqlid. In March, on the anniversary of the martyrdom of the Emam Jafar Sadeq, troops and SAVAK agents attacked the *madreseh* where Khomeini was preaching and arrested him, killing several students at the same time. He was released shortly afterward but continued his attacks on the government. He made a particularly strong speech on June 3, which was Ashura, and was arrested again two days later.[31] When the arrest became known, there were demonstrations in Tehran and several other major cities. Drawing force from the intense atmosphere of mourning for Emam Hosein, these demonstrations were repeated, and they spread widely in the days that followed. The shah imposed martial law and put troops on the streets, but hundreds of demonstrators (at least) were killed before the protests ended. These deaths, especially because they took place at Ashura, invited comparison with the martyrs of Karbala on the one hand, and the tyrant Yazid on the other.

Khomeini was released in August. But despite SAVAK announcements that he had agreed to keep quiet, he continued to speak out, and he was rearrested. Finally, he was deported and exiled in 1964 after a harsh speech attacking both the Iranian and U.S. governments for a new law that gave the equivalent of diplomatic immunity to U.S. military personnel in Iran:

> They have reduced the Iranian people to a level lower than that of an American dog. If someone runs over a dog belonging to an American, he will be prosecuted. Even if the Shah himself were to run over a dog belonging to an American, he would be prosecuted. But if an American cook runs over the Shah, the head of state, no one will have the right to interfere with him. . . .[32]

Shortly after the new law was passed in the Majles, a new U.S. loan of $200 million for military equipment was agreed—a conjunction all too reminiscent of the kinds of deals done with foreigners in the reign of Naser od-Din Shah. Initially Khomeini went in exile to Turkey, then to Iraq, and eventually (after the shah put pressure on the Iraqi government to remove him from the Shi'a center in Najaf) to Paris in 1978. Protest in Iran died down, aside from occasional manifestations at Tehran University and from members of the ulema. For the shah, the message from the episode appeared to be that he could govern autocratically and overcome short-term dissent with repression. In the longer term, he believed, his policies for development would bring benefits to ordinary people and secure his rule.

Khomeini

Ruhollah Khomeini was born in September 1902 in Khomein, a small town between Isfahan and Tehran. He came from a family of *seyyed* (descendants of the Prophet) whose patriarchs had been mullahs for many generations, and may originally have come from Nishapur. In the eighteenth century one of his ancestors had moved to India, where the family had lived in Kintur, near Lucknow, before his grandfather—known as Seyyed Ahmad Musavi Hindi—moved back to Persia and settled in Khomein in about 1839. He bought a large house there and was a man of property and status. Ahmad's son Mostafa studied in Isfahan, Najaf, and Samarra and married the daughter of a distinguished clerical family. Mostafa belonged to the upper echelons of the ulema, a cut above the mullahs who had to make a living as jobbing teachers, legal notaries, or preachers. This made him an important figure in the area, and it seems that it was while he was attempting to mediate in a local dispute that he was murdered in 1903, when Ruhollah, his third son, was only six months old.[33]

Ruhollah grew up in Khomein through the turbulent years of the Constitutional Revolution and the First World War, over which period Khomein was raided a number of times by Lori tribesmen. In 1918 his mother died in a cholera epidemic, leaving him an orphan as he was about to enter the seminary nearby in Soltanabad. It may be that the absence of his father as a child and becoming orphaned as a youth added impetus to the young Khomeini's ambition and drive to excel in his studies. Later he moved to Qom, where as a student of Shaykh Abdolkarim Ha'eri he wore the black turban of a seyyed. In Qom he received the conventional education in logic and religious law of a mullah, becoming a mojtahed in about 1936.[34] It was a young age for such an accomplishment, and a sign of his promise. From that time he began to teach and write. He was always a little unconventional, having an interest in poetry and mysticism (erfan) that more conservative mullahs would have disapproved of. He read Molla Sadra's *Four Journeys* and the *Fusus al-Hikam* of Ibn Arabi, and his first writings were commentaries on mystical and philosophical texts. In the 1930s he studied philosophy and erfan with Mirza Mohammad Ali Shahabadi, who as well as being an authority on mysticism believed in the importance of explaining religious ideas to ordinary people in language they could understand. Shahabadi opposed the rule of Reza Shah and also influenced Khomeini's politics.[35]

Khomeini had a strong sense of himself as well as the dignity of the ulema as a class, and always dressed neatly and cleanly—not affecting an indifference to clothes or appearance as some young mullahs did. He struck many people as aloof and reserved, and some as arrogant, but his small circle of students and friends knew him to be generous and lively in private. For his public persona as a teacher and mullah it was necessary for him to exemplify authority and quiet dignity. Through the 1940s and 1950s, as he continued to teach in Qom, it is perhaps correct to think of Khomeini as taking a position between the anti-colonial and anti-British activism of Ayatollah Kashani on the one hand, and the more conservative, withdrawn, quietist, less politically interventionist stance of Ayatollah Hosein Borujerdi on the other.[36] But Khomeini's combination of intellectual strength, curiosity, and unconventionality made him different from either. Potentially more creative and innovative, he still for the time being deferred to his superiors in the hierarchy of the ulema. Khomeini was made an ayatollah after the death of Borujerdi in March 1961, by which time he was already attracting large and increasing numbers of students to his lectures on ethics. He was regarded by some of them as their marja, their object of emulation.

The events of 1963–1964 made Khomeini the leading political figure opposed to the shah—along with Mossadeq, who was still under house arrest and thus effectively neutralized. Khomeini, though he disapproved of constitutionalism in private, had been careful to speak positively about the constitution in public.[37] His attack on the new law governing the status of the U.S. military was calculated to win over nationalists, some of whom might previously have been suspicious of a cleric. Intellectuals like Al-e Ahmad gave him their enthusiastic support. He was already applying the political method by which, through addressing popular grievances and avoiding pronouncements on issues that might divide his followers, he would later make himself a national leader.

But from 1964 Khomeini was out of Iran and, to all appearances, out of Iranian politics. In a sense, Iranian politics was itself exiled, taking place among Iranian students and others living abroad. Within Iran the press was controlled and censored, the elections continued to be rigged, and SAVAK pursued, arrested, and imprisoned Tudeh activists and other dissidents.

Oil Boom and Expansion

The land reform program went ahead from 1963, but with mixed results. The landlords who were to be expropriated were allowed to keep only one village each, but some landlords were able to evade the provisions—by giving their property to relatives, for example, or by creating mechanized farms, which were exempt. About two million peasants became landowners in their own right for the first time, and some were able to set themselves up on a profitable footing. But for many more the holdings they were given were too small to make a living, and there were large numbers of agricultural laborers who, because they had not had cultivation rights as sharecroppers before the reform, were left out of the redistribution altogether. Because the reform was accompanied by a general push for the mechanization of agriculture, there was suddenly less work for these laborers anyway. The net result was rural unemployment and an accelerating movement of people from the villages to the cities, especially Tehran, in search of jobs. It has been suggested that the rate of internal migration reached eight percent per year in 1972–1973,[38] and by 1976 Tehran had swelled to become a city of 4.5 million people.

In Tehran these people went to poorer parts on the southern edge of the city, to what were little better than shanty towns. They tended to settle down in groups from the same village or area. Often they would know a mullah also from the same area, and he would be accorded added authority in the prevailing circumstances of dislocation and uncertainty.[39]

Between 1963 and the latter part of the 1970s, Iran enjoyed a huge economic boom that saw per capita GNP rise from $200 to $2,000.[40] Industrial output increased dramatically in new industries like coal, textiles, and the manufacture of motor vehicles, and large numbers of new jobs were created to absorb the increase in population and the large numbers leaving agriculture. Industrial wages were low, however. Government spending expanded education and health services too—the number of children in primary schools went from 1.6 million in 1953 to more than 4 million in 1977; new universities and colleges were set up and enrollment rose from 24,885 to 154,215. Students at foreign universities grew in number from fewer than 18,000 to more than 80,000. The number of hospital beds went from 24,126 to 48,000. Improved living conditions, sanitation, and health services all contributed to a big drop in the infant mortality rate and a spurt in population growth that continued until the 1990s. In the mid-1970s half the population were under sixteen, and two-thirds were under thirty. This was to be the generation of the revolution.[41]

Investment rose dizzyingly as Iran benefited from a windfall bonanza of oil income—especially after the shah renegotiated terms with the oil consortium to give himself more control over production levels and prices. Then in 1973 the oil price doubled after the Yom Kippur war, and doubled again at the end of the year when the shah led the other OPEC countries to demand higher prices on the claim that oil had not kept pace with the price of other internationally traded commodities. Yet more money pumped into the system, though a large amount went back to the West—especially to the United States and the United Kingdom—in return for quantities of new military equipment. The shah bought more Chieftain tanks from the UK than the British army owned, and the very latest F-14 fighters from the United States.

But the economy was overheating, there was too much money chasing too few goods, there were bottlenecks and shortages, and inflation rose sharply—especially on items like housing rent and foodstuffs, and especially in Tehran. Initially, the shah blamed small traders for the price rises, and sent gangs (backed by SAVAK) into the bazaars to arrest so-called profiteers and hoarders. Shops were closed down, two hundred fifty thousand fines were issued, and eight thousand shopkeepers were given prison sentences—none of which altered the underlying economic realities by one iota. The arrests and fines joined a list of grievances felt by the bazaari artisans and merchants, who were already seeing their products and businesses edged aside by imports, new factories, suburban stores, and supermarkets.

There was a sense, including in government, that the developing economy had run out of control. In mid-1977 a new prime minister introduced a new, deflationary economic policy designed to restore some stability. But the result was a sudden jump in unemployment, as the growing number of arrivals in the cities either lost or failed to find jobs. Inflation and the sudden faltering of the economy were felt particularly by the poor, but to some extent by everyone. Rents were high for the middle-class engineers, managers, and professionals in Tehran, and those with a stake in new businesses felt the impact of deflation acutely.

Tehran in the 1970s was a strange place. Large numbers of very wealthy people—many wealthy to a degree most Europeans could only dream of—lived hard by people poorer than could be seen anywhere in western Europe. The city was already largely a city of concrete, with only a core of a few older palaces and government buildings. But despite the traffic and the ugliness, the older Iran was still there in the chadors on the streets and the call to prayer at dusk. The West, and especially the United States, were constant presences, from the Coca-Cola and Pepsi on sale everywhere to American cars and American advertising, but constant also (alongside continuing admiration for America and an associated desire for economic development) were a tension and a distaste for that American presence.

There were Americans everywhere in Tehran in the 1970s. Author and professor James A. Bill has estimated that between 800,000 and 850,000 Americans lived in or visited Iran between 1944 and 1979, and that the number resident there increased from fewer than 8,000 in 1970 to nearly 50,000 in 1979. Ten thousand were employed in defense industries around Isfahan alone. There were of course some Americans living in Iran who made an effort to understand the country, but many did not. For the most part, the Americans lived entirely separate lives, often living on American-only compounds and shopping in the U.S. commissary (the biggest of its kind in the world). Many British expatriates lived in a similar way. The American school in Tehran admitted only children with U.S. passports (unusual by comparison with American schools in other countries), and occasional suggestions that the children be taught something about Iran generally failed—a school board member said in 1970 that the policy had been "Keep Iran Out." In the mid-1960s an American hospital in Tehran took on some well-educated Iranian nurses to supplement its staff. The Iranians were not allowed to speak in Persian, even among themselves, and were excluded from the staff canteen, which was kept for U.S. citizens only. The Iranian nurses had to eat in the janitor's room. The hospital cared only for American patients, and one day when a desperate Iranian father tried to bring in his child, who had just been seriously injured by a car in the street outside, he was sent away to find transport to another hospital. Other Americans, notably those with the Peace Corps, worked alongside ordinary Iranians and were much appreciated. But the majority were in Iran for the money and the lavish lifestyle, which they could not have afforded at home:

> As the gold rush began and the contracts increased, the American presence expanded. The very best and the very worst of America were on display in the cities of Iran. As time passed and the numbers grew, an increasingly high proportion of fortune hunters, financial scavengers, and the jobless and disillusioned recently returned from Southeast Asia found their way to Iran. Companies with billion-dollar contracts needed manpower and, under time pressure, recruited blindly and carelessly. In Isfahan, hatred, racism and ignorance combined as American employees responded negatively and aggressively to Iranian society.[42]

Iranians returned the compliment. Incidents between U.S. residents and Iranians led to newspaper articles about drunken and lewd Americans, encouraging anti-American attitudes.

There was also another kind of tension within Iranian society. The young men of south Tehran, newly arrived from traditional communities in the countryside and either having no jobs or only poorly paid ones, saw (if they took a bus or taxi uptown) pretty young middle-class women sashaying up and down the streets flush with money, unaccompanied or with girlfriends, dressed in revealing Western fashions, flaunting their freedom, money, beauty, and from a certain point of view immorality.[43] On billboards, garish depictions of half-dressed women advertised the latest films. Status, and the lack of it, is not just about money; it is also about sex and desire. Tehran was a place of aspiration, but in the late 1970s it became for many a place of resentment, frustrated desire, and disappointed aspirations.

In an inspired passage Roy Mottahedeh described this time in Tehran as the time of *montazh*, when imported things were being assembled and put together in the city, often rather less than satisfactorily, and never quite complete—a time when everything in Tehran seemed to be "intimately connected with the airport":

> . . . in joking, Tehranis called all sorts of jerry-built Iranian versions of foreign ideas true examples of Iranian montazh.[44]

The most obvious examples of montazh were the ubiquitous Paykan cars assembled just outside Tehran from imported parts (to the design of the British Hillman Hunter), but the same principle could be seen or imagined at work elsewhere too: in corrupt property deals, in big buildings put up without enough cement, in the chaotic traffic, and in the new plaques and statues of the shah that appeared everywhere.

As the 1970s advanced, the political culture of the shah's regime became more repressive and hardened on the one hand, and more remote and attenuated on the other. SAVAK had a new target in those years—radical movements prepared to use violence against the regime. This notably included the Marxist Feda'i and the Mojahedin-e Khalq Organization (MKO), both of which fused Islam and Marxism. SAVAK expanded, and its use of torture became routine. In 1975 Amnesty International pronounced the shah's government to be one of the world's worst violators of human rights. The previous two tame parties in the Majles became one, called *Rastakhiz* (Resurgence), with a role simply to support and applaud the shah's efforts. Politics became a matter of who could be most sycophantic to the shah in public:

> The Shah's only fault is that he is really too good for his people—his ideas are too great for us to realize them.[45]

The shah himself rarely met ordinary Iranians. He went from place to place by helicopter and, following various assassination attempts, viewed parades and other events from inside a special bulletproof glass box. In 1971 he held an event at the historic sites of Persepolis and Pasargadae to celebrate, supposedly, the twenty-five-hundredth anniversary of the Iranian monarchy. This was *folie de grandeur* on a sublime scale. Heads of state from around the world were invited, but those from monarchies were given precedence. So Haile Selassie of Ethiopia was specially honored, while President Pompidou of France was set low in the precedence order. Pompidou took umbrage and sent his prime minister instead.[46] Thousands dressed up as ancient Medes and Persians, television coverage of the event was beamed around the world by satellite, and the distinguished guests drank champagne and other imported luxuries (the catering was laid on by Maxim's of Paris in three huge air-conditioned tents and fifty-nine smaller ones, and twenty-five thousand bottles of wine were imported for the event—rumors of the overall cost ranged as high as $200 million[47]). The shah made a speech claiming continuity with Cyrus, and a rebirth of ancient Iranian greatness.

But the Achaemenids meant little to most Iranians—they had probably never been to Persepolis, and what they knew of ancient Iran revolved around the stories of Ferdowsi's *Shahnameh* rather than what might or might not appear in Herodotus, or had been discovered at archaeological sites. There had long been an anticlerical, secularizing strand of nationalist thinking that appealed to the pre-Islamic, monarchical tradition of Iran, but it was a slender reed to carry this burden of regime self-projection. For most the Iranian heritage was an Islamic heritage, and the jollifications at Persepolis left them nonplussed. Khomeini denounced the event from Iraq, thundering that Islam was fundamentally opposed to monarchy in principle, that the crimes of Iranian kings had blackened the pages of history, and that even the ones remembered as good had in fact been "vile and cruel."[48] The shah also replaced the Islamic calendar with a calendar that took year one as the year of the accession of Cyrus, which again left most Iranians irritated and baffled.

For some members of the minorities in Iran, the reign of Mohammad Reza Shah was a good time of relative freedom and absence of persecution, in which some Jews and Baha'is in particular were able—especially through their cultural emphasis on education—to achieve a degree of prosperity. But poorer Jews in some towns continued to suffer as second-class citizens,[49] and through this period many Iranian Jews emigrated to the United States and Israel. The shah had passed a new Family Protection Law in 1967, which made divorce law fairer and more equal, and in particular made child custody dependent on the merits of the case in court rather than simply giving custody to the father.

The shah's rule was a mixture of failures and successes—neither all one nor all the other. Some of the vaunted economic and developmental achievements were impressive, while others were shallow and superficial. But in the end the important failures were primarily political—the shah had no program for restoring representative government, and his only solution for dissent was repression. If he had succeeded in making the monarchy truly popular, perhaps he could have sustained it for a time. Instead the monarchy became more remote and disconnected from the attitudes and concerns of ordinary Iranians. In a sense, paradoxically perhaps partly as a result of combating underground Marxists for so long, the shah made the mistake of a Marxist analysis: he thought that if he could just secure material prosperity through successful development, then everything else would fall happily into place. But few economies deliver continuous sustained growth indefinitely.

In 1977 the shah, if not actually under pressure from the new Carter administration in the United States then certainly aware that the Carter people were less sympathetic to repressive allies than their predecessors had been, began slowly to relax some of the instruments of repression. In February some political prisoners were released. Later on, court rules were changed to allow prisoners proper legal representation and access to civilian rather than military courts. The shah met representatives from Amnesty International and agreed to improve prison conditions. In May a group of lawyers sent a letter to the shah protesting at government interference in court cases. In June three National Front activists, including Karim Sanjabi, Shahpur Bakhtiar, and Dariush Foruhar, sent a bolder letter to the shah criticizing autocratic rule and demanding a restoration of constitutional government.

Later that month the Writers' Association, repressed since 1964, resurrected itself and pressed for the same goals—as well as for the removal of censorship (many of the leading members were Tudeh sympathizers or broadly leftist). In July the shah replaced Amir Abbas Hoveyda, his prime minister for twelve years, with Jasmshid Amuzegar, who was perceived to be more liberal. In the autumn more political associations formed or re-formed—including the National Front, under the leadership of Sanjabi, Bakhtiar, and Foruhar; and the Freedom Movement, closely allied with the National Front, under Mehdi Bazargan and Ebrahim Yazdi.[50]

On November 19 the Writers' Association held a poetry evening—the tenth in a series of such evenings—at the Goethe Institut. About ten thousand students were present, and this time the police tried to break it up. When the students poured into the streets to protest, the police attacked them, killing one, injuring seventy, and arresting about a hundred. But on this occasion civilian courts tried the students and quickly acquitted them.

While in exile, Khomeini kept up a stream of messages and speeches critical of the regime, which were smuggled into Iran and distributed, often using cassette tapes. Having developed his theory of opposition into a full-blown theory for Islamic government, he set this out in a book, based on lectures he gave in Najaf in 1970, with the title *Hokumat-e Eslami: Velayat-e Faqih* (Islamic Government: Regency of the Jurist).[51] In this text the Usuli thinking of the previous two centuries—a line of thought that had helped the ulema develop a hierarchy and had allowed them in effect to stand in for the Hidden Emam—was developed to its logical extreme: permission for the ulema to rule directly. This was the meaning of the term *velayat-e faqih*, which needs explaining. A *vali* was a regent or deputy, someone representing the person with real authority—it was the title taken by Karim Khan Zand in the eighteenth century, when he forbore to make himself shah. *Velayat* meant regency, guardianship, or deputyship—or rather, by extension, the authority of the deputy or regent. The term *faqih* signifies a jurist, an expert in Islamic law—*fiqh*. The logic of the concept was that the shari'a, derived from the word of God and the example of the Prophet, was there to regulate human conduct, and was the only legitimate law. In the absence of the Hidden Emam, the mojtaheds were the right people to interpret and apply the shari'a. So obviously, they were the right people to rule, too. Who else? From this point onward, Khomeini demanded the removal of the shah and the establishment of Islamic government. He delivered clear and consistent demands that the whole country could understand (at least they thought they could—what exactly Islamic government might mean in practice remained less clear), and that increasingly made him the focal point for opposition to the shah.

The principle of velayat-e faqih was not accepted by the ulema as a whole—indeed not accepted by very many. But since the First World War the ulema had been jostled and edged out of many of their traditional roles of authority in society by the secularizing Pahlavi monarchy. Under Mohammad Reza Shah the regime even attempted, in the late 1960s and 1970s (as part of the White Revolution program), to replace the traditional ulema with a new religious structure of mosques and mullahs answerable to the state. There was little popular enthusiasm for the state religion (*din-e dawlat*), but it succeeded in alienating the ulema as a whole even further from the shah. Ayatollahs Montazeri and Taleqani were arrested and sentenced to internal exile after disturbances at Tehran University and in Qom in 1970–1972.[52] But where Tudeh, the National Front, and the violent radicals were battered and disrupted by years of conflict with SAVAK, the informal nationwide network of mullahs and religious leaders—reaching into every social class, every bazaar guild, and every village—was still there in the late 1970s, as it had been in 1906. Its continuing presence reflected the enduring power of this alternative source of authority in Shi'a Iranian society. In the theory of velayat-e faqih and Khomeini, the ulema had the defining political principle and the leader that they had lacked in 1906.

By the end of 1977 the shah had alienated the ulema, alienated the bazaaris, and had created a large, poor, deracinated working class in Tehran. He had also alienated many of the educated middle classes—his natural supporters—through his repression and abuses of human rights. Some of these had in addition been radicalized by their experience of leftist politics in Europe in the late 1960s and 1970s. But there was another important influence on the thinking of this generation—Ali Shariati.

Shariati was born in 1933, near Sabzavar in Khorasan. He grew up to be a lively, highly intelligent, extroverted youth with a strong sense of humor, someone who enjoyed ridiculing his teachers. He was influenced by his father, who had been an advocate of progressive Islam in his own right, but also by writers like Hedayat and Western thinkers like Schopenhauer and Kafka. Later Shariati went to Mashhad University, and then to Paris, where he studied under Marxist professors, read Guevara and Sartre, communicated with the Martinique-born theorist and revolutionary activist Frantz Fanon, and took a doctorate in sociology (in 1964). His political activism also attracted the attention of SAVAK. Returning to Iran in 1965, he taught students in Mashhad and later in Tehran, attracting large numbers to his lectures, and wrote a series of important books and speeches. The general message was that Shi'ism provided its own ideology of social justice and resistance to oppression. This had been masked by a false Shi'ism of superstition and deference to monarchy (Black Shi'ism, Safavid Shi'ism), but the essential truths of the religion were timeless, centering on the martyrdom of Hosein and his companions. Shariati was not a Marxist, but he could be said to have recast Shi'a Islam in a revolutionary mold, comparable to the Marxist model: "Everywhere is Karbala and every day is Ashura."[53] For the shah's regime, he was too hot to handle. He was imprisoned in 1972, released in 1975, kept under house arrest, and allowed to go to England in 1977. He died there that June, apparently of a heart attack, though many Iranians believe he was murdered by SAVAK. Khomeini would never endorse Shariati's thinking directly, but was careful never to condemn it either. Shariati's radical Islamism, both fully Iranian and fully modern, was a strong influence on the generation of students that grew to adulthood in the 1970s.[54]

Through the inflation and the economic slump and deflation that followed, many Iranians—including well-off ones—had come to doubt their assumptions about steady growth and economic security. There had also been a number of incidents in which the shah had made himself look foolish or out of touch—the latest came on his visit to Washington at the end of 1977, when TV cameras caught him clinking champagne glasses with President Carter and weeping from tear gas on the White House lawn when the wind blew the wrong way from a nearby demonstration against his visit. An autocrat can get away with many things, but looking foolish undercuts him in the most damaging way.

Revolution

In January 1978 an article appeared in the paper *Ettela'at*, attacking the clergy and Khomeini as "black reactionaries." The article had been written by someone trusted by the regime and approved by the court, but had been refused by the more independently edited paper *Kayhan*. It twisted facts and invented fictions, suggesting that Khomeini was a foreigner (from his grandfather's birth in India and name, Hindi), a former British spy, and a poet (the last was true, and was intended to detract from his clerical seriousness because most ulema, with some backing from the Qor'an, disapproved of poetry).[55] The article immediately prompted a protest demonstration in Qom, in which thousands of religious students heaped abuse on the "Yazid government" and demanded an apology, a constitution, and the return of Khomeini. There were clashes with the police and a number of students were shot dead. The following day Khomeini, by now in Paris, praised the courage of the students and called for more demonstrations. Ayatollah Shari'atmadari, one of the most senior marjas at the time, condemned the shootings.

After a traditional mourning period of forty days, the bazaars and universities closed, and there were peaceful demonstrations in twelve cities, including in Tabriz, where again the police fired on the crowd, causing more deaths. The forty-day rhythm continued, like a great revolutionary lung, with the almost unanimous support of the ulema (though many of the clerics called for mourners to attend the mosques rather than to demonstrate). The demonstrations grew larger and more violent, with slogans like "death to the shah." After the end of May there was a lull (among other reasons, Ayatollah Shari'atmadari had urged people against further street demonstrations to avoid more deaths), but there was a violent incident in Mashhad in July where police fired on a crowd. On August 19 the Rex Cinema burned down in Abadan, an incident that is still controversial. About 370 people died in the fire. Government and opposition both accused each other, but events, trials, and investigations in later years indicate that a radical Islamic group with connections to ulema figures was responsible.[56] At the time, the mood was such that most blamed SAVAK.

By that time the demonstrations, which up to then had largely been an affair for middle-class students and members of the traditional bazaari middle class, were being augmented by strikes and other actions by factory workers—prompted by the government's deflationary policies.[57] In August there were many large demonstrations in the month of Ramadan, and more in early September. The shah's government banned the demonstrations and imposed martial law, but on September 8 there were huge protests in Tehran and other cities. Barricades were set up in the working-class areas of south Tehran. The government sent in tanks and helicopter gunships; the people on the barricades responded with Molotov cocktails. In Jaleh Square an unarmed crowd refused to disperse and were gunned down where they stood.

September 8 was thereafter called Black Friday, and the deaths increased the bitterness of the people toward the shah to such a pitch that compromise became impossible. All that was left was the implacable demand that the shah should go—the demand upon which Khomeini had insisted since 1970. By the autumn most other opposition groups had allied themselves to Khomeini and his program. Karim Sanjabi and Mehdi Bazargan flew to Paris, met with Khomeini, and declared their support for him in the name of the National Front and the Freedom Movement. Demonstrations and riots continued. The shah, by now increasingly ill with cancer, though this remained unknown to the public, veered between more repression and concessions, including the release of political prisoners and the dissolution of the Rastakhiz party. He appeared on television to say that he understood the message of the people, would hold free elections, and would atone for past mistakes.[58]

But it was all too late. As autumn went into winter, more and more workers spent more and more time on strike. The violence intensified again at the beginning of Moharram in December. In Qazvin, 135 demonstrators died when tanks drove over them. On the day of Ashura itself, December 11, more than one million people demonstrated in the streets of Tehran. After Ashura, street gangs roamed the capital at will. There were more and more signs that the army, which had experienced mass desertions, was no longer reliable. By this time, President Carter's support for the shah was clearly on the wane, and many Americans were leaving Iran after attacks on U.S.-owned offices and even the U.S. Embassy. The shah had lost control. On January 16, 1979, he left the country. On February 1, Khomeini flew back to Tehran.

8

Iran Since the Revolution

Islamic Revival, War, and Confrontation

When the existence of the Church is threatened, she is released from the commandments of morality. With unity as the end, the use of every means is sanctified, even cunning, treachery, violence, simony, prison, death. For all order is for the sake of the community, and the individual must be sacrificed to the common good.

—Dietrich of Nieheim, Bishop of Verden, 1411
(quoted by Arthur Koestler in *Darkness at Noon*)

In the Air France passenger jet that Ayatollah Khomeini took from Paris to Tehran—before it was even clear that the aircraft would be allowed to land—a Western journalist asked him what his feelings were about returning to Iran. He replied *Hichi*—"nothing."[1] This grumpy response to unimaginative journalism did not demonstrate a deep indifference to Iran or the well-being of the Iranian people, as has sometimes been claimed. Khomeini's reply has a gnomic quality that challenges interpretation.

Whether one approves of Khomeini or not, it is indisputable that when he arrived in Tehran on February 1, 1979, he was the focal point of the hopes of a whole nation. In some sense they reflected him and he them—at that moment, at least. It may be that the euphoric crowds welcoming him numbered as many as three million. This was in accordance with Khomeini's sense of himself—his idea of spiritual development was that of Ibn Arabi's Perfect Man.[2] Through contemplation, religious observance, and discipline, his aim was to approach the point at which his inner world reflected the world beyond himself—and, in turn, reflected and became a channel for the mind of God. As he left the aircraft, his car made its difficult way through the crowds from the airport to the Behesht-e Zahra cemetery for Khomeini to honor the martyrs killed in the demonstrations of the last few months. As he passed, the people chanted not just "*Allahu Akbar*" (God is Great) but also "*Khomeini, O Emam.*" In Shi'a mysticism (erfan), the Emam

and the Perfect Man were one and the same. No human being since the disappearance of the Twelfth Emam had been acclaimed with the title *Emam* (many senior ulema never accepted the title for Khomeini).[3] The followers and the crowds were not saying directly that Khomeini was the Hidden Emam returned to earth, but it was very close to it. Centuries before, the Arab poet Farazdaq saw the fourth Emam at Mecca, and afterward wrote:

> He lowers his gaze out of modesty. Others lower their gaze for awe of him. He is not spoken to except when he smiles.[4]

This is why Khomeini answered the pushy journalist on the aircraft as he did. The mojtahed on the path to becoming the Perfect Man had no place for feelings or the manifestation of feelings. He was at one with the crowds, and they with him, and both with God. Or so they believed.

The revolution of 1979 was not solely—and perhaps not even primarily—a religious revolution. Economic slump and middle-class disillusionment with the corruption and oppression of a regime many had previously supported were important factors, as was a nationalistic dislike of the unequal relationship with the United States. But the revolution drew great strength from its Shi'a form, which lent cohesion and a sense of common purpose to disparate elements—even those that were not overtly religious—and from the clarity and charisma of Khomeini, which albeit temporarily gave an otherwise disunited collection of groups and motivations a center and a unity. Unlike other revolutions in history—notably the Bolshevik revolution of 1917— the Iranian revolution was genuinely a people's revolution. The actions of a large mass of people were crucial to the outcome, and the immediate outcome, if not the longer-term result, was a genuine expression of the people's will.

In his last weeks the shah had appointed the National Front leader Shapur Bakhtiar as prime minister, and Bakhtiar had announced a program of measures in an attempt to restore constitutional government and some stability, including free elections (Bakhtiar had been imprisoned by the shah for several years at different times since 1953). But the National Front had disowned Bakhtiar, and Khomeini had pronounced his government illegal. Maintaining this line, upon his arrival Khomeini on February 5 appointed his own prime minister from the Freedom Movement, Mehdi Bazargan. Revolutionary Committees (*Komitehs*) were set up and began cooperating with deserters from the military, Tudeh, the Feda'i, and the MKO to take arms and attack buildings associated with the regime, including police stations and the SAVAK's notorious Evin prison. After a last stand by some members of the Imperial guard, on February 11 the military gave in and announced that they would remain neutral.[5] Bakhtiar resigned and went into hiding; he left the country two months later. From that point on, the revolutionaries were in control. The Komitehs rounded up senior figures of the Pahlavi regime, and a revolutionary tribunal operating out of a school classroom had them executed, including, on February 15, the former head of SAVAK, General Nassiri. Khomeini himself headed a Revolutionary Council that maintained contact with the Komitehs through the connections between mullahs. In that way he began inexorably to remove all rivals to his vision for the future of the country.

Komitehs were set up all over Iran, but not all of them were so susceptible to Khomeini's central control. In the northwest in particular, with its own regional and leftist tradition, revolutionary enthusiasm turned toward a drive for greater regional autonomy. Kurdistan plunged into outright rebellion and separatism. In the 1970s the shah had supported the Kurds in Iraq in armed resistance against the Iraqi government, but his support was intended only as leverage to pressure the Iraqis into concessions elsewhere. He dropped the Kurds as soon as it was convenient for him, and the Kurds in Iraq suffered terribly as their revolt was crushed. The episode again stimulated Kurdish nationalism, which had motivated previous separatist movements within Iran in the 1920s—under the charismatic leader Simko/Simitqu—and again in the 1940s. Of the many ethnic and religious minorities of Iran, the Kurds are the group with the most developed sense of a separate national identity, with strong links to the Kurds of Iraq, Turkey, and Syria. The Kurdish insurrection in Iran that followed the revolution was eventually crushed, but not without more bitter suffering—prefiguring the even worse treatment that was visited on the Kurds of Iraq later in the 1980s.

Even before he returned to Iran, Khomeini had been making speeches critical of the shah's leftist opponents. At the end of March 1979 he set the seal on the removal of the shah and the establishment of a state based on Islamic principles with a referendum that returned ninety-seven percent support for the establishment of an Islamic republic. In May Khomeini established the Revolutionary Guard Corps (*Sepah-e Pasdaran*) as a reliable military force to balance the army and to supplement the gangs of street fighters that became known as *Hezbollah*—the party of God. The extensive property of the shah's Pahlavi Foundation was transferred to a new *Bonyad-e Mostazefin* (Foundation for the Oppressed), which became a vehicle both for the projection of the regime's social policies and for political patronage.

The executions of old regime members shocked moderates and liberals (including Bazargan), as well as many of those around the world who had initially welcomed the fall of the shah. The killings stopped for a time in mid-March, but continued again in April, when Hoveyda was shot. Khomeini had initially called for moderation, but acquiesced to the pressure from young radicals urging revenge for the deaths of the previous year. The young Islamic radicals were his weapon against the rival groups that had participated in the revolution.[6] In April and May Khomeini was given a sharp reminder of the seriousness of the struggle and the consequences of failure, when several of his close supporters, including notably Morteza Motahhari, were assassinated.

The Shi'a ulema had probably never been as powerful as it was at the moment Khomeini returned from exile. But Khomeini was something of a parvenu among the senior ulema, and the Islamic regime he created reflected his highly individual personality at least as much as it did the nature of traditional Shi'ism. At the time of the revolution there were other senior figures who commanded great respect, but who were pushed aside by the enormous popularity of Khomeini immediately after his return from exile. The most prominent of these was Ayatollah Seyyed Kazem Shari'atmadari, who argued for a more moderate line in 1979 and was quickly silenced. Some of his supporters were executed. Khomeini later rescinded Shari'atmadari's status as *marja-e taqlid*—a wholly unprecedented step. The principle of *velayat-e faqih* was still a dubious novelty for many senior Shi'a figures, several of whom spoke out against it in 1980–1981. But they too were intimidated into silence. Khomeini and his supporters successfully consolidated their control, based on the principle of *velayat-e faqih*, but it never commanded universal support among the Iranian ulema.[7] A reassertion of Islamic values followed—including a reappearance of ulema as judges, and a reapplication of shari'a law. Although this has been moderated in some respects by laws passed centrally, some extreme practices like stoning for adultery (though infrequent) have continued and have attracted international criticism.

By the autumn of 1979 the liberals and moderates were looking increasingly marginalized. Over the summer, Khomeini had formed the Islamic Republic Party (IRP), and the first draft of the constitution, put together by Bazargan—similar to the constitution of 1906, minus the monarch—had been radically rewritten by the Assembly of Experts, which was dominated by ulema loyal to Khomeini. The Assembly of Experts had come together after an election marred by liberal and leftist boycotts and allegations of rigging. In its final form the constitution set up the system that still runs Iran today, and which still reflects Khomeini's idea of velayat-e faqih: that day-to-day government should be secular, but with ultimate power in the hands of a religious leader committed to Islamic government. The constitution set up an elected presidency, an elected Majles, and elected municipal councils, but it also established a Council of Guardians (twelve clerics and jurists) to vet and approve candidates before they could run for election, and to approve or veto legislation passed by the Majles. Above all, it confirmed Khomeini himself, and his successors, in the supreme position in the constitution. He had the right to appoint half the members of the Guardian Council, to approve the appointment of the president, and to appoint the head of the Revolutionary Guard Corps and the other heads of the armed forces. While Khomeini used the constitution to consolidate his gains, he was prepared throughout to use violent, extra-legal means to secure his ends, to take and keep the political initiative, and leave his opponents to debate over the rights and wrongs of what had happened. This last was a principle he claimed to have taken from the clerical politician of the 1920s, Modarres: "You hit first and let others complain. Don't be the victim and don't complain."[8]

Press freedom was also curtailed over the summer, in a concerted campaign. Hezbollah attacked newspaper offices, as well as the offices of political parties, forty newspapers closed down, and two of the biggest—*Ettela'at* and *Kayhan*—were taken over by the Bonyad-e Mostazefin. At the same time SAVAK, after the removal of its chiefs and officers by one means or another, was slowly being turned into an agency of the Islamic state (along with Evin prison). In 1984 it was renamed the Ministry of Intelligence and Security (MOIS).

In November 1979, prompted by the news that the shah had been allowed into the United States for treatment of his cancer (which finally killed him in July 1980), students broke into the U.S. Embassy and took the diplomats there hostage. Initially people thought this was just another student demonstration (something similar had happened in February), but when Khomeini backed the students and a continuation of the hostage crisis, Bazargan and his fellow Freedom Movement politicians resigned. Early in 1980 a new president, Abol-Hasan Bani Sadr, was elected under the new constitutional arrangements. He had general support, including from middle-class liberals. For the next year and a half he strove to resolve the hostage crisis, and to uphold principles of conventional legality and secular government. But like Bazargan before him, he ultimately failed and in 1981 was impeached by Khomeini.

Khomeini meanwhile exploited the hostage crisis to preserve a revolutionary fluidity and sense of crisis that enabled him to wrong-foot his opponents. He ordered purges to remove civil servants who were suspected of secularist or antirevolutionary attitudes, closed the universities to eject leftists and impose Islamic principles (they reopened, initially on a much reduced basis, in 1982), and used the Komitehs and Hezbollah to force women to wear the veil. The sense of continuing crisis was only enhanced by

President Carter's attempt to send helicopters to rescue the hostages in April 1980. The humiliation of the hostage crisis, the failed rescue, and the subsequent failure of Carter's reelection campaign all combined to entrench in ordinary Americans a hostile attitude to Iran that still hampers attempts at rapprochement between the two countries. (The hostages were eventually released just after Carter left office in January 1981.) Most Iranians, including radicals who supported the action at the time and some who participated in it, today agree that taking the hostages was a bad mistake.

In the early years of the revolution Khomeini and the IRP had to fight off some formidable enemies, both internal and external. But in each case, true to his guiding principles, it tended to be Khomeini who took the initiative, hitting his opponents with preemptive strikes—at least his internal adversaries. It has been argued that terror and repression were forced on the Iranian revolutionaries—who otherwise would have been humane and tolerant—by the turn of events, the pressure of war, and the viciousness of their enemies. But this argument does not stand up to scrutiny. Although he was reacting to events in a supple way, from the beginning Khomeini was fully aware that if he allowed his enemies to take the initiative, he might not get a second chance. He ruthlessly eliminated his opponents.

The two most serious challenges were from the MKO and Saddam Hossein. Having initially supported the revolution, the MKO were attacked by Khomeini in November 1980 (he labelled them *monafeqin*, the hypocrites—a term that recalled those who had apostatized after declaring loyalty to the Prophet Mohammad). He had their leader imprisoned for ten years on a charge of spying for the Soviet Union,[9] and Hezbollahis attacked the group's headquarters. The MKO fought back with demonstrations and street violence, and then with bombs, managing to kill many of Khomeini's supporters before their leadership was driven into exile. Two bombs at the headquarters of the IRP in June 1981 killed some seventy of Khomeini's closest companions and advisers, including his right-hand man, Ayatollah Beheshti. Large numbers of MKO supporters were killed (as many as several thousand, some of them executed publicly) or imprisoned.[10] From exile, at first in Paris and later in Iraq, the MKO kept up its opposition and its violent attacks. But in time it dwindled to take on the character of a paramilitary cult, largely subordinated to the interests of the Baathist regime in Iraq.

Khomeini and his supporters had also been fighting moves for autonomy in Azerbaijan, and the armed rebellion by the Kurdish Democratic Party (KDP) in Iranian Kurdistan, a rebellion not finally crushed until 1984. The last major political group not aligned to Khomeini and his followers were Tudeh, with whom most of the Feda'i had allied themselves after a split. They had supported Khomeini on the wooden-headed Marxist basis that the revolution of 1979 was a petty-bourgeois revolution that would be a prelude to a socialist one. In 1983 Khomeini turned on Tudeh, accusing them of spying for the Soviets and plotting to overthrow the Islamic regime. Seventy leading members were arrested; there were some executions and televised confessions. Tudeh and the Feda'i were banned, leaving the IRP and the small Freedom Party as the only ones still permitted to operate. The Freedom Party continues to this day in very restricted circumstances under its leader Ebrahim Yazdi.

War

In September 1980 Saddam Hossein's forces invaded Iran, beginning an eight-year war and intensifying pressure on the Iranian regime. Opinion differs over the origins of the Iran/Iraq war—whether Saddam opportunistically attacked Iran at a moment of perceived Iranian weakness, in the hope of snatching some quick gains in the Shatt-al Arab and elsewhere (attempting to put right a border dispute that had been resolved unfavorably for Iraq in the previous decade) or whether Iranian religious/revolutionary propaganda in 1979/1980, apparently directed at starting a revolution among Iraqi Shi'as and destroying his regime, left him little choice. But Saddam was the aggressor, invading and occupying Iranian territory. By the end of that immensely destructive war, Iranian talk of exporting religious revolution (one of the few concrete results of which was the Iranian contribution to the establishment of Hezbollah in Lebanon in the early 1980s) had faded. As many as one million Iranians were killed or injured, and a whole generation was stamped anew with the symbolism of Shi'a martyrdom. In addition to the regular army and the Pasdaran, large numbers of *Basij* volunteers were recruited, including boys as young as twelve. The regime constantly harped on Ashura, Hosein, and Karbala to maintain support for the war and to motivate the troops. The huge casualties on the Iranian side resulted partly from the human wave tactics they employed against the Iraqis, who were normally better equipped. The technological imbalance was the result of the policy of Western nations who, despite their declared neutrality, sent a variety of up-to-date weapons to the Iraqis while keeping the Iranians starved of spare parts for the weapons the shah had bought in the previous decade. The arsenal supplied to Iraq included chemical weapon technology that was used against Iranian soldiers as well as Kurdish civilians in the north of Iraq, whom Saddam treated as rebels. The war also had the effect of physically dividing Iranian Shi'as from the shrine cities of Najaf, Karbala, and Samarra.

Iraqi gains at the outset of the war, which caused huge damage in Khuzestan and the flight of hundreds of thousands of refugees, were wiped out by an Iranian counteroffensive in the spring of 1982, which recaptured Khorramshahr and forced Saddam to withdraw to the border. But the Iranians then amplified their war aims, demanding the removal of Saddam and huge war reparations. Thereafter it was the turn of the Iraqis to go on the defensive, but the Iranians were able to make only minor territorial gains, the most notable being the capture of the Fao peninsula in February 1986. The hope of a Shi'a uprising to support the Iranian attacks in southern Iraq proved an illusion—like Saddam's hope of an Arab uprising in Khuzestan in 1980—and the land war became a stalemate.

Beginning in 1984 Saddam attacked Iranian shipping in the Persian Gulf, trying to damage Iran's oil exports. The Iranians responded in kind, resulting in what became known as the Tanker War. The United States and other noncombatant nations moved ships into the Persian Gulf to protect shipping in international waters, but in July 1988 a U.S. warship, USS *Vincennes*, under a disastrously gung-ho commander, sailed into Iranian territorial waters in pursuit of some Iranian gunboats and after a series of bungles shot down an Iranian civilian airliner with a pair of surface-to-air missiles, killing

290. The Reagan administration gave explanations that contained more misleading inaccuracies and self-justifications than contrition, and later awarded the commander of *Vincennes* a campaign medal. Many Iranians still believe that the destruction of the airliner was not an accident but a deliberate act. Another less-than-glorious episode in the U.S./Iran relationship took place earlier, in 1986, when U.S. officials brought a pallet of spare parts for Iran's Hawk ground-to-air missiles from Israel to Tehran (plus a chocolate birthday cake from a kosher bakery in Tel Aviv and other presents) in what later became known as the Iran/Contra affair. The exposure and failure of the venture stood as another warning of the perils of making contact between the two countries, and of the divide of misunderstanding between them.[11]

As stalemate prevailed in the land war, the Iranians and Iraqis bombarded each other's capitals and other towns indiscriminately with long-range missiles, and with bombs dropped from aircraft, killing many civilians (the War of the Cities). Toward the end, Iraq had the upper hand in these exchanges, and in the land war was able to retake Iraqi territory at Fao and elsewhere, bringing the front line back almost exactly to where it had been in September 1980. Finally, with the terrible cost of the war mounting and no sign of the dream of a March to Karbala being realized, Khomeini was persuaded by Majles Speaker Akbar Hashemi Rafsanjani to accept what Khomeini called the chalice of poison. Rafsanjani, perhaps right for the wrong reason, had used the *Vincennes* incident to insist that the United States would never allow Iran to succeed in the war. Khomeini allowed President Khamenei (elected in 1981 and reelected in 1985) to announce in July 1988 that Iran would accept UN resolution 598, which called for a cease-fire.

Death and Reconstruction

Khomeini died on June 3, 1989, and his funeral at the Behesht-e Zahra cemetery drew crowds and scenes of mass emotion comparable only with those that had greeted his return from exile ten years before. At one point the coffin had to be rescued by helicopter from distraught mourners seeking pieces of his shroud as relics. Khomeini's last months had been overshadowed by the hard decision to end the war with Iraq, and this may have affected his health, but he was also suffering from cancer and heart disease. One significant event in these last months was what is conventionally called the fatwa against Salman Rushdie in February 1989 (some have suggested it would be more accurately described as a *hokm*—a religious judgment). It seems that Khomeini had been made aware of Rushdie's book *The Satanic Verses* some months earlier, but had dismissed it as unimportant (he had not even banned it from being imported). Reconsidering the question later—after demonstrations by Muslims in Britain and riots in Kashmir and Pakistan—he then delivered the fatwa as a deliberate act, to reassert his and Iran's claim to the leadership of Islam.[12] It was another classic Khomeini move, one that trumpeted Iran's Islamic and revolutionary uniqueness. But it also made more difficulties for those who might have wanted to bring Iran out of isolation into some kind of normality.

Another event occurred in these last months that illustrates again the degree to which Khomeini had been (and remained) an enigma even among the ulema. Early in January 1989 Khomeini sent a letter to the Soviet leader Mikhail Gorbachev, observing accurately that communism now belonged in the museum of history. Before he fell into the snare of materialistic capitalism, Khomeini said, Gorbachev should study Islam as a way of life. At first impression this seems an odd suggestion, but perhaps Khomeini sensed an affinity with Gorbachev—as an unconventional thinker hemmed in by unsympathetic and less imaginative minds. The form of Islam that Khomeini recommended upset many of his ulema colleagues—he commended to Gorbachev not the Qor'an nor any of the conventional works but instead the writings of Ibn Arabi, Avicenna, and Sohravardi. With the letter he sent three of his closest companions and pupils, versed in Islamic mysticism. Whatever his private thoughts, Gorbachev thanked them and expressed his pride at having received a personal letter from the Emam. But the letter attracted criticism from clergy in Qom, some of whom upbraided Khomeini in an open letter for having recommended mystics and philosophers. Khomeini responded with a "letter to the clergy" that vented the frustrations of a long life spent enduring the criticism of more tradition-minded mullahs:

> This old father of yours has suffered more from stupid reactionary mullahs than anyone else. When theology meant no interference in politics, stupidity became a virtue. If a clergyman was able, and aware of what was going on [in the world around him], they searched for a plot behind it. You were considered more pious if you walked in a clumsy way. Learning foreign languages was blasphemy, philosophy and mysticism were considered to be sin and infidelity. . . . Had this trend continued, I have no doubt the clergy and seminaries would have trodden the same path as the Christian Church did in the Middle Ages.[13]

Before the revolution, ascent through the ranks of the mojtaheds had been an informal process, but through the 1980s it became much more structured—policed and controlled by Khomeini and his followers.[14] As the hierarchy of Iranian Shi'ism came under control, so did doctrine: Khomeini was attempting to create out of the previous plurality a conformism to a single idea of Shi'ism. In the 1990s this development went further. Examinations were set up for aspiring mojtaheds, and political loyalty—and adherence to the velayat-e faqih—became more important than piety, depth of religious understanding, intellectual strength, or the approval of a loose group of senior clerics, as had previously been the case. A new group of political ayatollahs, selected in this new way, proliferated.[15] Others, more deserving in traditional terms, remained mere mojtaheds.

This meant that the revolution had instituted a religion controlled by the state and subordinated to state interests. The situation was oddly similar, from that perspective, to the *din-e dawlat* the shah had earlier attempted as part of the White Revolution—with the difference that this state was headed by a mojtahed rather than a monarch. By the mid to late 1990s some independent voices warned of the dangers of the new order. Notable among them was the thinker and theologian Abdolkarim Soroush, who called for a secular government and predicted that, otherwise, the compromises and hypocrisies of politics and government would discredit religion in Iran and alienate the young.[16] This is precisely what has happened. The corollary has been an underground resurgence among intellectuals of the nationalism of the 1920s and 1930s pattern, idealizing pre-Islamic Iran and blaming failures of development on the Arab conquest—appearing, ironically, to celebrate the Cyrus-nostalgia most had rejected from the lips of the last shah.[17]

Another voice to take a similar line has been Ayatollah Montazeri.[18] After the death of Beheshti, Montazeri had emerged in the 1980s as the figure most likely to succeed Khomeini as Supreme Leader. Montazeri had been a loyal supporter of Khomeini, and an important theorist for the principle of velayat-e faqih. But toward the end of the 1980s he fell out with Khomeini. The details of this are not entirely clear. Montazeri certainly sent a brave letter to Khomeini protesting the massacre in prison of thousands of political prisoners, mainly former members of the MKO. The massacre followed a final, absurd, doomed offensive by MKO military units from Iraq into Iranian territory just after the July 1988 cease-fire. Montazeri's letter to Khomeini was published:

> Three days ago, a religious judge from one of the provinces, who is a trustworthy man, visited me in Qom to express concern about the way your recent orders have been carried out. He said that an intelligence officer, or a prosecutor—I don't know which—was interrogating a prisoner to determine whether he still maintained his [old] position. Was he prepared to condemn the hypocrite organisation [the Mojahedin]? The prisoner said "Yes."' Was he prepared to take part in a [television] interview? "Yes," said the prisoner. Was he prepared to go to the front to fight the Iraqis? "Yes," he said. Was he prepared to walk into a minefield? The inmate replied that not everyone was prepared to walk over mines and, furthermore, the newly converted could not be expected to do so. The inmate was told that it was clear that he still maintained his [old] position, and he was duly dealt with. The religious judge's insistence that a decision should be based on a unanimous, not a majority, vote fell on deaf ears. He said that intelligence officials have the largest say everywhere and in practice influence others. Your Holiness

> might take note of how your orders, that concern the lives of thousands of people, are carried out.[19]

Some believe that the real rift was over the Iran/Contra arms deal—that Montazeri was left in the dark over the discussions with the United States and reacted badly when he found out. He also criticized the fatwa against Rushdie, saying that foreigners were getting the impression that Iranians were interested only in murdering people. Whatever the details, shortly before Khomeini's death in June 1989 it was made known that Montazeri would not follow Khomeini as Supreme Leader. Instead, Khomeini's close confidant Ali Khamenei took the role, having been promoted suddenly from *hojjatoleslam* to ayatollah—despite having had no very distinguished reputation as a scholar previously (several senior ayatollahs protested at Khamenei's elevation, with the extraordinary result that he became Supreme Leader but only a marja for Shi'as outside Iran). Since that time Montazeri has lived mainly under house arrest, and has made several statements against the conduct of the regime—arguing for a more limited role for the velayat-e faqih, for properly constitutional and democratic government, and an end to human rights abuses.

Despite the efforts of the regime to marginalize him, Montazeri is still the marja-e taqlid for many religious Iranians, along with others who keep a certain distance from the regime. Another important example is Grand Ayatollah Yousef Sanei, who has stated directly that the possession or use of nuclear weapons is unacceptable, and that Iran did not retaliate with chemical weapons against Saddam because marjas concurred that weapons of mass destruction as a whole were unacceptable. Sanei has also issued a fatwa against suicide bombings. Although Shi'as may have been responsible for the devastating suicide attack against the U.S. marine headquarters in Beirut in 1983, Lebanese Hezbollah later stopped using the tactic and since then to my knowledge Shi'a Muslims have not perpetrated suicide attacks.

These are just a few illustrations of the important fact that Iranian Shi'ism, let alone Shi'ism outside Iran, is bigger than the current Iranian religious leadership—something observers from outside the region too often fail to register. In recent years dissent from the regime party line has gathered strength among the Iranian ulema, and reform-minded thinkers like Mohsen Kadivar and Mohammad Mojtahed Shabestari have gained a following for their attempts to address current problems within an Islamic context in an intellectually honest and rigorous way.[20] In a sense, Shi'ism is doing something the religion has always done—legitimizing an alternative pole of authority to that power wielded by the dominant regime. At the same time, the moral authority of the ruling clique has withered just as the moral authority of the Bolsheviks withered.

Several commentators have remarked upon the caesura in Iranian politics created by the end of the Iran/Iraq war and the death of Khomeini.[21] The third event that marked this change was the election of Rafsanjani, the former Majles speaker, as president, in August 1989 (replacing Khamenei, who became Supreme Leader in place of Khomeini in June). As he became president, Rafsanjani announced a new era of reconstruction. Ali Ansari has called it the mercantile bourgeois republic, the period in which the bazaari middle class—long the bedrock of support for the political ulema—finally came into their kingdom.

The war had done huge damage to the Iranian economy and to the living standards of ordinary Iranians. Per capita income had fallen by at least forty percent since 1978.[22] In the border areas where the fighting had taken place, some 1.6 million people had been made homeless, and refineries, factories, government buildings, roads, bridges, ports, and irrigation works had all been destroyed. The country as a whole had to look after large numbers of badly injured ex-servicemen, including people suffering from the after-effects of chemical weapons, many of whom still suffer today. In addition, there were refugees from Iraq—a large number fled to Iran after the first Gulf War in 1991, when the United States and the UK encouraged a Shi'a revolt, and then stood aside while Saddam massacred the rebels—and from Afghanistan, where fighting had been raging since the Soviet invasion of 1979. By the end of the 1990s, Iran was hosting more than two million refugees. Unlike Iraq, Iran had come out of the war without a serious debt burden, but the need for reconstruction was great, and Iran's continuing international isolation was a handicap.

The war had an important unifying effect in the country, and the sacrifices made by ordinary people enhanced their sense of citizenship and commitment to the Islamic republic. The war was the first major conflict involving large numbers of ordinary Iranians since the early nineteenth century—perhaps since Nader Shah. But the commitment and sacrifices were not a blank check. People expected something back when the war was over. Rafsanjani promised them precisely this as he was elected. In particular, he promised development and an improvement in living standards for the poorest—the mostazefin—upon whom, as usual, the heaviest burdens had fallen.

But there was disagreement about the policy means to achieve these goals, and results were mixed. Since the revolution, for the necessity of the prosecution of the war but also to serve the declared aim of greater social equality, the regime had followed broadly statist economic policies. Now Rafsanjani, true to his bazaari origins and sympathies, tried to build the economy by pursuing greater market freedom. But disagreements within the regime hampered the effort—in particular, privatization measures went ahead and then were halted, amid accusations of mismanagement and corruption. Some progress and some expansion of the economy were achieved, but less than had been hoped. Industrial and agricultural production increased, as did exports—especially agricultural exports, and, notably, pistachio exports, in which Rafsanjani's own family had a significant stake. But the economy remained heavily dependent on oil, the oil industry remained inefficient for lack of international help to secure the most up-to-date technology, and that help was further blocked by U.S. economic sanctions, which sharpened through the 1990s as part of the policy of dual containment applied to both Iran and Iraq. Much investment in the economy went into a construction boom, which benefited the investors, but less so the mostazefin, if at all.[23]

By the midpoint of Rafsanjani's second term (1993–1997), there was widespread disappointment with his efforts. Living standards, especially for the less well off, had not improved in the way the people had been led to hope. Unemployment was increasing, partly as a result of sluggish economic performance but also because the population had continued to expand dramatically over the previous twenty years. Iran's rate of population growth was one of the highest in the world in this period—the total went from 33.7 million at the time of the 1976 census to 48.2 million in 1986 and to an estimated 68.5 million in 2007—though the rate of increase has now moderated. Tehran grew to a city of some 12 million people. Throughout the 1990s large numbers of new would-be workers were coming onto the job market each year.

Despite the problems, the first eighteen years of the Islamic republic had achieved important beneficial results for many ordinary Iranians. A determined push to improve conditions for the rural population succeeded where the Pahlavi regime had largely failed, introducing piped water, health services, electricity, and schools even in some of the most remote districts. Life expectancy lifted sharply, along with literacy rates (now around eighty percent—eighty-six percent for men and seventy-three percent for women). Perhaps the most important improvement, reflected in the literacy rate, was in education. Primary education was, at last, effectively extended to all. Iran is a country with a strong cultural appreciation of literacy, education, and intellectual attainment, and families made the most of the new opportunities.

The effect of the revolution on the position of women was typically mixed. They lost the better treatment at divorce that the last shah had introduced, which meant that fathers in principle got child custody—although in practice, as Ziba Mir-Hosseini's film *Divorce Iranian Style* demonstrated, women often manage to find ways around this principle in the divorce courts.[24] But women retained the vote. While polygamy and child marriage were made legal again, they almost never happen, except in some Sunni areas like Baluchistan. The imposition of the veil, along with encouragement from the religious hierarchy, allowed tradition-minded fathers to let their daughters attend schools, which were normally established on a single-sex basis. Girls took to this new opportunity with such energy and application that now sixty-six percent of students admitted to Iranian universities are women.[25] Given the pressure on families to make ends meet, many of these women take up jobs after university and work alongside men, and continue to do so even after marriage (though many also languish in unemployment). Some observers, notably Farah Azari, have remarked upon the way that orthodox, traditional Shi'ism has worked in the past to repress women and female sexuality in Iran, linking that to male anxiety in periods of social and economic change. There are still books to be written on the other distortions this has caused historically.[26] The success of women's education, and the greatly expanded importance of women in the workplace and in the economy, is a huge social and cultural change in Iran—one that in time, and combined with other factors, is likely to have profound consequences for Iranian society as a whole. Surveys have indicated that this is already emerging in more liberal attitudes toward education, the family, and work.[27] There are parallel changes in attitude away from religion toward more secular, liberal, and nationalistic positions.[28] Some clerics among the ulema are challenging the religious judgments on the status of women that were pushed through into law at the time of the revolution. These developments are not peripheral but are absolutely central to the future of the country.

Reform?

Women were some of the strongest supporters of President Khatami, who was elected in May 1997 with a reformist program. Without attacking the velayat-e faqih, Khatami called for proper constitutional government and for a halt to extra-judicial violence. He said several times that he believed his reform program was the last chance for the Islamic republic—that if reform were blocked, the people would demand secular government and overturn the theocratic regime altogether. But his reforms *were* blocked, and the regime became increasingly unpopular, especially among young people. Levels of attendance at mosques have plummeted. Over the last decade the hard-line regime has become more and more overtly self-serving, cynically using its religious trappings, and manipulating elections to keep vested interests in power.

Khatami's election was an unpleasant surprise for the hard-line leadership (they had supported his opponent Nateq Nuri), and they seemed to take some time to adjust to the changed conditions of politics that followed. Khatami won seventy percent of the vote in an election that captured the national imagination as none had done for years. This victory energized a new generation of young Iranians and gave them hope for the future. Unfortunately, Khatami was outmaneuvered by his opponents, and those hopes were disappointed. Some have suggested that he was a stooge for the hard-liners all along, but it is more plausible that he was just a bit too nice for politics—too unwilling, at the crucial moment in the summer of 2000, to risk a confrontation with the hard-liners that could have turned violent.

One question in Iranian foreign policy that always lurked in the background through this period was that of a resumption of diplomatic relations between Iran and the United States. On several occasions President Khatami made statements that seemed to suggest an openness to renewed contact with the United States, notably in an interview with Christiane Amanpour of CNN, broadcast in January 1998.[29] But it appeared that a block on renewed relations with America, like Iran's hostile attitude toward Israel, was a shibboleth the hard-line elements in the Iranian regime were unwilling to discard—a sign of keeping faith with the revolution. Some international commentators speculated that after the improvement of UK/Iran relations in the autumn of 1998, Britain would act as an honest broker between Iran and the United States, but this did not happen. It was difficult too for the U.S. government to make a serious effort at rapprochement, though President Bill Clinton and Secretary of State Madeleine Albright made a number of conciliatory statements in 1999 and 2000.

The murders of writers and dissidents in November and December 1998—events that became known afterward as the serial murders—were widely seen as an attempt by operatives within the MOIS to confront and discredit President Khatami. The victims included Dariush Foruhar, his wife Parvaneh, and other veterans of the initial phase of the revolution. One version of events says that Khatami was brought a tape that recorded a telephone call in which the killers—with Parvaneh audible in the background—had asked their bosses what they should do about her, because her husband was already dead. When Khatami successfully faced down that confrontation and secured the arrest of Saeed Emami and some of the other perpetrators, following up with a purge of the MOIS, many judged that he had strengthened both his own position and the reform process. But the arrests were followed by the detention of thirteen Jews in Shiraz on espionage charges, and again it seemed that disgruntled MOIS officials had arrested innocent people in order to portray the organization as bravely resisting some kind of Zionist plot. The arrests also had the effect of further embarrassing Khatami's efforts at international rapprochement. MOIS claimed at the time that a number of Muslims (nine, eight, three, or two according to different statements) had been arrested in connection with the same case. But details were hazy, and it seems that this was a screen to disguise the anti-Semitic aspect of the action. Eventually all the Jews were released, but some had been convicted in the interim of spying for Israel (for which the penalty can be death), and some of the releases were only on a provisional basis. That meant that the men might be rearrested should the MOIS find that convenient.

The question of the detainees and their uncertain future attracted renewed criticism of Iran and Iran's human rights record internationally. It also threw into harsh relief the situation of Jews in the Islamic republic. While there are still more Jews in Iran than anywhere else in the Middle East apart from Israel, it has been estimated that when Israel was established in 1948, there were at least 100,000 Jews living in Iran. By 1979, there were 80,000, and today estimates vary between 25,000 and 35,000.[30] This decline is mainly explained by the emigration of Iranian Jews to Israel and the United States especially. Plainly, there were both pull and push factors involved in that emigration, but the rate of emigration accelerated rapidly after 1979. After the revolution, in accordance with the Islamic injunction to protect the People of the Book, Khomeini held meetings with Jewish representatives and decreed that Jews should be protected. The constitution gave the Jewish community a fixed representation of one deputy in the Majles (the Armenian Christians and Zoroastrians are treated in a similar way, except that the Armenians have two deputies). Some of the stipulations in traditional shari'a law about the inferior legal status of Jews and other non-Muslims have been changed to make their treatment more equal, but many unequal distinctions remain. These include the rule that a convert to Islam inherits everything when a relative dies, while other claimants who do not convert get nothing. Under the Islamic republic the old anti-Semitism of some has simply dressed itself in anti-Zionist clothes (notwithstanding that many ordinary Iranians feel genuine indignation at Israel's treatment of the Palestinians). Many Jews feel that the political anti-Zionism of the regime has made anti-Semitism respectable, in the newspapers and in petty acts of persecution—for example, demands that Jews donate to anti-Zionist causes. The Jewish community generally survives, as at other times in the past, by making themselves unobtrusive and avoiding trouble. Given the ancient history of the Jews in Iran, and their rich and unique Iranian Jewish culture, this is a sad situation. In the United States and Israel, many Iranian Jewish families still uphold Iranian traditions—the celebration of Noruz, for example—and still speak Persian.

The position of the Baha'is has been worse, and many Baha'is have been imprisoned and executed since 1979 (one accusation leveled at them is that they have Zionist connections). Baha'is have been subject to intimidation and arrest, and to forced conversion. Having banned them from attending university as Baha'is, agents of the regime subsequently attacked those who had set up and participated in Baha'i study circles.

Although some in the West were disillusioned when President Khatami sided with the hard-line leadership in the summer of 1999 and let them break up student protests, it seemed that many Iranians agreed with him that evolutionary change was better than runaway violence. There was good reason to think he was right: after the experience of one revolution, it was understandable that Khatami and many other Iranians were unwilling to risk their hopes for change on the outcome of street violence.[31] Through all this period, the vigor of the expanded free press in Iran encouraged the belief that reform would prevail.

With the election of the strongly reformist sixth Majles in May 2000 (reform-oriented candidates secured 190 seats out of 290), many observers thought the reformers were at last in the driver's seat. Some people speculated that Iran might now move in the direction of a moderated form of religious supremacy, with the clerical element in the system guiding occasionally from the background, rather than taking a direct role as it had since 1979. But in retrospect, it seems that the attacks on former President Rafsanjani in that election campaign were a decisive error by the reformist press, in which they overreached themselves and drove an embittered Rafsanjani, who had previously tried rather ineffectually to arbitrate between the two camps, over to the hard-line side. Beginning in the summer of 2000, hard-line resistance to the reformist program stiffened and became more competent, perhaps reflecting Rafsanjani's advice. A sustained and targeted series of arrests and closures brought the flowering of the free press to an end.[32] Supreme Leader Ayatollah Ali Khamenei intervened personally to prevent the new Majles from overturning the press law that facilitated this crackdown (passed by the previous Majles in the last months of its term). And the Majles generally found themselves blocked by hard-line elements in the Iranian system from making any significant progress with the reform program. If ever Khatami missed the chance to confront the hard-line leadership over his popular mandate for reform—a confrontation that was probably unavoidable if the reform project was to succeed—this was surely the time. But the moment passed, the free press faded, and the hard-line party regained confidence. The testing of the Shahab III medium-range missile in July 2000 also marked a new phase of sharpened international concern over Iranian weapons programs and nuclear ambitions.

9

From Khatami to Ahmadinejad, and the Iranian Predicament

"The empires of the future are the empires of the mind."

—Winston Churchill (speech at Harvard University, September 6, 1943)

Since 1979, Iran has followed a lonely path of resistance to the global influence of Western values—particularly that of the United States. One could see this as a reflection of the Iranians' continuing sense of their uniqueness and cultural significance. The Iranian revolution in 1979 was the harbinger of Islamic revival more widely, showing that previous assumptions about the inevitability of development on a Western model in the Middle East and elsewhere had been misguided. As often before, others followed, for better or worse, where Iran had led. Some hoped in the late 1990s that the Khatami reform movement might show the way out of Islamic extremism at the other end, but although there is good evidence that Iranians are today more skeptical of religious leadership and more inclined to secularism than most other nationalities in the Middle East,[1] that hope appears, at least for the moment, to have been premature.

The failure of the West fully to take advantage of the opportunity offered by a reformist president in Iran already looks like a bad mistake. One such opportunity came after the September 11, 2001, attacks in the United States when members of the Iranian leadership (not just Khatami, but also Khamenei) condemned the terrorist action in forthright terms, and ordinary Iranians showed their sympathies with candlelit vigils in the streets of Tehran—more evidence of the marked difference of attitude between Iranians and other Middle Eastern peoples. Another opportunity came after Iran gave significant help to the coalition forces against the Taliban later in 2001, helping to persuade the Northern Alliance to accept democratic arrangements for post-Taliban Afghanistan.[2] In 2002 Iranians were rewarded with President George W. Bush's "Axis of Evil" speech, which lumped Iran with Iraq and North Korea. Finally, the Bush administration ignored an Iranian offer in the spring of 2003 (shortly after the fall of Baghdad), via the Swiss, for bilateral talks toward a Grand Bargain that appeared to promise a possible resolution of the nuclear issue and de facto Iranian recognition of Israel.

The purpose of all this is not to reinforce the cringing sense of guilt that bedevils many Western observers who look at the Middle East. It is not All Our Fault, and no doubt if the Iranians had been in the position of strength that Britain was between 1815 and 1950, or that the United States has been in since then, they would have behaved as badly, and quite possibly worse. The Iranians also missed opportunities for rapprochement in the Khatami years. But too often we have gotten things wrong, and that has had a cost. It is important to see events from an Iranian perspective, to see how we got things wrong, and to see what needs to be done in order to get them right. The most important thing is this: if we make commitments and assert certain principles, we must be more careful to mean what we say and to uphold those principles.

The Iranian reaction after 9/11 shows in high relief the apparent paradox in Iranian attitudes to the West, in general, and to the United States, in particular. As we have seen, Iranians have real historical grounds for resentment that are unique to Iran and that go beyond the usual postures of nationalism and anti-Americanism. But among many ordinary Iranians there is also a liking and respect for Europeans and Americans that goes well beyond what one finds elsewhere in the Middle East. To some extent this is again a function of the Iranians' sense of their special status among other Middle Eastern nations. Plainly, different Iranians combine these attitudes in different ways, but the best way to explain this paradox is perhaps to say that many Iranians (irrespective of their attitude to their own government, which they may also partly blame for the situation) feel snubbed, abused, misunderstood, and let down by the Westerners they think should have been their friends. This emerges in different ways—including in the rhetoric of politics, as is illustrated by a passage from a televised speech by Supreme Leader Khamenei on June 30, 2007:

> Why, you may ask, should we adopt an offensive stance? Are we at war with the world? No, this is not the meaning. We believe that the world owes us something. Over the issue of the colonial policies of the colonial world, we are owed something. As far as our discussions with the rest of the world about the status of women are concerned, the world is indebted to us. Over the issue of provoking internal conflicts in Iran and arming with various types of weapons, the world is answerable to us. Over the issue of proliferation of nuclear weapons, chemical weapons and biological weapons, the world owes us something.[3]

The troubled course of the relationship between Iran and the West has entered a new and more confrontational phase under President Ahmadinejad. His June 2005 election campaign was successful because, with the organizational backing of the Pasdaran, he articulated the discontent of the poor and the urban unemployed, manipulating yet again Shi'a indignation at the arrogance of power. His opponent in the final stage of the election was former President Hashemi Rafsanjani, who for many Iranians represented the worst of the corrupt cronyism of the regime. But many voted for Ahmadinejad simply because for once they had a chance to vote for someone who was not a mullah. Most foreign observers, often unduly influenced by their contacts in prosperous, reform-inclined north Tehran, were taken completely by surprise at the result. Prior to his election Ahmadinejad, who had visited poorer parts of the country that had not seen a politician for years, emphasized economic and social issues; his religious enthusiasm and his urge to cut a figure in international relations has blossomed only since then. The election was far from fair or free—many reformists openly boycotted it, in protest at the exclusion of their candidates by the Guardian Council. In the second round Ahmadinejad received at most sixty percent of the vote in a sixty percent turnout—less than forty percent of the total number of electors. In the first round of the elections, with a wider field of candidates, he was the first choice of only six percent of the voters.

In the summer of 2005 Niall Ferguson warned that Ahmadinejad could be the Stalin of the Iranian revolution. Ahmadinejad may have the instincts and aspirations of a Stalin, but the political position in Iran is not so open to his ambitions, and he seems unlikely to prove a figure of the same fierce, sinister intelligence. For months the Majles blocked—in the end, successfully—his appointment of favorites and hangers-on to his cabinet. It seemed unlikely then, and seems even more unlikely now, that Ahmadinejad can deliver on his promises to the poor. His economic management has been heavily criticized within Iran, and his introduction of gasoline rationing in the summer of 2007 seems likely to undercut his populism further. After the introduction of the gas rationing, a poll appeared to show that 62.5 percent of the people who voted for Ahmadinejad in 2005 would not do so again.[4] But if the nuclear confrontation with the West, for which he has been the figurehead, leads to sanctions, it could give him and the regime as a whole an alibi for their failure yet again to deliver on the economy and jobs.

Some observers of the situation in Iraq and Iran have warned apocalyptically of the danger of a nuclear-armed Iran controlling a Shi'a-dominated Iraq, a resurgent Shi'a Hezbollah in Lebanon, and a rising (Sunni) Hamas in the West Bank and Gaza, combined with Iranian-backed Shi'a movements erupting in Bahrain and along other parts of the southern coast of the Persian Gulf. This is not a combination that Israel (let alone others) can afford to be complacent about, and the threats of President Ahmadinejad, even if more rhetoric than real, are still significant and influential.

But all is not quite as it may seem. In the wider Middle East, with the possible exception of Hezbollah in Lebanon, Shi'as show little enthusiasm for Iranian-style Islamic rule. For Shi'ism as a global phenomenon, the velayat-e faqih looks increasingly like a radical step too far, and otherwise the most extreme voices in Islam come from the Sunni side. Under the influence of Al-Sistani and Moqtada al-Sadr, Iraqi Shi'as have maintained an independent line, though more attacks and provocations by Sunni insurgents may push them further into the arms of the Iranians. Iran has an influence on Shi'a Iraq, and the Iranians tend to see themselves as the protectors of the Iraqi Shi'as—as they do for Shi'as elsewhere. But the Shi'ism of southern Iraq, centered on the great shrines of Najaf (the tomb of Ali), Karbala, and Samarra, has an authority of its own, independent of Iranian Shi'ism, which is centered on the theological schools of Qom. Iraqi Shi'as do not necessarily trust the Iranians. And many ordinary Iranians do not much like seeing their government spending money and effort on behalf of foreigners—whether Iraqis, Lebanese, or Palestinians—when plenty of Iranians lack jobs, housing, and decent living conditions.

The ruling regime in Iran has many faults, but it is more representative than most in the Middle East outside Israel (though the trend is not encouraging—the Majles elections of 2004 and the presidential elections of 2005 were more interfered with and less free than previous elections). Despite repressive measures by the state, Iran is not a totalitarian country like the Soviet Union during the Cold War. It is a complex polity, with different power centers and shades of opinion among those in power. There is space for dissent—within certain boundaries. Iran still has the potential for self-generated change, as has been recognized by observers from Paul Wolfowitz to Reza Pahlavi, the son of the last shah. Important independent Iranian figures like Shirin Ebadi and dissidents like Akbar Ganji have urged that Iran be left alone to develop its own political solutions. One theory of Iranian history, advanced by Homa Katouzian and others,[5] is that Iran lurches from chaos to arbitrary autocracy and back again. There is certainly some evidence of that in the record. Perhaps increased political freedom would merely unleash chaos, and no doubt there are pragmatists within the current Iranian regime who make just that argument for keeping things as they are. One could interpret the crisis of the reform movement in 2000, followed by the press crackdown, as another episode in the Katouzian cycle. There are signs of disillusionment and nihilism among many young Iranians after the failure of the Khatami experiment.[6] But I don't believe in that kind of determinism. There is real social and political change afoot in Iran, in which the natural dynamic toward greater awareness, greater education, and greater freedom is prominent. Other Europeans in the seventeenth century used to say that England was a hopelessly chaotic place, full of incorrigibly violent and fanatical people who clamored to cut off their king's head. A century later England was the model to others for freedom under the law and constitutional government.[7]

There are grounds for some cautious optimism. The preparedness of Iran and the United States in the spring of 2007 to speak to each other openly and directly for the first time since the hostage crisis is in itself a great step forward that looked impossible—from the perspective of both sides—a year or two ago. The talks are about Iraq. A priority for those talks must be to induce Iran to end the attacks on U.S. and British servicemen in Iraq by Shi'a militia that have caused too many deaths and terrible injuries (the frequency of the attacks seems, in the winter of 2007/2008, to be diminishing). But attempts to lay a major part of the blame for the current problems in Iraq at the door of the Iranians have been dishonest. When the U.S. government presented a dossier in February 2007 detailing allegations that Iran had supplied components for explosive devices to attack coalition armored vehicles, the number of deaths they connected to such attacks was 187, and the validity of the allegations was disputed.[8] At that time the total number of casualties among U.S. and coalition servicemen in Iraq was more than three thousand. Overwhelmingly, coalition servicemen have been killed and wounded not by Shi'a militias backed by Iran, but by Sunni insurgents backed by—whom? Presumably by elements within countries like Jordan and Saudi Arabia.[9] But we don't hear so much about that. Iran has been accused of trying to destabilize the new Iraqi government. But why would Iran wish to do that when Iraqi Shi'as sympathetic to Iran are running that government already? Like the capture of the British sailors and marines in the spring of 2007, Iranian involvement in Iraq is better explained not as aggrandizement aimed at any other outcome, but rather as a reminder from the Iranians to the United States and Britain that Iran has permanent interests on her borders. The Iranian regime, as pragmatism would suggest, has always insisted on its desire for stability in both Iraq and Afghanistan.

It does not look like a good time, with Ahmadinejad in power, for the West to attempt a rapprochement with Iran. But willy-nilly, the United States and Britain need Iranian help in Iraq and Afghanistan, and in the region in general. This is a simple reflection of the fact that Iran is a permanent and important presence in the Middle East, and that Iran has been the prime beneficiary of the removal of the Taliban and Saddam, Iran's former enemies. The present government of Iran is far from perfect, but there are other governments in the Middle East that are as bad or worse—on democracy or human rights—whom we have few scruples about describing as close allies. If we can deal respectfully with Iran as a partner and an equal—and not merely, as too often in the past, as an instrument to short-term ends elsewhere—we might be surprised at how far even the current hard-line regime would go in taking up the partnership. Then we would see the beneficial effects a better relationship could have within Iran. The Iranian leadership is not just Ahmadinejad, and his leverage in the Iranian system is less than it appears. The wider leadership circle—those who coordinate decisions in the Supreme National Security Council—is substantially the same as it was in 2003, when it authorized the Grand Bargain offer.

There are many bleak aspects to the current situation in Iran. The arrests of women and visiting academics in the spring of 2007 were yet another retrograde step. Arrests to enforce the dress code (which relaxed significantly in the Khatami period) and prevent so-called immorality in public, such as a couple holding hands or kissing, intensified at the same time.[10] Khatami's purge of the MOIS has been reversed and many of those suspected of complicity in the serial murders of 1998 have returned. Peaceful demonstrations are broken up and demonstrators arrested and held for extended periods. It is sad beyond words that the president of a country with such a diverse and profound intellectual heritage—and such an ancient and important Jewish presence—should seek to make a splash with a conference for an international rag bag of wild-eyed Holocaust deniers and an exhibition of offensive and inane cartoons. But the propensity of the Iranian regime to Holocaust denial did not begin with Ahmadinejad, just as Iranian support for Hamas and Hezbollah, and their attacks on Israel, goes back many years. Ahmadinejad's call for Israel to be wiped off the map—or according to a more precise translation, "erased from the page of time"—was foolish and irresponsible.[11] His position on the problem of Israel and the Palestinians—that Israel was created for European Jews as a manifestation of European guilt after the Nazi Holocaust, and that the Israelis should go back to Europe—was ignorant and crass. The Jews of Israel came from a wide variety of countries over a long period, including large numbers in the last two decades from the former Soviet Union. Plainly the shock of the Holocaust was one factor in the establishment of Israel, but so too was the poor position of Jews in Islamic countries at that time. In the years immediately after the establishment of the state of Israel in 1948, roughly equal numbers came from Islamic countries on the one hand, and from Europe on the other (including, for example, around 260,000 from Morocco, 129,290 from Iraq, 29,295 from Egypt, 229,779 from Romania, 156,011 from Poland, and 11,552 from Germany in the period 1948–1955[12]). Of course, many tens of thousands of Iranian Jews went to Israel in those years also. In that period Jews in the Middle East, just as much as the Jews of Europe, were seeking a country in which they could be masters of their own destiny—in which they could resist persecution with their own means, as opposed to hoping uncertainly for the friendly intervention of non-Jewish state powers, as had always been the case in the Diaspora. Anti-Semitism had not been just a European phenomenon, and in some degree the present problem of relations between Muslims in the Middle East and Israelis is merely a transformed and relocated version of the old problem of how the majority of Islamic peoples of the Middle East related to the minority of Jews (and other *dhimmis*) in their midst.

Notwithstanding the real need for a solution to the suffering of the Palestinians, for Ahmadinejad to expect the Israelis to return to their former status as second-class citizens and victims in the Middle East is unrealistic political posturing.

The Nuclear Dispute

Ahmadinejad's provocative remarks about Israel have sounded the more threatening because of the continuing dispute over Iran's nuclear program. Most Western states have suspected Iran of trying to acquire a nuclear weapon capability, which if acquired would be a contravention of Iran's commitments under the Nuclear Non-Proliferation Treaty (NPT) and associated agreements. The Iranians claim they have no nuclear weapon ambitions and say, correctly, that the other NPT signatory states are bound to assist Iran's civil nuclear program under *their* NPT commitments. The International Atomic Energy Agency (IAEA) has found no evidence of an Iranian nuclear weapon program. But after the discovery of undeclared nuclear sites at Arak and Natanz in 2002, the IAEA has said that the Iranians have repeatedly failed to meet safeguards obligations, and that it could not be confident that there were no further undeclared nuclear activities or materials in Iran. The IAEA's chairman, Dr. Mohamed El Baradei, has called for greater cooperation and openness from the Iranians to dispel legitimate suspicions about an Iranian nuclear weapon program. Others have pointed out that Iran was not obliged to declare the sites at Arak and Natanz, because they were not yet operational. In the autumn of 2005 the IAEA declared that Iran was not in compliance with the NPT safeguards agreement. Since then, the UN Security Council has called upon Iran to suspend uranium enrichment, and has imposed sanctions.

Uranium enrichment is achieved by spinning uranium gas in a centrifuge to separate out the more fissile uranium 235 isotope from the less fissile uranium 238 isotope. Uranium 235 is the isotope needed for nuclear reactions, and uranium containing a higher than normal proportion of Uranium 235 is described as "enriched." Uranium enriched to between two and three percent is satisfactory for a civil nuclear reactor but needs to be further enriched to ninety percent or more for a nuclear weapon. This is the problem: civil uranium enrichment is a legitimate activity under the NPT. But once the enrichment process has begun, the difference between enrichment to levels consistent with civil use and the levels necessary for weapons is difficult to verify from outside. Iran has been enriching uranium since April 2006, and estimates for the time needed to gather enough highly enriched uranium for a bomb have ranged from two to eight years, depending on the number of centrifuges and the efficiency of their operation.

The Israeli and U.S. governments have made plain that they cannot accept Iran's acquisition of a nuclear weapon. But within Iran, Ahmadinejad and other politicians have presented opposition to their program as Western blocking of Iranian civil nuclear power, and the dispute has produced an upsurge of nationalist feeling in favor of Iran's right to nuclear power. This shades ambiguously into support in some quarters for Iran to *be* a nuclear power—that is, a power with nuclear weapons, like Pakistan, India, Israel, France, Russia, the UK, and the United States. Meanwhile, as the clock ticks and the centrifuges spin, Israel warns that it will take military action to destroy the Iranian nuclear (weapon) program if it is not halted by other means. Some of the rhetoric against Iran in the United States can be dismissed as ignorance and political scare mongering. Israeli concerns cannot.

It may be that the Iranian leadership is determined to acquire a nuclear capability. If so, even Israeli or U.S. bombing campaigns could not stop it indefinitely—the processes could be dispersed and concealed in deep underground bunkers, if they have not been already. And Iran could do enormous damage to the United States and her allies in retaliation. But the declaration by Iranian religious leaders against ownership of nuclear weapons should be given some credence. Possession of a capability to produce a nuclear weapon, as opposed to an actual weapon, would be almost as desirable for the Iranian regime as a weapon itself—it would have most of the deterrent effect of an actual weapon, and the only real utility of nuclear weapons is deterrence. That may be the real Iranian aim—but even that may not be a fixed, determined aim. If Iran were able to normalize its relations with the United States, remove the threat of regime change, and obtain even a limited version of the sort of security guarantees U.S. allies enjoy, the perceived need for a nuclear weapon capability would be much reduced, if not removed altogether. That may be part of the significance of the Grand Bargain offer of 2003. Either way, the United States should at least attempt to resolve the problem in this way before seriously considering military action. It should always be a principle to exhaust diplomacy before contemplating an act of war. That is the minimum that the soldiers and civilians who might die in the event of war have a right to expect of their governments. U.S./Iranian diplomacy has barely yet begun. It may be that after the National Intelligence Estimate of November 2007, and the revelation it contained, that the U.S. intelligence agencies collectively believed that Iran had halted its nuclear weapon program in 2003, negotiation toward a normalization of relations may have become a little easier. At least the danger of conflict appears for the moment to have receded.

Empire of the Mind?

The deeper, reflective, humane Iran is still there beneath the threatening media headlines. Iranian cinema is one of the most remarkable phenomena of the country since the revolution. Banned from the themes of violence and sex regarded by Hollywood as indispensable, Iran has produced a cinema of unique poetic artistry and universal appeal that has won many international prizes. Directors like Abbas Kiarostami, Jafar Panahi, Mohsen Makhmalbaf, and his daughter Samira Makhmalbaf have become internationally recognized through films like *The Apple*, *10*, *Taste of Cherry*, *The Circle*, *Blackboards*, and *Colour of God*. Many of these films develop subjects dealing with the mistreatment of women, the vulnerability of children, the effects of war, the distortions of Iranian politics and society, and other themes critical or tending to be critical of the Islamic regime. Some say that many Iranians, especially young Iranians, never watch these films, choosing instead to see

Hollywood-style film romances that never get an outing in the West. But this cinema nonetheless shows the enduring greatness, the potential, the confidence, and the creative power of Iranian thought and expression.

Iran and Persian culture have been hugely influential in world history. Repeatedly, what Iran has thought today, the rest of the world (or significant parts of it) has believed tomorrow. At various stages Iran has truly been an Empire of the Mind, and in a sense it is still—Iranian culture continues to hold together an ethnically and linguistically diverse nation. Iran is poised now to take on a bigger role in Iraq, Afghanistan, and the region generally than it has taken for many years. But is Iran an empire of the future? In other words, can Iran take the role of importance and influence in the Middle East and the wider world that is her due?

This has to be considered doubtful. One element of the doubt is whether the wider world community will allow Iran that role. But another doubt, the main doubt, is whether today's Iran, governed by a narrow and self-serving clique, is capable of that wider role. In the past, at its best, Iran attained a position of influence by fostering and celebrating her brightest and best minds—by facing complexity honestly, with tolerance, and by developing principles to deal with it. Today Iran is ruled by merely cunning minds, while the brightest and best emigrate or are imprisoned, or stay mute out of fear. A generation of the best-educated Iranians in Iran's history have grown up (more than half of them women) only to be intimidated and gagged. Iran's international position has been one of extreme isolation for over twenty years, and when one of Iran's sharpest and most humane minds, Shirin Ebadi, won the Nobel Peace Prize in 2003, the enthusiasm with which she was feted in the wide world contrasted dismally with the way she was ignored by the Iranian government on her return. Since 1979 Iran has challenged the West, and Western conceptions of what civilization should be. That might have been praiseworthy in itself, had it not been for the suffering and oppression, the dishonesty and disappointment that followed. Could Iran offer more than that? Iran could, and should.

Notes

Preface—The Remarkable Resilience of the Idea of Iran

1. Gobineau, the earliest theorist of Aryan racial theories, served as a diplomat in the French Embassy in Tehran in the 1850s.

Chapter 1—Origins: Zoroaster, the Achaemenids, and the Greeks

1. Accessed from the University of Pennsylvania's Web site, www.museum.upenn.edu/new/research/Exp_Rese_Disc/NearEast/wines.html.

2. A. T. Olmstead, *History of the Persian Empire: Achaemenid Period* (Chicago: University of Chicago Press, 1948), 22–23.

3. The nature of the early Zoroastrian religion is subject to great difficulties of interpretation, on the surface of which I can barely make a scratch. I have relied heavily on Alessandro Bausani, *Religion in Iran: From Zoroaster to Bahu'u'llah* (New York: Bibliotheca Persica, 2000); see also Mary Boyce, *A History of Zoroastrianism, Volume One: The Early Period* (Leiden: Brill, 1975), and Shahrokh Razmjou, "Religion and Burial Customs," in *Forgotten Empire: The World of Ancient Persia* (London: I. B. Tauris, 2005), 150–180.

4. Bausani, *Religion in Iran*, 10–11; see also Mary Boyce, *Zoroastrianism: A Shadowy but Powerful Presence in the Judaeo-Christian World* (London: Dr. William's Trust, 1987), 9.

5. Though Bausani, *Religion in Iran*, doubted this explanation as too simplistic, 29–30, it is an attractive intellectual model with an obvious read-across to the way early Christianity assimilated some previous religious forms, while literally demonizing others as superstition or witchcraft.

6. Though in the earliest times Ahriman's direct opponent was Spenta Mainyu—*Bounteous Spirit*—rather than Ahura Mazda, who was represented as being above the conflict.

7. Boyce, *Zoroastrianism*, 8.

8. Bausani, *Religion in Iran*, 53.

9. The late Mary Boyce believed that Zoroastrianism became better known to the Jews after the end of the Achaemenid Empire, through these diaspora communities (Boyce, *Zoroastrianism*, 11).

10. See Richard C. Foltz, *Spirituality in the Land of the Noble: How Iran Shaped the World's Religions* (Oxford, UK: Oneworld, 2004), 45–53, and Edwin Yamauchi, *Persia and the Bible* (Grand Rapids, MI: Baker Book House, 1990), 463–464, for a counter to the Boyce thesis.

11. Daniel D. Luckenbill, *Ancient Records of Assyria and Babylonia* (London: Histories and Mysteries of Man, 1989), 115–120.

12. James Pritchard, *Ancient Near Eastern Texts Relating to the Old Testament with Supplement*, 3rd ed. (Princeton, NJ: Princeton University Press, 1969), 316.

13. Patricia Crone, "Zoroastrian Communism," in *Comparative Studies in Society and History* 36 (July 1994): 460.

14. Maria Brosius, *Women in Ancient Persia, 559–331 BC* (Oxford: Clarendon Press, 1998), 198–200 and passim.

15. Olmstead, 66–68, quoting later Greek sources.

16. Alessandro Bausani, *The Persians* (London: Book Club Associates, 1975), 20.

17. Josef Wiesehöfer, *Ancient Persia* (London: I. B. Tauris, 2006), 33 and 82. An alternative reading of the evidence would be that Darius murdered the real Bardiya (and possibly his brother Cambyses before him) to gain the throne. He then had to crush a series of loyalist rebellions and concoct a cover story.

18. Ibid., 67–69.

19. Alexandra Villing, "Persia and Greece," in *Forgotten Empire: The World of Ancient Persia* (London: I. B. Tauris, 2005), 236–249.

20. See Villing, 230–231.

21. Olmstead, 519–520.

22. Boyce, *A History of Zoroastrianism*, 78–79.

Chapter 2—The Iranian Revival: Parthians and Sassanids

1. Wiesehöfer, 134.

2. Ibid., 145.

3. Habib Levy, *Comprehensive History of the Jews of Iran*, H. Ebrami, ed. (Costa Mesa, CA: Mazda Publishers, 1999), 113–115.

4. I have taken these lines from an eighteenth-century translation of Plutarch, "by Dacier and others" published in Edinburgh in 1763. In the modern Penguin edition of *The Bacchae* (Harmondsworth: 1973), Phillip Vellacott translated the same lines: *"I am bringing home from the mountains / A vine-branch freshly cut / For the gods have blessed our hunting."*

5. "Arsacid Dynasty," in *Encyclopedia Iranica* (New York: Routledge, 1982–).

6. Ibid.

7. Bausani, *Religion in Iran*, 12; Wiesehöfer, 149.

8. "Arsacid Dynasty," in *Encyclopedia Iranica.*

9. Levy, 113.

10. "Mithraism," in *Encyclopedia Iranica.*

11. Touraj Daryaee, *Sasanian Persia: The Rise and Fall of an Empire* (London: I. B. Tauris, 2007); Wiesehöfer, 160.

12. Homa Katouzian, *Iranian History and Politics: The Dialectic of State and Society* (London: Routledge, 2007).

13. Daryaee, *Sasanian Persia.*

14. Wiesehöfer, 161; "Shapur I," in *Encyclopedia Iranica.*

15. Anthologized in Seamus Heaney and Ted Hughes, eds., *The School Bag* (London: Faber and Faber, 1997), 183–186.

16. Daryaee, *Sasanian Persia.*

17. See Touraj Daryaee, *Sahrestaniha-i Eransahr: A Middle Persian Text on Late Antique Geography, Epic, and History* (Costa Mesa, CA: Mazda Publishers, 2002).

18. Bausani, *Religion in Iran*, 107.

19. Ibid., 83–96.

20. Daryaee, *Sasanian Persia.*

21. Bausani, *Religion in Iran*, 89.

22. Ibid., 89, 118, and 120; Daryaee, *Sasanian Persia.*

23. Bausani, *Religion in Iran*, 87.

24. For Pelagius the best book, an important book, is B. R. Rees, *Pelagius: Life and Letters* (Woodbridge, UK: Boydell and Brewer, 1998). My account of Augustine would be disputed by some, who still uphold his theological positions (reasserted in the sixteenth century and later by Calvinists), but the facts of his time as a Manichaean are not disputed. Much recent Christian theology has turned away from many Augustinian positions, favoring more Pelagian attitudes. An interesting aspect of the dispute is that Pelagius maintained that man could perfect himself and attain salvation by his own efforts; Augustine insisted that salvation could only come by the aid of God's grace. There is a similarity between Pelagius's ideas on this point and the thinking of some Islamic thinkers, notably Ibn Arabi (see Chapter 3).

25. Bausani, *Religion in Iran*, 86.

26. Also Sprach Zarathustra: "*wenn ich frohlockend sass, wo alte Götter begraben liegen, weltsegnend, weltliebend neben den Denkmalen alter Weltverleumder*"—"*if ever I sat rejoicing where old gods lay buried, world-blessing, world-loving, beside the monuments of old world-slanderers.*"

27. "Shapur I," in *Encyclopedia Iranica.*

28. Daryaee, *Sasanian Persia.*

29. Bausani, *Religion in Iran,* 11–13. See page 15 for Bausani's explanation of the later redaction of the Zoroastrian Pahlavi texts in the ninth century.

30. "The Sassanids," in *Encyclopedia Iranica;* Ammianus Marcellinus, vol. 2, 457–503, Loeb Classics.

31. Ibid.; Daryaee, *Sasanian Persia.*

32. Ibid.

33. Crone, 448. She considered the religious movement to be a life-affirming reaction to gnosticism rather than an outgrowth of Manichaeism (461–462), and followed an alternative chronology of events that set the death of Mazdak after Khosraw's accession to the throne. Many aspects of the Mazdak episode are disputed.

34. Mohammad ibn Jarir al-Tabari, *The Sasanids, the Byzantines, the Lakhmids, and Yemen,* vol. 5 of *History of al-Tabari,* edited and translated by C. E. Bosworth (Albany: State University of New York Press), 135 and note. The story also appears in Western accounts, but some of them give the woman as Kavad's wife.

35. Wiesehöfer, 190.

36. Bausani, *Religion in Iran,* 101.

37. Ibid., 100; Daryaee, *Sasanian Persia.*

38. Al-Tabari, 149.

39. Edward Gibbon, *The History of the Decline and Fall of the Roman Empire* (London: Printed by A. Strahan for T. Cadell and W. Davies, 1802), vol. 7, 149–151 (the passage draws on the Byzantine historian Agathias).

40. "The Sassanids," in *Encyclopedia Iranica.*

41. Steven Runciman, *A History of the Crusades* (Harmondsworth: Penguin, 1991), 10–11.

42. "The Sassanids," in *Encyclopedia Iranica.*

Chapter 3—Islam and Invasions: The Arabs, Turks, and Mongols

1. Modern colloquial Persian is in many ways simplified from the written form of classical Persian, and the Persian of young Iranians now is changing further, borrowing many words from English, via films, television, and the Internet.

2. The interpretation of the Prophet's dealings with the Jews of Medina is a controversial subject. See Bertold Spuler, *The Age of the Caliphs: A History of the Muslim World* (Princeton, NJ: Markus Wiener Publishers, 1995), 11–12; Norman A. Stillman, *The*

Jews of Arab Lands: A History and Source Book (Philadelphia: Jewish Publications Society, 1979), 11–16.

3. See Abdelwahab Bouhdiba, *Sexuality in Islam* (New York: Routledge, 1985),19–20 and passim.

4. See for example Ira M. Lapidus, *A History of Islamic Societies* (Cambridge: Cambridge University Press, 2002), 30.

5. Richard N. Frye, *The Golden Age of Persia: The Arabs in the East* (London: Weidenfeld and Nicolson, 1975), 64–65.

6. Aptin Khanbaghi, *The Fire, the Star and the Cross: Minority Religions in Medieval and Early Modern Iran* (London: I. B. Tauris, 2006), 25.

7. Bausani, *Religion in Iran*, 118.

8. Ibid., 111–121.

9. Ibid., 111; for the changes after the conquest see *The Cambridge History of Iran: From the Arab Invasion to the Saljuq*, vol. 4 (London: Cambridge University Press, 1975), 40–48.

10. Ibid., 63–64.

11. Hugh Kennedy, *The Court of the Caliphs* (London: Phoenix, 2005), 134–136.

12. Ehsan Yarshater, "The Persian Presence in the Islamic World," in *The Persian Presence in the Islamic World*, Richard Hovannasian and Georges Sabagh, eds. (Cambridge: Cambridge University Press, 1998), 70–71.

13. Frye, *The Golden Age of Persia*, 122–123; Bausani, *Religion in Iran*, 143.

14. Bausani, *The Persians*, 84–85.

15. Mehdi Nakosteen, *History of the Islamic Origins of Western Education, AD 800–1350* (Boulder: University of Colorado Press, 1964), 20–27.

16. Quoted in Frye, *The Golden Age of Persia*, 150.

17. Bausani, *Religion in Iran*, 121–130; see also Khanbaghi, 20–27.

18. Quoted in Crone, 450.

19. Persian transliterated from Reza Saberi, *A Thousand Years of Persian Rubaiyat: An Anthology of Quatrains from the Tenth to the Twentieth Century Along with the Original Persian* (Bethesda, MD: Ibex Publishers, 2000), 20; for the translation I am grateful to Hashem Ahmadzadeh and Lenny Lewisohn for their help. The selection of poetry that follows here is a personal one and includes a disproportionate number of rubaiyat—largely because the quatrain form is shorter than the other main verse forms and enabled me to incorporate more poetry from a variety of poets in a short space, and to include the original Persian.

20. Jerome Clinton, "A Comparison of Nizami's *Layli and Majnun* and Shakespeare's *Romeo and Juliet*," in *The Poetry of Nizami Ganjavi: Knowledge, Love and Rhetoric*, K. Talattof and J. Clinton, eds. (New York: Palgrave Macmillan, 2000), xvii.

21. Ibid., 72–73.

22. Idries Shah, *The Sufis* (London: Octagon Press, 1964), xiv.

23. A. J. Arberry, *Classical Persian Literature* (London: George Allen/Ruskin House, 1958), 67.

24. Mehdi Aminrazavi, *The Wine of Wisdom: The Life, Poetry and Philosophy of Omar Khayyam* (Oxford: Oneworld Publications, 2007), 25–27.

25. Ibid., 199–200.

26. Saberi, 75; translation by Axworthy, Ahmadzadeh, and Lewisohn. There are examples of quatrains where Fitzgerald took greater liberties with the originals.

27. Aminrazavi, 131–133; Ehsan Yarshater, ed., *Persian Literature* (New York: Bibliotheca Persica Press, 1988), 148–150.

28. Saberi, 78; translation by Axworthy, Ahmadzadeh, and Lewisohn.

29. A. J. Arberry, *The Ruba'iyat of Omar Khayyam: Edited from a Newly Discovered Manuscript Dated 658 (1259–60) in the Possession of A. Chester Beatty Esq.* (London: Emery Walker Ltd., 1949), 14; Ahmad Saidi, ed. and trans., *Ruba'iyat of Omar Khayyam* (Berkeley: University of California Press, 1992), 36; translation by Axworthy, Ahmadzadeh, and Lewisohn.

30. For Sufism generally, see especially Leonard Lewisohn, *The Heritage of Sufism, Volume I: Classical Persian Sufism from Its Origins to Rumi (700–1300)* (Oxford: Oneworld, 1999), and Annemarie Schimmel, *Mystical Dimensions of Islam* (Chapel Hill: University of North Carolina Press, 1975).

31. Lewisohn, *The Heritage of Sufism*, 11–43; Marshall Hodgson, *The Venture of Islam*, vol. 2 (Chicago: University of Chicago Press, 1974), 203, 209, 213, 217–222, 293, 304.

32. *The Cambridge History of Iran, Volume 5: The Saljuq and Mongol Periods* (London: Cambridge University Press, 1968), 299.

33. Arberry, *Classical Persian Literature*, 90–91.

34. R. Gelpke, *Nizami: The Story of Layla and Majnun* (Colchester: Bruno Cassirer, 1966), 168.

35. Clinton, 25.

36. Leonard Lewisohn and C. Shackle, eds., *Attar and the Persian Sufi Tradition: The Art of Spiritual Flight* (London: I. B. Tauris, 2006), 255; and L. Lewisohn, "Attar, Farid al-Din," in Lindsay Jones, ed., *Encyclopedia of Religion, 15-Volume Set* (New York: MacMillan Reference Books, 2005), 601—cf. Nietzsche: *Was aus Liebe getan wird, geschieht immer jenseits von Gut und Böse—That which is done out of love, always takes place beyond Good and Evil.*

37. Farid al-Din Attar, *The Conference of the Birds*, Afkham Darbandi and Dick Davis, eds. and trans. (London: Penguin Classics, 1984), 57–75.

38. David Morgan, *Medieval Persia 1040–1797: History of the Near East* (London: Longman Publishing Group, 1988), 88–96 and passim.

39. *The Cambridge History of Iran, Volume 5*, 313–314; based on John Andrew Boyle, ed. and trans., *The History of the World-Conqueror (Juvayni)* (Cambridge: Harvard University Press, 1958), 159–162.

40. Ibid., 337.

41. Levy, 245.

42. Jalal al-Din Rumi, *The Masnavi, Book One*, Jawid Mojaddedi, ed. and trans. (New York: Oxford University Press, 2004), 4–5.

43. Saberi, 257; translation by Axworthy and Ahmadzadeh.

44. William C. Chittick and Peter Lamborn Wilson, eds. and trans., *Fakhruddin Iraqi: Divine Flashes* (London: Paulist Press, 1982), 34.

45. Ibid., 36.

46. Baqer Moin, *Khomeini: Life of the Ayatollah* (London: I. B. Tauris, 1999), 47. These are deep waters; the idea of the Perfect Man refers back to Sohravardi, Neoplatonism, and possibly to the personifications (daena, fravashi) and angels in Zoroastrianism; see also Henry Corbin, *En Islam Iranien: Aspects Spirituels et Philosophiques*, vol. 2 (Paris: Gallimard, 1971), 297–325.

47. Henry Corbin, *Spiritual Body and Celestial Earth: From Mazdean Iran to Shi'ite Iran* (Princeton: Princeton University Press, 1977), 139; the similarity to the earlier extracts describing the daena is obvious.

48. Chittick and Wilson, 60.

49. G. M. Wickens, trans., *The Bustan of Sa'di* (Leiden: 1974), 150.

50. Edward Granville Browne, *A Literary History of Persia: Volume II, From Firdawsi to Sa'di* (Cambridge: Cambridge University Press, 1969), 530.

51. Saberi, 274; translation by Axworthy and Ahmadzadeh.

52. Ibid., 277; translation by Axworthy and Ahmadzadeh.

53. Arberry, *Classical Persian Literature*, 331. There is more than an echo of this poem in Matthew Arnold's *Dover Beach*.

54. Arberry, 43; I am grateful to Lenny Lewisohn for his translation. Compare with Thomas Hardy's poem "Moments of Vision":

That mirror
Which makes of men a transparency
Who holds that mirror
And bids us such a breast-bare spectacle see
Of you and me?

55. And not just Iranians—Western commentators have agonized over whether such poems, addressed to a Beloved in the third person singular—which in Persian is gender neutral—are homoerotic or conventionally heterosexual. The answer, given the absence of clear gender markers, such as one finds in other poems, is surely that the ambiguity is deliberate. One might more profitably reflect how appropriate the neutral third person is to the higher meaning of the Beloved, i.e., to God.

56. P. Natil Khanlari, ed., *Divan-e Hafez* (Tehran: 1980), ghazal 197; also quoted in John W. Limbert, *Iran: At War with History* (Boulder, CO: Westview Press, 1987), 144.

57. Saberi, 384; Saberi's translation.

58. *The Cambridge History of Iran, Volume 5*, 546–547.

59. Jürgen Paul, "L'invasion Mongole comme revelateur de la société Iranienne," in *L'Iran face à la domination Mongole* (Tehran: 1997), 46–47 and passim.

60. Cf. Mostafa Vaziri, *Iran as Imagined Nation: The Construction of National Identity* (New York: Marlowe and Company, 1994), passim.

61. Ibn Khaldun, *The Muqaddimah: An Introduction to History* (London: Routledge and Kegan Paul, 1967), 353–355; E. Gellner, "Tribalism and the State in the Middle East," in *Tribes and State Formation in the Middle East* (London: I. B. Tauris, 1991), passim.

Chapter 4—Shi'ism and the Safavids

1. The following draws largely on Moojan Momen, *An Introduction to Shi'i Islam: The History and Doctrines of Twelver Shi'ism* (New Haven, CT: Yale University Press, 1987), 28–33 and passim.

2. See for example James A. Bill and John Alden Williams, *Roman Catholics and Shi'i Muslims: Prayer, Passion, and Politics* (Chapel Hill: University of North Carolina Press, 2002), 1–7.

3. Kathryn Babayan, *Mystics, Monarchs and Messiahs: Cultural Landscapes of Early Modern Iran* (Cambridge: Harvard Center for Middle Eastern Studies, 2002), xxxviii.

4. Ibid., xxxix.

5. *Encyclopedia Iranica* "Esmail" (Savory); see also Andrew J. Newman, *Safavid Iran: Rebirth of a Persian Empire* (London: I. B. Tauris, 2006), 9–12.

6. "Esmail," in *Encyclopedia Iranica* (Savory).

7. Newman, 24–25 , passim.

8. The extent of Shi'ism in Iran before 1500 and the changes thereafter have been thoroughly explored by Rasul Ja'farian, *Din va Siyasat dar Dawrah-ye Safavi* (Qom: 1991).

9. Foltz, 134.

10. V. Minorsky, ed. and trans., *Tadhkirat al-Muluk: A Manual of Safavid Administration* (London: Gibb Memorial Trust, 1980), 33–35.

11. See Willem Floor, *The Economy of Safavid Persia* (Wiesbaden, Germany: 2000), and Rudolph Matthee, *The Pursuit of Pleasure: Drugs and Stimulants in Iranian History 1500–1900* (Princeton, NJ: Princeton University Press, 2005).

12. C. A. Bayly, *Imperial Meridian: The British Empire and the World 1780–1830* (London: Longman, 1989), 30; J. Foran, "The Long Fall of the Safavid Dynasty: Moving Beyond the Standard Views," in *The International Journal of Middle East Studies*, no. 24 (1992): 281–304 (passim); Mansur Sefatgol, "Safavid Administration of Avqaf: Structure, Changes and Functions, 1077–1135/1666–1722," in *Society and Culture in the*

Early Modern Middle East: Studies on Iran in the Safavid Period (Leiden: Brill Academic Publishers, 2003), 408.

13. See Willem Floor, *Safavid Government Institutions* (Costa Mesa, CA: Mazda Publishers, 2001) and Minorsky.

14. "Molla Sadra Shirazi," in *Encyclopaedia Iranica* (Sajjad Rizvi). "Molla" and "Mullah" are the same word, but I refer to Molla Sadra in this way in an attempt to distance him from modern connotations that could be misleading.

15. Roy Mottahedeh, *The Mantle of the Prophet* (Harmondsworth: Penguin, 1987), 179.

16. Yarshater, *Persian Literature*, 249–288, and, notably, the quotation from Bausani, 275.

17. Levy, 293–295; see also Eliz Sanasarian, *Religious Minorities in Iran* (Cambridge/New York: Cambridge University Press, 2000), 45.

18. To get a sense of this, albeit in a description from a later period, the relationship between the Jewish family and their village mullah in Dorit Rabinyan's *Persian Brides* (Edinburgh: George Braziller Publishers, 1998) is vivid and memorable.

19. Mottahedeh, 203. The thinker Ali Shariati (1933–1977) also attacked the Shi'ism of the Safavid period (Black Shiism) but arguably was addressing deficiencies of religious practice in his own time rather than making a historical point. His priority was to encourage a resurgence of true Shi'ism (Red Shi'ism)—a revolutionary Shi'ism of social justice—see Chapter 7.

20. See Rudolph Matthee, "Unwalled Cities and Restless Nomads: Firearms and Artillery in Safavid Iran," in *Safavid Persia: The History and Politics of an Islamic Society* (London: I. B. Tauris, 1996), and Michael Axworthy, "The Army of Nader Shah," in *Iranian Studies* (December 2007).

21. Matthee, *The Pursuit of Pleasure*, 61.

22. Ibid., 50–56.

23. Roger Savory, *Iran Under the Safavids* (Cambridge: Cambridge University Press, 2007), 232.

24. Matthee, *The Pursuit of Pleasure*, 58–60.

25. Ibid., 91–92, 92n. The evidence comes not just from Western observers at court, but also from Persian sources; the Shaykh ol-Eslam of Qom had the temerity to criticize the shah's drinking and was lucky to escape execution for it.

26. Newman, *Safavid Iran*, 99; "Part of this struggle for the hearts and minds of the 'popular' classes."

27. See V. Moreen, "Risala-yi Sawa'iq al-Yahud [The treatise Lightning Bolts Against the Jews] by Muhammad Baqir b. Muhammad Taqi al-Majlisi (d. 1699)," in *Die Welt des Islams* 32 (1992), passim.

28. J. Calmard, "Popular Literature Under the Safavids," in *Society and Culture in the Early Modern Middle East: Studies on Iran in the Safavid Period* (Leiden: Brill Academic Publishers, 2003), 331.

Chapter 5—The Fall of the Safavids, Nader Shah, the Eighteenth-Century Interregnum, and the Early Years of the Qajar Dynasty

1. This version is taken from Sir John Malcolm, *History of Persia: Containing an Account of the Religion, Government, Usages, and Character of the Inhabitants of That Kingdom* (London: Murray, 1829), 399–400; but a number of Persian and other sources give the same story—cf. Mohammad Kazem Marvi, 18, and Fr. Judasz Tadeusz Krusinski, *The History of the Late Revolutions of Persia* (London: 1740; New York: Arno Press, reprint 1973), 62–64.

2. Matthee, *The Pursuit of Pleasure*, 92–94; Babayan, 485; Lewisohn, *The Heritage of Sufism, Volume I*, 132–133.

3. Birgitt Hoffmann, ed. and trans., *Persische Geschichte 1694–1835 erlebt, erinnert und erfunden—das Rustam at-Tawarikh in deutscher Bearbeitung* (Bamberg, Germany: Aku, 1986), 203–204, 290; Krusinski, 121–122; Michael Axworthy, *The Sword of Persia: Nader Shah, from Tribal Warrior to Conquering Tyrant* (London: I. B. Tauris, 2006), 31–33.

4. Bayly, 30; Foran.

5. Krusinski, 196–198.

6. Axworthy, *The Sword of Persia*, 142.

7. N. D. Miklukho-Maklai, "Zapiski S Avramova ob Irane kak istoricheskii Istochnik," in *Uchenye Zapiski Leningradskogo gosudarstvennogo universiteta. Seriia vostokovedcheskikh nauk*, Part 3 (Leningrad.: 1952), 97.

8. Basile Vatatzes (ed. N. Iorga), *Persica: Histoire de Chah-Nadir* (Bucharest, Romania: 1939), 131–133.

9. Levy, 360–362; Axworthy, *The Sword of Persia*, 169.

10. The full significance of Nader's religious policy is covered admirably in Ernest Tucker's *Nadir Shah's Quest for Legitimacy in Post-Safavid Iran* (Gainesville: University Press of Florida, 2006).

11. See Axworthy, *The Sword of Persia*, 249–250; as well as Axworthy, "The Army of Nader Shah." The size of the army is corroborated from a number of sources, and is plausible given earlier trends.

12. Bayly, 23 (Ottoman and Moghul figures); Floor, *The Economy of Safavid Persia*, 2; Charles Issawi, *The Economic History of Iran, 1800–1914* (Chicago: University of Chicago Press, 1971), 20; Willem Floor, "Dutch Trade in Afsharid Persia" *Studia Iranica*, Tome 34, fascicule 1, 2005 .

13. Axworthy, *The Sword of Persia*, 280–281.

14. Mirza Mohammad Mahdi Astarabadi, *Jahangusha-ye Naderi*, translated into French by Sir William Jones as the *Histoire de Nader Chah* (London: 1770) (original Persian text edited by Abdollah Anvar, Tehran, 1377), 187.

15. *The Cambridge History of Iran*, vol. 7, 63–65.

16. Floor, *The Economy of Safavid Persia*, 3.

17. Ibid.

18. Ibid., 2–3; Issawi, 20.

19. Floor, "Dutch Trade in Afsharid Persia," 59.

20. Notably by Ann K. S. Lambton, "The Tribal Resurgence and the Decline of the Bureaucracy in the Eighteenth Century," in *Studies in Eighteenth-Century Islamic History* (Carbondale and Edwardsville: Southern Illinois University Press, 1977). For this paragraph see also *The Cambridge History of Iran*, vol. 7, 506–541 (Richard Tapper); Richard Tapper, *Frontier Nomads of Iran: A Political and Social History of the Shahsevan* (Cambridge: Cambridge University Press, 2006), 1–33; and Gellner.

21. Hasan-e Fasa'i, *History of Persia Under Qajar Rule* (New York: Columbia University Press 1972), 4.

22. Ibid., 52–54.

23. Malcolm, 125.

24. *The Cambridge History of Iran*, vol. 7, 125.

25. See Hamid Algar, "Shi'ism and Iran in the Eighteenth Century," in *Studies in Eighteenth-Century Islamic History* (Carbondale and Edwardsville: Southern Illinois University Press, 1977).

26. Mottahedeh, 233; a similar process took place in the later Roman Empire with the title of senator and other honorifics.

27. Momen, 238–244; Nikki R. Keddie (Ghaffary), *Qajar Iran and the Rise of Reza Khan 1796–1925* (Costa Mesa, CA: Mazda Publishers, 1999), 94–96.

28. For example, Hasan-e Fasa'i, 101–102.

29. *The Cambridge History of Iran*, vol. 7, 142–143.

30. Malcolm, 217.

31. Denis Wright, *The English Amongst the Persians: Imperial Lives in Nineteenth-Century Iran* (London: I. B. Tauris, 1977), 4–5.

32. *The Cambridge History of Iran*, vol. 7, 331–333; Hasan-e Fasa'i, 111.

33. Ibid., 334; Keddie, *Qajar Iran and the Rise of Reza Khan 1796–1925*, 22.

34. Ibid., 335–338.

35. Nikki R. Keddie, *Modern Iran: Roots and Results of Revolution* (New Haven, CT: Yale University Press, 2006), 42–43.

36. Laurence Kelly, *Diplomacy and Murder in Tehran: Alexander Griboyedov and Imperial Russia's Mission to the Shah of Persia* (London: Tauris Parke Paperbacks, 2006), 190–194.

37. Nikki R. Keddie, "The Iranian Power Structure and Social Change 1800–1969: An Overview," *International Journal of Middle East Studies* 2 (January 1971): 3–4; *The Cambridge History of Iran*, vol. 7, 174–181.

38. Keddie, *Qajar Iran and the Rise of Reza Khan 1796–1925*, 17; *The Cambridge History of Iran*, vol. 7, 174.

Chapter 6—The Crisis of the Qajar Monarchy, the Revolution of 1905–1911, and the Accession of the Pahlavi Dynasty

1. Abbas Amanat, *Pivot of the Universe: Nasir al-Din Shah and the Iranian Monarchy, 1831–1896* (Berkeley: University of California Press, 1997), 252.

2. Levy, 427.

3. Ibid., 430.

4. Haideh Sahim, "Jews of Iran in the Qajar Period: Persecution and Perseverence," in *Religion and Society in Qajar Iran* (London: RoutledgeCurzon, 2005), 293–310.

5. Sanasarian, 45–46.

6. Hasan-e Fasa'i, 256–260.

7. Amanat, 44, 66.

8. For a case study of the Qashqai tribe bringing out these points, see Lois Beck, "Women Among Qashqai Nomadic Pastoralists in Iran," in *Women in the Muslim World* (Cambridge: Harvard University Press, 1979).

9. Keddie, *Qajar Iran and the Rise of Reza Khan 1796–1925*, 26–28; Amanat, 113–117.

10. *The Cambridge History of Iran*, vol. 7, 182–183.

11. Amanat, 428–429; *The Cambridge History of Iran*, vol. 7, 180.

12. Ibid., 180.

13. Ibid., 401–404 (Greaves).

14. Quoted in Ervand Abrahamian, "The Causes of the Constitutional Revolution in Iran," *International Journal of Middle East Studies* 10 (August 1979): 400.

15. Nikki R. Keddie, "Sayyid Jamal Al-Din Al-Afghani," in *Pioneers of Islamic Revival* (London: Zed Books, 2005), 24 (I drew on Keddie also for the last part of the previous paragraph).

16. Levy, 397.

17. *The Cambridge History of Iran*, vol. 7, 199–200.

18. Abrahamian, "The Causes of the Constitutional Revolution in Iran," 404.

19. Ibid., 408–409.

20. Levy, 490–491.

21. Mottahedeh, 221–222; Vanessa Martin, *Islam and Modernism: The Iranian Revolution of 1906* (London: I. B. Tauris, 1989), 193–195.

22. Ibid., 223; Moin, 22.

23. Levy, 498–507.

24. *The Cambridge History of Iran*, vol. 7, 206–207; Said Amir Arjomand, *The Turban for the Crown: Islamic Revolution in Iran* (London: Oxford University Press, 1988), 46.

25. Morgan Schuster, *The Strangling of Persia* (London: T. Fisher Unwin, 1912), 219.

26. Ali Ansari, *A History of Modern Iran Since 1921: The Pahlavis and After* (London: Longman, 2003), 22.

27. Accessed at http://www.gwpda.org/Dunsterville/Dunsterville_1918.htm.

28. For the contrary view see Homa Katouzian, "Riza Shah's Legitimacy and Social Base," in *The Making of Modern Iran: State and Society Under Riza Shah, 1921–1941* (London: RoutledgeCurzon, 2003), 16–18.

29. Ansari, *A History of Modern Iran Since 1921*, 21–22.

30. Homa Katouzian, *State and Society in Iran: The Eclipse of the Qajars and the Emergence of the Pahlavis* (London: I. B. Tauris, 2000), 165; Arjomand, 60; Keddie, *Qajar Iran and the Rise of Reza Khan 1796–1925*, 74.

31. Wright, 181; Katouzian, *State and Society in Iran*, 233; also Keddie, *Qajar Iran and the Rise of Reza Khan 1796–1925*, 79; Michael Zirinsky, "Imperial Power and Dictatorship: Britain and the Rise of Reza Shah, 1921–1926," *International Journal of Middle East Studies* 24 (November 1992): passim.

32. Arjomand, 62–63.

Chapter 7—The Pahlavis and the Revolution of 1979

1. Vita Sackville-West, *Passenger to Teheran* (London: Tauris Parke Paperbacks, 1991; 1st ed., 1926), 100–101; Keddie, *Qajar Iran and the Rise of Reza Khan 1796–1925*, 79.

2. Stephanie Cronin, "Paradoxes of Military Modernisation," in *The Making of Modern Iran: State and Society Under Riza Shah, 1921–1941* (London: RoutledgeCurzon, 2003), 44 and passim.

3. Issawi, 376.

4. Ervand Abrahamian, *Iran Between Two Revolutions* (Princeton, NJ: Princeton University Press, 1982), 143.

5. Issawi, 375–379.

6. Rudolph Matthee, "Education in the Reza Shah Period," in *The Making of Modern Iran* (London: RoutledgeCurzon, 2003), 140 and passim.

7. Kamran Talattof, *The Politics of Writing in Iran: A History of Modern Persian Literature* (Syracuse, NY: Syracuse University Press, 2000), 53–62. The story that all Hedayat's

works had been banned by Ahmadinejad was carried in the *Guardian* in an article by Robert Tait on November 17, 2006, but when I visited Iran in November 2007, I was told that only one of his works had been banned.

8. Yarshater, *Persian Literature*, 336–380.

9. Abrahamian, *Iran Between Two Revolutions*, 143; Katouzian, "Riza Shah's Legitimacy and Social Base," 29–30.

10. Ansari, *A History of Modern Iran Since 1921*, 56–59.

11. Ibid., 68.

12. Katouzian, "Riza Shah's Legitimacy and Social Base," 26–32.

13. Abrahamian, *Iran Between Two Revolutions*, 163 (the shooting) and 158–161; Ansari, *A History of Modern Iran Since 1921*, 64.

14. Ibid., 164.

15. Katouzian, "Riza Shah's Legitimacy and Social Base," 32–33.

16. Levy, 544–546.

17. Accessed at http://users.sedona.net/~sepa/sardarij.html and www.wiesenthal.com/site/apps/s/content.asp?c=fwLYKnN8LzH&b=253162&ct=285846.

18. Ansari, *A History of Modern Iran Since 1921*, 110.

19. Ibid., 78–85.

20. Homa Katouzian, *Sadeq Hedayat: The Life and Legend of an Iranian Writer* (London: RoutledgeCurzon, 2003), 13–14; Katouzian rather dryly suggests that the reorientation would have shifted as easily in the other direction if Axis powers had occupied Iran.

21. Mottahedeh, 98–105; Abrahamian, *Iran Between Two Revolutions*, 125–126.

22. Ibid., 164.

23. Moin, 105.

24. Keddie, *Modern Iran*, 130; Daryiush Bayandor's researches toward a new book on the coup argue plausibly that the role of the secret services was rather less significant than previously thought and that of the clergy and their bazaari supporters was rather more significant.

25. Mottahedeh, 287–323; George Morrison, ed., *History of Persian Literature from the Beginnings of the Islamic Period to the Present Day* (Leiden, UK: Brill Academic Publishers, 1981), 201–202 (Kadkani); for Simin Daneshvar's revelations, see Talattof, 160.

26. Ansari, *A History of Modern Iran Since 1921*, 133.

27. Abrahamian, *Iran Between Two Revolutions*, 420.

28. Issawi, 375–382.

29. Quoted in Ali Ansari, *Iran, Islam and Democracy: The Politics of Managing Change* (London: Chatham House, 2000), 38–39.

30. Keddie, *Modern Iran*, 145; Robert Graham, *Iran: The Illusion of Power* (London: Croom Helm, 1978), 69.

31. Moin, 107–108.

30. Keddie, *Modern Iran,* 145; Robert Graham, *Iran: The Illusion of Power* (London: Croom Helm, 1978), 69.

31. Moin, 107–108.

32. Ibid., 123.

33. Ibid., 1–8.

34. The best account of such an education is Mottahedeh's brilliant *Mantle of the Prophet.*

35. Moin, 42–44.

36. Ibid., 64.

37. Keddie, *Modern Iran,* 147.

38. Ibid., 152.

39. Abrahamian, *Iran Between Two Revolutions,* 535–536.

40. Keddie, *Modern Iran,* 158.

41. Abrahamian, *Iran Between Two Revolutions,* 430–431.

42. James A. Bill, *The Eagle and the Lion: The Tregedy of American-Iranian Relations* (New Haven, CT: Yale University Press, 1988), 379–382.

43. Farah Azari, "Sexuality and Women's Oppression in Iran," in *Women of Iran: The Conflict with Fundamentalist Islam* (London: Ithaca Press, 1983), 130–132 and passim, drew attention to the sexual aspect of the revolution in an insightful chapter, and Mottahedeh, 273, makes a similar point.

44. Mottahedeh, 270–272.

45. Quoted in Abrahamian, *Iran Between Two Revolutions,* 419.

46. Ansari, *A History of Modern Iran Since 1921,* 173.

47. Bill, *The Eagle and the Lion,* 183–184.

48. Mottahedeh, 328.

49. For a vivid picture of the lives of the Jews of Shiraz in this period, see Laurence D. Loeb, *Outcaste: Jewish Life in Southern Iran* (New York: Routledge, 1977).

50. Abrahamian, *Iran Between Two Revolutions,* 500–504.

51. Moin, 152–156.

52. Momen, 256–260.

53. Keddie, "Sayyid Jamal Al-Din Al-Afghani", 236

54. Ibid., 208–245; Abrahamian, *Iran Between Two Revolutions,* 464–473.

55. Moin, 186.

56. This judgement is based on contributions to the Gulf 2000 Internet forum in the spring of 2007; particularly on a contribution from Ali Sajjadi, who investigated the case for a Radio Farda report.

57. Abrahamian, *Iran Between Two Revolutions,* 510–513.

58. Ibid., 519.

Chapter 8—Iran Since the Revolution: Islamic Revival, War, and Confrontation

1. Or alternatively, *hich ehsasi nadaram*—"I have no feelings."

2. See Chapter 3.

3. With the partial exception, in the context of ghuluww rhetoric, of Shah Esma'il I (see Chapter 4).

4. I am grateful to Baqer Moin for this quotation, and his thoughts on this subject, and the insights in his book *Khomeini.*

5. Abrahamian, *Iran Between Two Revolutions*, 526–529.

6. Moin, 207–208.

7. Roy 1994, 173, claims that none of the most senior ayatollahs (the grand ayatollahs) supported the velayat-e faqih in 1981—except Montazeri, Khomeini's pupil.

8. Moin, 214.

9. Momen, 294.

10. Ansari, *A History of Modern Iran Since 1921*, 233.

11. Bill, *The Eagle and the Lion*, 1–2.

12. Moin, 282–283; Chris Rundle, *From Colwyn Bay to Kabul: An Unexpected Journey* (Stanhope: 2004), 146–150.

13. Quoted in Moin, 275–276.

14. Momen, 298–299.

15. Ansari, *A History of Modern Iran Since 1921*, 244–245.

16. For further exposition of Soroush's ideas on this point, see Ansari, *Iran, Islam and Democracy*, 75.

17. See Katouzian, *Sadeq Hedayat*, 5–6, and Mottahedeh, 383–384.

18. See the interview published in the *Mideast Mirror*, January 20, 2000, 15, among other statements.

19. Moin, 279.

20. David Menashri, *Post-Revolutionary Politics in Iran: Religion, Society and Power* (London: Routledge, 2001), 35–38.

21. See Anoush Ehteshami, *After Khomeini: The Iranian Second Republic* (London: Routledge, 1995), passim; and Ansari, *Iran, Islam and Democracy*, 52–53.

22. Keddie, *Modern Iran*, 264.

23. Ibid., 264–266.

24. See also Ziba Mir-Hosseini, "Women, Marriage and the Law in Iran," in *Women in the Middle East* (Basingstoke, UK: Macmillan, 1992).

25. 2003 figures—Keddie, *Modern Iran*, 286.

26. Afsaneh Najmabadi, *Women with Mustaches and Men Without Beards: Gender and Sexual Anxieties of Iranian Modernity* (Berkeley: University of California Press, 2005), gives thought-provoking analysis on the theme of gender in Iranian history.

27. Azadeh Kian-Thiébaut, "From Motherhood to Equal Rights Advocates: The Weakening of the Patriarchal Order," *Iranian Studies* 38 (March 2005): passim.

28. Brought out most clearly in the comparative surveys carried out by Mansour Moaddel, which also back up Kian-Thiébaut—for example, 49 percent of Iranians surveyed believed love was more important than parental approval when marrying (41 percent thought the contrary), where in Iraq the split was 71 percent for parental approval and 26 percent for love. In Saudi Arabia, the tallies were 50 percent for parental approval and 48 percent for love. Surveys are accessible at www.psc.isr.umich.edu/research/tmp/moaddel_values_survey.html.

29. The interview is discussed in detail in Ansari, *Iran, Islam and Democracy*, 133–137.

30. Sanasarian, *Religious Minorities in Iran*, 47, 47n; 48, 48n. Others have suggested that the number of Jews in 1948 may have been as high as 140,000 to 150,000.

31. Shirin Ebadi said something very much to this effect—that one revolution is enough—in a speech she gave at the Hay-on-Wye literary festival in May 2006.

32. For discussion of the crackdown on the free press in the summer of 2000, see Ansari, *Iran, Islam and Democracy*, 211–217.

Chapter 9—From Khatami to Ahmadinejad, and the Iranian Predicament

1. For example, 27 percent of Iranians surveyed by Mansour Moaddel took part in religious services once a week or more, compared with 33 percent in Iraq, 42 percent in Egypt, 44 percent in Jordan, and 45 percent in the United States. Fifty-five percent of Iranians thought Western cultural invasion was a very serious problem, compared with 64 percent of Egyptians, 68 percent of Iraqis, 70 percent of Saudis, and 85 percent of Jordanians. Asked whether they were primarily Muslim or country nationalists, 61 percent of Iranians said Muslim and 34 percent said nationalist. In Iraq it was 63 percent Muslim and 23 percent nationalist; in Jordan, 72 percent Muslim and 15 percent nationalist; in Saudi Arabia, 75 percent Muslim and 17 percent nationalist; and in Egypt, 79 percent Muslim and 10 percent nationalist. In Iran 60 percent thought men made better political leaders than women, compared with 72 percent in Saudi Arabia, 84 percent in Egypt, 86 percent in Jordan, 87 percent in Iraq, and 22 percent in the United States. However, other findings suggested that, perhaps because they have had more experience with it, Iranians were less enthusiastic about democracy as the best form of government than others in the region. Accessed at www.psc.isr.umich.edu/research/tmp/moaddel_values_survey.html.

2. For details of Iranian support against the Taliban, see the report from James Dobbins (leader of the U.S. delegation to the talks in Bonn that set up the coalition), *Washington Post*, July 22, 2007.

3. Translated transcript from Mideastwire.com.

4. Poll by Baztab.com; reported to Gulf 2000 (a Web discussion forum) by Meir Javedanfar.

5. Katouzian, *Iranian History and Politics*; see also Mansour Moaddel, *Islamic Modernism, Nationalism and Fundamentalism: Episode and Discourse* (Chicago: University of Chicago Press, 2004).

6. For these, and for a brilliant snapshot of the general attitudes of at least some young Iranians, see Nasrin Alavi, *We Are Iran: The Persian Blogs* (London: Portobello Books, 2005); also R. Varzi, *Warring Souls: Youth, Media and Martyrdom in Post-Revolution Iran* (Durham: University of North Carolina Press, 2006).

7. One of those historical facts that modern Britons, left bereft of their own history by their education system, often forget to remember.

8. One hundred seventy in the United States and seventeen in Britain. Figures taken from BBC, http://news.bbc.co.uk/1/hi/world/middle_east/6351257.stm, and the *Daily Telegraph*, www.telegraph.co.uk/news/main.jhtml?xml=/news/2006/06/25/wirq225.xml &sSheet=/news/2006/06/25/ixnews.html.

9. On July 15, 2007, the *Los Angeles Times* reported, on the strength of comments by (anonymous) senior U.S. military officers, and others, that although the finger had been pointed at Iran and Syria, the largest number (45 percent) of foreign suicide bombers and insurgents in Iraq were from Saudi Arabia (plus 15 percent from Syria and Lebanon, and 10 percent from North Africa—figures for Iran were not given, presumably because they were off the bottom end of the scale). Suicide attacks have systematically killed larger numbers of civilians and soldiers in Iraq than other kinds of attacks, and they have been predominantly, if not entirely, carried out by Sunni insurgents. The same source claimed that 50 percent of all Saudi fighters in Iraq came there as suicide bombers. The article commented: "The situation has left the U.S. military in the awkward position of battling an enemy whose top source of foreign fighters is a key ally that at best has not been able to prevent its citizens from undertaking bloody attacks in Iraq, and at worst shares complicity in sending extremists to commit attacks against U.S. forces, Iraqi civilians and the Shiite-led government in Baghdad."

10. In April 2007 the Iranian Supreme Court overturned murder verdicts against a group of Basijis convicted of killing people they regarded as immoral in the southeastern city of Kerman (in 2002). The victims included a couple that were betrothed, who had been abducted while on their way to view a house they had been hoping to live in together after their marriage. The Supreme Court accepted the men's defense that they believed

they had been justified (on the basis of guidance from Ayatollah Mesbah Yazdi), after giving warnings, in killing people they regarded as immoral. It was thought that there could have been as many as eighteen such killings in Kerman, and similar murders in Mashhad and Tehran as well (http://news.bbc.co.uk/2/hi/middle_east/6557679.stm).

11. The formula had been used before by Khomeini and others, and had been translated by representatives of the Iranian regime as "wiped off the map." Some of the dispute that has arisen over what exactly Ahmadinejad meant by it has been rather bogus. When the slogan appeared draped over missiles in military parades the meaning was pretty clear. It was partly to address Ahmadinejad's remarks, but also because it has often been passed over, that I have paid some moderate attention to the history of Iran's Jews in this book.

12. Martin Gilbert, *Israel: A History*. (London: Black Swan, 1999), 639.

Select Bibliography

Abrahamian, Ervand. *Tortured Confessions: Prisons and Public Recantations in Modern Iran.* Berkeley: University of California Press, 1999.

______. *Khomeinism: Essays on the Islamic Republic.* Berkeley: University of California Press, 1993.

______. *Iran Between Two Revolutions.* Princeton, NJ: Princeton University Press, 1982.

______. "The Causes of the Constitutional Revolution in Iran." *International Journal of Middle East Studies* 10 (August 1979): 381–414.

______. "The Crowd in Iranian Politics 1905–1953." *Past and Present* (December 1968): 184–210.

Al-Tabari, Mohammad ibn Jarir. *The Sasanids, the Byzantines, the Lakhmids, and Yemen* (vol. 5 of the *History of al-Tabari*) C. E. Bosworth, ed. and trans. Albany: State University of New York Press, 1999.

Alavi, Nasrin. *We Are Iran: The Persian Blogs.* London: Portobello Books, 2005.

Algar, Hamid. "Shi'ism and Iran in the Eighteenth Century." *Studies in Eighteenth-Century Islamic History,* Thomas Naff and Roger Owen, eds. Carbondale and Edwardsville: Southern Illinois University Press, 1977.

Amanat, Abbas. *Pivot of the Universe: Nasir al-Din Shah and the Iranian Monarchy, 1831–1896.* London: I. B. Tauris, 1997.

Aminrazavi, Mehdi. *The Wine of Wisdom: The Life, Poetry and Philosophy of Omar Khayyam.* Oxford: Oneworld , 2005.

Ansari, Ali. *Confronting Iran: The Failure of American Foreign Policy and the Next Great Crisis in the Middle East.* London: Hurst Books, 2006.

______. "Persia in the Western Imagination." *Anglo-Iranian Relations Since 1800,* Vanessa Martin, ed. Abingdon, UK: Routledge, 2005.

______. *A History of Modern Iran Since 1921: The Pahlavis and After.* London: Longman, 2003.

______. *Iran, Islam and Democracy: The Politics of Managing Change.* London: Chatham House, 2000.

Arberry, A. J., ed. and trans. *Classical Persian Literature.* Abingdon: RoutledgeCurzon, 2004; 1st ed., 1958.

______. *Fifty Poems of Hafiz.* Cambridge: Cambridge University Press, 1947.

———. *The Ruba'iyat of Omar Khayyam: Edited from a Newly Discovered Manuscript Dated 658 (1259–60) in the Possession of A. Chester Beatty Esq.* London: Emery Walker Ltd., 1949.

Arjomand, Said Amir. *The Turban for the Crown: Islamic Revolution in Iran.* Oxford: Oxford University Press, 1988.

Astarabadi, Mirza Mohammad Mahdi. *Jahangusha-ye Naderi,* translated into French by Sir William Jones as the *Histoire de Nader Chah.* London: 1770; original Persian text ed. Abdollah Anvar, Tehran: 1377 (1998).

Atabaki, Touraj, *Iran and the First World War: Battleground of the Great Powers.* London: I. B. Tauris, 2006.

———. *Azerbaijan: Ethnicity and Autonomy in Twentieth-Century Iran.* London: British Academic Press, 1993.

Attar, Farid al-Din. *The Conference of the Birds,* Afkham Darbandi and Dick Davis, eds. and trans. London: Penguin Classics, 1984.

Avery, Peter. *The Collected Lyrics of Hafiz of Shiraz.* London: Archetype, 2007.

Axworthy, Michael. "Diplomatic Relations Between Iran and the UK in the Early Reform Period, 1997–2000." *Iran's Foreign Policy: From Khatami to Ahmadinejad,* Anoush Ehteshami and Mahjoob Zweiri, eds. London: Ithaca Press, 2008.

———. "The Army of Nader Shah." *Iranian Studies* (December 2007).

———. "Basile Vatatzes and His History of Nader Shah." *Oriente Moderno* 2 (2006): 331–343.

———. *The Sword of Persia: Nader Shah, from Tribal Warrior to Conquering Tyrant.* London: I. B. Tauris, 2006.

Azari, Farah. "Sexuality and Women's Oppression in Iran." *Women of Iran: The Conflict with Fundamentalist Islam.* London: Ithaca Press, 1983.

Babayan, Kathryn. *Mystics, Monarchs and Messiahs: Cultural Landscapes of Early Modern Iran.* Cambridge: Harvard Center for Middle Eastern Studies, 2002.

Bakhash, Shaul. *The Reign of the Ayatollahs: Iran and the Islamic Revolution.* London: I. B. Tauris, 1985.

Bausani, Alessandro. *Religion in Iran: From Zoroaster to Bahu'u'llah.* New York: Bibliotheca Persica, 2000.

———. *The Persians.* London: Book Club Associates, 1975.

Bayat, Mangol. *Iran's First Revolution: Shi'ism and the Constitutional Revolution of 1905–1909.* Oxford: Oxford University Press, 1991.

———. *Mysticism and Dissent: Socioreligious Thought in Qajar Iran.* Syracuse, NY: Syracuse University Press, 1982.

Bayly, C. A. *Imperial Meridian: The British Empire and the World 1780–1830.* London: Longman, 1989.

Beck, Lois. "Women Among Qashqai Nomadic Pastoralists in Iran." *Women in the Muslim World,* Lois Beck and Nikki Beck Keddie, eds. Cambridge: Harvard University Press, 1978.

Berquist, Jon L. *Judaism in Persia's Shadow: A Social and Historical Approach.* Minneapolis, MN: Wipf and Stock Publishers, 1995.

Bill, James A. *The Eagle and the Lion: The Tragedy of American-Iranian Relations.* London and New Haven, CT: Yale University Press, 1988.

Bill, James A., and John Alden Williams. *Roman Catholics and Shi'i Muslims: Prayer, Passion, and Politics*. Chapel Hill: University of North Carolina Press, 2002.

Bly, Robert, with Leonard Lewisohn. *The Winged Energy of Delight: Selected Translations*. London: HarperCollins, 2004.

Bouhdiba, Abdelwahab. *Sexuality in Islam*. London: Routledge, 1985.

Boyce, Mary. *Zoroastrianism: A Shadowy but Powerful Presence in the Judaeo-Christian World*. London: Dr. William's Trust, 1987.

_______. *Zoroastrians: Their Religious Beliefs and Practices*. London: Routledge and Kegan Paul, 1979.

_______. *A History of Zoroastrianism, Volume One: The Early Period*. Leiden: Brill, 1975.

Boyle, John Andrew, ed. and trans. *The Cambridge History of Iran, Volume 5: The Saljuq and Mongol Periods*. London: Cambridge University Press, 1968.

_______. *The History of the World-Conqueror (Juvayni)*. Cambridge: Harvard University Press, 1958.

Briant, Pierre. *From Cyrus to Alexander: A History of the Persian Empire*. Winona Lake, IN: Eisenbrauns, 2002.

Brosius, Maria. *Women in Ancient Persia, 559–331 BC*. Oxford: Clarendon Press, 1998.

Browne, Edward Granville. *A Literary History of Persia: Volume II, From Firdawsi to Sa'di*. Cambridge: Cambridge University Press, 1969.

Bruinessen, Martin van. "A Kurdish Warlord on the Turkish-Persian Frontier in the Early Twentieth Century: Ismail Aqa Simko." *Iran and the First World War: Battleground of the Great Powers*, Touraj Atabaki, ed. London: I. B. Tauris, 2006.

Buchta, Wilfried. *Who Rules Iran? The Structure of Power in the Islamic Republic*. Washington, DC: Washington Institute for Near East Policy, 2000.

Calmard, J. "Popular Literature Under the Safavids." *Society and Culture in the Early Modern Middle East: Studies on Iran in the Safavid Period*, A. J. Newman, ed. Leiden: Brill, 2003.

The Cambridge History of Iran (7 vols). Cambridge: Cambridge University Press, 1961–1991.

Chittick, William C., and Peter Lamborn Wilson, eds. and trans. *Fakhruddin Iraqi: Divine Flashes*. London: Paulist Press, 1982.

Christensen, A. *L'Iran sous les Sassanides*. Copenhagen: 1944.

Clinton, Jerome W. "A Comparison of Nizami's *Layli and Majnun* and Shakespeare's *Romeo and Juliet*." *The Poetry of Nizami Ganjavi: Knowledge, Love and Rhetoric*, K. Talattof and J. Clinton eds. New York: Palgrave Macmillan, 2000.

_______. *The Tragedy of Sohrab and Rostam*. University of Washington Press (Rev. ed.), 1996.

Cole, Juan R. I. *Sacred Space and Holy War: The Politics, Culture and History of Shi'ite Islam*. London: I. B. Tauris, 2002.

Colledge, Malcolm A. R. *The Parthians*. London: 1967.

Corbin, Henry. *Spiritual Body and Celestial Earth: From Mazdean Iran to Shi'ite Iran*, Nancy Pearson, trans. Princeton, NJ: Princeton University Press, 1977.

_______. *En Islam Iranien: Aspects Spirituels et Philosophiques*, 4 vols. Paris: Gallimard, 1971.

Crone, Patricia. "Zoroastrian Communism." *Comparative Studies in Society and History* 36 (July 1994): 447–462.

Cronin, Stephanie. "Britain, the Iranian Military and the Rise of Reza Khan." *Anglo-Iranian Relations Since 1800*, V. Martin, ed. Abingdon, UK: Routledge, 2005.

_______. "Paradoxes of Military Modernisation." *The Making of Modern Iran: State and Society Under Riza Shah, 1921–1941*. S. Cronin, ed. London: RoutledgeCurzon, 2003.
Curtis, J. E., and Nigel Tallis, eds. *Forgotten Empire: The World of Ancient Persia*. London: I. B. Tauris, 2005.
Curtis, Vesta Sarkhosh, and Sarah Stewart, eds. *Birth of the Persian Empire* (*The Idea of Iran*, vol. 1. London: 2005.
_______. *The Age of the Parthians* (*The Idea of Iran*, vol. 2). London: 2007.
Curzon, Lord G. N. *Persia and the Persian Question*. London: Cass, 1966.
Daryaee, Touraj. *Sasanian Persia: The Rise and Fall of an Empire*. London: I. B. Tauris, 2007.
_______. *Sahrestaniha-i Eransahr: A Middle Persian Text on Late Antique Geography, Epic, and History*. Costa Mesa, CA: Mazda Publishers, 2002.
Ehteshami, Anoush. *After Khomeini: The Iranian Second Republic*. London: Routledge, 1994.
Encyclopedia Iranica, Ehsan Yarshater, ed. New York: Routledge, 1982–.
Fasa'i, Hasan-e. *History of Persia Under Qajar Rule*. Heribert Busse, trans. New York: Columbia University Press, 1972.
Fischer, Michael M. J. *Mute Dreams, Blind Owls and Dispersed Knowledge: Persian Poesis in the Transnational Circuitry*. Durham, NC, and London: Duke University Press, 2004.
Floor, Willem. *Love and Marriage in Iran: A Social History of Sexual Relations in Iran*. Washington, DC: 2007 (forthcoming).
_______. *Dastur al-Moluk: A Safavid State Manual*. Costa Mesa, CA: Mazda Publishers, 2006.
_______. "Dutch Trade in Afsharid Persia" *Studia Iranica*, Tome 34, fascicule 1, 2005, 43–93.
_______. *The History of Theater in Iran*. Washington, DC: Mage Publishers, 2005.
_______. *Safavid Government Institutions*. Costa Mesa, CA: Mazda Publishers, 2001.
_______. *The Economy of Safavid Persia*. Wiesbaden, Germany: 2000.
_______. *The Afghan Occupation of Safavid Persia, 1721–1729*. Paris: Association pour l'avancement des éudes iraniennes, 1998.
_______. *Labour Unions, Law and Conditions in Iran (1900–1941)*. Durham, UK: University of Durham, 1985.
_______. *Industrialization in Iran, 1900–1941*. Durham, UK: University of Durham, 1984.
Foltz, Richard C. *Spirituality in the Land of the Noble: How Iran Shaped the World's Religions*. Oxford: Oneworld Publications, 2004.
Foran, J. "The Long Fall of the Safavid Dynasty: Moving Beyond the Standard Views." *The International Journal of Middle East Studies*, no. 24 (1992): 281–304.
Frye, Richard N. *The Golden Age of Persia: The Arabs in the East*. London: Weidenfeld and Nicolson, 1975.
_______. *The Heritage of Persia*. London: Weidenfeld and Nicolson, 1962.
_______. *Iran*. London: George Allen & Unwin Ltd., 1954.
Garthwaite, Gene. *The Persians*. Oxford: 2005.
_______. *Khans and Shahs: A Documentary of the Bakhtiyari in Iran*. Cambridge: Cambridge University Press, 1983.
Gellner, E. "Tribalism and the State in the Middle East." *Tribes and State Formation in the Middle East*, J. Kostiner and P. S. Khoury, eds. London: I. B. Tauris, 1991.
Gelpke, R. *Nizami: The Story of Layla and Majnun*. Colchester, UK: Bruno Cassirer, 1966.

Ghani, Cyrus. *Iran and the Rise of Reza Shah: From Qajar Collapse to Pahlavi Power*. London: I. B. Tauris, 1998.

Gibbon, Edward, *The History of the Decline and Fall of the Roman Empire*. London: Printed by A. Strahan for T. Cadell and W. Davies, 1802.

Gilbert, Martin. *Israel: A History*. London: Black Swan, 1999.

Graham, Robert. *Iran: The Illusion of Power*. London: Croom Helm, 1978.

Harney, Desmond. *The Priest and the King: An Eyewitness Account of the Iranian Revolution*. London: I. B. Tauris, 1997.

Heaney, Seamus, and Ted Hughes, eds. *The School Bag*. London: Faber and Faber, 1997.

Herrmann, Georgina. *The Iranian Revival*. Oxford: Elsevier-Phaidon, 1977.

Hodgson, Marshall G. S. *The Venture of Islam*. Chicago: University of Chicago Press, 1974.

Hoffmann, Birgitt, trans. and ed. *Persische Geschichte 1694–1835 erlebt, erinnert und erfunden—das Rustam at-Tawarikh in deutscher Bearbeitung*. Bamberg, Germany: Aku, 1986.

Issawi, Charles. *The Economic History of Iran, 1800–1914*. Chicago: University of Chicago Press, 1971.

Ja'farian, Rasul. "The Immigrant Manuscripts: A Study of the Migration of Shi'i Works from Arab Regions to Iran in the Early Safavid Era." *Society and Culture in the Early Modern Middle East: Studies on Iran in the Safavid Period*, A. J. Newman, ed. Leiden: Brill, 2003.

_______. *Din va Siyasat dar Dawrah-ye Safavi*. Qom: 1991.

Jones, Lindsay, ed. *Encyclopedia of Religion*, 15-vol. set. New York: MacMillan Reference Books, 2005.

Katouzian, Homa. *Iranian History and Politics: The Dialectic of State and Society*. London: Routledge, 2007.

_______. "Riza Shah's Legitimacy and Social Base." *The Making of Modern Iran: State and Society Under Riza Shah, 1921–1941*, S. Cronin, ed. London: RoutledgeCurzon, 2003.

_______. *Sadeq Hedayat: The Life and Legend of an Iranian Writer*. London: RoutledgeCurzon, 2002.

_______. *State and Society in Iran: The Eclipse of the Qajars and the Emergence of the Pahlavis*. London: I. B. Tauris, 2000.

Keddie, Nikki R. *Modern Iran: Roots and Results of Revolution*. New Haven, CT: Yale University Press, 2006.

_______. *Women in the Middle East: Past and Present*. Princeton, NJ: Princeton University Press, 2006.

_______. "Sayyid Jamal Al-Din Al-Afghani." *Pioneers of Islamic Revival*, Ali Rahnema, ed. London/Beirut/Kuala Lumpur: Zed Books, 2005.

_______. *Qajar Iran and the Rise of Reza Khan 1796–1925*. Costa Mesa, CA: Mazda Publishers, 1999.

_______. "The Iranian Power Structure and Social Change 1800–1969: An Overview." *International Journal of Middle East Studies* 2 (January 1971): 3–20.

Kelly, Laurence. *Diplomacy and Murder in Tehran: Alexander Griboyedov and Imperial Russia's Mission to the Shah of Persia*. London: I. B. Tauris, 2002.

Kennedy, Hugh. *The Court of the Caliphs*. London: Phoenix, 2005.

Khaldun, Ibn. *The Muqaddimah: An Introduction to History*, Franz Rosenthal, trans. London: Routledge and Kegan Paul, 1967.

Khanbaghi, Aptin. *The Fire, the Star and the Cross: Minority Religions in Medieval and Early Modern Iran*. London: I. B. Tauris, 2006.

Khanlari, P. Natil, ed. *Divan-e Hafez*. Tehran: 1980.

Kian-Thiebaut, Azadeh. "From Motherhood to Equal Rights Advocates: The Weakening of the Patriarchal Order." *Iranian Studies* 38 (March 2005): 45–66.

Krusinski, Fr. Judasz Tadeusz. *The History of the Late Revolutions of Persia*. London: 1740; New York: Arno Press, 1973.

Lambton, Ann K. S. *Landlord and Peasant in Persia: A Study of Land Tenure and Land Revenue Administration*. London: I. B. Tauris, 1991.

_______. *Theory and Practice in Medieval Persian Government*. London: Variorum, 1980.

_______. "The Tribal Resurgence and the Decline of the Bureaucracy in the Eighteenth Century." *Studies in Eighteenth-Century Islamic History*, Thomas Naff and Roger Owen, eds. Carbondale and Edwardsville: Southern Illinois University Press, 1977.

Lapidus, Ira M. *A History of Islamic Societies*. Cambridge: Cambridge University Press, 2002.

Levy, Habib. *Comprehensive History of the Jews of Iran*, H. Ebrami, ed. Costa Mesa, CA: Mazda Publishers, 1999.

Lewisohn, Leonard, ed. "Attar, Farid Al-Din." *Encyclopedia of Religion*, 15-vol. set, Lindsay Jones, ed. New York: MacMillan Reference Books, 2005.

Lewisohn, Leonard, and C. Shackle, eds. *Attar and the Persian Sufi Tradition: The Art of Spiritual Flight*. London: I. B. Tauris, 2006.

_______. *The Heritage of Sufism, Volume I: Classical Persian Sufism from Its Origins to Rumi (700–1300)*. Oxford: Oneworld, 1999.

Limbert, John W. *Iran: At War with History*. Boulder, CO: Westview Press, 1987.

Lockhart, Laurence. *The Fall of the Safavi Dynasty and the Afghan Occupation of Persia*. Cambridge: 1958.

_______. *Nadir Shah: A Critical Study Based Mainly Upon Contemporary Sources*. London: Luzac, 1938.

Loeb, Laurence D. *Outcaste: Jewish Life in Southern Iran*. New York: Routledge, 1977.

Luckenbill, Daniel D. *Ancient Records of Assyria and Babylonia*. London: Histories and Mysteries of Man, 1989.

Luft, Paul. *Iran Unter Schah Abbas II (1642–1666)*, PhD dissertation. Göttingen: 1968.

Makdisi, George. *The Rise of Humanism in Classical Islam and the Christian West: With Special Reference to Scholasticism*. Edinburgh: Edinburgh University Press, 1990.

Malcolm, Sir John. *History of Persia: Containing an Account of the Religion, Government, Usages, and Character of the Inhabitants of that Kingdom*. London: Murray, 1829.

Manz, Beatrice. *The Rise and Rule of Tamerlane*. Cambridge: Cambridge University Press, 1989.

Martin, Vanessa. *Islam and Modernism: The Iranian Revolution of 1906*. London: I. B. Tauris, 1989.

Marvi Yazdi, Mohammad Kazem. *Alam Ara-ye Naderi*, Mohammad Amin Riyahi, ed. Tehran 1374, 3rd ed., 1995.

Matthee, Rudolph P. *The Pursuit of Pleasure: Drugs and Stimulants in Iranian History 1500–1900*. Princeton, NJ: Princeton University Press, 2005.

_______. "Education in the Reza Shah Period." *The Making of Modern Iran*, S. Cronin, ed. London: RoutledgeCurzon, 2003.

_______. *The Politics of Trade in Safavid Iran: Silk for Silver, 1600–1730*. Cambridge: Cambridge University Press, 1999.

_______. "Unwalled Cities and Restless Nomads: Firearms and Artillery in Safavid Iran." *Safavid Persia: The History and Politics of an Islamic Society*, Charles Melville, ed. London: I. B. Tauris, 1996.

Melville, Charles, ed. *Safavid Persia: The History and Politics of an Islamic Society*. Cambridge: I. B. Tauris, 1993.

Menashri, David. *Post-Revolutionary Politics in Iran: Religion, Society and Power*. London: Routledge, 2001.

Miklukho-Maklai, N. D. "Zapiski S Avramova ob Irane kak istoricheskii Istochnik." *Uchenye Zapiski Leningradskogo gosudarstvennogo universiteta. Seriia vostokovedcheskikh nauk*, part 3. Leningrad: 1952.

Minorsky, V., ed. and trans. *Tadhkirat al-Muluk: A Manual of Safavid Administration*. London: Gibb Memorial Trust, 1980, 2nd repr.; 1st ed., 1943.

Mir-Hosseini, Ziba. "Women, Marriage and the Law in Iran." *Women in the Middle East*, Haleh Afshar, ed. Basingstoke, UK: Macmillan, 1992.

Moaddel, Mansour. *Values and Perceptions of the Islamic and Middle Eastern Publics*. New York: 2007; findings of surveys also available at www.psc.isr.umich.edu/research/tmp/moaddel_values_survey.html.

_______. *Islamic Modernism, Nationalism and Fundamentalism: Episode and Discourse*. Chicago: University of Chicago Press, 2004.

Moin, Baqer. *Khomeini: Life of the Ayatollah*. London: I. B. Tauris, 1999.

Momen, Moojan. *An Introduction to Shi'i Islam: The History and Doctrines of Twelver Shi'ism*. New Haven, CT: Yale University Press, 1985.

Moreen, V. "Risala-yi Sawa'iq al-Yahud (The Treatise Lightning Bolts Against the Jews), by Muhammad Baqir b. Muhammad Taqi al-Majlisi (d. 1699)." *Die Welt des Islams* 32 (1992).

Morgan, David. *The Mongols*. Oxford: Blackwell Publishers, 1990.

_______. *Medieval Persia 1040–1797: History of the Near East*. London: Longman Publishing Group, 1988.

Morrison, George, ed. *History of Persian Literature from the Beginnings of the Islamic Period to the Present Day*. Leiden: Brill, 1981.

Morton, A. H. "The chub-i tariq and Qizilbash Ritual in Safavid Persia." *Études Safavides*, J. Calmard, ed. Paris and Tehran: 1993.

Mottahedeh, Roy. *The Mantle of the Prophet*. Harmondsworth, UK: Penguin, 1987.

Najmabadi, Afsaneh. *Women with Mustaches and Men Without Beards: Gender and Sexual Anxieties of Iranian Modernity*. Berkeley: University of California Press, 2005.

_______. *The Story of the Daughters of Quchan: Gender and National Memory in Iranian History*. Syracuse, NY: Syracuse University Press, 1998.

Nakosteen, Mehdi. *History of the Islamic Origins of Western Education, AD 800–1350*. Boulder: University of Colorado Press, 1964.

Newman, Andrew J. *Safavid Iran: Rebirth of a Persian Empire*. London: I. B. Tauris, 2006.

______. "Baqir al-Majlisi and Islamicate Medicine: Safavid Medical Theory and Practice Re-examined." *Society and Culture in the Early Modern Middle East: Studies on Iran in the Safavid Period*, Andrew J. Newman, ed. Leiden/Boston: Brill, 2003.

______. "The Myth of the Clerical Migration to Safavid Iran." *Die Welt des Islams* 33 (1993): 66–112.

Olmstead, A. T. *History of the Persian Empire*. Chicago: University of Chicago Press, 1948.

Parsons, Anthony. *The Pride and the Fall: Iran 1974–1979*. London: Cape, 1984.

Paul, Jürgen. "L'invasion Mongole comme revelateur de la société Iranienne." *L'Iran face à la domination Mongole*, Denise Aigle, ed. Tehran: 1997.

Perry, J. R. *Karim Khan Zand*. Oxford: Oneworld, 2006.

______. *Karim Khan Zand: A History of Iran, 1747–1779*. Chicago/London: University of Chicago Press, 1979.

Pritchard, James B. *Ancient Near Eastern Texts Relating to the Old Testament with Supplement*, 3rd ed. Princeton, NJ: Princeton University Press, 1969.

Rabinyan, Dorit. *Persian Brides*. Edinburgh: George Braziller Publishers, 1998.

Razmjou, Shahrokh. "Religion and Burial Customs." *Forgotten Empire: The World of Ancient Persia*, J. E. Curtis and N. Tallis, eds. London: I. B. Tauris, 2005.

Rees, B. R. *Pelagius: Life and Letters*. Woodbridge, UK: Boydell and Brewer, 1998.

Rizvi, Sajjad H. *Mulla Sadra Shirazi: His Life and Works and the Sources for Safavid Philosophy*. Oxford: Oxford University Press on behalf of the University of Manchester, 2007.

Roy, Olivier. *The Failure of Political Islam*. London: I. B. Tauris, 1994.

Rumi, Jalal al-Din. *The Masnavi, Book One*, Jawid Mojaddedi, ed. and trans. New York: Oxford University Press, 2004.

Runciman, Steven. *A History of the Crusades*. Harmondsworth, UK: Penguin, 1991.

Rundle, Chris. *From Colwyn Bay to Kabul: An Unexpected Journey*. Stanhope: The Memoir Club, 2004.

Saberi, Reza. *A Thousand Years of Persian Rubaiyat: An Anthology of Quatrains from the Tenth to the Twentieth Century Along with the Original Persian*. Bethesda, MD: Ibex Publishers, 2000.

Sackville-West, Vita. *Passenger to Teheran*. London: Tauris Parke Paperbacks, 1991; 1st ed., 1926.

Sahim, Haideh. "Jews of Iran in the Qajar Period: Persecution and Perseverence." *Religion and Society in Qajar Iran*, Robert Gleave, ed. London: RoutledgeCurzon, 2005.

Saidi, Ahmad, ed. and trans. *Ruba'iyat of Omar Khayyam*. Berkeley: University of California Press, 1992.

Sanasarian, Eliz. *Religious Minorities in Iran*. Cambridge/New York: Cambridge University Press, 2000.

Savory, Roger. *Iran Under the Safavids*. Cambridge: Cambridge University Press, 1980.

Schimmel, Annemarie. *Mystical Dimensions of Islam*. Chapel Hill: University of North Carolina Press, 1975.

Schuster, Morgan. *The Strangling of Persia: A Record of European Diplomacy and Oriental Intrigue*. London: T. Fisher Unwin, 1912.

Sefatgol, Mansur. "Safavid Administration of Avqaf: Structure, Changes and Functions, 1077–1135/1666–1722." *Society and Culture in the Early Modern Middle East: Studies on Iran in the Safavid Period*, Andrew J. Newman, ed. Leiden: Brill, 2003.

_______. "The Question of Awqaf Under the Afsharids." *Studia Iranica: Cahiers*, vol. 21/*Materiaux pour l'Histoire Economique du Monde Iranien*, Rika Gyselen and Maria Szuppe, eds. Paris: 1999.

Sha'bani, Reza. *Tarikh-e Ijtima'i-ye Iran dar 'asr-e Afshariyeh*. Tehran: 1986.

Shah, Idries. *The Sufis*. London: Octagon Press, 1964.

Spuler, Bertold. *The Age of the Caliphs: A History of the Muslim World*. Princeton, NJ: Markus Wiener Publishers, 1995.

Stillman, Norman A. *The Jews of Arab Lands: A History and Source Book*. Philadelphia: Jewish Publications Society, 1979.

Subrahmanyam, S. "Un Grand Derangement: Dreaming an Indo-Persian Empire in South Asia 1740–1800." *Journal of Early Modern History*, vol. 4. Leiden: Brill, 2000.

Tabataba'i, Muhammad Husayn. *Shi'ite Islam*. New York: 1979.

Talattof, Kamran. *The Politics of Writing in Iran: A History of Modern Persian Literature*. Syracuse, NY: Syracuse University Press, 2000.

Tapper, Richard. *Frontier Nomads of Iran: A Political and Social History of the Shahsevan*. Cambridge: Cambridge University Press, 1997.

_______, ed. *The New Iranian Cinema: Politics, Representation and Identity*. London: I. B. Tauris, 2002.

Tucker, Ernest S. *Nadir Shah's Quest for Legitimacy in Post-Safavid Iran*. Gainesville: University Press of Florida, 2006.

Varzi, R. *Warring Souls: Youth, Media and Martyrdom in Post-Revolution Iran*. Durham: University of North Carolina Press, 2006.

Vatatzes, Basile, (ed. N. Iorga) *Persica: Histoire de Chah-Nadir*. Bucharest, Romania: 1939.

Vaziri, Mostafa. *Iran as Imagined Nation: The Construction of National Identity*. New York: 1993.

Villing, Alexandra. "Persia and Greece." *Forgotten Empire: The World of Ancient Persia*. London: I. B. Tauris, 2005.

Wickens, G. M., trans. *The Bustan of Sa'di*. Leiden: 1974.

Wiesehöfer, Josef. *Ancient Persia*. London: I. B. Tauris, 2006.

Woods, John E. *The Aqquyunlu: Clan, Confederation, Empire: A Study in 15th/9th Century Turko-Iranian Politics*. Minneapolis, MN: Bibliotheca Islamica, 1976.

Wright, Denis. *The English Amongst the Persians: During the Qajar Period 1787–1921*. London: Heinemann, 1977.

Yamauchi, Edwin M. *Persia and the Bible*. Grand Rapids, MI: Baker Book House, 1990.

Yarshater, Ehsan. "The Persian Presence in the Islamic World." *The Persian Presence in the Islamic World*, Richard Hovannasian and Georges Sabagh, eds. Cambridge: Cambridge University Press, 1998.

_______, ed. *Persian Literature*. Albany, NY: Bibliotheca Persica Press, 1988.

Zirinsky, Michael P. "Imperial Power and Dictatorship: Britain and the Rise of Reza Shah, 1921–1926." *International Journal of Middle East Studies* 24 (November 1992): 639–663.

Index

MICHAEL AXWORTHY

is a Lecturer at the Institute of Arab and Islamic Studies at the University of Exeter in England. From 1986 to 2000 he served in the British Foreign Service; from 1998 to 2000 he was the Head of Iran Section of the Foreign and Commonwealth Office. The author of *The Sword of Persia*, a biography of the Persian monarch Nadir Shah, Axworthy publishes widely in the field of Iranian history. He lives in Cornwall, England.